SPORTS AND LAW:
CONTEMPORARY ISSUES

Edited by
HERB APPENZELLER

THE MICHIE COMPANY
Law Publishers
CHARLOTTESVILLE, VIRGINIA

This book is dedicated in
loving memory of

Joy Cronland Dennis

whose life has given meaning
to Faith, Hope, and Love.

ACKNOWLEDGMENTS

Sports and Law: Contemporary Issues is the result of the unselfish effort of many people. Although it is impossible to personally recognize each one, I am grateful for their help.

I wish especially to thank the following:

— The contributing authors, who so generously shared their experience and expertise and made the book possible.

— Millie Dunkel for typing various parts of the manuscript.

— Elizabeth Dunn, who has written and published a variety of articles for over fifty years. She served as editor for Reader's Digest Books and shared her expertise in editing many of the sections in addition to making valuable suggestions on the style and organization of the book.

— Lynne Gaskin, a legal scholar who made timely suggestions that improved the book.

— Dianna LeBaube for her tireless effort and for her unusual diligence in typing and retyping the entire manuscript in a spirit of cooperation and friendship.

— Dabney Oakley of The Michie Company, who has been the man behind the scenes with the many details that are essential to the publication of a book.

— W. R. Rogers, President, and Samuel Schuman, Academic Dean, of Guilford College for their constant support and encouragement.

— *Athletic Business* for permission to reprint Herb Appenzeller's article on "Educational Exploitation."

— *Update,* the American Bar Association publication, for permission to reprint Teri Engler's article on "Violence in Sports."

— The *Insurance Counsel Journal* for permission to reprint John Fagen's article entitled "Ski Area Liability for Downhill Injuries."

— The Michie Company for permission to reprint James Oshust's section on "The Law of Public Assembly Facilities" and Chester Lloyd's section on "Emergency Medical Plans for Large Crowds" from *Successful Sport Management.*

TABLE OF CONTENTS

		Page
Introduction		xiii

Chapter 1. Sports Litigation — A Perspective 1
§ 1.1. Athletic Director (by Herb Appenzeller) 1
§ 1.2. Athlete (by Reggie Kenan and Pella Stokes) 3
§ 1.3. Athletic Trainer (by Jerald Hawkins) 6
§ 1.4. Attorney (by Bynum Hunter) 8
§ 1.5. Coach (by Richard Borkowski) 11
§ 1.6. Official (by Gerald Austin) 13
§ 1.7. Product Liability Expert (by Maria Dennison) 14

Chapter 2. Administrative Issues 17
§ 2.1. Implications of the *Seattle* Decision (by Samuel Adams) 17
    § 2.1(A). Shift From Product Liability to Responsibility of Coaches and School Districts 17
    § 2.1(B). Failure to Warn 18
    § 2.1(C). Failure to Instruct 19
    § 2.1(D). Negligence of the Seattle School District 19
    § 2.1(E). Implications of the *Seattle* Decision 20
    § 2.1(F). Conclusion 22
§ 2.2. Sports, the Law and Due Process (by Harry Mallios) 22
    § 2.2(A). Sports-Related Legal Issues 23
    § 2.2(B). Concern: Administrator, NCAA, Congress 24
    § 2.2(C). What Is Due Process of Law? 26
    § 2.2(D). Requirements to Ensure Due Process 27
    § 2.2(E). Conclusion 29
§ 2.3. Warnings and Waivers (by Gary Nygaard) 30
    § 2.3(A). Inherent Risk 30
    § 2.3(B). Warnings 31
    § 2.3(C). Waivers 34
    § 2.3(D). Conclusion 36
§ 2.4. Public Responsibilities of Amateur Sports Organizations (by Glen M. Wong & Richard J. Ensor) 36
    § 2.4(A). Access to Public Records 36
    § 2.4(B). Public Access to Televised College Football Games 39
    § 2.4(C). The Court of Appeals 41
    § 2.4(D). The Supreme Court's Decision 42
    § 2.4(E). Public Funding of Athletic Facilities 44
    § 2.4(F). Delegation of a Public Responsibility 44
    § 2.4(G). Conclusion 47
§ 2.5. Title IX: After *Grove City* (by Linda Carpenter) 48
    § 2.5(A). Significance of *Grove City* to Physical Education and Sports Programs 51

		Page
§ 2.5(B).	What Is the Future of Title IX?	52
§ 2.5(C).	Conclusion	52
§ 2.6.	Legislating Against Violence in Sports (by Rick Horrow)	53
§ 2.6(A).	The Pressure to Perform	54
§ 2.6(B).	Sports in Court — The Present Score	57
§ 2.6(C).	Conclusion	60
§ 2.7.	"He Said What"?! Defamation in Sports (by David R. Maraghy)	61
§ 2.7(A).	The Law of Defamation	61
§ 2.7(B).	The *New York Times* Rule — Constitutional Privilege	65
§ 2.7(C).	Public Figures — Position, Public Controversy, Public Interest or Public Official	68
§ 2.7(D).	Rule of Repose	76
§ 2.7(E).	Conclusion	78

Chapter 3. Coaching Issues 79

§ 3.1.	Employment of Coaches: Is the Right to Hire the Right to Fire? (by Herb Appenzeller)	79
§ 3.1(A).	The Secondary School Coach	79
§ 3.1(B).	Tenure and Dismissal	79
§ 3.1(C).	Racial Discrimination	82
§ 3.1(D).	Reverse Discrimination	84
§ 3.1(E).	Sex Bias	84
§ 3.1(F).	Constitutional Rights	87
§ 3.1(G).	Employment Issues on the Collegiate Level	92
§ 3.1(H).	Conclusion	98
§ 3.2.	Certification of Coaches (by Robert B. Turner)	99
§ 3.2(A).	Preparation of Coaches	101
§ 3.2(B).	Legal Ramifications	105
§ 3.2(C).	Conclusion	107
§ 3.3.	The Coach as Codefendant: Football in the 1980's (by Richard A. Lester)	108
§ 3.3(A).	The Role of the Coach	109
§ 3.3(B).	Provide Quality Equipment	110
§ 3.3(C).	Maintenance of Equipment	110
§ 3.3(D).	Failure to Warn	111
§ 3.3(E).	Precautionary Steps	112
§ 3.3(F).	Providing Adequate Insurance	113
§ 3.3(G).	Conclusion	113

Chapter 4. Student-Athlete Issues 115

§ 4.1.	Athletes' Rights: Fact or Fiction (by C. Thomas Ross)	115
§ 4.1(A).	Are Athletes' Rights Legal?	115
§ 4.1(B).	A Landmark Case in Athletes' Rights	116
§ 4.1(C).	Categories of Athletes' Rights	116
§ 4.1(D).	Conclusion	117
§ 4.2.	Educational Exploitation of Athletes (by Herb Appenzeller)	118

Page

§ 4.2(A). Pressures Make It Difficult for Athletes to Get
            Good Education 119
§ 4.2(B). Education Malpractice Becoming a Powerful
            Factor in the Profession 120
§ 4.2(C). Judicial Interference Would Disrupt Adminis-
            tration of Schools 122
§ 4.2(D). It Is Time to Meet the "Exploitation" Challenge . 123
§ 4.2(E). Conclusion 123
§ 4.3. The Athlete With Disabilities (by Julian V. Stein) 124
§ 4.3(A). Legalized Discrimination 125
§ 4.3(B). Problems Confronting Individuals With Disabil-
            ities 125
§ 4.3(C). Progress in Sport for the Disabled 126
§ 4.3(D). A Look to the Future 127
§ 4.3(E). Conclusion 128
§ 4.4. The College Participant: Student Athlete or Paid Profes-
         sional? (by David K. Stotlar) 128
§ 4.4(A). Athletic Scholarship Differs From Other Finan-
            cial Aid 129
§ 4.4(B). Contractual Relationship of Athletic Scholar-
            ship 130
§ 4.4(C). Workers' Compensation 133
§ 4.4(D). Taxation of Athletic Scholarship 136
§ 4.4(E). Conclusion 138
§ 4.5. The Athletic Scholarship as Contractual Basis for a Prop-
         erty Interest in Eligibility (by Brian Porto) 139
§ 4.5(A). Property Right 140
§ 4.5(B). State Action 141
§ 4.5(C). A "Liberty" Interest 146
§ 4.5(D). Legal Contract 149
§ 4.5(E). Enforcement Procedures 155
§ 4.5(F). Conclusion 157

Chapter 5. Sports Medicine Issues 159
§ 5.1. The Legal Status of the Athletic Trainer (by Boyd B. Baker
         and Phillip B. Parry) 159
§ 5.1(A). States Require Licensure for Physical Thera-
            pists 159
§ 5.1(B). Categories Regarding Physical Therapy Laws ... 160
§ 5.1(C). Statutory Requirements by States 162
§ 5.1(D). Conclusion 162
§ 5.2. Drug Testing in Sports (by Kenneth S. Clarke) 163
§ 5.2(A). The Banned List 164
§ 5.2(B). Informed Consent 164
§ 5.2(C). Prevention of a False Positive 165
§ 5.2(D). Prevention of a False Negative 166
§ 5.2(E). Confidentiality 166

                                                                Page

§ 5.2(F).   Accurate Information 166

§ 5.2(G).   Appeal 167

§ 5.2(H).   Conclusion 167

§ 5.3.   Emergency Medical Services for Large Crowds (by Chester Lloyd) 167

§ 5.3(A).   Introduction 167

§ 5.3(B).   Duty to Provide an Emergency Medical Capability 168

§ 5.3(C).   Standards and Guidelines Specify the Scope of Treatments 168

§ 5.3(D).   Other Facilities and State Laws May Dictate Level of Care 169

§ 5.3(E).   The Emergency Medical System in Action 170

§ 5.3(F).   Planning for Emergency Medical Response 171

§ 5.3(G).   Program Complexity 176

§ 5.3(H).   Conclusion — Program Benefits 177

Chapter 6. Officials and Spectator Issues 179

§ 6.1.   Violence in Sport (by Teri Engler) 179

§ 6.1(A).   Is Winning Everything? 179

§ 6.1(B).   The Chicken or the Egg? 181

§ 6.1(C).   Courts as Referees 181

§ 6.1(D).   Enforcing Civility 183

§ 6.1(E).   How Much Risk to Assume 184

§ 6.1(F).   "I Didn't Mean It" 186

§ 6.1(G).   Statutory Control 187

§ 6.1(H).   Conclusion 188

§ 6.2.   Officials and the Law: Rights and Liabilities (by Melvin S. Narol) 188

§ 6.2(A).   Recovery for Injuries 189

§ 6.2(B).   Intentional Injuries 189

§ 6.2(C).   Negligent Injuries 190

§ 6.2(D).   Workers' Compensation 193

§ 6.2(E).   Liability for Player Injuries 197

§ 6.2(F).   Before the Game 198

§ 6.2(G).   During-the-Game Inspection 200

§ 6.2(H).   Liability for Game Rulings 202

§ 6.2(I).   Conclusion 206

§ 6.3.   Spectators, Too, Sue (by Betty van der Smissen) 206

§ 6.3(A).   Participatory Risks 206

§ 6.3(B).   Crowd Control 209

§ 6.3(C).   Safe Premises 211

§ 6.3(D).   Conclusion 212

Chapter 7. Equipment and Facilities Issues 215

§ 7.1.   Product Liability: A Legal Dilemma (by Maria Dennison) ... 215

§ 7.1(A).   Liability for Design Defects and Failure to Warn 216

Page

§ 7.1(B). Historical Efforts to Address the Problem 219

§ 7.1(C). Tort Reforms at the State Level 219

§ 7.1(D). Federal Product Liability Reform: What It Would Accomplish 221

§ 7.1(E). The Search for a Federal Legislative Solution ... 222

§ 7.1(F). Federal Preemption of State Law 222

§ 7.1(G). Standard of Liability for Design and Failure to Warn 223

§ 7.1(H). Who Is Responsible in a Product Liability Action? 224

§ 7.1(I). Punitive Damages 225

§ 7.1(J). Where Do We Go From Here? 227

§ 7.1(K). Conclusion 227

§ 7.2. Effective Design and Upkeep of Gymnastic Facilities (by Marc Rabinoff) 228

§ 7.2(A). Growth of Gymnastics 229

§ 7.2(B). Attempt by Equipment Manufacturers to Follow Standards 229

§ 7.2(C). Recommendations for Upkeep of Gymnastic Equipment 231

§ 7.2(D). Conclusion 233

§ 7.3. Ski Area Liability for Downhill Skiers (by John K. Fagen) .. 233

§ 7.3(A). Historical Development of Ski Area Liability for Downhill Injuries 234

§ 7.3(B). Attacks on Assumption of Risk as a Defense 236

§ 7.3(C). Conclusion 246

§ 7.4. The Law of Public Assembly Facilities (by James Oshust) ... 246

§ 7.4(A). Introduction 246

§ 7.4(B). Need for Legal Assistance 246

§ 7.4(C). Access and Availability of Facility 247

§ 7.4(D). Access to Records, Booking Schedules and Operational Details 249

§ 7.4(E). Access to Premises 249

§ 7.4(F). Search and Seizure 251

§ 7.4(G). Crowd Control 251

§ 7.4(H). Availability of Required and Desired Accouterments 252

§ 7.4(I). Conclusion 253

Index 255

INTRODUCTION

Sports litigation is on the rise in America's litigious society as the sports industry continues to grow. Sport is no longer just "fun and games" but a multi-billion dollar industry that involves millions of participants. The American sports environment is filled with many troublesome issues which ultimately lead to litigation. The issues of the 1980's are no longer just traditional contract disputes and allegations of negligence. Rather, there has been a clear trend toward more — and more diverse — issues that have a tremendous impact on the sports industry. Sports issues involve athletes, administrators, athletic trainers, coaches, equipment manufacturers, officials, operators of sports facilities, physicians, and even the unsuspecting spectator. No one associated with sport is immune from litigation.

Legal developments in sport receive daily attention from the media. This publicity, combined with a great interest in sport, from Little League to professional competition, has created a new awareness of sports law. "Sports law" is a recent term used by many people, but it is simply law as it applies to sports. It has been described as a developing specialty area of the legal profession. As the number of sports-related lawsuits escalates, so does the number of attorneys who are called upon to apply legal principles to the sports industry. John Weistart and Cym Lowell, in *The Law of Sports,* note that attorneys deal with a variety of legal disciplines that include "agency, antitrust, communications law, constitutional law, contracts, criminal law, labor law, property, tax, and torts." Since the early 1960's attorneys have been joined by legal scholars who have been gathering information, analyzing, and explaining the emerging phenomenon of sports law.

Sports and Law: Contemporary Issues is composed of topical sections written by thirty-three professionals with expertise and experience in the field of sports law. These professionals have identified contemporary legal issues in sport and their implications for the sports industry. While these issues apply to sport at all levels of competition, the text concentrates on sports-related issues on the amateur level.

Sports and Law: Contemporary Issues is divided into chapters that deal with those issues most frequently involved in sports litigation. Chapter 1, "Sports Litigation — A Perspective", views litigation as seen by the various participants of sport. Chapter 2, "Administrative Issues", considers issues that confront the sports administrator and includes sections on the implications of the Seattle decision, due process, warnings and waivers, public responsibilities of amateur sports organizations, Title IX after the Grove City decision, legislating against violence in sport, and defamation of character. Chapter 3, "Coaching Issues", looks at three critical issues confronting coaches: the employment of coaches, certification of coaches, and the coach as codefendant in the '80's. Chapter 4, "Student-Athlete Issues", includes sections on the rights of student-athletes, educational exploitation, disabilities, paid student-athletes, and the athletic scholarship and its implications for athletic participation. Chapter 5, "Sports Medicine Issues", considers the legal status of the athletic trainer, drug testing, and emergency medical services for large crowds. Chapter 6, "Officials and Spectator Issues", covers violence in sport, the sports official and the law, and spectators and the law. Chapter 7, "Equipment and Facilities Issues", contains sections on product liability, gymnastic facilities, ski area liability, and the law of public assembly facilities.

Because of the complexity of sports-related issues, the reader may find that the sections overlap at times. This can be positive reinforcement of the material and points to what the issues have in common. No attempt has been made to alter the authors' opinions, which may at times be subject to controversy. This should allow the reader to evaluate directly an author's point of view and supporting facts. Footnotes appearing in the original draft of the sections have been omitted or incorporated into the textual material as appropriate.

While it is important to identify contemporary sports-related issues that affect society, it is far more important that a book such as *Sports and Law: Contemporary Issues* encourage administrative, judicial and legislative action that will minimize abuses in sport, produce laws and regulations setting standards and guidelines to improve sport, and provide new directions for the sports industry.

ABOUT THE AUTHORS

SAMUEL ADAMS, Ed.D.
Professor of Physical Education
Washington State University
Pullman, Washington

Sam Adams has written over twenty articles relating to athletics. He is co-author of *Assessment of Physical Education and Athletic Programs and Personnel* and editor of *Catastrophic Injuries in Sports, Avoidance Strategies.* He is a lecturer at state, regional, and national conferences on athletic problems and assessment and liability in sports. He was named the Faculty Member of the Year in 1980.

HERB APPENZELLER, Ed.D.
Director of Athletics and Professor of Sport Management
Guilford College
Greensboro, North Carolina

Herb Appenzeller is the author of six books in the area of law and sports and numerous articles in the area of law and physical education and sports. He is the co-author of *Successful Sport Management* and a lecturer on the national level in the field of law and sports. He is the co-author of *Sports and the Courts Quarterly,* Executive Director of the Sport Studies Foundation, President of Sports Executive, Inc., a member of the board of directors for the National Association of Sports Officials and a board member to the Sports Medicine Foundation of America.

GERALD AUSTIN, Ed.D.
Principal, Weaver Education Center
Greensboro, North Carolina

Gerald Austin has officiated basketball and football for 25 years on the high school, small and major college level, and now professionally. He has been an official for the Atlantic Coast Conference for nine years before joining the National Football League.

BOYD BAKER, Ed.D.
Associate Professor
Department of Exercise and Sport Sciences
University of Arizona
Tucson, Arizona

Boyd Baker teaches two graduate courses: "Physical Education and the Law" and "Legal Aspects of Sports Administration" at the University of Arizona. He has conducted legal workshops and seminars in eight western states. He has written extensively in the area of sport law. Boyd Baker serves on the Board of Advisors of the Sport Studies Foundation, the Board of Governors of the American Alliance for Health, Physical Education, Recreation and Dance (AAHPERD). He is also on the Board of Directors of AAHPERD, Southwest District. He is Commissioner of Officials for the Arizona Interscholastic Association, Region III.

RICHARD BORKOWSKI, Ed.D.
Director of Physical Education and Athletics
Episcopal Academy
Merion, Pennsylvania

Richard Borkowski has an extensive background in teaching and coaching. He lectures throughout the United States in the area of physical education and sports law. He has published numerous articles in the field of physical education and sports and serves as a consultant and "expert witness" for numerous law firms.

LINDA CARPENTER, Ph.D., J.D.
Professor of Physical Education
Brooklyn College
Brooklyn, New York

Linda Carpenter is a member of the New York Bar. She is a lecturer on the national level and has written numerous articles for professional journals. For ten years she has been a board member of A Very Special Place, Inc., an organization that helps mentally retarded adults. She has written *Gymnastics for Girls and Women*.

KENNETH CLARK, Ph.D.
Director, Sports Medicine
United States Olympic Committee

Kenneth Clarke has held positions with the Chicago Heart Association, the University of Illinois Division of Rehabilitation Education, the American Academy of Orthopedic Surgeons, and the American Medical Association. He has been the coordinator of the American Medical Association's Committee on Medical Aspects of Sports. Kenneth Clarke founded the National Athletic Injury (Illness Reporting System (NAIRS)). He served as professor and department head at Penn State University and was Dean of the College of Applied Life Studies at Illinois University. He has been Director of Sports Medicine at the United States Olympic Committee since 1981. He had edited four books on sports medicine for professional societies and has published widely in medical and educational journals. He was Chairman of the NCAA Committee on Competitive Safeguards and Medical Aspects of Sports. He served as a consultant to the National Coordinating Council for Drug Education on drug matters in sports. He is a Fellow of both the American Academy of Physical Education and the American College of Sports Medicine. He is a recipient of the University of Illinois' Alumni Merit Award and the Arthur B. Steinhaus Distinguished Alumni Award from George Williams College.

MARIA DENNISON
Director of Washington Operations for the Sporting Goods Manufacturing Association
Washington, D.C.

Maria Dennison has authored numerous articles and a book on corporate political action committees. She is a frequent industry spokesperson and regularly appears before Congress as an expert witness on consumer affairs, international trade and recreation issues. She is a member of Women in Governmental Relations and the National Press Club. She was named as an Outstanding Young Woman of America in 1982.

TERI ENGLER, J.D.
Law Education Consultant
Evanston, Illinois

Teri Engler has a Law degree from Loyola University in Chicago, Illinois. She has taught at Loyola Law School and supervised law student-teachers in the Chicago area high schools. She wrote the Illinois supplement to the national *Street Law* text and has conducted numerous workshops on legal topics. She has written numerous articles on law-related topics and is a co-author of *Sports and Law*. She is a member of the Illinois Bar.

RICHARD ENSOR, M.S.
Law School
Seton Hall University
South Orange, New Jersey

Richard Ensor is a former sports information director at Saint Peter's College in Jersey City, New Jersey and assistant athletic director at St. Louis University. He is currently a second year law student at Seton Hall University Law School in South Orange, New Jersey where he is director of its Sports Law Forum. He has a Masters Degree in Sport Management from the University of Massachusetts, Amherst.

JOHN FAGEN, L.L.B.
University of Michigan Law School
Ann Arbor, Michigan

John Fagan received his B.G.S. (with distinction) from the University of Michigan and graduated from the University of Michigan Law School. His material in this book won first prize in the 1981 Legal Writing Contest.

JERALD HAWKINS, Ed.D., A.T.C.
Chairman, Department of Sport Studies
Guilford College
Greensboro, North Carolina

Jerald Hawkins is the Sports Medicine Coordinator at Guilford College. He is a certified athletic trainer and exercise physiologist. He is the author of several publications on sport injury management, personal fitness and exercise physiology, including his role as editor and contributing author of *Sports Medicine: A Guide For Youth Sports.*

RICK HORROW, J.D.
Executive Director
Miami Sports and Exhibition Authority
Miami, Florida

Rich Horrow received his J.D. degree from the Harvard Law School. He has written extensively in the area of sports law and is the author of *Sports Violence: The Interaction Between Private Lawmaking and the Criminal Law.* He was the drafter and principal advisor for the Sports Violence Act of 1980 and 1981, and the Sports Violence Arbitration Act of 1982. He is the Chairman of the American Bar Association's Task Force on Sports Violence and the Vice-President of Sports Lawyers' Association. He has appeared on ABC, CBS and NBC television and radio shows and lectured to colleges and universities on sports violence. He is the commentator for WTVJ Channel 4 in Miami, a nationally syndicated "Sports in the Courts" series. He is a member of the Florida Bar and an Adjunct Professor of Law at Nova University.

BYNUM HUNTER, J.D.
Attorney in the Law Firm of Smith, Moore, Smith, Schell and Hunter
Greensboro, North Carolina

Bynum Hunter received his undergraduate and law degree at the University of North Carolina at Chapel Hill. He is the attorney for the Atlantic Coast Conference and active in sports law litigation. Fellow, American College of Trial Lawyers. Fellow, American Bar Foundation. Member: North Carolina and American Bar Associations International Association of Insurance Counsel.

REGGIE KENAN
Assistant District Attorney
Goldsboro, North Carolina

Reggie Kenan attended Guilford College where he achieved All America honors in football (NAIA). He attended Campbell University Law School and is a member of the North Carolina Bar.

RICHARD LESTER, J.D.
General Counsel, Riddell, Inc.
Bensenville, Illinois

Richard Lester is a graduate of the University of Kansas Law School. He was an attorney in private practice in Kansas City, Missouri from 1972 until 1979. At the present time he is the general counsel for the Riddell Sporting Goods Company.

CHESTER LLOYD, M.A.
Consultant
West Orange, New Jersey

Chester Lloyd is a specialist in the delivery of emergency care for mass gatherings and/or large facilities. For the last ten years, he has been involved with the planning, training, and patient care aspects of emergency medical services. His experience includes work as coordinator of emergency medical teams for large-capacity stadiums. He completed his Master of Science degree at the University of Illinois, Urbana-Champlaign, where he researched medical preparedness at mass gatherings. Currently, he serves as an independent consultant, providing advice on emergency medical response for entertainment and sport facilities, in corporate offices or industrial settings, and at any facility or event which attracts large crowds.

HARRY MALLIOS, Ph.D.
Professor of Sport Law
Miami University
Coral Gables, Florida

Harry Mallios served as Athletic Director at Miami University from 1979 to 1983. He is the faculty representative to the NCAA for the University and serves as special advisor to the Provost of the University. He has published extensively in the area of constitutional law and, in particular, tort liability and due process of law. Harry Mallios was a member of the Miami University's football teams that participated in the 1951 Orange Bowl and 1952 Gator Bowl.

DAVID MARAGHY, J.D.
Graham, Miles and Bogan
Greensboro, North Carolina

David Maraghy is a graduate of the Wake Forest University Law School where he was the editor of "Notes and Comments" for the Wake Forest University Law Review. He served as clerk for Chief Justice Susie Sharp of the North Carolina Supreme Court. He is general chairman for the Greater Greensboro Open Golf Tournament (1986). He will be a partner with Pro's, Inc., Richmond, Virginia. He is an adjunct professor at Guilford College and has been an assistant lacrosse coach.

MELVIN NAROL, J.D.
Attorney in the firm of Jamieson, Moore, Peskin and Spicer
Princeton, New Jersey

Melvin Narol is an authority on legal issues confronting sport officials and active in sports law. He is a partner with the law firm of Jamieson, McCardell, Moore, Peskin and Spicer, Princeton, New Jersey and a member of the New Jersey Bar and District of Columbia Bar. Melvin Narol is an active high school basketball official. He has authored numerous articles on the legal rights and liabilities of sports officials which have appeared in *Referee, Trial* Magazines and *The National Law Journal.* He is consultant for officials' associations in several states and a lecturer before both lawyers and sports officials' associations. He is Chairman of the Board of Directors of the National Association of Sports Officials and serves as Chairman of the Committee on Sports Officials and Other Non-Playing Personnel of the American Bar Association's Forum Committee on the Entertainment and Sports Industries.

GARY NYGAARD, Ph.D.
Professor of Health and Physical Education
University of Montana
Missoula, Montana

Gary Nygaard is the co-author of *Law for Physical Educators and Coaches* and *A Coach's Guide to Sport Law.* He is the author of "You and the Law" in *Coaching Young Athletes.* He teaches a course at the university in legal issues in physical education and sport.

JAMES OSHUST
Managing Director
Greensboro Coliseum Complex
Greensboro, North Carolina

James Oshust's career in facility management began with his appointment as General Manager of the Sioux Falls, South Dakota Arena and Coliseum Complex. He also served as Promotion Director, Toledo Sports Arena. Other appointments have been as General Manager of the Niagara Falls Convention Center, the Mid-South Coliseum, Memphis, Tennessee. He is a graduate of Ohio State University's School of Journalism (Radio-TV News), and has served as publicity representative for Holiday On Ice Shows, Inc. He has also worked in commercial television production. At one time he held the offices of Executive Vice-President and General Manager of the St. Louis Stars Professional Soccer Club, North American Soccer League. He is a member of the Board of Directors of the International Association of Auditorium Managers.

PHILLIP PARRY
Plainview High School
Plainview, Texas

Phillip Parry is a native of Kansas. He received his B.S. degree from Emporia State in Emporia, Kansas. He received his M.S. degree from the University of Arizona in Tucson, Arizona. He is Head Athletic Trainer for Plainview High School, Plainview, Texas.

BRIAN PORTO, Ph.D.
University of Indiana Law School
Bloomington, Indiana

Brian Porto taught political science at Yankton College in Yankton, South Dakota and at Macalester College in St. Paul, Minnesota. He has written several articles for publication on amateur sports and the law. He has a chapter in *Government and Sport: Public Policy Issues.* At the present time, Brian Porto is completing work for a J.D. degree at Indiana University's Law School.

MARC RABINOFF, Ed.D.
Professor of Physical Education and Recreation
Metropolitan State College
Denver, Colorado

Marc Rabinoff was a nationally certified gymnastic judge from 1968 to 1980. He was a coach of men and women's gymnastic teams on the collegiate level. He is involved in gymnastics at the local, state and national level. He has written numerous articles in the area of sport law, safety and product liability and lectures on the same topics. He is the chairman of the Safety Committee of the Education and Safety Division of the United States Gymnastics Federation. During the summers of 1982, 1983 and 1984 he conducted workshops at Metropolitan State College. He has written a chapter entitled "Raising the Level of Awareness in Gymnastics Safety" for the *USGF Gymnastic Manual.*

C. THOMAS ROSS, J.D.
Craige, Brawley, Liipfert and Ross
Winston-Salem, North Carolina

Tom Ross has a varied sports background and is a speaker and writer on the topic of sports and physical education law. He is the Past Chairman, ABA Special Committee on Youth Education for Citizenship and Past Chairman, ABA Commission on Public Understanding About the Law. He is author of *Sports and Law* and co-editor of *Sports and the Courts Quarterly.*

JULIAN STEIN, Ed.D.
Professor of Physical Education
George Mason University
Fairfax, Virginia

Julian Stein has been an active participant in ASCSA. He was chairman for the Adapted Physical Education Academy for the National Association for Sport and Physical Education and Editor of *Challenge, Outlook, IROC Briefings* and *Practical Pointers* series of the American Alliance for Health, Physical Education, Recreation and Dance. He is a reviewer for the Journal of Physical Education, Recreation and Dance. Julian Stein has participated in over 800 workshops and seminars nationally and internationally. He is a clinician on the President's Council on Physical Fitness and Sports and the Director of the National Capital Regional Clinic on Physical Fitness and Sports. He has been the chairman of AAHPERD's Task Force on progress for the Mentally Retarded and Consultant for the Programs for the Handicapped and Executive Director for the Unit on Programs for the Handicapped.

PELLA STOKES, J.D.
Attorney
Greensboro, North Carolina

Pella Stokes attended Guilford College where he achieved success as a scholar-athlete. He signed a professional baseball contract with the Cincinnati Reds of the National League. He is a graduate of Wake Forest University Law School and a member of the North Carolina Bar. He works in the area of sport law and is an agent for athletes who enter professional sports.

DAVID STOTLAR, Ed.D.

Assistant Professor of Physical Education
Iowa State University
Ames, Iowa

David Stotlar was formerly the track coach at the University of Utah. As an assistant professor of physical education at Iowa State University, he teaches the Legal Aspects of Physical Education and Sports course. He also teaches Sports Administration at the graduate level. He has published several articles on legal issues in physical education and sports for professional journals.

ROBERT TURNER, Ed.D.

Assistant Professor of Physical Education
Averett College
Danville, Virginia

Robert Turner received his doctorate from the University of North Carolina at Greensboro with an emphasis on the psychological aspects of physical education and sports. He has been an educational administrator for eleven years, a golf coach, and a professor of physical education. He has conducted numerous workshops on the legal aspects of physical education and sport for public school personnel. In addition he has participated in workshops dealing with invitational education. He has published many articles in the field of physical education and sports and was a contributing editor to *Youth Sports: A Search For Direction.*

BETTY van der SMISSEN, Ph.D., J.D.

Professor/Director School of HPER
Bowling Green State University
Bowling Green, Ohio

Betty van der Smissen is a member of the Kansas Bar. She has written numerous articles for professional journals and is the author of *Legal Liability of Cities and Schools for Injuries in Recreational Parks.* Her latest book is *Legal Liability and Risk Management.* She is a lecturer in the area of physical education, recreation and sports law on the national level.

GLENN WONG, Ph.D., J.D.

Assistant Professor of Sport Management
University of Massachusetts
Amherst, Massachusetts

Glenn Wong has written numerous articles in the area of sport law and is co-author of *The Law and Business of Sports.* He is an attorney and a member of the Massachusetts Bar. He teaches sport law, sport finance and business and sport labor relations at the University. He is a member of the American Bar Association's Forum Committee on Entertainment and Sports Law. He negotiates contracts for professional athletes.

CHAPTER 1

SPORTS LITIGATION — A PERSPECTIVE

§ 1.1. Athletic Director.

By Herb Appenzeller

There is widespread disagreement today over the effect litigation is having on sport. Critics of sports litigation bitterly deplore the unprecedented rise in the number of lawsuits, with enormous awards becoming the rule and not the exception. These outspoken critics insist that lawsuits are out of control and, if allowed to continue, will inevitably destroy sports.

I disagree. I'd like to argue just as vehemently that litigation may be the only remedy for correcting the abuses that have plagued sport for all too long.

Reflect back on the time before sports litigation. I vividly remember the decade of the forties, when I experienced sport as a high school and college athlete and later as a young and inexperienced high school coach.

One of my friends played on an opposing high school football team that had replaced the traditional leather helmet with the new, shiny plastic one. The entire team was excited and proud of the helmets because they were the first area team to adopt them. But my friend was struck a hard blow to the head in our game and became one of the first casualties of a helmet-related injury. An autopsy revealed that his death had been caused by the blow to the head, but a contributing factor was that his helmet did not fit properly. No one thought of suing anybody — it just was not the thing to do.

During my senior year in high school, I sustained a very serious injury, but when a popular assistant coach advised me to wait until the end of the season to see a doctor, I agreed. I paid the price later in life, but once again no one thought of suing anyone.

Medical examinations were rare in the forties. I do not remember one being given prior to participation in any sport in high school or college. I do recall a physician in the locker room before our seventh game in college. We were undefeated and on the list of practically every major post-season bowl. I saw the team physician injecting Novocain into players who were injured in the previous game. These players had not practiced all week, but suddenly crutches, slings and braces were discarded for football uniforms. It was like magic — until halftime, when the painkiller wore off. But even the players who were injected and reinjured considered it all part of the game and never thought of a lawsuit.

There were other abuses, too. A well-known college football coach failed to honor his scholarship commitments to over a dozen players. He terminated their scholarships by a penny postcard that wished them well — somewhere else. The disappointed athletes stoically accepted their fate as a hazard of the sport, and once again no one thought of pursuing the matter in court.

As a novice coach I witnessed the agony of a young teacher when a student under his care died from a baseball injury that safety precautions could have

1

prevented. Just weeks later a fellow coach went through the torture that accompanies a fatal accident when one of the students in a group he was supervising drowned in a muddy lake. No qualified lifeguard was present, yet no one thought of litigation. After all it was 1950 and lawsuits against teachers and coaches just were not in style.

Nor was I blameless. As a young high school coach I allowed the trainer to pass out pregame "pep pills" to eager athletes who firmly believed that these pills gave them an edge over their opponents. And how many times did I misjudge a broken bone for a mere sprain and simply tape it, encouraging the athlete to continue in practice or in the game since, after all, "When the going gets tough, the tough get going." My poor judgment concerned me, but I never thought it would lead me to the courtroom. In those days, a special bond existed between the athlete and the coach.

Not only did we not go to court in the forties and fifties; we had no sympathy for the few who did dare to sue. A popular football player was injured during an intersectional game and was left unattended on the sideline for the remainder of the game and during the long train trip back to campus. He sued his coach because he felt that he had been an outstanding prospect for professional baseball until his injury. He demanded compensation for his injury, which he blamed on the negligence of the coach. We sympathized with him until we learned he was suing the coach. Once again you just did not sue for a sports injury in those days.

These attitudes prevailed, in my opinion, until the mid-sixties, when a New Jersey court found a school district guilty of negligence in a gymnastic case and awarded the injured student in excess of a million dollars. Soon after, a California court awarded an athlete crippled in a football scrimmage over $300,000. These two cases received national attention and launched a new era in sports, often referred to as the "injury industry" or the "sue syndrome." Not only did the injury cases reach the courts in record numbers; cases were brought that involved the rights of athletes, due process, discrimination and just about any other reason for suit. The defendants were the athletes themselves, coaches, officials, spectators, administrators, team physicians, athletic trainers, manufacturers of sports equipment, and owners and operators of sports facilities. Truly no one associated with sports is now immune from litigation.

As a participant in sport, a former coach (baseball, basketball, football, and track) and an athletic director for 37 years, I have never wanted to be involved in a lawsuit. As a result, I work extremely hard to prevent situations that might result in litigation. And I am not the only one. Legitimate litigation and the awareness that negligent conduct can lead to a lawsuit has brought dramatic changes that are beneficial to sport.

In recent years the manufacturers of football helmets have borne the brunt of injury-related lawsuits. The crisis among the manufacturers caused many to give up the production of helmets. But those who continued to produce helmets have come up with an approved helmet that offers the coach, player, and manufacturer some feeling of security. The National Operating Commission on Standards for Athletic Equipment (NOCSAE) has formulated safety standards intended to decrease the number of head injuries in football and reduce the number of helmet-related lawsuits.

Now the attention is beginning to turn from the helmet to the coach who teaches the techniques of blocking and tackling. To avoid a day in court, the coach must now abide by the rules and avoid teaching butt blocking and head tackling. The athlete has become the beneficiary of such improvement, which came about, in part, because lawsuits threatened the very existence of the game of football.

The lack of a thorough physical examination or any examination at all has been a deep concern to many people. Today we are providing more physical examinations prior to participation in sport than ever before. This is progress! Medical experts advise physicals prior to participation to protect the athlete from serious problems. They point out that the black athlete is particularly susceptible to certain diseases — especially hypertension — and needs a careful examination because these diseases can be alleviated with treatment, enabling the athlete to participate in sports with safety. More and more physicians are beginning to specialize in sports medicine, and today legislatures in many states are passing laws designed to provide medical safety for the athlete. North Carolina recently passed a law requiring by 1984 a qualified athletic trainer for all schools that sponsor interscholastic athletic teams. Once again, the athlete benefits from the change.

One additional example is noteworthy. When the American Academy of Pediatrics urged the curtailment of the trampoline it shocked educators everywhere. Legal authorities supported the action of the Academy because they felt that no one could successfully win a trampoline injury case after the Academy's stand on the issue. Because of the threat of litigation, many schools locked up their trampolines and discontinued their use in physical education activities and competitive sports. But that wasn't the end of it. Many sports organizations joined with the American Alliance for Health, Physical Education, Recreation and Dance on a position paper setting definitive guidelines for using the trampoline. It pointed out that the major problem often came from incompetent instructors and spotters, not defective equipment. As a result the trampoline has been restored to most programs — but with safety guidelines designed to protect the participant.

It is the courts that accentuate the importance and welfare of the individual, it is the courts that attempt to end discrimination of every sort in sport, and it is the courts that curb the rising violence that often takes place in the sports arena.

The courts are making sports participation better. Participants now enjoy the safest equipment, finest facilities, and best medical care and coaching ever — thanks to litigation.

---

§ 1.2. Athlete.

By Reggie Kenan and Pella Stokes

Mention the word "court" among sports fans and many will automatically think of a basketball or tennis court. In a sports setting, however, "court" can often mean a court of law. The reality of today's litigious society has reached both law and sport and caused them to be entwined. At the same time athletes have become conscious of the factors that lead to litigation.

The opinions in this section are the result of our involvement in sport as participants, in addition to personal observation and interaction with many athletes. The emphasis is on litigation in amateur sport. However, issues involving litigation on the amateur sports level can often be traced to professional sport with its potential for financially rewarding careers.

While individual athletes may look at sport litigation differently, the issues that lead to litigation remain more constant and produce similar results in the majority of situations that come before the courts. Although many athletes consider injuries to be an inherent part of sports participation, an increasing number of athletes are seeking to recover damages for sport-related injuries that are caused by forces not commonly associated with that sport. The most frequent claim for relief is the allegation that the injury was caused by someone's negligence.

As athletes in baseball and football, we gave no serious thought to litigation resulting from sports participation. Our goals were similar: participate in sport and receive a college degree, but not necessarily in that order. Today, as attorneys, it has become obvious to us that athletes are now involved in sports litigation for many reasons.

Regardless of the particular sport, there always remains the potential for injury to the athlete. It is in this area that the majority of litigation seems to occur in amateur sport. It is difficult to participate in any sport without some thought of potential injury and without assuming risks that are common to physical competition. Athletes, however, rarely contemplate all the injuries that can be caused by the negligent acts of others. For example, a shortstop or second baseman in baseball generally assumes that opposing players will attempt to slide into him when he pivots to complete a double play. When an opposing player fails to slide and chooses to run full force into the man pivoting, striking him and causing severe injury, the possibility of a lawsuit based on negligence becomes a reality. This hypothetical example can easily apply to other sport, and illustrates the fact that unreasonable and deliberate acts can lead to litigation. Typically, athletes have not considered litigation in similar situations until recently, when publicity and awareness of individual rights have increased the potential for judicial remedies.

Many male athletes tend to consider themselves "macho"; they — and some female athletes — pride themselves on accepting injuries from excessively rough play as the sign of a strong athlete. This self-image causes many athletes to avoid legal action because they view it as a sign of weakness, even when a valid cause of action exists. But negligence is not the only theory that can be the basis of a lawsuit by an injured athlete. Intentional or willful conduct can also form the basis of litigation when participants ignore the rules of the game and disregard the safety of others. Athletes report that they are more inclined to seek judicial relief when the injury is the result of deliberate and willful conduct rather than negligent conduct.

Regardless of whether an injury in sports competition is the result of negligence or intentional action to injure, someone must be found liable if litigation is pursued. Liability may be found in competing participants, coaches, administrators, physicians, spectators, manufacturers of sports equipment and owners of sports facilities. Athletes generally place trust in those with whom they associate on a sports level.

Athletes today are making legal claims for a lack of due process. The most important due process claim usually involves the loss of eligibility. Ineligibility may result from good conduct violations, age restrictions, transfer rules, grade point deficiencies or other causes.

Many amateur athletes, realistically or not, view participation in sport as a step toward professional sports with a high potential income. Therefore, for due process purposes, eligibility may be classified as a property interest. Some athletes report that when they were recruited by colleges they were assured that participation at a particular school would enable them to "make it" in professional sport. Some people argue that sport participation is not a property right. Others contend that it is and that the freedom to choose employment is a guaranteed right of all citizens. But the prevailing feeling seems to be that the chance to participate in professional sport should not be taken away without proper justification.

In addition to due process, athletes are particularly aware of the equal protection clause of the fourteenth amendment, regarding discrimination based on race, sex and handicap. The athlete of today is unwilling to be denied participation in sport because of discrimination. And it is true that discriminatory acts not only disrupt sports teams but also cause athletes to distrust coaches or administrators who create unfavorable situations.

Most athletes realize that laws do not change inherent human reactions, and that therefore better communication is essential in order to eliminate discrimination. But athletes also recognize that to ensure equal opportunity to demonstrate their athletic ability, the use of legal remedies is available as a last resort.

To determine how athletes look at litigation, it is important to examine the effect it has upon the individual athlete. The effect of litigation can manifest itself in psychological, physical and economic terms.

When an athlete resorts to legal action rather than retaliation in the arena, some damage may be done to the individual's self-image. Even in situations in which the athlete is injured by willful and intentional conduct, the athlete may lose some self-confidence, due to fear of retaliation and another injury.

It is also possible for psychological reactions to affect physical play. Athletes involved in legal action during a playing season often report that their performance is weakened by tension or anxiety and, because of this, they are often ambivalent about the value of litigation.

In the end, the most significant reason for litigation by the athlete may be economics. When a future in professional sport is jeopardized by acts that result in injury, an athlete will in all probability view litigation as protection for that possible career. Sport, like our legal system, emphasizes the dollar and thus prompts athletes to seek monetary relief in the courts for actions that take place in the sports arena.

Though athletes look at litigation in a variety of ways, the issues remain the same and the courts of law have secured an important place in athlete's lives. When sport itself is of primary concern and the athlete's welfare becomes secondary, litigation is possible. The threat of litigation alone may protect the rights of athletes and assist in the maintenance of rules guaranteeing respect and protection for all sports participants.

---

§ 1.3. Athletic Trainer.

By Jerald Hawkins

The field of sports litigation as it relates to sports medicine is as broad and complex as the field of sports medicine itself. From physician to physical therapist, from exercise physiologist to athletic trainer, the threat of litigation is a source of concern. Traditionally, sports medicine litigation has been most commonly experienced by physicians accused of medical malpractice and other medical and health care professionals charged with professional malfeasance, misfeasance or nonfeasance. Today, however, there exist a multiplicity of sources for litigation within the realm of sports medicine. The most common areas of concern for nonphysician sports medicine professionals are: (1) sports injury care and (2) exercise testing, prescription and instruction.

The prevention, care and rehabilitation of sport-related injuries, often termed "athletic training," is performed by a vast array of persons in our society. Because of its direct involvement with health care, athletic training encompasses a host of duties and responsibilities which, if performed incorrectly may result in further injury or even death. The most pressing issues regarding the practice of sports injury care today may be: (1) the determination of who is qualified to provide athletic training services, (2) the licensing or certifying of these persons, and (3) the development of a standard of practice for evaluating the extent to which athletic trainers perform in an acceptable manner.

The most universally recognized form of professional recognition for athletic trainers is certification by the National Athletic Trainers Association. Although other organizations also certify trainers, NATA is the oldest and most prestigious certifying agency. To receive NATA certification, a candidate must pass a comprehensive certification examination after having graduated from a NATA-approved college program or having completed equivalent academic requirements and a minimum of 1800 hours of internship under the direct supervision of a NATA-certified trainer. Because of the rigorous nature of these requirements, NATA certification is granted to only those persons who demonstrate a high level of expertise in all phases of sports injury care.

Unfortunately, NATA certification in most states does not provide the trainer with the legal right to employ many of the injury management techniques upon which certification is based. At the present time only a very few states license or certify athletic trainers for the practice of sports injury management. Therefore, by statement or implication, most states limit the practice of sports injury management to physicians, physical therapists, and others who have been specifically identified in state statutes governing health care practices. The result of such a dilemma is that highly qualified, professionally recognized athletic trainers are often forced to perform their injury management services outside the letter of the law. Except in a handful of states, this problem's importance continues to be ignored by those outside of sports medicine.

A related issue with significant legal implications is the absence of a "standard of practice" for athletic trainers. Most professions which are related to the provision of services, especially in the general area of health care, have a "standard of practice" or set of criteria by which the quality of services rendered may be objectively evaluated. While it is true that NATA standards provide criteria for performance evaluation relative to certification, there is no universally accepted "job description" or "standard of practice" for athletic trainers. The development of standard performance criteria for athletic trainers is currently being discussed by a variety of professional organizations. In the meantime, the nearest thing to such a document is the *Role Delineation Study* produced by the NATA in an attempt to provide a comprehensive description of the athletic trainer's role.

It is the concern of many sports medicine professionals that the *persona non grata* legal status of athletic trainers in most states constitutes fertile grounds for litigation. The absence of a standard of practice for trainers does little to assuage these feelings of concern.

The second general area in which sports medicine litigation is likely to be seen is that of exercise testing, prescription and instruction. In the midst of America's "fitness boom", we see the proliferation of fitness-related programs. Unlike the current situation in sports injury management, there are universally recognized guidelines for safely testing and prescribing exercise for healthy adults. There have also been various levels of certification developed by the American College of Sports Medicine, the YMCA and other reputable fitness-related organizations. Unfortunately, except for specific organizational requirements (e.g., YMCA requirement that fitness leaders be "certified" according to YMCA standards), there exists, in most states, no legal criteria which fitness instructors, exercise leaders, spa managers, etc. must meet in order to perform fitness tests and prescribe exercise programs based upon those tests. Fortunately, however, the threat of fitness programming-related litigation appears to impact most directly upon those with little or no professional preparation in exercise science. It should be of less concern to those qualified persons who meet the standards of the American College of Sports Medicine, American Heart Association, YMCA or other such organizations, providing of course that they perform within the standards to which they subscribe. It is to be hoped that the widespread problem of unqualified staff members in fitness-related programs will be addressed through appropriate legislation before needless injuries or deaths place this issue on already-crowded court dockets across our nation.

Litigation is a word that very few sports medicine professionals like to consider. However, improved standards of performance and increased awareness of the need for qualified sports medicine personnel will continue to reduce the risk of injury to the recipients of sports medicine services and of litigation for those who perform those services.

§ 1.4. Attorney.

By Bynum Hunter

Lawyers know that litigation can involve just about everything under the sun. The term "sports litigation" also covers a wide range of legal subjects. The term "sports law" covers an even broader spectrum than sports litigation because there are many legal matters involving sport that seldom result in litigation. *Black's Law Dictionary* defines "litigation" as follows: "A judicial controversy. A contest in a court of justice, for the purpose of enforcing a right." Almost any litigation pertaining to sport, either directly or indirectly, comes under the heading of "sports litigation." There are many types of cases in this category, including products liability, antitrust, constitutional rights, contracts, discrimination, labor disputes, and negligence cases. Even tax cases, patent cases, and criminal cases can come under the heading of "sports litigation." As we all know, television has had a tremendous impact on sport, and, as would be expected, there has arisen litigation in that area which is highly important to the sports industry, both amateur and professional, as well as to the public in general.

In one of the more significant sports litigation cases to arise in recent times, *National Collegiate Athletic Association v. Board of Regents,* 104 S. Ct. 2948 (1984), the United States Supreme Court invalidated the lucrative football television contracts between the NCAA and two major networks, ABC and CBS (also involved was WTBS), on the grounds that antitrust laws were violated. This decision has created substantial problems not only for the NCAA but for major colleges fielding football teams, primarily in the form of loss of revenues with which to operate other intercollegiate sports programs which produce little or no revenue. For the 1984 football season, the NCAA had no television plan, the College Football Association (CFA) (made up of more than 60 major universities) had a television plan with ABC, and the Pac-Ten and Big Ten Conferences had a plan with CBS. Other major conferences and schools, most of which were also CFA members, had various plans with television producers, mostly on a regional basis. However, the revenues being generated under these new plans apparently were much less than under the invalidated NCAA football television plan.

What the future holds for college football television is uncertain. New solutions are being sought, but it is likely there will be further litigation in this area. At least one suit, *Association of Independent Television Stations, Inc. v. The College Football Association,* CIV-84-2283 R (W.D. Okla. Sept. 13, 1984), pending at the time of this writing, challenges the validity of the new CFA and Pac-Ten and Big Ten television plans, primarily on antitrust grounds.

Ironically, professional sport fares better in some respects under the antitrust laws than does college sport. Perhaps the most important sports litigation case of all time is *Federal Baseball Club of Baltimore, Inc. v. National League of Professional Baseball Clubs,* 259 U.S. 200 (1922), where the United States Supreme Court ruled, in effect, that professional baseball is immune from the antitrust laws. That decision stands to this day. However, no other professional sport enjoys this immunity. In *Toolson v. New York Yankees, Inc.,* 346 U.S. 356 (1953), the Supreme Court reaffirmed the baseball antitrust exemption pointing out that because Congress had never seen fit to abolish the court-ruled baseball antitrust exemption, Congress presumably did not intend that baseball should be subjected to antitrust regulation. There is really no way to explain why professional baseball should have antitrust immunity and any other sport should not, particularly where amateur sport is involved. However, Congress has allowed limited antitrust immunity for certain *professional* sports. The Sports Broadcast Act of 1961, 15 U.S.C. §§ 1291-1295, allows an antitrust liability exemption for the pooled sale of telecasting rights for professional football, baseball, basketball, and hockey leagues, but no others, and the Act does not apply to intercollegiate athletics. The Act does protect college and high school football in that it requires the blacking out of professional football telecasts on Friday evenings and Saturdays from the second Friday in September to the second Saturday in December within 75 miles of the game site of any college or high school game scheduled to be played on such a date, 15 U.S.C. § 1293. Perhaps Congress at some point will see fit to enact legislation similar to the Sports Broadcast Act for the benefit of intercollegiate athletics. Such legislation could help solve some of the problems created by the Supreme Court's invalidation of the NCAA football television plan. However, the new United States Football League (USFL) has apparently opted not to come under the Sports Broadcast Act and evidently intends to enter into an agreement with a network to televise some of its games on Saturdays commencing with the 1986 season. Such an agreement could pose further problems for college football television.

Any time a new professional league is formed in any sport to compete with one already in existence it can be expected that a rash of litigation will follow, usually when players "jump" from one league to the other. This was certainly true in the days of the American Basketball Association (ABA) when a number of prominent professional players left the NBA to play for ABA teams, and vice versa. These cases basically involved alleged breaches of contract and many involved alleged tortious interference with contractual relationships. The ABA was a bonanza for most professional basketball players in that it caused their salaries to increase dramatically. On the other hand, there were many bitter disappointments when certain ABA clubs folded and players who thought they had valuable contracts found out those clubs were unable to pay.

The inception of the USFL will likely spawn considerable litigation. In fact, the USFL recently has levied a $1.3 billion lawsuit against the National Football League (NFL), claiming, among other things, antitrust violations.

Another significant area of sports litigation is in the enforcement of rules such as those promulgated by the NCAA and the various conferences throughout the country. Many of these cases arise in the context of an athlete being declared ineligible for one reason or another. These cases can involve a combination of claims for discrimination, antitrust violations, and deprivation of constitutional rights. Recently the NCAA adopted an eligibility requirement known as Proposition 48, which would require a student-athlete to have at least a C average (2.0) in high school and a combined score of at least a 700 (out of a possible 1600 total — math and verbal) on the Scholastic Aptitude Test (SAT) in order to be eligible to participate in intercollegiate athletics at an NCAA member school. Proposition 48 was to go into effect in August of 1986, but the NCAA has postponed its implementation. If and when Proposition 48 does go into effect, it is almost a certainty that litigation will follow. Proposition 48 makes good sense, but there is considerable opposition. Certain studies indicate that minorities may have difficulty in attaining a score of at least 700 on the SAT. Of course, the purpose of the SAT is to give some indication as to whether or not a student-athlete can pass college work. A score of 700 on the SAT is not particularly high. It seems that a requirement such as Proposition 48 should be encouraged because the requirement would likely motivate most young people who aspire to be college student-athletes to work harder in high school. Several years ago the Atlantic Coast Conference (ACC) required a combined score of at least 800 on the SAT in order to be eligible to participate in intercollegiate athletics at an ACC school. A lawsuit was brought challenging the so-called "800 Rule," but before that litigation ran its course the ACC decided to drop the rule. Also, at that time the NCAA used what was known as the "1.6 Rule," a formula which combined a student-athlete's high school class standing and SAT scores. The "1.6 Rule" was somewhat less stringent than the "800 Rule." There was litigation over the "1.6 Rule," and eventually the NCAA abandoned it. It seems clear that almost any type of scholastic eligibility requirement which is adopted by the NCAA or any of the conferences is likely to receive a court challenge sooner or later.

If an attorney becomes involved in sports litigation, it will most likely involve a sport-related personal injury. These are basically negligence cases. There are hundreds of reported cases in this area, and there has been personal injury litigation in just about every sport. There are probably more reported decisions in this area than in any other type of sports litigation. These cases may involve participants, spectators, coaches, officials, and others. There are also many products liability personal injury cases. The football helmet cases have received wide attention, but almost any item of sports equipment may become the subject of a products liability action against the manufacturer. There are also medical malpractice cases against doctors which claim negligence in the treatment of athletic injuries; in those cases the relationship of the doctor to the school or team may be significant. Claims for workers' compensation benefits may arise, although it is usually held by the courts that workers' compensation acts are not applicable to college athletes. The increase in sports litigation in the personal injury area has been dramatic over the last ten to fifteen years. Given the current state of litigiousness among our citizens, we will likely see many more types of sports injury lawsuits.

§ 1.5. Coach.

By Richard Borkowski

For the last decade or so, the 50-yard-line bench and the legal bench have become related. In early days, sport seemed almost mystically immune from litigation. Coaches seldom gave a second thought to the possibility of becoming involved in a lawsuit related to their profession. Such is not the case today. To some degree that attitude has come full cycle. The fear of being part of a lawsuit is now as common as the fear of losing the big game. We now see sports law courses, films, conferences, workshops, and a steady stream of articles on a coach's legal responsibilities. Knowledge and sensitivity in this area are increasing — and well they should. The coaching profession, like every other, is caught in our present litigious society.

But for all the concern and well-meaning efforts of school administrators, professors, business managers and even lawyers, the dilemma of the current lawsuit explosion will not be substantially corrected until we listen to those at the center of this crisis. I refer to the coaches. We need to know how they feel about what is happening.

For the past thirteen years, in my role as a consultant and expert witness, I have talked with over a hundred coaches who have been defendants in sport-related lawsuits. I have also been part of a national workshop dealing with the legal responsibilities of coaches.

The general response of coaches already involved in a lawsuit and of those not yet involved is practically identical. There is first a feeling of disbelief: "You mean someone's going to sue me?" Then a feeling of righteous indignation: "After all the time and effort I've given to girls' lacrosse for twenty years, I'm being sued because someone broke her wrist." Coaches find it difficult if not impossible to accept the fact that someone on their team will sue them. As one coach has said: "This whole know-your-legal-responsibility stuff is for the birds!"

People involved in coaching are concerned, upset and angry. "I work seven days a week," said one coach, "average twelve cents an hour, give most of that away on pizzas, never get to spend more than two hours in a row with my children until they try out for my team, and now someone wants to sue me! What the . . . is going on!"

Many other coaches are not as outspoken but have similar feelings. People who have given so much to our society are suddenly being questioned as to their professionalism and credibility. Nothing can be more debilitating. An 0 and 10 season is nothing compared to the traumatic experience of a lawsuit.

Several years ago I was part of the successful defense of an outstanding coach in the State of New York. The day after the coach was found not guilty of negligence he resigned from coaching. Sport cannot afford to lose such quality leadership.

Yes, the coaching ranks are concerned — yes, even angry. The solution begins when we understand that simple fact.

It is time to move, however, from anger to action. There are things the coaching profession can and should be doing to combat the present proliferation of lawsuits. The following suggestions are those that have already proven successful in preventing a lawsuit or in defending a coach.

1. Forget the "It'll never happen to me" attitude.
2. Move from your view of your legal responsibilities to learning how the legal system views them.
3. Realize the bottom line is an improved situation for the athlete. In reality the preponderance of lawsuits are related to injuries ranging from broken bones to paralysis to death. The best way to avoid and minimize the chances of a lawsuit is to run a "safety first, last, and always" program. It protects athletes and you. When you get down to the basics of any legal responsibility program, you are really talking about safety: "How can I best care for my athlete?"
4. Realize that courts say coaches can be considered negligent, and therefore candidates for litigation, when they fail in their duty to:
   a. Properly prepare/condition a participant for the activity. Don't send the cross-country team out for a ten-mile run on the first day of practice.
   b. Properly instruct the athlete. Teach everyone the skills he or she will need in a progressive sequence. Don't see who can tackle before you teach your players how to properly tackle.
   c. Provide proper equipment and facilities. A wall behind the basketball backboard must be covered with a mat. Failure to do so would probably be considered negligence because it is foreseeable that players may get hurt if their normal actions bring them in contact with the wall. Foreseeability, always a critical issue in determining negligence, is nothing more than common sense. It is foreseeable, for example, that a student will get a cauliflower ear if he wrestles the entire season without a headgear, or that chances of a drowning increase when a lifeguard is not on duty.
   d. Properly supervise the participants. The most-cited reason for suing coaches is permitting people to participate without supervision and/or leaving the area of participation. Not being there at practice breaks a basic rule of safety.
   e. Warn participants about the dangers of the specific activity. Nothing seems to incur the wrath of coaches more than this established legal requirement. Coaches must inform and warn every player, prior to and during the season, about the dangers of the particular activity. The more informed the individual, the better-prepared the individual. If a warning prevents one student from being injured, it is worth it. Warnings can and should be presented within the normal context of the coaching procedure. The courts have determined this to be a legal requirement, and we are all playing in that court!

A coach who properly conditions, instructs, provides good equipment, and proper facilities, supervises, and warns his players of inherent risks falls into what the courts call a reasonable, prudent person or professional. And that is the best any court can require.

When talking to coaches about how they can meet their legal responsibilities and still have creative, vigorous and valuable programs, I suggest a list of do's and don'ts. The essence of these hints falls into what I call the three C's of safety, the basis of legal responsibility:

1. *Caring.* People who clearly care about the people they coach beyond the win/lose consideration generally avoid lawsuit entanglements.
2. *Credibility.* It is important to promote the public relations of safety the same way we promote our sport. Let students, faculty, administration, and community know what you are doing to increase the overall safety of the program. For example, hold a clinic for the girls' lacrosse team's parents that includes a talk by the trainer, a demonstration of warm-up exercises, and a talk about rules of safety.
3. *Continuation.* The hardest of the three C's. Not only must one demonstrate care and credibility, one must continually demonstrate these qualities. Supervision must be 100 percent and continuous.

The Three C's can be summarized by one big C — Common Sense.

Every athletic program has a new opponent. It is not an opponent who is a 290-pound all-world defensive tackle nor an opposing team's 6'5" female basketball player. It is the litigiousness of our society. Sport has not escaped this trend. Coaches must realize that more than formations and uniforms have changed in athletics. The ultimate answer is what we've been doing forever — creating a game plan. In this case we need a defensive game plan that starts and ends with the well-informed, reasonable and prudent professional — and that includes understanding legal responsibilities. Such awareness can keep you *on* the court, rather than *in* the court. Now that is common sense.

---

§ 1.6. Official.

By Gerald Austin

As I was watching a basketball game one day, a play occurred that caused me to think, "What implications does that play have for the official covering the action?" A player had stolen the ball and broken away for a sure basket. As he was going up to dunk the ball, the player from whom the ball had been stolen came in hard from behind and drove the shooter head-over-heels into the supports under the basket. A two-shot foul was called. The official had enforced the rule as it is written. But are there legal ramifications for an official when a player is injured? Let me pursue the subject from a position of "What if . . . ."

In a football game an end is going up to catch a pass downfield and the cornerback, in an attempt to bring the receiver down and jar the ball loose, hits him with a forearm to the head — but there is no flag. The player does not get up but is taken off the field on a stretcher. Is the covering official liable for negligence? Is the entire crew liable?

Many times in basketball a player driving to the basket releases the ball and then crashes into a defensive player under the basket. There is no call because the official has determined the player was not in a position to play defense. However, what if the offensive player does not get up because he has injured his knee, which eventually requires surgery. Is the official negligent if he doesn't call a foul? Has he permitted rough play that could lead to any type of legal action? If the official makes a call, does it protect him from being liable?

The rules of basketball state that if a player becomes injured during a live ball, the official shall hold his whistle until the ball becomes dead or the player's team gains control. More often than not officials will stop the action so that an injured player may be attended to by the trainer. Most officials are becoming more cognizant of players becoming injured and are stopping play. I believe this is being done out of a sense of safety and concern for the players.

Let's look at another aspect of possible litigation that seems to have implications for officials: the rowdy and uncontrolled crowd behavior at some athletic contests. Several officials with whom I have talked have stated emphatically that if the organization responsible for control of the fans and the well-being of the officials did not take the necessary action to ensure their safety, they would definitely take legal action. The uncontrolled, boisterous conduct of more and more spectators at games is one of the major concerns of officials. Officials are looking to game administrators to provide for their safety and protection before, during and after the game.

I am not aware of any litigation involving game officials at present. I do remember two lawsuits several years ago involving basketball officials. One was by two officials who were dropped from a conference because they were "blackballed" by a coach of that conference. The judge ruled that they were to be reinstated unless the conference had documented evidence of their incompetence. The other case was when a coach kicked an official as they were leaving the floor. The coach had to apologize publicly and agree to conduct himself in an appropriate manner during the next season.

Officials have not been a party to very many lawsuits involving athletic events. Let us hope it stays that way.

---

§ 1.7. Product Liability Expert.

By Maria Dennison

The sporting goods industry is in trouble. And the cause of the trouble is the current state of product liability law.

Did you know that ten years ago there were 14 football helmet manufacturers and that today there are two that control the market? That of the $42 wholesale price of a football helmet $11 goes to product liability insurance and litigation costs? That when new helmets were strapped on by nearly 500,000 football players in the fall of 1984, more than $5 million of the price of the helmets was already set aside for product liability expenses? That manufacturers and school districts are paying millions of dollars to injured victims for accidents not involving a defective product? And that in recent years state courts have held sporting goods manufacturers liable for:

— Injuries that were not their fault?
— Injuries caused by misuse of products?
— Failure to warn sufficiently that sports involve risk?
— Improvements to products?

Causes of these conditions, as viewed by industry, include the following:

— Judicial expansion of theories of liability that bring the manufacturer closer to the status of insurer;
— Relaxation of state and federal evidentiary rules;
— Continuous erosion of traditional defenses available to industry;
— Diminishing demand for individual responsibility;
— Expansion of the plaintiff's bar in number, skill and ingenuity;
— The seeking from a manufacturer of millions of dollars in damages for a design aspect of a product that has been in wide use for many years but which is nevertheless redesigned in the jury room;
— Jury responsibility for determining how many dollars should be assessed against a defendant to punish him or make an example of him for some alleged misconduct that is more than negligent but less than criminal.

The dilemma these legal trends pose for the sports community is well illustrated by the following story:

It is a fine afternoon in Small-Town, U.S.A., and a football game is in progress on the school field. The score is tied, it is fourth down, and three yards to go for a touchdown. Johnny takes the ball and bulls his way through an equally determined defense. A cheer goes up from his teammates — he made it! But Johnny does not get up.

He's sustained a paralyzing injury that will change his life, a tragedy that years ago would have been uncompensated and probably accepted as bad luck.

Not so today. Today, Johnny may seek compensation from the school, the coach, and the helmet manufacturer. And he has a good chance of winning a large injury award to meet his lifelong financial needs.

True, Johnny has suffered a tragic injury and there are expenses to be paid. But what about the concept of fault? And of deterrence? Will the coaches be any more able to prevent accidental injuries? And can football helmets be made that will absolutely prevent head and neck injuries? More likely, schools may decide to bar football on their playing fields and helmet manufacturers may look for another product to make.

Liability problems are not limited to football. For example, a Columbia, Maryland newspaper has reported that an injured player filed a $2.2 million lawsuit against the Maryland Catholic Youth Organization for an eye injury received during a basketball game. The referees had allegedly failed "to take proper and reasonable precautions in exercising ordinary care to assure the safety of the players."

Manufacturers, merchandisers, sports officials and school districts are held responsible for accidents which they have no way of controlling. The result: Manufacturers are being litigated into extinction, schools are thinking about eliminating sports programs, and trial lawyers who receive $1.16 for every dollar an injured player receives are looking for more "deep pockets." Nor is compensation uniform. Injuries compensated in one state are ignored in another.

Product liability is a national problem requiring a national solution. Uncertainties and imbalance in the product liability tort litigation system will continue in the absence of a uniform statute at the federal level. Over the years, a maze of conflicting state court decisions and a hodgepodge of state statutes have inhibited manufacturers from implementing technological improvements to products and have produced the high legal and business costs shouldered by the consuming public. And those increased prices have made U.S. manufacturers less price competitive with their foreign counterparts. A federal law could go far in creating fairness and balance between the interests of sports product sellers and product users.

CHAPTER 2

ADMINISTRATIVE ISSUES

§ 2.1. Implications of the *Seattle* Decision.

By Samuel Adams

A court decision in February, 1982, *Thompson v. Seattle Public School District,* an unpublished decision, opened a new era in sport litigation with far-reaching implications for sport at all levels: youth, interscholastic, intercollegiate and professional. In that case a young man was awarded $6.3 million in a lawsuit against the Seattle school district and a coach for a football injury that left him a quadriplegic in 1975. The young player was a 15 year old sophomore at the time of the injury. He was injured when he was running with the football and lowered his head to ward off tacklers. He was hit on the top of his helmet, causing an injury to his spinal cord. The player sued his coach for failure to warn of the dangers inherent in football and for improper instruction in coaching.

§ 2.1(A). Shift From Product Liability to Responsibility of Coaches and School Districts.

Most liability suits in sport in earlier years were based on equipment, or what is termed product liability. This case presents a shift from product liability and manufacturers of sports equipment to coaches and school districts. The court also brought into focus the limits of the "assumption of risk" doctrine, which had been one of the main defenses in sports injury litigation cases. Cym Lowell and John Weistart, writing in *The Law of Sports,* define assumption of risk in the following manner: "This doctrine states that a party who voluntarily assumes a risk of harm arising from the conduct of another cannot recover if harm in fact results."

Lowell and Weistart cite four circumstances in which assumption of risk may arise. The circumstance which applies most closely to injuries to athletes is "when one is explicitly aware of a risk caused by the potential negligence of another, and yet proceeds to encounter it voluntarily." The authors also point out that in ordinary cases involving the assertion of negligence liability the court will consider the duty owed by the defendant to the plaintiff to ameliorate unreasonable risks to the plaintiff and the duty owed by the plaintiff to himself: "[I]t may be stated as a general rule that voluntary, *'sui juris'* participants in lawful sporting activity assume, as a matter of law, all of the ordinary and inherent risks in the sport, as long as the activity is played in good faith and the injury is not the result of an intentional or wilful act."

This general rule applied until the *Seattle* case, as illustrated by *Vendrell v. School District #26C,* 376 P.2d 406 (Or. 1962). In this case a high school football player was rendered a paraplegic as the result of a broken neck sustained when he tried to use his head as a battering ram to ward off opposing tacklers (as in the *Seattle* case). When the player brought suit to

17

recover for his injuries, the court denied recovery. After noting that he had received extensive training, practice, and play under the competent instruction and supervision of his coaches, the court stated that the general rules of participant non-recovery in football were that

> The playing of football is a body-contact sport. The game demands that the players come into physical contact with each other constantly, frequently with great force. The linesmen charge the opposing line vigorously, shoulder to shoulder. The tackler faces the risk of leaping at the swiftly moving legs of the ball-carrier and the latter must be prepared to strike the ground violently. Body contacts, bruises, and clashes are inherent in the game. There is no other way to play it. No prospective player need be told that participants in the game of football may sustain injury. That fact is self-evident. It draws to the game the manly. They accept the risk, blows, clashes, and injuries without whimper.

The fact that you may be injured in a collision sport such as football is no longer self-evident. In fact, courts have held that sport, with the exception of boxing are not inherently dangerous; they only become dangerous by the way they are conducted.

The two major charges in the *Seattle* case were: failure to warn sufficiently and failure to properly instruct. During the trial, the plaintiff's lawyers also charged that the Seattle school district administration was negligent in not providing a specific football teaching curriculum and safety manual for coaches, and did not have a formal evaluation procedure for coaches. These allegations influenced the decision of the jurors.

The football coach and the Seattle school district conducted their football program in a manner which was usual and customary for most high schools in the United States. As the Seattle school district's athletic director at the time stated in the *Seattle Times*: "We follow the general practices of districts throughout the country. If we're doing it wrong, all districts in the country are doing it wrong." Interviews with the jurors after the trial did not produce specific reasons for their opinions nor suggestions for remedial action. School districts throughout the country have been left with the monumental problem of what their coaches and school districts must do to prevent litigation in the future, not only in football but in any sport, physical education, intramurals and any activity that involves movement or risk.

§ 2.1(B). Failure to Warn.

In developing a program for safety in sports to help ensure the safety of participants and serve as a defense against litigation, districts must consider the more specific charges presented during the *Seattle* trial:

> a. Players were not adequately warned about the dangers of lowering the head when running with the football, nor of making primary contact with the top of the helmet.
> b. Players were never specifically warned that if they struck another player with the top of the helmet they could sustain a neck injury which could result in becoming a quadriplegic.

c. Players' parents were never warned of the specific injuries which their son could sustain in football, and specifically they were never told he could become a quadriplegic.

d. Players were never informed of the specific anatomical damage which could occur to the neck if the head was used as a primary point of contact.

e. Coaches did not provide written or illustrative material on the proper way of running with the football, or the specific dangers of lowering the head while running with the ball, or of using the head as a primary point of contact.

§ 2.1(C). Failure to Instruct.

a. Coaches failed to utilize written warnings, illustrative charts, and safety films in instructing players about the dangers of lowering their heads.

b. Coaches did not use effective drills, nor a sufficient variety of instructional methods, to teach players how to run safely with the ball and to ensure that they would not lower their heads.

c. Players were not adequately informed regarding the reason for the "spearing rule" in football.

d. Players were not sufficiently warned, chastised or penalized if they lowered their head when making contact with another player.

e. Coaches did not inform the players about the Points of Emphasis, contained in the 1975 *National Federation Football Rule Book,* related to the use of the helmet in making primary contact with another player.

§ 2.1(D). Negligence of the Seattle School District.

a. The district failed to certify coaches.

b. The district failed to maintain and evaluate district-wide injury reports.

c. The district failed to properly monitor injury rates and their causes and solutions.

d. No person within the school or district was specifically assigned responsibility as a safety officer for athletics.

e. Coaches were not required to attend clinics, and the district did not pay for their voluntary participation.

f. The district failed to provide coaches with enough current information and data regarding football injuries and the dangers of using the helmet as the primary point of contact.

g. The district had few written sports safety regulations or guidelines.

h. Coaches were not required to utilize standardized instructional techniques or materials.

i. The district provided no football curriculum or safety manual to coaches.

     j. There was no formal evaluation of coaches.

     k. A sophomore was allowed to play varsity football.

     l. Coaching activities were inadequately supervised and monitored.

§ 2.1(E). Implications of the *Seattle* Decision.

The *Seattle* case, while very frightening and perhaps even threatening to the continuation of athletic programs is positive in many respects. The case has created a renewed emphasis on the safety and welfare of the participant in sports. Although most school districts and coaches have always emphasized the safety aspect of sports, taught correct techniques and supervised properly, they are now much more sensitive to recording their procedures and evaluating themselves and their programs to serve the best interests of student athletes. Other implications and recommendations include:

1. Parents and students should sign an "Assumption of Risk" form. Although this would not be a legal advantage, it could discourage some litigation.

2. Parents should be required to sign a "Consent and Release" form. The wording of the release should be narrow in scope and related specifically to participation in practice and game activities.

3. Districts should give consideration to adopting written guidelines or policies concerning the following:

    a. There should be written minimum qualifications for the selection of coaches. This may lead to certification of coaches, which appears to be a step in the right direction. A set of written procedures and criteria for the selection of coaches should be developed. If an administrator assigns unqualified personnel to coach, the administrator and district may be held liable for that person's conduct.

    b. General safety guidelines and procedures in the form of manuals should be developed for each sport activity.

    c. Continuing education for coaches should be required. Paying for coaches' fees and expenses at clinics, workshops and seminars should be considered.

    d. Instructional guides and materials for each sport should be developed. This should include a progressive sequence in teaching skills, drills used and proper techniques.

    e. Sports library and audiovisual materials related to sports safety should be expanded.

    f. Coaches should be required to maintain standardized injury reports and to submit them to a central office for compilation and analysis. Daily injury report forms should be developed, as well as forms for doctors' reports, treatment and authorization to return to activity. A student's forms should be retained until the age of majority.

    g. Coaches of high-risk sports should be required to develop daily practice schedules and to retain such records for three years.

    h. Coaches should be required to have cardiopulmonary resuscitation (CPR) training.

4. Parents and athletes should be provided written information regarding the potential catastrophic injuries which can occur in each sport, the proximate causes of such injuries and the player's responsibilities in avoiding actions which can cause such injuries. Such forms would require the signature of the student's parents and should be kept on file until the age of majority. The dangers involved should be spelled out in very specific terms. All foreseeable dangers should be demonstrated methods of avoidance and safety techniques should be taught.

5. Coaches should be provided with current informational, instructional and illustrative materials dealing with physical conditioning, training and sports safety. This implies that activities which can prove to be dangerous or injurious to health unless proper conditioning and progression is followed can create a potentially liable situation. Coaches must be aware of the muscular strength and cardiovascular conditioning necessary for various levels of skills. If an activity or condition such as climate (e.g., extreme humidity) requires special training, proper training procedures must be followed. If an activity has a progressive sequence of skills, the lower level of skills must be mastered before the higher level of skills is attempted. All activities must be within the limits of the participants.

6. Coaches must be closely screened and evaluated by qualified personnel regarding their qualifications and performance. Files should be maintained on the qualifications of coaches and their continuing education activities. Coaches must be held responsible for knowing and teaching proper techniques. They must also be abreast of correct methodology.

7. The instructional and safety programs at each school should be audited by a qualified person on an ongoing basis. Program content and methods should be evaluated in terms of effectiveness in providing appropriate information and skill development.

8. The responsibility and authority of building administrators, activity coordinators and athletic office staff should be clearly defined in terms of:
    a. selection, orientation and supervision of coaches;
    b. auditing and enforcement of district policies and procedures; and
    c. evaluation of coaches and athletic activity coordinators.

9. Continuous evaluation of policies, procedures, coaches and all segments of the athletic program should be carried out. Guidelines for this evaluation should be written and responsibility for doing it should be designated. Evidence that it is being done should be recorded.

10. Record-keeping is essential protection. Written planning not only assists in the development of high-quality coaching, it also documents procedures in case of litigation. Records should be kept for at least three or four years. If a serious injury has occurred the records for the athlete should be kept until the age of majority.

It is recommended that whatever steps are taken in response to the *Seattle* case be predicated on the following questions:

1. Is it reasonable to believe that the action will effectively and significantly reduce the number or severity of catastrophic injuries?
2. Does the action have the potential of reducing or discouraging litigation?
3. Will the action reduce the probability of the district being found negligent in case of litigation?
4. Does the action actually increase the liability to the district by establishing policies and procedures which may not be followed to the letter by administrators or coaches?

§ 2.1(F). Conclusion.

In sum, the *Seattle* case has made school districts aware that they need specific written guidelines, objectives, and procedures for their programs in order to fulfill their legal responsibilities while keeping the best interests of student-athletes a top priority.

It has also made coaches more aware of the quality of their planning and instruction. Coaches are more safety-conscious and more aware of the need for being up-to-date in proper training practices and techniques. Coaches are now looking for all foreseeable dangers in their sports and this is producing a safer environment for sport participants.

---

§ 2.2. Sports, the Law and Due Process.

By Harry Mallios

During the last decade, sports-related issues reviewed by courts of law have increased dramatically. As a result, considerable critical literature has produced a striking order of events with an almost revolutionary impact upon the administration of athletic programs. The issues which confronted athletic administrators during this time resulted largely from mandates that arose in the aftermath of federal legislation and litigation involving sports programs. The outcome of this legislation or litigation has altered the way athletic associations, educational institutions, coaches and student athletes, or any combination of these, have resolved their conflicts. In many instances, accepted procedures owe their genesis to the outcome of litigation or legislation which set legal parameters as guidelines for the athletic administrator.

Educational institutions, coaches and student athletes are constantly subjected to varying degrees of penalty for violation of rules and regulations. As a result, athletic associations and athletic conferences which have imposed penalties have them tested in the courts. Just as the severity of the infraction may vary, so also does the appropriate penalty and its method of application and determination. The penalties which are most severe are those that place an institution on probation, suspend or terminate the employment of a coach or suspend or terminate the sports eligibility of a student athlete. Penalties such as these have been challenged in court because the penalties were considered unfair or the procedure was considered arbitrary. Invariably the level of inquiry regarding the action taken involves constitutional questions.

This section deals with the increasing prominence of the due process clause of the fifth and fourteenth amendments to the United States Constitution. The legal aspect of due process is more accurately expressed by cases involving the exercise of authority against athletic associations, athletic conferences, educational institutions, coaches and student athletes.

§ 2.2(A). Sports-Related Legal Issues.

In 1975, the National Collegiate Athletic Association (NCAA) adopted a policy during its 70th annual convention incorporating the provision of "due process of law" when dealing with student athletes. The National Association of Collegiate Directors of Athletics (N.A.C.D.A.) exhibited interest in establishing a clear perspective of due process during its convention that same year.

Although athletic directors may not be lawyers, they are being called upon with greater frequency to make decisions which fall directly within the encompassing parameters of the legal environment. As a result, it is necessary that an educational institution and athletic administrator establish a clear understanding of the judicial view in athletic administrative functions generally and the legal status of "due process of law" particularly.

In the majority of instances, legal questions are dealt with in the absence of formal legal training. In a larger and more practical way, however, educational institutions and athletic administrators should no longer assume that their actions will not be questioned. Athletic administrators should be cognizant of the diversity between the law and "common notions" of the law in the administration of their official duties.

The prominence of Title IX legislation has done much to create an awareness of the law as it relates to sex equity in sports programs. The recent *Grove City* decision by the United States Supreme Court continues to shape the legislative impact of Title IX and is reflected in the attempt by Congress to amend Title IX by expanding it institutionally, as opposed to the programmatic application held by the Supreme Court.

There has been a large number of cases brought before the courts challenging the constitutionality of imposed penalties against institutions, coaches or student athletes. An example of this was reported in the June 6, 1984, issue of the Chronicle of Higher Education, highlighting a university basketball coach's ongoing challenge of the NCAA's right to order his suspension for rule violations in the basketball program which allegedly took place prior to and after his arrival at the university. The coach filed suit seeking a restraining order blocking his suspension from coaching, claiming he would be denied, without "due process of law," his property right to be actively employed in his professional career. The educational institution, as a member of the NCAA, was placed in the position that required it to take "appropriate actions" against staff members who violate rules. The threshold question is whether a university can enforce such a severe penalty as suspension against a staff member without satisfying due process requirements. In a statement prepared for the court, Samuel Lionel, the attorney for the coach, stated: "Every precept of due process was ignored by the NCAA when he was not permitted to defend himself properly . . . . The NCAA established a terrible precedent of trying the case and then bringing him in to defend himself."

Following testimony, the NCAA responded to enforcement proceedings and procedures employed by the committee on infractions and its investigative staff by stating that it stood by the procedures of the Association and supported its staff members. The NCAA statement went on to say that the hearing was "the most extensive hearing procedure for a single institution in NCAA history."

The case, which attracted national publicity, has been before the courts for approximately seven years. A decision was reached in June, 1984, favoring the coach. The Las Vegas district court ruled that the NCAA violated the coach's "due process" rights. The NCAA indicated that it would appeal the decision to the Nevada Supreme Court and continued legal action seems certain.

A similar case was decided approximately one month earlier by the United States Supreme Court in which a high school football coach/athletic director's job was terminated. The question of violation of the constitutionally protected right of "due process of law" was the issue. The Supreme Court of the United States affirmed a lower court's ruling that the coach/athletic director had a "property interest" in his position of employment. The high school coach had been dismissed by the school board following one year of employment although he had been promised two years of employment by the school board. The U.S. Court of Appeals for the Seventh Circuit said that the coach/athletic director had been illegally dismissed, and as a result, had been denied his constitutional protection of due process. It added that he had a property interest in such employment. Curtailment of employment seems to be a major penalty since it places careers in jeopardy, and, therefore, courts require a great degree of circumspection on the part of those who impose such a penalty.

§ 2.2(B). Concern: Administrator, NCAA, Congress.

Athletic administration is assuming greater legal significance as many administrators question the frequency of penalties directed against them as violations of their constitutional rights. Judicial decisions indicate that those who would seek to impose penalties of a severe nature which impair or jeopardize an individual's career should be aware of the propriety of procedures and limitations as imposed by law.

Athletic administrators initiating disciplinary action against a coach or student athlete must proceed in a fair and legal manner. This does not mean that an athletic administrator, educational institution, athletic association or conference cannot impose penalties. The implication is clear, however, that failure to proceed in a fair, reasonable and constitutional manner may result in litigation.

When a severe penalty is contemplated against a student athlete, the NCAA suggests guidelines which state:

> [T]he member institution should notify the student athlete concerned and afford him an opportunity for an informal hearing before the faculty athletic representative, director of athletics, or other appropriate institutional authority before action is taken, it being understood that the hearing opportunity should not delay or set aside the member's obligations . . . .

The obligations mentioned above are recommended in the Association's *Policies and Practices for Intercollegiate Athletics,* and the policy stipulated: "[T]his hearing opportunity will avoid possible mistaken actions affecting the student-athlete's eligibility and should satisfy due process procedures if any be required." This recommended policy suggests a course of action for member institutions to follow when dealing with student athletes and applying Association regulations. This suggested course of action should be standard procedure in any serious matter affecting the status of a student athlete. Certainly, the rudiments of due process rights are more than extended if such procedures are followed by the NCAA policies.

Media coverage and publicity which surround the controversy involving sanctions or penalties assessed against member institutions, coaches or student athletes for rule violations are widespread. This controversy caused the Congress of the United States to undertake an investigation into NCAA practices during the middle 1970's to determine whether methods employed in the Association's investigatory procedures afford due process protection. The House Subcommittee on Oversight and Investigations reviewed procedures by the NCAA's Committee on Infractions and heard a number of complaints from those who felt they had been deprived of fundamental rights as a result of measures taken or penalties imposed by the NCAA.

And, more recently, it was reported that U.S. Senator Howard Metzenbaum would hold hearings on whether colleges are required to continue student athletes' grants-in-aid until graduation, provided they are making progress toward a degree. A televised report by the Center for Athletes' Rights and Education (CARE) aroused Senator Metzenbaum's interest in the limitation imposed by the NCAA on the length of time scholarships are awarded. NCAA legislation allows member institutions to award grants-in-aid for periods of one year. Following the one-year award period, student athletes may have their scholarship aid renewed or not renewed. If the scholarship aid is not renewed, the student athlete must be informed of the right to appeal the decision of nonrenewal.

An example of how due process may be included in the appeal procedure is as follows:

1. Procedures for appeal must have been established by the institution.
2. A notice of nonrenewal of scholarship aid must be received by the student.
3. A notice of the right to be heard must be received by the student.
4. The hearing body must be impartial.

Congress is getting involved because some critics of the NCAA allege that it is not doing anything about the student athletes who do not graduate after scholarship aid has been withdrawn. John L. Toner, the President of the NCAA, and members of the NCAA Council reject such a claim and feel that Congress should not be involved in such matters.

§ 2.2(C). What Is Due Process of Law?

It is well-documented that member institutions, student athletes and coaches have been subjected to varying penalties for violation of rules and regulations. The penalties have ranged from a reprimand to institutional probation for one or more years, suspension or termination of a coach and student athletes' suspension or termination of eligibility for participation. Just as the degree of the infraction varies, so may the degree of penalty vary when imposed by an athletic association or institution. Court challenges continue to question the severity of the penalty assessed in its application and violation of "due process of law."

What does the "due process of law" mean and what are the legal implications of this term? More importantly, does due process apply to student athletes who are disciplined for an alleged rule violation? Does due process apply to a coach who may be disciplined for an alleged rule violation and does it apply to member institutions that are disciplined by an athletic association or conference?

The Constitution of the United States responds not once but twice to such questions when it states that no person shall be deprived of life, liberty or property without "due process of law." The fifth amendment to the Constitution places such restraints upon the federal government, and the fourteenth amendment establishes the same limitation when state action is involved. In determining whether "state action" exists, some legal scholars argue the constitutional application affects only public as opposed to private action. The NCAA is a private organization comprising a voluntary membership of institutions. The Association has among its membership, however, both public and private institutions. Insofar as public institutions are concerned, an association with such institutions within its membership would fall within the concept of state action. Private institutions, some argue, may not be held to the same constitutional due process standard. The question raised in private action, however, is whether the state has so insulated itself into a position of interdependence that it must be recognized as a joint participant in a constitutional sense.

Due process and the legal implication associated with this term is a complex and, quite often, misunderstood concept. As a result, the attempt to define due process is not an easy task. The original significance of the idea underlying "due process of law" was that a person should not be deprived of his life, liberty or property except in accordance with the procedures established by law. As a result, due process was invoked to challenge the validity of arbitrary assertions of executive power.

To understand the complexity of the expression, it seems appropriate to continue to develop the breadth and scope of the term. In *Hannah v. Larche,*

363 U.S. 420 (1960), former Chief Justice Earl Warren of the United States Supreme Court stated: "[D]ue process is an elusive concept. Its exact boundaries are indefinable and its content varies according to specific factual contexts."

Additionally, in *Palko v. Connecticut,* 302 U.S. 319 (1937), Supreme Court Justice Benjamin Cardozo felt that for due process to be violated, the deprival of a right must "violate a principle of justice so rooted in the traditions and conscience of our people as to be ranked as fundamental." Another definition of due process, found in *Pennoyer v. Neff,* 95 U.S. 714 (1877), is that the term "means a course of legal proceedings which have been established in our system of jurisprudence for the protection and enforcement of private rights."

Charles Adam White, former chairman of the NCAA's Committee on Infractions and a professor of constitutional law at the University of Texas, stated in the September 1978 issue of *NCAA News* that due process "is going to vary depending upon the possible consequences to the person in question." This rationale places the issue in proper perspective; namely, that "due process of law" may indeed vary depending upon: (1) the seriousness of the infraction, (2) the possible consequences to the institution or individual in question and (3) the degree of sanction or penalty imposed. These three items are the basic considerations embraced in the concept of due process. Further reinforcement lies in the distinction by White that there is no one way of describing what is required, but rather, they vary according to the circumstances. Thus, when the violation of a rule or regulation requires only a moderate penalty, the procedures required for satisfying due process are not the same as when probation or suspension of employment or eligibility could be a possible penalty. How severe the penalty must be to reach constitutional status is cloudy; however, it seems clear that if the proceedings involve a serious penalty, several fundamental constitutional safeguards are required.

§ 2.2(D). Requirements to Ensure Due Process.

Contemporary due process protection finds safeguards which are embraced and found in its two dimensions — "substantive" and "procedural." Both aspects are equally subject to legal review. "Substantive" due process involves the rule, regulation or legislation being violated; namely, is it fair and reasonable? The principle or precept must have a function and it must be clearly related to the fulfillment of that function. "Procedural" due process, on the other hand, has at its focal point the questioning of the decision-making process which is followed in determining whether the rule or regulation has been violated and the penalty, if any, that is imposed. In other words, when measuring "substantive" due process, does the rule or legislation have a purpose and is it clearly related to the accomplishment of that purpose? In applying elements of "substantive" due process, an institution or individual being penalized has the legal right to seek to make a rule or legislation invalid if it does not satisfy the legal parameters of "substantive" due process.

The second aspect of due process equally subject to court review deals with "procedural" due process. The balancing process of notice comes first. This shall be clearly stated: a charge of what rule or regulation has been violated and what act is thought to have been committed which makes it appropriate to impose a serious penalty. Basically, the requirement of such a degree of specificity is simply to give the accused an opportunity to know what to defend against and to know reasonably well in advance what is thought to have been violated so as to make useful the next level of the requirement itself, that is, the hearing.

There must be a hearing, particularly if the application of a severe penalty seems imminent. This hearing need not be a formal or ceremonial undertaking, but it must at least provide an opportunity to appear and, generally, to be present while those who are presenting charges state their position. Essentially, this hearing could make certain that whoever is making the critical decision governing the future outcome of the case will make it on the basis of information which has been shared and the basis that one can speak informally as to the nature of the evidence presented.

There is a requirement of impartiality on the part of the group or individual who makes the decision. The right of "impartiality" is that a court would likely require a degree of detachment in the group or individual making the critical judgment.

An issue which causes confusion and controversy and remains a subject of disagreement with the courts on the issue of due process is whether the accused may be accompanied by an advisor or an attorney. There have been cases which have rejected the notion that the accused has a right to have an attorney present. However, the changing scene suggests that attorneys-at-law will probably be allowed access to the hearings in which consequences may be serious. At the same time, the attorney may play a limited function; that is, he may advise but not necessarily be given the prerogative to engage in the customary adversary role pursued in court.

And, finally, although it may not be a constitutional requirement, a hearing which could place an institution on probation, relieve a coach of his duties or declare a student athlete ineligible should have a transcript of the proceedings on file for future use in the event of litigation. This is not to suggest an elaborate or costly mechanism nor a court stenographer, but possibly a tape recording of the entire proceedings. This suggestion is made in the spirit of fairness, because to the extent that you can persuade a court of law that the hearing was fundamentally fair, the court is unlikely to intervene and make an independent review of the entire transaction.

Due process, of course, would entail the most exhausting provisions to ensure that justice is served in the criminal courts. The outcome of such a court trial could mean incarceration, and if such a liberty is taken away, exhaustive procedures are necessarily required. It could hardly be otherwise, for "due process of law" in criminal proceedings requires that trials be conducted according to the prescribed forms and judicial procedure of the state for the protection of the individual rights and liberties of its citizens. This implies that the nature of the penalty imposed should relate to the procedures followed, or, stated another way, the greater the degree of penalty, the more process that is due. As a result, due process varies upon the magnitude of the penalty, the right being violated and the relationship of the individuals. Something different is called for in a criminal trial as opposed to an NCAA athletic conference or institutional investigation. And while "due process of law" means adequate notice, a fair hearing, impartiality and an opportunity to present one's side of an issue, the touchstone is reasonableness and fairness. Whether a criminal trial or an NCAA infractions case, the quality of procedural due process will vary as a legal requirement according to the gravity of the penalty and the extent of jeopardy in which an individual is placed.

§ 2.2(E). Conclusion.

It could be that those who have an oblique concept of the parameters of due process may feel that certain action taken is violative of specific rights. All citizens, of course, are guaranteed fundamental rights under the Constitution and simply because one is a student athlete, coach or member institution would not cause one to forfeit these rights. However, unless one is trained and familiar with the complexity of the legal environment, the full meaning and depth of the term could easily be misconceived and misunderstood. In *Davis v. Ann Arbor Public Schools,* 313 F. Supp. 1217 (E.D. Mich. 1970), the court noted a generally held misconception regarding due process when it stated: "The plaintiff misconceives the law. . . . '[A] full-dress judicial hearing with the right to cross examine witnesses' is not required for due process."

The NCAA, although challenged numerous times, has been consistently sustained in cases challenging procedures taken in enforcement cases. In the previously mentioned case in which the college basketball coach was upheld in his claim of a due process violation by the NCAA, the decision by the court has been viewed as a crack in the dike by some, insofar as the NCAA's invulnerability is concerned. However, it is the first of many steps to be taken in what will be a long and time-consuming journey through the rising tiers of authority in the courts. It may be well for the critics who condemn the action of the NCAA Committee on Infractions to note that they should not fall into the trap of equating the requirements of "due process of law" with one's personal views of desirable procedure. The NCAA, in particular, has fared well in convincing those who have reviewed its imposed penalties and sanctions that the nature of the hearing and the proceeding itself have been fundamentally fair.

As a practical matter, while the athletic administrator need not be an attorney, it is clear, indeed, that constitutional guarantees afforded citizens in general apply equally as well to educational institutions, administrators, coaches and student athletes. The immediate, practical and constitutional result of this is clear: the courts are reviewing with less hesitancy claims presented by aggrieved parties charging a violation of protected rights. This legal development, which has accelerated markedly during the past decade, continues to the present. In light of the changing nature in the attitude of today's courts, it is suggested that a primary concern regarding the imposition of penalties which jeopardize an individual's career should be minimum standards of "due process of law," the touchstone of which is fairness.

It should be remembered that the circumstances of the procedural steps taken and not necessarily the penalty assessed will determine whether litigation is justified and, indeed, "due process of law" has been served. Athletic administrators cannot ignore the fact that for whatever reason, good or bad, the legal dimension of sport-related issues are being reviewed and assuming new proportions.

§ 2.3. Warnings and Waivers.

By Gary Nygaard

The use of warnings and waivers is a significant issue in sports injury litigation. In recent years, our judicial system has stated emphatically that players must be informed of the risks they face when they choose to participate in a sport. Consequently, the proper use of warnings of inherent risks is essential. Waivers, on the other hand, are not as highly regarded by our courts, and their use may be questionable and is certainly limited. At present, there seems to be some confusion about the proper use of warnings and waivers. This section discusses the concepts of inherent risk, warnings and waivers. Recommendations and examples are provided to illustrate the way warnings should be used and the way waivers may be used. In addition, this section presents a discussion of the limitations of waivers.

§ 2.3(A). Inherent Risk.

It is essential that athletes be aware of the risks they face when they play a sport, and that they face only those risks that are inherent in the sport. In football being tackled is an inherent risk, but being tackled on a field lined with unslaked lime is not. In basketball a player may make contact with a padded wall, but he should not make contact with an unreinforced glass window. In baseball a player may slide on a rough surface, but should not slide through large rocks and broken glass. In each example the latter risk is not an inherent risk, and only inherent risks may be assumed by players. An inherent risk is one that occurs during the normal play of a sport and within the rules of the sport on a safe facility by trained players who have had sound instruction, have proper equipment and know, understand and appreciate the risks of the sport.

The last part of this definition of an inherent risk is important to this discussion about warnings and waivers. It is not enough that athletes are subjected only to inherent risks. They must also be aware of these risks. Further, our judicial system expects a three-layered level of awareness of risks so that players know, understand and appreciate the inherent risks of a sport. An offhand, one-time mention of risks in a sport is insufficient. Warnings are necessary, and these warnings should be clear and apparent to athletes so that they know (have a concept of in the mind), understand (know of the meaning or importance) and appreciate (be fully aware of the importance or magnitude) the warning.

Two recent case law examples illustrate the extent to which players should know, understand and appreciate the inherent risks of a sport. In *Passantino v. Board of Education of City of New York,* 395 N.Y.S.2d 628 (N.Y. 1977), a baseball lawsuit, a player was able to recover over $1,800,000, in part because of improper warnings. The young man was on third base when the sign was flashed for a squeeze play. As the pitch was thrown the player broke for home. The batter missed the bunt attempt and the catcher caught the ball and blocked home plate. In an attempt to jar the ball loose the player made a head-first slide and suffered a crippling injury. The injured player was an experienced baseball player and had never been taught to slide head first, only feet first. The court held that this was insufficient and that in addition to teaching the feet-first slide the coach should have warned the player of the danger of sliding head first. On appeal this award was reduced to $1,000,000, and on further appeal was dismissed. This illustrates a disturbing feature of sport injury litigation: the law is whatever it decides to be on a given day.

A similar case occurred in Seattle, Washington, with a high school football player who became a quadriplegic because of an injury in a game. The player was a running back and lowered his head in an attempt to get past a tackler, suffering the traumatic injury in the attempt. His lawyers asserted that the player was not properly warned of the dangers of lowering his head while carrying the football. The court initially awarded the young player $6,300,000.

In both examples, the players were aware of the proper techniques, but they did not know, understand and appreciate the risks associated with the failure to use the proper techniques. They did not sufficiently know, understand and appreciate the risks inherent in the sport. One result of the football lawsuit was the following warning to be read and signed by parents and players prior to football practice in King County, Washington:

> I understand that the dangers and risks of playing or practicing to play tackle football include, but are not limited to, death, serious neck and spinal injuries which may result in complete or partial paralysis, brain damage, serious injury to virtually all internal organs, serious injury to virtually all bones, joints, ligaments, muscles, tendons, and other aspects of the muscular skeletal system, and serious injury or impairment to other aspects of my body and general health and well-being . . . .

This is certainly a frightening list of inherent risks, but it is designed to help parents and players to know, understand and appreciate the risks of football before the players are allowed to participate. For football this warning of and by itself may not be sufficient. Players will need to be repeatedly reminded of the inherent risks in football. They will need to be reminded of the warning on their football helmet. They will need to be warned about the unique risks associated with specific skills in football. They may need to watch a film that is available which depicts the effect of a permanently crippling injury on a young football player so that they know, understand and appreciate the full implications of a permanently paralyzing injury on a young person.

§ 2.3(B). Warnings.

It is apparent that players must be warned about inherent risks in an activity. The more dangerous the sport, the more important are these warnings, but no sport is completely free of risk. It is a good idea to put warnings in writing and read through the written warning with players and parents if the sport is a particularly hazardous one and the players are minors. A written warning, *signed* and *dated* by players and parents and stored in a record file, does two things. First, if it is properly written, it can be used to show that the coach is aware of and has tried to make players aware of the risks in a sport. Second, if it is in written form, signed and stored, it can be used to prove the appropriateness of a coach's *a priori* planning. Since sound planning is a legal duty of a coach, a warning can help indicate the coach's thoroughness in planning. If the warning is not in written form, it is more difficult to use it to support your contention that players were warned and that you have recognized beforehand the importance of good warnings.

If a sport or sports equipment has general warnings associated with it, it is important to post and emphasize these warnings whenever possible. Football has such warnings, specifically the National Operating Committee on Safety in Athletic Equipment warning on the helmet. Football players need to be reminded to read this warning when they put on or inspect their helmet. Trampoline activities also contain general warnings. Because of severe injuries on the trampoline and subsequent lawsuits, warnings need to be posted on and near each trampoline. These warnings should be supplied by the manufacturer. In addition, the nature of trampoline activities has changed, and in beginning trampoline classes no somersaulting should be attempted.

The following warning should be posted on trampolines:

> Warning — Crippling injuries can occur during somersaults. Somersaulting should never be attempted without an overhead safety harness operated by a trained instructor. Refer to instruction manual. Almost all the benefits and enjoyment of the Trampoline can be obtained by learning the non-somersaulting, twisting skills and routines provided in the manual furnished with this Trampoline. Any activity involving motion or height creates the possibility of accidental injury. This equipment is intended for use ONLY by properly trained and qualified participants under supervised conditions. Use without proper supervision could be DANGEROUS and should NOT be undertaken or permitted. Before using, KNOW YOUR OWN LIMITATIONS and the limitations of this equipment. If in doubt, always consult your instructor. Always inspect for loose fittings or damage and test stability before each use.

Included in this section is a warning used for racquetball classes at the University of Montana. The following factors were considered in developing this warning, for the reasons mentioned. Warnings should be written in clear and unambiguous language that is appropriate to the age and intelligence level of the players. In addition to written warnings, verbal warnings should be used repeatedly, especially when play becomes too aggressive or too dangerous. Remember, a one-time warning, written or verbal, may be insufficient. As a personal example, I have taught racquetball to college students for a number of years. I use the warning contained herein and emphasize the danger of eye injuries and the need to always wear eyeguards.

My students are not minors and should be able to appreciate the necessity for eye protection, but in every class I must constantly remind the students to put their eyeguards on. For comfort or cosmetic reasons, a number of players prefer to not wear them, and I have to insist repeatedly they do.

A warning should contain a description of the demands and stresses the sport places on a player. It is especially important that a description of the cardiorespiratory stress be given so that your players can begin to appreciate the physiological demands the sport will place on them.

A warning should acknowledge that injuries can occur in the sport and that it is impossible to ensure the safety of the participant. Following this statement it is a good idea to provide a description of the most common inherent risks in the sport along with safeguards to which you expect players to adhere. After a thorough reading and discussion of the inherent risks in a sport, it is a good idea to solicit questions from players. If the warning is not clear, players may have questions and should be given the opportunity to ask them and then given honest, unbiased answers to their questions.

Following this list of inherent risks and a session for questions and answers, it is a good idea to include a statement that asks the player to acknowledge that he or she is physically fit for the sport. Of course, if physical examinations are a part of your sports program, this information should come to you from the examining physician. In the example provided herein, the students may or may not have had a recent physical, but they are not minors, and I want them to certify to me that they are sufficiently fit and have no conditions that will preclude them from the sport. Similarly, since the warning form may be used for beginning or advanced racquetball, I want the players to certify that they have sufficient skill to take part in the activity at the appropriate level. Needless to say, the players will be evaluated early on in the class to assure that their assertions about their skill level were accurate.

Finally, before the players are permitted to participate, they must sign and date the warning sheet and return it to me. I will keep the form until the end of the quarter or, in the event of an injury, until it is no longer needed.

YOU MUST READ AND SIGN THIS WARNING
BEFORE YOU PARTICIPATE

Every sport contains inherent risks and it is impossible to ensure the safety of players. Racquetball is a reasonably safe sport as long as certain guidelines are followed. It can develop aerobic and anaerobic fitness. It places physiological stresses on you comparable to basketball or handball. If you have any physical condition that precludes you from such activities, please obtain a physician's consent to participate, and play with caution.

Eye injuries can occur in racquetball. For that reason, eyeguards are mandatory for this class. These are protective devices, but cannot ensure eye safety. *DO NOT LOOK AT A BALL WHILE IT IS BEING HIT.* A racquetball can come off a racquet at speeds in excess of 120 mph. *TURN YOUR FACE AWAY FROM ALL SHOTS.*

Racquetball is played in a 20 x 20 x 40 court. Learn court presence, i.e., know where you are in relation to the walls, and to your fellow competitor. Racquetball is not a collision sport, please don't make it one. Avoid crowding a fellow competitor. Give him or her room for a complete swing, including follow-through. *BE SURE YOUR WRIST STRAPS ARE ALWAYS SECURE.*

It is perhaps inevitable that you will be hit by a ball. This is painful, and will cause a bruise which should be iced as soon as possible. From my experience, if you are hit by a ball or racquet it's generally *your* fault. Give each other room to play and shoot without contact. In the event of a real or potential "hinder," immediately stop play and replay the point.

Racquetball is a game of sudden stops or starts. I recommend wearing two pairs of socks, cotton inner and woolen outer. *USE ONLY COURT SHOES. DO NOT USE RUNNING SHOES.* The higher soles and sharper edges of running shoes tend to produce ankle injuries.

When entering a court, always knock or flick the lights off and back on. Wait for the door to be opened from *WITHIN*.

Do you have questions?

I have read the preceding and certify that I am physically fit for this racquetball class. I further attest that I have sufficient experience to enable me to participate in this class. I fully know, understand and appreciate the risks inherent in the sport of racquetball. I am voluntarily participating in this activity.

Signature	Age	Date

It is not necessary to list every conceivable risk that may occur in a game in a warning. It is important to list three categories of risks. First, if the sport has any potential for serious injury (i.e., eye injuries in racquetball), that risk should be mentioned. Second, if the sport contains any risks that are unique to the sport (i.e., being hit by a racquet of an opponent), those risks should be listed. Third, if the sport has risks that frequently appear (being struck by a racquetball), it is important to mention them. Specificity in sport is a principle in training for a sport and in motor learning. It is also a principle in writing a warning, as most sports contain unique risks which the players must know, understand and appreciate. Obviously, when the sport is a new one, or new to your players, warnings are especially important because the players may have no idea what risks are included in the play of the sport.

§ 2.3(C). Waivers.

A waiver is a form of an exculpatory (fault-freeing) agreement. The main feature of an exculpatory agreement is to relieve one party of all or a part of its responsibility to another. An exculpatory agreement or clause (a waiver) is considered a contract and has presented a conflict between two fundamentals of law, the fundamental tenet of contract law that all persons should have the freedom to contract as they wish and the fundamental principle of negligence law that one should be responsible for negligent acts which cause injury to others. This conflict has been resolved in various ways and has resulted in some confusion regarding the validity of waivers. Exculpatory clauses are not the favorite of courts, but in some circumstances they have been upheld.

Some very broad, general waivers have been upheld. In some of these instances, the contracting party may not even be aware that he or she had agreed to a waiver, but the waiver is so broad and pertains to risks that should be a common knowledge and, consequently, has been held to be valid. The next time you go to a major league baseball game, read the back of the ticket stub you are given. In addition to its use as a rain check, you may be surprised to find that you have agreed to a general waiver. One that I have reads as follows:

> The holder assumes all risks and danger incidental to the game of baseball including specifically (but not exclusively) the danger of being injured by thrown bats and thrown or batted balls, and agrees that the participating clubs, their agents and players are not liable for injuries resulting from such causes.

Waivers have been upheld for highly skilled, semiprofessional or professional performers in high-risk sports. Examples include an experienced runner in a 10,000-meter road race, a ski jumper, an experienced scuba diver, a member of the pit area at a demolition derby and automobile racers. In each of these instances, the participants were experienced adults engaged in or near to the high-risk activity.

Despite these examples, our judicial system does not look favorably upon waivers and has used a heightened degree of judicial scrutiny when interpreting exculpatory agreements. The courts fear that an acceptance of waivers may lead to dangerous conditions. As of this writing there are at least nine factors that may void a waiver. The presence of any one of these factors may be enough to make a waiver useless except as a warning and as an indication of planning. The first of these factors is important to sports programs because so many of our sports programs involve young people. People who are not of legal age, minors, cannot be held to a contract such as a waiver. If players are minors, they cannot waive their right to hold coaches or administrators liable. They do not have the maturity and knowledge to do so. Many waivers have two places for signatures, one for the player and one for the parents or guardians if the player is a minor. In this case, the parents or guardians may waive their right to sue, but the player cannot, and the parents or guardians cannot waive their child's right to bring suit. When books on physical education or athletic administration state that waivers have little practical value, this is the reason. Most of those books are written for the administration of school recreation, physical education or athletic programs with minors as participants.

Other factors which may void a waiver include the following:

1. a strong public policy which prohibits waivers;
2. one party in a clearly dominant position, as in boss-employee;
3. fraud or misrepresentation within the waiver;
4. the use of force or duress to sign the waiver;
5. ambiguity — both parties should know what they are signing, and what they are signing should be conspicuous and result from free and open bargaining;
6. a waiver that is unreasonable;
7. the presence of wanton, intentional or reckless misconduct; and
8. the signature accepting the waiver separated from the actual exculpatory clause.

If the members of your team are not minors and none of the above conditions exist, there is a chance that a waiver may be upheld.

In *Williams v. Cox Enterprises, Inc.,* 283 S.E.2d 367 (Ga. App. 1981), the following waiver was upheld for an experienced runner:

In consideration of acceptance of this entry, I waive any and all claims for myself and my heirs against officials or sponsors of the 1977 Peachtree Road Race for injury or illness which may directly or indirectly result from my participation. I further state that I am in proper physical condition to participate in this event . . . .

The application described the course as one of the most difficult 10,000-meter courses in America, with heat, humidity and hills combining to make the race a grueling event.

§ 2.3(D). Conclusion.

It is very important that warnings be given to players about the inherent risks in a sport. These warnings should enable players to know, understand and appreciate the risks they will encounter in that sport. Warnings should be thorough, cover the significant risks in the sport and be written in a language players will understand. It is strongly recommended that warnings be in written form and that the written warning be signed by the players and kept by the coaches. Additional reminders about inherent risks should be given repeatedly throughout the season.

Waivers may be used, but, because of the limitations described herein, may be of little value. Again, they seem to be of value for participants who are experienced and who are about to engage in a high-risk sport. They have little value for minors.

---

§ 2.4. Public Responsibilities of Amateur Sports Organizations.

By Glenn M. Wong & Richard J. Ensor

Public amateur athletic organizations have certain duties that they must fulfill to the public as a condition of their corporate existence and as required in their charters of incorporation. This section will focus on areas of responsibility owed the public by public or quasi-public organizations. Three such organizations are: the National Collegiate Athletic Association (NCAA), an amateur athletic association consisting of public and private colleges and universities; the University of Tennessee (U.T.), a state university; and the Boston Athletic Association (B.A.A.), a charitable corporation organized to run the Boston Marathon. Attention will be given to four issues: access to public records, public access to televised college football games, public funding of athletic facilities and the delegation of a public responsibility.

§ 2.4(A). Access to Public Records.

As a public or quasi-public organization, an organization may be required to comply with certain restrictions that differ from those placed on private organizations. One difference is that it may be required to open its records for public inspection.

The three court cases which follow illustrate the conflicts which arise when organizations try to protect the confidentiality of their files. The overall issue involves weighing the right of the public to be informed against the organization's need to protect the confidentiality of its files.

The first of these cases, *Seal v. Birmingham Post,* 8 Med. L. Rptr. 1633 (1982), involved Edward Seal, the principal of Butler High School in Huntsville, Alabama, who instituted a lawsuit against the Birmingham Post newspaper, two reporters and its editor for defamation. Seal contended that the defendants falsely reported that he gave money to Bobby Lee Hurt, a Butler High School basketball star, because he threatened to transfer to another school. Seal alleged that the newspaper incorrectly reported that he used basketball gate receipts to pay for Hurt's dental work. The newspaper also reported that Hurt chose to attend the University of Alabama at Huntsville because of financial pressure brought to bear by an alumnus of Butler High School who was linked to Seal. The NCAA conducted an investigation into allegations of rule violations by Hurt. This case, along with libel litigation, involved pre-trial procedures in which the Birmingham Post newspaper sought to have the NCAA appear in court with its confidential files regarding Hurt.

The NCAA requested a court order to protect its files, but a Kansas district court denied it. The court gave the following reasons for denying the NCAA's request:

1. In Kansas, the scope of discovery is to be liberally constructed so as to provide the parties with information essential to . . . insure the parties a fair trial;

2. In Kansas, only the news media has the privilege to withhold information deemed to be confidential;

3. Plaintiffs' contention that if the information contained in its files is made public, that then the NCAA will be powerless to gain information regarding alleged violations of its rules, is outweighed by the importance of the defendants needing access to relevant information that may lead to admissible evidence to defend itself from the allegation of libel so that the defendants may continue to exercise, without fear, their rights under the First Amendment to the Constitution of the United States; and,

4. Plaintiffs have failed to show that any of the statements that may be contained in the files of the NCAA are privileged communication or that the Court should prohibit their release to the defendants for the reasons above set out.

The Kansas district court issued a subpoena to the NCAA requiring it to produce "all documents and correspondence" relating to its investigation of Edward Seal, Bobby Lee Hurt and the University of Alabama at Huntsville.

The NCAA appealed the adverse decision to the Kansas Supreme Court, claiming that the documents in question related to confidential investigations conducted by the NCAA and the Southeastern Conference pertaining to possible rule infractions by the University of Alabama at Hunstville in the recruitment of high school basketball star Bobby Lee Hurt.

The Kansas Supreme Court decided in favor of the Birmingham Post newspaper when it commented that: "The case presented a dispute between an interest of confidentiality, on one hand, and the need of the defendants to defend themselves in a libel action." It said that: "While we recognize the interest in preserving the confidential nature of these memoranda is substantial, it must give way to assure all the facts will be available for a fair determination of the issues in the libel action." One justice dissented and noted that:

When I weigh the conflicting interests in the material sought to be discovered, I come down on the side of protecting the public interest. The public has an overwhelming interest in fostering and supporting the self-regulation engaged in by the Colleges and Universities under the auspices of the NCAA.

While these cases have not received widespread publicity (in part because the cases were unreported), they will pose serious problems for the NCAA if they set a trend.

There have been other cases in which the public has challenged the privacy of the NCAA or its member institution's files. For instance, in *Arkansas Gazette Co. v. Southern State College,* 620 S.W.2d 258 (Ark. 1981), the publisher of the Arkansas Gazette sued the Arkansas Intercollegiate Athletic Conference (A.I.C.) to require it to disclose the amount of money each of the ten-member Arkansas colleges and universities awarded its student athletes.

The A.I.C., in arguing against the disclosure of this information referred to a previous Arkansas case, *McMahan v. Board of Trustees of University of Arkansas,* 499 S.W.2d 56 (Ark. 1973), in which the court held that lists of people receiving complimentary football tickets did not have to be made public. A.I.C. contended that its proceedings came under the public exceptions clause of the Arkansas Freedom of Information Act, since it dealt with information about student athletes.

The Arkansas Supreme Court found that the A.I.C. was not an educational agency and therefore could not close its records to the public. The court recognized that the Arkansas Gazette was only interested in the total dollar amounts awarded by each school, not each student's individual award. Therefore, the court reversed the lower court's decision with directions to release the information, holding that information maintained by an athletic conference as to gross amounts of monies dispensed by member institutions during the school year was not included under the public exceptions clause. The court concluded that since the information in question was not protected material under the federal Family Education Rights Privacy Act of 1974, the requested disclosures did not violate a student's reasonable expectation of privacy.

As more states enact "sunshine" or open meeting laws to their civil codes, the ability of the NCAA to protect itself from public access to its records may continue to be challenged. This may especially be true since many of the NCAA's member institutions are either state institutions or state supported institutions.

The court's unwillingness to protect the NCAA files and records could prove damaging to the NCAA's ability to police itself since the basis of enforcement is self-investigation and policing. If potential witnesses are worried about anonymity, they may become reluctant to participate. This could have a serious impact on the investigation and enforcement policies (if this precedent is followed). The NCAA's status as a voluntary association has often had the effect of insulating it from outside interference in its matters, but there may be litigation in the state and federal court systems which could result in restricting the association's powers. It is also possible that the power of the

NCAA may be limited by such diverse means as antitrust law and due process considerations with respect to student athletes and coaches.

§ 2.4(B). Public Access to Televised College Football Games.

The NCAA was given authority by its member institutions in 1952 to administer live telecasting of college football games. While the details of the television plan have varied throughout the years, the plan has generally accomplished the following:

1. limited the number of live television appearances an NCAA member could make in a year;
2. prevented individual member institutions from contracting on an individual basis with national, local, and cable companies;
3. fixed revenue amounts for rights fees allocated by the NCAA to member institutions whose teams appeared as part of the network television contract; and,
4. allocated a percentage of the total television contract for the NCAA's operating budget.

The College Football Association (C.F.A.) was formed to promote the interests of its Division I-A member schools within the NCAA. The C.F.A. is composed of 63 NCAA Division I-A member institutions and includes five of the major football-playing conferences, the Big Eight, Southeast, Southwest, Atlantic Coast Conference and Western Athletic Conference, and major independents such as Notre Dame, Pittsburgh, Penn State and Boston College. The only major football-playing schools which are not C.F.A. members are those schools in the Pacific Ten and Big Ten Conferences.

In 1979, the C.F.A. began to feel that its voice in the formulation of football television policy was diluted in the 800-plus membership, of the NCAA and that the institution was not reflective of its own members' importance in obtaining a national television contract.

As such, the C.F.A. negotiated a contract of its own with NBC television for the 1982 and 1983 football seasons. The NBC contract was more attractive to C.F.A. members in terms of rights, fees and appearances than the 1982-1985 agreements that the NCAA had with ABC and CBS. While C.F.A. member institutions were considering whether to accept the NBC pact, the NCAA indicated that doing so would be in violation of NCAA rules and that disciplinary sanctions would result. This caused many C.F.A. members who originally had approved the C.F.A.-NBC contract to vote against accepting it. As a result of the C.F.A.'s failure to contract with NBC and continued dissatisfaction with the NCAA's television policy, the University of Georgia and the University of Oklahoma brought suit in November, 1981. In *Board of Regents of University of Oklahoma v. National Collegiate Athletic Association,* 546 F. Supp. 1276 (W.D. Okla. 1982), they challenged the NCAA's exclusive control over televised football and contended that the NCAA violated the Sherman Antitrust Act by its exclusive television contracts with two major networks, ABC and CBS.

The NCAA argued that the television package was beneficial to its membership as a whole and accomplished two important purposes. First, it protected the live gate of college and high school football games, which resulted in higher attendance at games. In support of this argument the NCAA pointed to an increase in total attendance for NCAA football games in all but one year from 1953 until 1983.

Second, the NCAA contended that its plan had the positive effect of spreading television revenues and exposure to a greater number of member institutions.

The NCAA also contended that limitations on the number of television appearances a member institution could make allowed a greater number of institutions to appear on television, which resulted in the schools receiving substantial rights fees. In addition to the revenues, these institutions received invaluable television exposure and extensive media attention. As a result, the recruitment efforts of these institutions were enhanced.

The NCAA maintained that uncontrolled televising of football games would result in the creation of a football superpower group, since a limited number of institutions would be attractive to television. With increased revenues, exposure and media attention to the superpower group, the NCAA predicted that the disparity among the member institutions would be increased. This would be contrary to the NCAA policies and purposes of the NCAA since it "would place irresistable temptations for the development of winning teams, thereby threatening the future of the sport."

A federal district court judge ruled in favor of Oklahoma and Georgia on September 15, 1982, issuing a 98-page opinion in support of his decision. Judge Burciaga, in issuing an injunction against the NCAA noted that the television contracts between the NCAA and ABC, NBC and the Turner Broadcast System were in violation of the Sherman Antitrust Act and were therefore void. Judge Burciaga held that "the right to telecast college football games is the property of the institutions participating in the games, and that right may be sold or assigned by those institutions to any entity at their discretion." He found that the television football controls exercised by the NCAA constituted price fixing, output restriction, a group boycott and an exercise of monopoly power over the market of college football television. He found that the membership of the NCAA agreed to limit production to a level far below that which would occur in a free market situation. In addition, Judge Burciaga was not persuaded that the televising of college football games would have any negative impact on game attendance at nontelevised games.

Judge Burciaga disagreed with the NCAA that the television controls helped maintain competitive balance among the football programs of various schools. In his reasoning, he compared the telecasting policies of NCAA football to those of NCAA basketball. The NCAA does not control the televising of regular season basketball games. These arrangements are left to the individual member institutions and conferences which have contracted with various national and local television and cable companies. Judge Burciaga rejected the NCAA's contention that televising football was distinguishable from televising basketball; in fact, he held that "the market in television basketball is to be persuasive guidance of how a free market in television football would operate."

Judge Burciaga's decision rendered illegal the NCAA's television contracts with ABC and CBS for $131.75 million each and Turner Broadcasting System for $18 million. Therefore, his decision voided a total of $481.5 million in television contracts.

On September 17, 1982, the NCAA returned to Judge Burciaga and requested a stay of his order invalidating the NCAA's football television contracts. This request was rejected by Judge Burciaga. The NCAA then appealed the rejection of the stay to the court of appeals, which granted the NCAA's request on September 22, 1982. This allowed the television contract to remain in effect during the 1982 football season pending the NCAA's appeal of Judge Burciaga's decision. NCAA member institutions were unable to sell broadcast rights on an individual basis for the 1982 season.

This had an immediate effect on the University of Oklahoma and the University of Southern California, which had sold the rights of their game on September 25, 1982, to Katz Sports, an independent broadcast syndicator. The telecast of this game was prevented by the stay of the district court decision granted by the court of appeals.

§ 2.4(C). The Court of Appeals.

The NCAA appealed the case to the 10th Circuit Court of Appeals, 707 F.2d 1147 (10th Cir. 1983), which heard the case in November, 1982. On appeal, the NCAA argued that Judge Burciaga incorrectly concluded that there was price-fixing in the awarding of television contracts since there was "vigorous competition among the networks" in bidding for the national television contracts. It further argued that the court erred in its conclusion that the NCAA was not a voluntary association.

In May, 1983, the court of appeals upheld the district court ruling, in a 2-1 decision. The court found that the television plan constituted an illegal *per se* price fixing and rejected all of the NCAA's arguments to the contrary.

The court disagreed with the NCAA's contention that the plan promoted live gate attendance at games, stating that since the plan involved a concommitant reduction in viewership, the plan did not result in a net increase in output and so was not procompetitive. The argument that the plan allowed the NCAA to promote balanced competition was rejected because the court held that to endorse such a position was to argue that competition will destroy the marketplace. Such an endorsement would defeat the policy of the Sherman Act. The court reasoned that competitive balance could be developed by less restrictive governance. Thirdly, the court declined to view the television plan as competitively justified by the need to compete with other television programs. This was because the plan eliminated competition between producers of football and hence was illegal *per se*. The court of appeals decided that the anticompetitive limits on price and output of television production were not offset by any procompetitive aspects of the television plan, even if it were not *per se* illegal.

In June, 1983 United States Supreme Court Justice Bryon White, a former All-America football player at Colorado, granted the NCAA a stay pending a decision by the Supreme Court on whether it would review the case. This had the effect of extending the television plan through the 1983 football season. In December, 1983, the Supreme Court granted a review of the case and oral arguments were heard in March, 1984.

§ 2.4(D). The Supreme Court's Decision.

On June 27, 1984, in *National Collegiate Athletic Ass'n v. Board of Regents of University of Oklahoma,* 104 S. Ct. 2948, a 7-2 decision, the United States Supreme Court struck down the NCAA's 1982-1985 Football Television Plan because it violated federal antitrust law. The effect of this ruling was felt immediately with networks, producers, syndicators, advertisers and NCAA member institutions scrambling to implement broadcast schedules for the 1984 season.

Justice John Stevens wrote the Supreme Court's opinion upholding the decisions of the district and appeals court. It rejected the stringent *per se* illegal test, however, as the basis for its decision when it commented: "Rather what is critical is that this case involves an industry in which the horizontal restraints (horizontal price-fixing and output limitations) on competition are essential if the product is to be available at all."

The Court believed that the NCAA's television plan by restraining prices and output had "a significant potential for anticompetitive effects." It emphasized this point when it said:

> Individual competitors lose their freedom to compete. Price is higher and output lower than they would otherwise be, and both are unresponsive to consumer preference. A restraint that has the effect of reducing the importance of consumer preference in setting price and output is not consistent with this fundamental goal of antitrust law. Restrictions on price and output are the paradigmatic examples of restraints of trade that the Sherman Act was intended to prohibit. At the same time, the television plan eliminates competitors from the market, since only those broadcasters able to bid on television rights covering the entire NCAA can compete. Thus, as the District Court found, many telecasts that would occur in a competitive market are foreclosed by the NCAA's plan.

Discussing the position of NCAA football within the marketplace the Court noted:

> It inexorably follows that if college football broadcasters be defined as a separate market — and we are convinced they are — then the NCAA's complete control over those broadcasters provides a solid basis for the District Court's conclusion that the NCAA possesses market power with respect to those broadcasts. "When a product is controlled by one interest, without substitutes available in the market, there is monopoly power."
> . . .

Thus, the NCAA television plan on its face constitutes a restraint upon the operation of a free market, and the findings of the District Court establish that it has operated to raise price and reduce output. Under the Rule of Reason, these hallmarks of anticompetitive behavior place upon petitioner a heavy burden of establishing an affirmative defense which competitively justifies this apparent deviation from the operations of a free market."

Turning to the NCAA's contentions, the Court rejected each one, stating that it did not agree with the NCAA's arguments that its television plan protected live gate attendance or maintained a competitive balance. It therefore concluded:

The NCAA plays a critical role in the maintenance of a revered tradition of amateurism in college sports. There can be no question but that it needs ample latitude to play that role, or that the preservation of the student-athlete in higher education adds richness and diversity to intercollegiate athletics and is entirely consistent with the goals of the Sherman Act. But consistent with the Sherman Act, the role of the NCAA must be to *preserve* a tradition that might otherwise die; rules that restrict output are hardly consistent with this role. Today we hold only that the record supports the District Court's conclusion that by curtailing output and blunting the ability of member institutions to respond to consumer preference, the NCAA has restricted rather than enhanced the place of intercollegiate athletics in the Nation's life. Accordingly, the judgment of the Court of Appeals is affirmed.

After the NCAA's proposed television plan was defeated, the Division 1-A and I-AA member institutions adopted three binding principles for the 1984 season that included the following:

1. There shall be no televising of collegiate football games on Friday nights, and any afternoon football televising on that day of the week must be completed by 7 p.m. local time in each location in which the program is received.
2. No member institution shall be obligated to televise any of its games, at home or away. No member institution may make any arrangements for live or delayed televising of any game without the prior consent of its opponent institution.
3. The gross rights fee paid for each 1984 national telecast or cablecast shall be subject to an assessment of 4 percent to be paid to the NCAA by the home institution. The assessment will be used to fund the costs of the NCAA postgraduate scholarship program and football-related NCAA services. A "national telecast" is defined as a football game televised or cablecast simultaneously to at least 20 million homes in at least 30 states, or televised or cablecast to 50 percent of U.S. television homes as reported by the 1984 Edition/No. 52 of Television and Cable Factbook and all updates to that publication issued prior to August.

§ 2.4(E). Public Funding of Athletic Facilities.

In *Lester v. Public Building Authority,* No. 78491 (Chancery Ct. Knox County, Tenn. 1983), suit was brought by faculty members against the University of Tennessee to block funding and construction of a $30 million Assembly and Sports Center on the University of Tennessee campus. The Center was to be financed by the State of Tennessee for $7 million, Knox County, Tennessee, $10 million and the University of Tennessee, $13 million.

The faculty members insisted that appropriations from the state could place their salaries and raises in jeopardy. They also argued, as Knox County residents, that their taxes would be increased because of funding pledges made by the County, that such pledges were made illegally and that the taxpayers would suffer substantial losses unless the pledges were enjoined.

The controversial case was settled out of court when a compromise was reached. The University agreed to provide full information to its Faculty Senate regarding the funding of the Center. It also agreed to not make additional requests over the $7 million already appropriated for the Center while continuing efforts to secure funds for the proposed new library. The University stated that the athletic department would assume the cost of any construction overruns if they occurred. It also agreed that current and future pledges for the Center along with unrestricted gifts to the athletic department and revenues from the operation of the arena and other operations of the athletic department would be used first to retire the bonds issued for the construction of the Center. A final agreement was the assurance by the University that it would not use funds appropriated by the Tennessee General Assembly for academic budgets and salaries, increases in student activity fees without consultation from appropriate student representatives or unrestricted gifts to the University except those designated to the athletic department.

While this case was not decided in a court of law, the issues raised are potential problems in the area of public funding of athletic facilities. The faculty members were successful in pressuring school officials by litigation to allow faculty input into university projects in return for the promise not to delay the funding and construction of the Center.

David Burkhalter, the faculty's lawyer, stated: "The significant thing about the settlement is that it is legally binding and sets a clear priority. It means that the University has recognized that the faculty has a right to say how University money should be spent, and that's unprecedented at the University of Tennessee."

§ 2.4(F). Delegation of a Public Responsibility.

The Boston Athletic Association (B.A.A.) is a nonprofit corporation. Its original purpose was amended in 1982 to include the encouragement of sport and the promotion of physical exercise with particular emphasis on long-distance running events.

The Board of Directors of the Association felt a need for sponsorship revenues to maintain the successful operation of the Boston Marathon. In April, 1981, the Board gave William Cloney, the Association's president, authority to negotiate and execute agreements in its name as he deemed them to be in the Association's best interests. Cloney discussed the possibility of promoting the Boston Marathon with Marshall Medoff, the sole incorporator, officer, director and shareholder of International Marathons, Inc. (I.M.I.). I.M.I.'s purpose was sales and sports. Cloney and Medoff reached an agreement that included the following:

1. I.M.I. would be the exclusive promoter of the Boston Marathon with rights to make five major and five minor sponsorship contracts as well as to involve an unlimited number of companies that would supply services to the B.A.A.
2. With the exception of the Japanese market, all radio, television and movie rights in the Marathon were assigned to I.M.I.
3. The exclusive use of the Boston Marathon and B.A.A. logo and name were transferred to I.M.I.
4. While the B.A.A. reserved the right to decline any or all sponsors, the approval of a sponsor, would not be unreasonably withheld.
5. The I.M.I. agreed to pay the B.A.A. an annual sponsorship fee of $400,000 with all sponsorship revenues over that amount payable to I.M.I. If sponsorship in a particular year fell below $400,000, the B.A.A. could agree to accept less.
6. Every five years the sponsorship fee could be increased according to the change in the Consumer Price Index.

The final terms of the agreement provided that the annual fee did not require the B.A.A. to be paid by sponsors' revenues. The agreement was to extend and review itself automatically from year to year as the annual fee was paid. This agreement was entered into without the knowledge of the B.A.A.'s board.

Medoff signed contracts with nine corporate sponsors while serving as the B.A.A.'s agent for the Boston Marathon and raised $700,000 for the 1982 Marathon. The contracts varied in terms, length and monies paid to the B.A.A. for the sponsorships. Seiko, for example, paid $400,000 for the rights to be the official presenter and timer and it agreed to pay $450,000 in 1984. Eastman Kodak, the official photographer paid $50,000 in 1982 which was to increase to $95,000 in 1984. Medoff was considering a change in the day of the race from Monday (Massachusetts' state holiday of Patriot's Day) to a Sunday for broader national television coverage.

When the Board of Directors learned of the Cloney-Medoff agreement later that year, it declared that Cloney exceeded his authorization. In *Boston Athletic Ass'n v. International Marathons, Inc.,* 467 N.E.2d 58 (Mass. 1984), the Board then instituted a lawsuit on behalf of the B.A.A. against I.M.I. to prevent it from representing itself to the public as the Association's agent. It declared that the contract signed by Cloney and Medoff violated Massachusetts laws and that Cloney exceeded his authority by entering into the agreement.

A hearing was held and the hearing examiners disapproved the contract: "No charitable organization . . . shall agree to pay a professional solicitor or its agents . . . in the aggregate a total amount in excess of 15 percent of the total moneys, pledges, or other property raised or received by reason of any solicitation activities or campaigns, including reimbursement for expenses incurred."

The I.M.I. appealed and the superior court refused to review the decision because it was a moot question. The supreme court affirmed the superior court's refusal to consider the decision. On the question of the validity of the contract it noted: "We hold the contract between the BAA and IMI to be void and unenforceable. The defendant is, however, entitled to recovery in *quantum meruit* for the services it rendered in obtaining sponsorship contracts for the running of the Marathon in 1982."

Regarding the delegation of authority by the Board to Cloney it stated: "Persons dealing with a corporation are presumed to know the extent of its powers. An officer of a nonprofit organization cannot have apparent authority to encumber the principal function of the corporation and to divert the substantial earning capacity of the corporation to private benefit."

The court concluded:

> It is entirely inconsistent with the nonprofit nature of the organization to permit such a substantial segment of the revenue earning capacity of the Marathon to be used as a vehicle for personal gain. For the foregoing reasons, the Board of Governors of the BAA was not empowered to delegate to Cloney the right to make this contract with IMI.

Cloney, as a result of the decision facing forced resignation, retired from the B.A.A. board. He defended his action by commenting: "I had the authority to sign this much-maligned contract. I should note Mr. Medoff has fulfilled his end of the contract. At no time was there any question of procedures being followed, agreements being made, and contracts being signed."

Cloney noted that "for the first time, the BAA has a substantial financial cushion of some half-million dollars."

The emphasis on corporate sponsorship by the B.A.A. changed after the Marathon's legal battles. Timothy W. Kilduff, a member of the B.A.A. Board and its spokesperson, observed: "There's a world of difference between selling the Boston Marathon and subsidizing the race . . . . [T]he main difference is that there is no interest in profit. Profit is not the objective of what we're doing."

Marshall Medoff disagreed with these sentiments when he responded: "This business about commercializing the race was baloney from the start. They're intent on doing exactly the same program as we did, only they can't do it as well."

According to the B.A.A., many traditional sponsors of the Marathon disengaged themselves from the race after Medoff became involved. Prudential Insurance Company, Bristol-Myers, Kodak, Coca-Cola, Anheuser-Busch and Asics Tiger dropped out as sponsors after Medoff took over the operation.

By the time of the 1983 race, however, the B.A.A. had solved many of the corporate complaints by lowering the sponsorship fees and adding new sponsors to replace those companies that had discontinued sponsorship.

The B.A.A.-I.M.I. controversy is interesting in that the court pointed out, in dramatic fashion, the importance it places on public organizations, such as athletic organizations, to maintain responsibility entrusted to them by the public. While the Boston Marathon is a significant event in the world of sport, the principles espoused in this decision would be applicable to the Little League Association, the NCAA and similar nonprofit voluntary organizations.

§ 2.4(G). Conclusion.

There is limited judicial precedent in the areas discussed in this section. The public responsibilities of amateur athletic organizations, however, are a new and developing area of law which has already had a significant impact an amateur athletics.

(1) *Access to Public Records.*

Since state codes differ in coverage, language and interpretation, future litigation may be important in establishing guidelines for the NCAA and other amateur athletic associations regarding access to public records.

It is difficult to determine where the court will balance the individual's right of privacy with the public's right to know and access to information. The court must consider and weigh two important, countervailing constitutional guarantees. The cases mentioned in this section indicate that the trend may be toward the public's right to know and access to previously confidential records. This may result in an increase in the sources of information available to the public while simultaneously reducing the amount of information the association may be able to keep confidential. This may result in potential witnesses being reluctant to testify if they believe that their testimony may be made public. Investigators for organizations such as the NCAA may become more circumspect in their questioning, and the information they incorporate into memoranda may be reduced. The accessibility of records may negatively impact on the ability of these organizations to investigate and may thereby hinder their efforts to maintain their public responsibility of preserving amateurism.

(2) *Public Access to Televised College Football Games.*

The Supreme Court, in establishing that the NCAA had a public responsibility to provide a free and open market for college football telecasts, has raised a number of questions. In addition to the scheduling of games and revenues for both the individual schools and the NCAA, important questions remain concerning NCAA governance and the legality of any national television plan that seeks to place controls and limitations on the marketplace.

Many college administrators feel that the television plan is the smallest problem facing the NCAA. Wesley N. Posvar, Chancellor of the University of Pittsburgh, characterized the situation as follows: "The least important aspect of this is the television situation. I think there has been a polarization by that vote Tuesday. The potential for unraveling discipline and rules and order in intercollegiate athletics is the major issue. If we didn't have an NCAA, we'd have to reinvent it."

(3) *Public Funding of Athletic Facilities.*

In *Lester v. Public Building Authority,* No. 78491 (Chancery Ct. for Knox

County, Tenn. 1983), the University of Tennessee's faculty members were successful in pressuring the University's officials into a compromise over the question of how state money was to be spent. It could be argued that this case might have been won by the University on its merits. While this may be true, time is of the essence in many facility projects, and delays could prove costly in the long run.

The significance of *Lester* is that affected parties may have a public responsibilities argument on which to base claims, and courts may be willing to hear such suits. The question is how the court can balance competing public duties of the need for fiscal responsibility versus the need to accommodate the sport-going public in a responsible manner. If available dollars to universities continue to shrink and tax dollars are used to make up the difference, litigation such as the *Lester* case may become common. The success of the faculty in *Lester* demonstrates how affected parties, by keeping vigilant, may proceed on financial issues involving public institutions.

(4) *Delegation of a Public Responsibility.*

The B.A.A. court decisions illustrate dramatically the importance that the judiciary places on athletic organizations to maintain the responsibility entrusted to them by the public.

Marshall Medoff argued unsuccessfully that the I.M.I. contract was lawful since the B.A.A. had on its own never cleared over $25,000, while his contract guaranteed it $400,000 annually. William Cloney seemed empowered to act as the board's agent based on his previous record of negotiating all sponsorship and broadcast contracts on his own.

When dealing with an organization in which the public has placed a trust, however, it seems that an individual should consider the higher degree of scrutiny that such an arrangement may receive from the courts.

Laws governing nonprofit or charitable organizations will differ from state to state. Regardless of the state, however, an amateur voluntary athletic organization such as the B.A.A. should be cognizant of the problems experienced by the B.A.A. because of the overly broad and general powers it delegated to its chief executive officer. The courts, based on the decision in the B.A.A. case, may expect that such organizations keep tight control over the actions and policies instituted by officers in the corporation's behalf.

---

§ 2.5. Title IX: After *Grove City.*

By Linda Carpenter

The impact of Title IX on physical education and athletic programs has been massive, and, in the midst of its second decade, Title IX continues to provide ample fodder for debate.

Title IX states in part: "[N]o person in the United States shall, on the basis of sex, be excluded from participation in, be denied the benefits of, or be subjected to discrimination under any education program or activity receiving

Federal financial assistance . . . ." Section 901(a) of the Education Amendments of 1972, 20 U.S.C. § 1681(a) (1976).

At its enactment in 1972, Title IX joined other anti-discrimination legislation, such as Title VI of the Civil Rights Act of 1964, and the Rehabilitation Act of 1973 and the Age Discrimination Act of 1975 soon followed it. But Title IX applies only to educational settings, whereas the other three apply to all federally assisted programs. In each of the four pieces of legislation, however, the possible withdrawal of federal financial aid has been used as a threat, and the apprehension of that threat has proven so effective that actual withdrawal has seldom been necessary.

Secondary and post-secondary schools were required to be in compliance with Title IX by July, 1978, but, long before then, extensive changes were being made in physical education and athletic programs in the name of Title IX.

The wording of Title IX is simple, but the regulations developed to implement its details were far from simple. Three years passed before final regulations were issued, and even then confusion remained. The only thing that seemed clear was that Title IX, whatever it required of an educational institution, would change the face of women's sports.

Today, barriers to the participation of girls and women in sports have been markedly reduced. Competitive athletics for girls and women have been expanded and now include well developed national championships. Most men's and women's departments of physical education and athletic programs which, before Title IX, existed separately have been merged under the leadership of a male chairman or athletic director. The number of positions available for coaches of women's teams has grown; yet the percentage of females in those positions has declined. Administrative leadership positions have, since Title IX, become increasingly occupied by males, so that in 1984 almost 87% of women's intercollegiate sports programs were directed by males.

These changes have been caused or at least hastened by Title IX. The lack of clarity of the applicability and requirements of Title IX did not deter the invocation of its name to add impetus to change within physical education and sports.

The courts have not been free of the confusion surrounding Title IX. For example, the courts have questioned the enforcement scope of Title IX: is it to be applied on an institution-wide basis or only to those specific programs within the institution which receive federal funding? If enforcement is applicable only on a program-specific basis, then, even though a sports program might openly discriminate on the basis of sex, it would not fall within the jurisdiction of Title IX except in the unlikely event that the sports program specifically received federal funds.

Grove City College v. Bell, 104 S. Ct. 1211 (1984), answered the question of program specificity. Grove City College, a private, coeducational undergraduate college in Pennsylvania, received no federal funds except Basic Educational Opportunities Grants (BEOG), which were provided to about six percent of its student body of 2200. The grants were awarded directly to the students, but, before the grants could be released to them, the college was required by the Department of Education to sign a Title IX Assurance of Compliance form. The college refused to sign. As a result, funds were terminated. Administrators and students from Grove City College then joined in a suit which finally worked its way to the Supreme Court and was decided in February, 1984.

From the beginning, Grove City College was an unlikely target for enforcement. There was never any allegation of discrimination. In the Supreme Court's opinion, Justice Powell noted: "One would have thought the Department [of Education], confronted as it is with cases of national importance that involve actual discrimination, would have respected the independence and admirable record of this college. But common sense and good judgment failed to prevail." Earlier in the trek of *Grove City* to the Supreme Court, in August, 1982, the Third Circuit, 687 F.2d 684 (1982), defined and ruled on the two main issues which would determine the applicability of Title IX to physical education and sports. First, the Third Circuit held that, since Grove City College was a recipient of federal funding, it was required to comply with Title IX. Second, a definition of "program" was worked out. The definition of "program" would turn out to be the central issue in Title IX.

The Department of Education argued in favor of an institution-wide definition of "program." It argued that all departments within an institution are ultimately controlled by the university; therefore, the university can force its departments to alter discriminatory policies if necessary.

The Third Circuit, in the absence of any case precedent, agreed with the Department of Education and ruled that "program" (not defined in the original Title IX) meant "institution." Therefore, if discrimination existed within a department which received no federal funds while other areas of the institution received funding, all federal funds could be withdrawn from that institution.

After the Third Circuit decision, the students and administrators of Grove City College applied to the Supreme Court to hear the case. The Court agreed. In the year and a half which passed before the Supreme Court ruled in the case, the Department of Education, which is charged with enforcing Title IX, reversed its previous position and, in August, 1983, submitted a brief, urging the Supreme Court to restrict the Department's enforcement power by defining "program" more narrowly. Although the stand taken by the Department of Education was of no real importance in the *Grove City* case because there were no allegations of discrimination, the stand was vitally important to the future of Title IX.

In arriving at its decision in *Grove City*, the Supreme Court found it necessary not only to address the question of "program-specific" versus "institution-wide enforcement", but also the question of direct versus indirect funding. It seems clear that if a specific department received direct federal funding the jurisdiction of Title IX would be invoked. However, Grove City College, as an institution, never directly received federal funds; only a few of its students did. And so without first deciding whether this type of funding makes Grove City College a "recipient" of federal funds, it is impossible to reach the more critical question of the meaning of "program."

The Court decided unanimously that federal funding, even as indirect as the BEOG's in the *Grove City* case, is sufficient to make the institution a "recipient" within the meaning of Title IX.

On the second question of the meaning of "program" (program-specific or institution-wide) the Court adopted the narrow interpretation that Title IX enforcement is limited to the specific program actually touched by financial aid.

It should be noted that, although the Court decided contrary to the decision of the Third Circuit that Title IX enforcement is program-specific, it did not offer a definition of "program." Regardless of the ultimate definition of "program," it is no longer possible to interpret "program" as "institution."

§ 2.5(A). Significance of *Grove City* to Physical Education and Sports Programs.

What is the significance of the *Grove City* case to physical education and sports programs? Federal funding does not often enter the program areas of physical education or sports, even indirectly. Therefore, Title IX after *Grove City* probably cannot be enforced in those areas.

Some have expressed hope that because federal funding formed a portion of the construction money for gymnasia and stadia on campuses, the activities carried on within such facilities would have been sufficiently touched by federal funding to be subject to Title IX. But tying facilities to programs carried on within them is too tenuous to invoke the provisions of Title IX. In light of the rapid and massive cancellation of Office of Civil Rights Title IX investigations following the *Grove City* decision, it is apparent that jurisdiction over sex discrimination in physical education and sports programs is not going to be sought out by the Office of Civil Rights.

Others have suggested that scholarship disbursements to athletes, some of which include federal funds administered by the college's financial aid office, would be sufficient to carry Title IX's antidiscrimination jurisdiction to entire athletic programs. It now appears unlikely, however, that anything beyond the scholarships themselves would be subject to Title IX enforcement. Auburn University provides an example of this. Investigations begun by the O.C.R. prior to the *Grove City* decision revealed discriminatory activities within the athletics program at Auburn University. The O.C.R. dropped its case except that portion concerning scholarships within a few days after the *Grove City* decision. So, it seems the Office of Civil Rights will not attempt to use scholarships to reach deeper.

It now seems that the federally funded scholarship of a student is not carried around campus to the student's various activities giving the Office of Civil Rights an opportunity to enforce Title IX and other antidiscrimination legislation. Instead, an athlete with such a scholarship must not be discriminated against in the awarding of the scholarship, but may be discriminated against by the English Department, for instance, if the department itself received no federal funding.

Some large institutions receiving massive financial aid claim they will not use *Grove City* as a means of retrogressing to discriminatory tactics previously abandoned due to Title IX (tracing federal funds to find programs free of federal funds is too complex to make such retrogression possible). Goodwill is also proposed as a deterrent to retrogression.

However, in the matter of discrimination it is unwise to depend on goodwill. The reality of this became evident when at several colleges the scholarships of women athletes were cancelled within days of the *Grove City* decision.

§ 2.5(B). What Is the Future of Title IX?

Soon after the *Grove City* decision, a number of bills were placed before the House and the Senate for clarification and redefinition of the broad scope Congress had intended for Title IX. If Congress passes these or similar bills, in this or forthcoming sessions, the interpretation of "program" will no longer be left to the courts; it will have been defined by Congress.

Senate Bill 2568, often referred to as the Omnibus Bill because it included Title IX's antidiscrimination legislation, provided for some specific changes in the wording and definitions of Title IX. For instance, "program or activity" became "recipient," thus defeating the narrow definition presented by *Grove City*. Furthermore, the bill proposed the removal of "program or activity" from the enforcement section and replaced it with "recipient"; thus, federal funds would have been in jeopardy if sex discrimination existed anywhere on campus.

Although sponsored by a majority of senators, the Omnibus Bill had a difficult time getting out of committee. The opponents of the bill feared that, in its reaffirmation and definition of terms, the bill might have expanded the enforcement scope of Title IX and its companion legislation to unintended proportions. Congress adjourned without passing Bill 2568 or any of its companions, but additional bills have already been introduced in the 1985-1986 Congress.

§ 2.5(C). Conclusion.

It is difficult to predict the future of Title IX, but in the absence of clarifying legislation, Title IX is of very little use in creating physical education and athletics programs free of sex discrimination.

If Title IX's identity remains defined by *Grove City*, female sports participants and their programs might, by some benevolent stroke of good fortune, continue to move toward a future where sex discrimination is not "part of the game." The awareness of sex discrimination which grew out of Title IX, whether it was enforced or not, might move us all to better things, even in a world after *Grove City*. More likely there will be a reduction in the opportunities for women. The rapid reduction of scholarships for women at some colleges after the *Grove City* decision supports this, and the NCAA's plan to equalize the number of sports offered on each campus for men and women also might be looked upon with distrust. In any case, it is clear that even if Title IX's enforcement powers do not do away with sex discrimination, the past impact of Title IX can never be erased.

§ 2.6. Legislating Against Violence in Sports.

By Rick Horrow

A Harris Poll released in April, 1983, indicates that half of the nation's sports fans think sports are too violent. Nearly eight of ten fans are concerned about violence in boxing and hockey and seven of ten in football.

A recent report compiled for the Institute of Sports and Social Analysis emphasizes the detrimental effects of excessive sports violence on both the youngsters who play and the spectators who watch. The five years of research conducted in preparing my book *Sports Violence: The Interaction Between Private Lawmaking and the Criminal Law* also convinces me that excessive violence will continue to increase as long as the pressures and incentives to be violent remain.

Here are some examples of the more serious incidents of sports violence in recent years:

On August 22, 1965, Juan Marichal (San Francisco Giants) used his baseball bat to land a crushing blow to the head of John Roseboro (Los Angeles Dodgers), producing a celebrated settlement before trial.

On September 21, 1969, Wayne Maki (St. Louis Blues) retaliated against a swing by Ted Green (Boston Bruins) by using his hockey stick on Green "like a logger splitting a stump." Green sustained a serious concussion and massive hemorrhaging. Two brain operations were only partially successful, and Green would never fully recover.

On September 16, 1973, Charles "Booby" Clark (Cincinnati Bengals), upset because his team was losing a game, hit Dale Hackbart (Denver Broncos) on the back of the head with his right forearm while Hackbart was on one knee with his back toward Clark after an interception. The blow left Hackbart with three broken vertebrae, muscular atrophy in his arm, shoulder and back and a loss of strength and reflex in his arm.

On January 4, 1975, Dave Forbes (Boston Bruins), returning to play after a stay in the penalty box, struck Henry Boucha (Minnesota North Stars) in the face with the butt end of his hockey stick, then jumped the fallen player and punched him until pulled away by a third player. Boucha suffered a fracture of the eye socket and required 25 stitches to close facial cuts.

On December 9, 1977, Kermit Washington (Los Angeles Lakers), after engaging in an on-court scuffle with another player, punched Rudy Tomjanovich (Houston Rockets) full force in the face. Tomjanovich suffered a broken jaw and a fractured nose and skull.

On October 28, 1979, Steve Luke (Green Bay Packers) — one of the Hit Brothers — struck Norm Bulaich (Miami Dolphins) in the face with his forearm. Bulaich's jawbone was broken in two, and the bones around one eye were splintered; he would never play again.

On January 11, 1980, Dave Cowens (Boston Celtics) landed a hard left to the face of "Tree" Rollins (Atlanta Hawks) in response to an early tie-score play. Both sustained blows to the face before being separated by coaches, players and referees. For their on-court brawl, both players were ejected from the game.

On November 28, 1982, linebacker Stan Blinka (New York Jets) smashed his arm into the head of John Jefferson (Green Bay Packers) as the wide receiver ran a route over the middle before the ball left the quarterback's hands. Jefferson had to leave the game. Said Packers' former Coach Bart Starr: "The player does not have the ball, and there is no attempt to tackle him — that's the act of a hoodlum, and hoodlums should not have the privilege of playing in our game."

Unfortunately, these incidents are symptomatic of the alarming trend toward excessive violence in all professional sports. In one recent National Hockey League season, for example, penalties totaled a record 22,329 minutes, a 25% increase over the preceding year. Football is no better. In a recent season, 1,638 National Football League players missed two or more games with "serious injuries," and studies have revealed that football is so physically debilitating that a pro's life span is significantly shorter than that of most males. With basketball players throwing elbows and baseball players knocking down batters and sliding in with their spikes flailing, excessive violence has become an issue even in what the casual fan would consider "noncontact" sport. As athletes become more competitive and as the pressures to succeed become stronger, the possibility of violent conduct during the game increases.

While most "during-the-game sports violence" is rightfully considered just part of the game, many exceptionally severe acts must be dealt with by the league and — if the league fails — by the courts.

Not surprisingly, most persons involved in professional sport — players, managers, coaches, owners, league officials — would prefer to keep all sports issues, including violence and injuries, a "family matter." By and large, actions which would quickly result in civil and often criminal charges if committed any place other than the playing field or court have seldom been held answerable to the same law which checks tempers and protects the vulnerable in other situations. And, when sports cases have gone to court, difficulties have arisen in applying general assault and battery laws to sports-specific situations and in drawing the fine lines between what the sport allows — even demands — and the excessive, unwarranted act of violence.

§ 2.6(A). The Pressure to Perform.

The mentality that all violence — even exceptionally severe violence — is just part of the game is taught almost from the cradle. From their earliest training, athletes are taught to be tough and play tough. In high school, promising players must demonstrate the ability to play a "hard-nosed" game if they hope for a college scholarship. In college, the only hope for making the pros is to emulate the pros.

Once the "skills" of violence are learned, players are pressured explicitly and implicitly by teammates, coaches and management to continue their violent conduct. In modern hockey, for example, players are forced to fight when challenged or risk being branded as cowards. Violence and intimidation in excess of that permitted by the rules of the game are becoming integral parts of strategy. Players fight because it has become a condition of the job.

In football intense competition against teammates for roster positions — and against opponents for victory — leads to the mentality that the law of survival is the only law that governs. In testimony before the Hackbart court former coaches John Ralston of Denver and Paul Brown of Cincinnati admitted that it was normal behavior in the NFL for players to "disregard the safety of opposing players."

Furthermore, most players accept the fact that some less talented players must be more violent to compensate for inferior ability. Thus, the sports establishment appears to condone the actions of certain "enforcers" even though these actions go beyond those which would be tolerated from more skilled players.

According to some, team management is responsible for applying pressure as well. If Jack Tatum is to be believed, Oakland Raiders owner Al Davis was about to pay Tatum less because he "was not hitting like he did earlier in his career"; Tatum was allegedly "paid to be a warhead." Since Davis told him that anyone who came near him should be "knocked to hell," Tatum "went for an intimidating hit" on August 12, 1978 — the one that paralyzed Darryl Stingley — rather than attempt the interception, "because of what owners expect when they give him his paycheck."

For excessive violence, which goes beyond what most everyone considers "part of the game," there is a strong tendency to avoid the courts and deal with such conduct "within the family." However, since most of this conduct is condoned and accepted — in fact, encouraged — by members of the league, it is hard to imagine how such a group could effectively regulate excessive sports violence.

In an attempt to keep disputes "within the family," each league informally decides what type of conduct it will and will not tolerate. In hockey normal fighting is tolerable, stick swinging is not. In football, though the league and its players tolerate the occasional during the game fight and exceptionally severe clip or late hit, the line is transgressed by a blatant cheap shot well after the play is over or by a malicious forearm or punch.

Once each league develops its own "law," most management suggests that the league's internal disciplinary proceedings provide an adequate means of controlling players' behavior in the hockey rink and on the football field. The league, they say, knows the sport better than any court does; if the courts get involved, the game will become more tame, less competitive and less appealing, and the minute the courts have the power to litigate the game, a "Pandora's Box" will be opened. For one thing, they argue, the leagues mete out punishment evenly, whereas court decisions will vary from jury to jury and state to state. For another, they say, court action will only serve to increase hostility among players who must compete against each other frequently and thus might actually encourage more violence. Finally, they claim, the games will lose their competitive edge and excitement if players must worry about going to jail for a clip in football or slashing in hockey.

The players seem to have adopted a similar attitude. According to a Washington Capitals' executive, most players feel that they "are subject to league rules, and not local rules, once they sign their contracts." One hockey player, advocating a novel legal approach, insisted that "there is no such thing as a lawsuit, discipline is handled by league officials, and that's that." The general consensus is that most players think it is taboo to bring the courts into sports.

In theory, then, each league has the power to mete out severe fines and suspensions for excessively violent conduct. Some members of the sports establishment believe that their systems have reduced excessive violence. While there is some merit to this claim, the typical small fines and short suspensions have no deterrent value whatsoever. The penalties are usually too lenient, given the nature of the offense and the high income of the average professional athlete. For example, in October, 1977, the NFL engaged in "the first suspension by the Commissioner, for on the field behavior in almost 10 years — and the first for violence against another player for a flagrant personal foul." The incident involved a "deliberate forearm blow" to the head of the player after the player had caught the ball and was in the clutches of a tackler. The punishment was suspension for one game and a loss to the player of approximately $2,000. The response of the suspended player: "It don't faze me at all."

In the world of the professional athlete a "conviction" by the league may bring with it a certain amount of outright respect. Further, even if the fines were more severe, some players claim that their teams pay the fines. Not only do these players suggest that this means that they can ignore the fine, but they maintain that "the team should pick it up because they expect you to do what you get fined for."

Of course, there are other reasons why players support the prevailing attitude that sports cases do not belong in the courtroom. Even if some players thought they could go to court to protect themselves, the unwritten "macho code" in reality prevents it. One hockey player warned that going to court "probably goes against the unwritten rule of survival of the fittest. If you can't survive on the ice, don't go running to the courts for protection." Victims will settle it "their own way." While most of those interviewed adamantly argued that there is no "conspiracy" to prevent lawsuits, Ed Garvey, former Executive Director of the NFL Players' Association, notes that many players fear that "court involvement will hurt their chances of getting ahead." The fear of being condemned as "a clubhouse lawyer" is a real one. One NHL player went so far as to suggest that "the fear of being labeled is the only reason that players don't go to court." Some players fear that taking a legal claim "outside the family" will result in an informal blacklisting around the league.

While most players who would avoid the courts are motivated by fear, others are motivated by "a love of the game." With the tremendous salaries and benefits afforded by the league, many players feel that sport has "been too kind to them to drag it through the courts." In football, for example, the 1978 average NFL salary was $62,585 — a 13.2% increase over 1977's $55,288 average. The minimum salary was $26,000 in 1980, an $8,000 increase since 1974. Players are also protected by a retirement plan, a life insurance plan, a major medical plan and dental coverage. Therefore, it is easy to understand the position that "most players are happy and love the game." Even those who are victims of the game's violence would prefer to keep things within the family if they believe — as many do — that court interference would "destroy what they've got." Even the "liberals" realize that their paychecks are too good to risk.

§ 2.6(B). Sports in Court — The Present Score.

Despite the enormous pressures working to avoid sports violence litigation, an increasing number of cases are reaching the courts. The civil and criminal justice systems have power to deal with excessive sports violence through laws prohibiting assault and battery. The argument used most often to justify the courts' involvement in during-the-game violence is advanced by Gary Flakne, County Attorney for Hennepin County, Minnesota, and prosecutor in the leading American "sports violence case," State v. David Forbes. He states:

> The mere act of putting on a uniform and entering the sports arena should not serve as a license to engage in behavior which would constitute a crime if committed elsewhere. If a participant in a sporting event were allowed to feel immune from criminal sanction, merely by virtue of his being a participant, the spirit of maiming and serious bodily injury . . . may well become the order of the day.

But most incidental contact is a normal and legitimate part of the game; other contact is harmful, malicious, repugnant and no doubt illegal. The key question, therefore, is: where do you draw the line between the two? In at least one case in each major sport, courts have grappled with this problem.

Many of the cases involving sports violence demonstrate that the law is not very clear. A football player may be liable for something he does on the field, yet a hockey player may not be liable for something he does in the rink. A player may be liable in Louisiana and not liable in Illinois. Much of the problem is caused by the fact that judges and juries must interpret laws which were not written to cover sports violence cases.

Typically, the legal battle pits the plaintiff (or the "state," if it is a criminal case) — trying to prove that the athlete intended an assault and battery — against the defendant athlete — trying to prove either that he acted in self-defense or out of an "involuntary reflex" or that, by playing in the game, the victim "consented to" the contact or "assumed the risk" of getting hurt. Sometimes the team will be sued under the theory that as an employer it is responsible for its employees' actions. The team can also be sued under the theory that its "supervision" is negligent if it allows a violent player to play. All of these legal theories are used daily in courtrooms with relative ease; yet, in sports violence cases, they are quite different to prove.

The popular view is that people participate in athletics out of love for the game, not out of a malicious desire to harm an opponent. Therefore, it is much harder to make the case that one athlete intended to injure another one. If an athlete argues that he acted in self-defense, the general principle is that he could have used whatever force was necessary to protect himself.

Some athletes have argued that their actions were the product of an involuntary reflex to act or that their victims "assumed the risk." Most courts agree there is some merit to this argument, but the familiar problem arises:

drawing the line separating conduct that is consented to as part of the game and conduct that is beyond the scope of consent and thus is illegal.

Even if the cases were absolutely clear on what contact is or is not legal during a game, there are a number of other problems that have kept the courts out of this area in the past. First, many prosecutors simply do not want to file a criminal charge against an athlete for something he does during a game. In the criminal system, this is basically the decision of the prosecutor, and most seem to feel they have enough "real crime" to deal with without getting involved in applications of the criminal code for behavior on the playing field.

Second, some argue that the courts should stay out of this area because criminal penalties have little deterrent value, since most players do not think they are breaking the law. The fact that the four major hockey assault cases have all ended in an acquittal or a hung jury reinforces this argument.

Third, courts have generally been unsuccessful in the past because of the problem of convincing jurors, some of them sports fans, that some violent conduct should be illegal even if it occurs during the game. There are no statutes dealing specifically with sports violence. "Juries," argues Maricopa County (Phoenix) Attorney Charles F. Hyder, therefore "have no real sense of the standards and norms in the area." Even if jurors grasp the facts of a particular incident and understand the context of the sport, it is difficult for them to decide that the athlete they may have seen many times on television or read about in the newspaper actually broke the law.

Realistically, then, there are a number of significant and serious problems when the courts become involved in litigating sports violence. In fact, the sports establishment is probably correct when it argues that most disputes should be kept "within the family."

Indeed, in recent years, each sport has made some changes with a view toward policing its game. In football, concern in 1978 led to a formal written statement from Commissioner Rozelle that "violence on the playing field would not be tolerated and that multi-game suspensions might be employed as enforcement." Further, the rule instructing NFL officials to be quicker in whistling a play dead when the quarterback is in the grasp of a tackler, adopted at the 1979 Annual Meeting, has worked as well as the league had hoped. Miami Dolphin Coach Don Shula commented that "tacklers are not driving crowns of helmets into ribs or backs as often. The threat of penalty has forced many tacklers to concentrate on keeping their faces up and merely 'wrapping up' the quarterbacks." The quarterback, since 1980, is protected by a quick whistle any time he is in the grasp of the tackler behind the line of scrimmage. In the past, the quick whistle was in effect only when the quarterback was in the pocket. The NFL has also developed a Joint Committee on Player Safety and Welfare for the purpose of deliberating on rules that "could adversely affect player safety."

In hockey the NHL Players' Association has prompted the NHL leadership to at least discuss the prospect of establishing new rules and penalties aimed at reducing fighting and violence. In basketball the NBA has been trying to crack down on violence after the Tomjanovich affair. Former Commissioner Larry O'Brien emphasized that "we will not tolerate violence in any form" and fined and suspended eight players, one coach and even one referee that year for excessive acts of during-the-game violence.

If the sports establishment can be convinced that sports violence is more illegal than entertaining, reform will be much easier, and a number of significant changes will be possible. First, a change in many of the "safety oriented" rules of the game will be easier to achieve. In hockey, for example, the rule concerning fighting penalties could be toughened. An automatic suspension for fighting could be introduced (as in Olympic hockey) so that any player can refuse to fight without losing face with his peers and coaches. Referees' standards could be upgraded so rules are consistently and completely enforced. Second, the system could increase its emphasis on skill development at lower age levels. Coaches must be instructed that there is a purpose to amateur sports beyond that of training professionals. Third, the media could begin an effort to educate the sporting public to be sensitive to the distinction between subtle skills and overt illegal violence.

So how do we solve the problem?

In 1980, I helped draft the Sports Violence Bill that was introduced into the U.S. House of Representatives by Ohio's Ronald Mottl. The bill suggested that a professional athlete who knowingly used excessive force and thereby caused a risk of significant injury to another could be fined as much as $5,000 and imprisoned for as long as one year. The intent of the bill was clearly not to send athletes to jail, or even to fine them, but rather (1) to uniformly define the line separating normal, aggressive, "part of the game" play from excessive physical force and (2) to force the professional sports leagues to implement and enforce this standard internally, before an incident reached the government.

Though the bill attracted a good deal of attention through three sets of hearings before the House Judiciary Subcommittee on Criminal Justice, questions such as "Why federal government intervention?" and "Why a jail sentence?" confused and distorted the real issue: that someone must define a clear standard, enforce violations and therefore deter future incidents such as blatant cheap shots in football, stick-swinging and skate-slashing in hockey, fistfighting in basketball and the intentional "beanball" in baseball.

Most experts agree that the primary responsibility for this challenge rests with the pro sports leagues. They have the expertise and power to deal with the problem effectively if they choose to do so. In fact, since the proposed 1980 criminal bill (which did not survive committee hearings), the NFL has developed new blocking and quarterback-protection rules, major league baseball has instructed umpires to eject pitchers they believe intended to throw at batters and the NBA has broadened the grounds for technical fouls — all steps in the right direction. But, a further effort is needed to assure that the pro sports leagues continue to take the lead in protecting their players.

This may be further encouraged through the Sports Violence Arbitration Act that was introduced in the U.S. House of Representatives by Tom Daschle (Democrat of South Dakota). The bill would require all major sports leagues to establish an arbitration tribunal that would create financial incentives for clubs and players to refrain from encouraging or engaging in violent conduct.

The tribunal could impose fines upon a club and hold the club financially liable for any unnecessary violent conduct by its players. The financial liability of a club would include paying the salary of an injured player during the convalescence period following an injury, paying the injured player's medical expenses, paying damages to the injured player if he is prevented from playing in subsequent seasons and possibly paying damages or awarding a draft choice to the injured player's club for loss of services.

Additionally, substantial fines could be imposed upon the club for failure to supervise noticeably violent tendencies of a player. The tribunal also could suspend without pay the player who engages in unnecessary violent conduct. A grievance procedure, patterned after procedures followed by the Federal Mediation and Conciliation Service, would be the means of imposing punishment on clubs and players.

As this bill progresses through congressional committees, there is bound to be considerable controversy. But the bill responds to the criticisms of the previous effort by (1) removing the criminal penalty and (2) allowing the pro sports leagues to take primary responsibility for policing themselves.

While we must expect criticism, we must remember that if some decisive action is not taken to reinforce to the sports establishment that excessive sports violence is more illegal than entertaining, the next incident may require a eulogy.

§ 2.6(C). Conclusion.

A Harris poll released in 1983 indicates that half of the nation's sports fans think sports are too violent. Excessive violence will continue to increase as long as the pressures and incentives to be violent remain. Exceptionally severe acts of violence must be dealt with by governing organizations and if this fails, by the courts.

If many acts of sports violence took place anywhere but on the playing field or court, the actions would result in civil and often criminal charges. Most persons involved in professional sports, however, prefer to keep violence and injuries a "family matter." When sports cases have gone to court, difficulties have arisen in applying general assault and battery laws to sports-specific situations.

From their earliest training, athletes are taught that violence is just part of the game. Violence and intimidation are becoming part of the game strategy and in some situations a condition of the job.

Despite the enormous pressures to avoid sports violence litigation, an increasing number of cases are reaching the courts. Many of the cases demonstrate that the law is not very clear. A football player may be liable for something he does on the field, yet a hockey player may not be liable for something he does in the rink. A player might be liable in Louisiana but not in Illinois. The problem is caused in part by the fact that judges and juries must interpret laws which were not written to cover sports violence cases.

The Sports Violence Bill was intended to uniformly define the line separating normal, aggressive play from excessive physical force and to force the professional sports leagues to implement and enforce this standard internally. The bill did not survive committee hearings of Congress.

The Sports Violence Arbitration Act would require all major sports leagues to establish an arbitration tribunal that would create financial incentives for clubs and players to refrain from violent conduct. The bill will undoubtedly result in controversy, but it responds to previous criticism of the Sports Violence Bill by removing the criminal penalty and allowing professional sports leagues to assume the primary responsibility for policing themselves.

Some action is needed to reinforce to the sports establishment that excessive sports violence is more illegal than entertaining before it is too late to prevent a major incident.

§ 2.7. "He Said What"?! Defamation in Sports.

By David R. Maraghy

The earliest decision involving defamation in "sports" found by this author is the case of *McFadden v. Morning Journal Association,* 51 N.Y.S. 275 (App. Div. 1898). In this case the New York Supreme Court held it libelous *per se* for the defendant newspaper to publish a fictional account of a rowing race between two young women for the affections of a young man:

> The occasion was the great Prospect Park quarter-mile junior singles, for the Cupid Cup. Miss Nellie McFadden (a prize for Aladdin), and sweet Mamie Barton (you'd sure lose your heart on), had both set their caps for young Frederick Bohn; so, with a friend and relation, they went to the park, to give demonstration ('twas just before dark), by rowing a race, — an aquatic love chase, — of their love for this perfectly proper Don Juan.

§ 2.7(A). The Law of Defamation.

This chapter reviews defamation — "the taking from one's reputation" — in the world of sport. W. Prosser in *The Law of Torts* § 111, at 739 (4th ed. 1971), defines defamation as "that which tends to injure 'reputation' in the popular sense; to diminish the esteem, respect, goodwill or confidence in which the plaintiff is held, or to excite adverse, derogatory or unpleasant feelings or opinions against him."

The various defenses and privileges regarding a defamation allegation will be examined here, as will a recent decision making a distinction between statements disparaging performance and actual defamation. In *Andres v. Williams,* 405 A.2d 121 (Del. 1979), the athletic director at Delaware State College reported to the college athletic council that the plaintiff, employed by the college as a sports writer and statistician, "did not work within the supervisor structure, that he incurred excessive telephone bills, that he was unavailable to coaches and team members, that he also worked for a newspaper and thus had a conflict of interests, that he did not arrange press conferences and that he had not attended athletic events." Not surprisingly, the plaintiff's one-year employment contract with the college was not renewed.

The court, citing *The Restatement of Torts* § 559, found that the critical statements by the athletic director were not of the level that would "lower [Andres] in the estimation of the community or deter third persons from associating or dealing with him, nor do they injure reputation in the popular sense. Prosser, *Law of Torts* (1971) Section 111." The language, therefore, did not constitute defamation, and the court affirmed the trial court in granting the defendant's motion for summary judgment against the plaintiff.

There are two forms of defamatory publication: libel and slander. "Publication," a necessary element of the tort, is the means of communication of the defamatory statement to a third party. Libel originally referred to the written or printed word while slander was of an oral character. The distinction "is one of embodiment in some permanent physical form" and leaves the plaintiff to prove actual damage in claims of slander, whereas in libel cases the damage is assumed to be greater because the language is in a permanent form.

There are four exceptions to a plaintiff's requirement of proof in a slander action. No actual proof of damage is necessary to support an actionable slander claim when the slander (1) imputes a crime, (2) imputes a loathsome disease, (3) adversely affects trade, business or profession or (4) imputes unchastity of a woman.

Generally, defamatory words may be divided into two types: a statement defamatory "upon its face" or a statement which requires the aid of outside evidence to convey its defamatory meaning. A slanderous statement imputing one of the four exceptions cited above has been labeled "slander *per se* " or slander which is "actionable *per se*." Similarly, many courts apply this rule to libel so that a libelous statement imputing one of the exceptions is "libel *per se*." Any other libel is libel *per quod*; i.e., the plaintiff must prove the defamatory meaning and how it damaged him. Other decisions are based on the proposition that any libel is actionable because it is more permanent than the spoken word and accordingly more widely circulated.

In cases of slander in sport the courts use the term defamation *per se*, that is, defamation "upon its face" and therefore actionable. Two instances where courts have considered this issue of whether or not defamation *per se* was present can be found in *Fawcett Publications, Inc. v. Morris*, 377 P.2d 42 (Okla. 1962), and *Chuy v. Philadelphia Eagles Football Club*, 595 F.2d 1265 (3d Cir. 1979).

In *Fawcett* the plaintiff was a member of the 1956 Oklahoma University football team. An article entitled "The Pill That Can Kill Sports" published in a 1958 issue of True Magazine published by the defendant alleged that the Oklahoma players were illegally using amphetamines:

> The "lifter" (amphetamine user) can and does become heroic, boisterous, pugnacious, or vicious . . . . These results are what make amphetamines useful in the field of athletics. They promote aggression, increase the competitive spirit, and work the same as the epinephrine (adrenalin) produced in your body. The adrenal cortex, however, is wiser than victory-hungry coaches and athletes . . . .

The *Fawcett* court found that the article was "defamatory on its face" and libelous *per se,* in that it exposed "the entire O.U. team to public hatred and contempt and tends to deprive the team and its membership of public confidence. The reader was unequivocally informed that members of the team illegally used amphetamine."

An additional aspect of the *Fawcett* decision is the issue of the plaintiff's right to institute a libel action, since he was not specifically named in the libelous article. The court noted a distinction between "class libel," in which an individual may not maintain an action for derogation of a class, and "group libel," in which under the right circumstances an action may lie. Discounting size of the group alone as a conclusive factor, the court found that since the article was libelous *per se,* it libeled every member of the team, even though not specifically named. The average reader, reasoned the court, could identify the plaintiff with the libelous statement since he was a regular and constant player and not part of a changing element of that group.

In *Chuy,* the team physician for the Philadelphia Eagles told a reporter that the plaintiff suffered from polycythemia vera, a blood condition which manufactured blood cells that formed embolisms. The plaintiff contended that these comments were defamatory *per se,* in that they imputed to him a "loathsome disease." In rejecting this contention, the court recited the history in this area, which traditionally considered a "loathsome disease" to be one of special social repugnance, limited primarily to sexually communicable venereal disease and leprosy. Polycythemia vera is of unknown origin and is neither contagious nor attributed in any way to socially repugnant conduct. Finally, the court found that since Chuy's career as a football player had already ended due to an unrelated injury he could not support a defamation action by contending that the physician's statements affected his trade or profession.

There exist several privileges, or defenses, to any defamation action. The oldest axiom is that truth is a defense to any civil action for libel or slander. A privileged statement is one which but for the occasion on which or the circumstances under which it is made would be defamatory and actionable. The privilege concept evolved as public policy to further the right of free speech in a matter of public or social interest. Privileges can be absolute — judicial and legislative proceedings — or qualified — acting in public interest, acting in one's own interest, reports of public proceedings and fair comment on matters of public concern. A major portion of this effort deals with a constitutional privilege established and developed in a line of cases beginning with *New York Times Co. v. Sullivan,* 376 U.S. 254 (1964), when statements have been made concerning "public figures." There are, however, several instructive cases on other aspects of privilege.

In *Sellers v. Time Inc.,* 299 F. Supp. 582 (E.D. Pa. 1969), the United States District Court for the Eastern District of Pennsylvania found the privilege of fair reporting on judicial proceedings established under the common law. The defendant had published an article indicating that the plaintiff golfer had been sued because he made a golf shot which went backwards, striking a partner in the eye and causing a loss of sight. In granting the defendant publisher's motion for summary judgment, the court noted that the article did not lose its privilege because of its allegedly "flippant" or "smart alecky" style of reporting.

Several cases demonstrate the privilege of fair comment in sports. In *Conkwright v. Globe News Publishing Co.,* 398 S.W.2d 385 (Tex. Civ. App. 1965), William "Red" Conkwright brought a libel action against the publisher of a newspaper article stating that the plaintiff, "who shouldn't be coaching anything, is coaching the Houston receivers." The court deemed the article privileged as a published opinion, calling it a reasonable comment or criticism concerning a public matter and published for general information.

The plaintiff in *Cohen v. Cowles Publishing Co.,* 273 P.2d 893 (Wash. 1954), was a jockey complaining of a newspaper article reporting that he had a cowardly and particularly unskillful ride in a recent race. The court noted that persons "who present their work or products to the public for its approval and acceptance, thereby subject it to public criticism, and honest comment upon it is privileged."

A coach's privilege, unique but nevertheless sensible, was recognized by the court in *Iacco v. Bohannon,* 245 N.W.2d 791 (Mich. App. 1976), although the exact nature of that privilege was never identified in traditional terms. A high school basketball coach suspended his team captain for an alleged lack of loyalty to the team. This action resulted in a lawsuit by the former player against the coach and the school district alleging libel and slander. The coach had gathered together the team and in their presence announced the suspension of the plaintiff, who could be reinstated only by an overt "and sustained demonstration of team loyalty. We must see and hear your faith in your team's ability to win." The court determined that the coach had a duty to criticize the performance of the players as members of the team and to act in a fashion which would promote the maximum team effort. Protected by such a qualified privilege, no action would lie against the coach. In addition to granting summary judgment for the defendant coach, the court ruled proper summary judgment in favor of the defendant school district based on governmental immunity.

The more recent decision of *Institute of Athletic Motivation v. University of Illinois,* 170 Cal. Rptr. 411 (Cal. App. 1981), found a privilege based upon a section of the California Civil Code which tracked the common law privileges noted earlier. The court stated that a publication or broadcast is privileged if made:

> In a communication, without malice, to a person interested therein, (1) by one who is also interested, or (2) by one who stands in such relation to the person interested as to afford a reasonable ground for supposing the motive for the communication innocent, or (3) who is requested by the person interested to give the information.

The plaintiff was a corporation founded in the late 1960's by clinical psychologists Bruce Ogilvie and Thomas Tutko. It had developed a questionnaire purporting to identify certain personality traits predictive of athletic success, titled "Athletic Motivation Inventory" (A.M.I.). The A.M.I. form was given as a psychological test to coaches and athletes, and A.M.I. was widely used by high schools, colleges and athletic organizations, both private and professional.

Defendant Rainer Martens, a professor of physical education at the University of Illinois with a Ph.D. in sports psychology, wrote a four-page letter criticizing A.M.I., which was sent to numerous professional athletic organizations and to several sports magazines. Among other assertions, the letter stated that Ogilvie and Tutko, contrary to their claims of supporting evidence, "have been unwilling or unable to provide any evidence that A.M.I. . . . is reliable or valid." Without such documentation, the letter continued, the offering of that psychological test on a commercial basis constituted an "unethical practice" according to the standards of the American Psychological Association. The letter also called upon various sports organizations to expose A.M.I. The court ruled the letter to be defamatory as a matter of law "in that it has a tendency to affect the integrity and business reputation of the plaintiff." The issue then became whether or not Martens's defamatory statements were somehow privileged.

The California court ruled Martens's communication a privileged one to interested persons within the meaning and intent of the Civil Code. The court also stated, however, that this privilege might be abused and the protection of the privilege lost, due to the publisher's lack of belief in truth. No such abuse was found, however, because Martens, a sports psychologist, afforded to persons interested (coaches) reasonable ground for supposing his motive for communicating to be innocent. While evidence of a less than innocent motive existed, the jury chose not to be swayed in that direction.

Finally, the court noted that the primary focus of the communication was an "academic professional marketplace of ideas" and did not involve any private aspect of individual or corporate life. The plaintiff here entered the arena of public controversy by offering the A.M.I. to the athletic community, and by representing it as a valid indicator of behavioral response.

§ 2.7(B). The *New York Times* Rule — Constitutional Privilege.

The most litigated question in sports-related defamation is whether or not plaintiff is a public figure. If he is, he must prove actual malice on the part of the defendant before a recovery will be allowed.

In the case of *New York Times Co. v. Sullivan*, 376 U.S. 254 (1964), the Supreme Court decided that the first and fourteenth amendments, guaranteeing freedom of speech and press, prohibited a public official from recovering damages for a defamatory falsehood concerning his official conduct unless he could prove that the statement was made with "'actual malice' — that is with the knowledge that it was false or with reckless disregard of whether it was false or not." This qualified privilege is a constitutional one which has become known as the *New York Times* rule. According to the Court, the freedom of expression upon public issues is secured by the first amendment, a necessary safeguard "to assure unfettered interchange of ideas for the bringing about of political and social changes desired by the people." We are a nation committed "to the principle that debate on public issues should be uninhibited, robust, and wide-open, and that it may well include vehement, caustic, and sometimes unpleasantly sharp attacks on government and public officials". The *New York Times* Court acknowledged that "erroneous statement is inevitable in free debate, and that it must be protected if the freedoms of expression are to have the 'breathing space' that they need to survive." Any rule compelling a critic of official conduct to guarantee the truth of all factual assertions, or else to suffer libel judgments, amounts to "self-censorship."

In order to show actual malice in a defamation action, thereby overcoming the privilege of the *New York Times* rule, the evidence given by a public official plaintiff must be clear and convincing.

Two years later, in the case of *Rosenblatt v. Baer,* 383 U.S. 75 (1966), the Supreme Court defined the public official to whom the *New York Times* rule would apply as "government employees who have, or appear to the public to have, substantial responsibility for or control over the conduct of governmental affairs."

The *New York Times* rule was further extended from public officials to public figures in one of the most significant and frequently cited libel cases from the world of sport, *Curtis Publishing Co. v. Butts,* 388 U.S. 130 (1967). This case established an additional aspect to the *New York Times* rule, which stated, in effect, that when the standards of investigation and reporting ordinarily adhered to by responsible publishers are not met, damages for defamation may be awarded.

The case arose due to an article, in the March 23, 1963 issue of the Saturday Evening Post, entitled "The Story of a College Football Fix." At the time, Butts was Athletic Director at the University of Georgia, with overall responsibility for the administration of its athletic program. Although Georgia is a state university, Butts actually was employed not by the state but by the Georgia Athletic Association, a private corporation. The plaintiff, a well-known and respected figure in the coaching profession, had previously served as head coach at the University; he was negotiating with a professional team at the time of the defamatory statement.

The article alleged that prior to the clash between Alabama and Georgia, Butts had disclosed to the Alabama coach "Georgia's plays, defensive patterns and all the significant secrets Georgia's football team possessed." The basis of the article was an affidavit offered by one George Burnett, an insurance salesman, who had overheard a telephone conversation between Butts and Alabama's head coach, Paul "Bear" Bryant, a week before the game. Supposedly Burnett gave his notes of the conversation to Georgia head coach Johnny Griffith, and the episode ended in Butts's resignation, allegedly for health and business reasons. The conclusion of the article boasted: "The chances are that Wally Butts will never help any football team again . . . . The investigation by university and Southeastern Conference officials is continuing; motion pictures of other games are being scrutinized; where it will end no one so far can say. But careers will be ruined, that is sure."

Before the *New York Times* decision, a jury had returned a verdict of libel in favor of Butts in the amount of $60,000 general damages and $3,000,000 punitive damages. The trial court reduced the total to $460,000.

In reviewing the appeal the Court considered its recent decision and reasoning in *New York Times.* Further, the Court noted that Butts "commanded a substantial amount of independent public interest at the time of the publications . . . [and] would have been labeled public figures under ordinary tort rules." The Court concluded that the similarities and differences between libel actions involving public officials and those involving public figures like Butts required the slightly altered *New York Times* standard. Such libel actions affecting "public figures" could not be left entirely to state libel laws, without any constitutional safeguard, but neither were the vigorous requirements of *New York Times* the only solution.

In affirming the lower court's decision the Supreme Court allotted three full pages to description of the grossly inadequate investigation undertaken by The Saturday Evening Post in preparing the article. The most elementary precautions had been ignored, and the Post writer assigned to the story was not well-informed on football. These facts gave ample support to the finding of "a departure from the standards of investigation and reporting ordinarily adhered to by responsible publishers."

The *Butts* case offered an often-quoted statement of how the status of a "public figure" is attained: by position alone "or by his purposeful activity amounting to a thrusting of his personality into the 'vortex' of an important public controversy." One year later, the Supreme Court offered fresh insight into the standard of "actual malice" in *St. Amant v. Thompson*, 390 U.S. 727, (1968). The Court cited favorably *Garrison v. Louisiana*, 379 U.S. 64 (1964), an earlier opinion requiring that a defamation plaintiff show that a false publication has been made with a "high degree of awareness of probable falsity."(Note that both *Garrison, supra,* and St. Amant are nonmedia defendants.) The *St. Amant* Court held that:

> [R]eckless conduct is not measured by whether a reasonably prudent man would have published, or would have investigated before publishing. There must be sufficient evidence to permit the conclusion that the defendant in fact *entertained serious doubts as to the truth of his publication.* Publishing with such doubts shows a *reckless disregard* for truth or falsity and demonstrates *actual malice.* [Emphasis added.]

The next decision with lasting ramifications in this area is *Gertz v. Robert Welch, Inc.,* 418 U.S. 323 (1974), which indicates two methods by which someone may become a "public figure" and to whom should be applied the *New York Times* standard in any defamation action:

> For the most part those who attain this status have assumed roles of especial prominence in the affairs of society. Some occupy positions of such persuasive power and influence that they are deemed public figures for all purposes. More commonly, those classed as public figures have thrust themselves to the forefront of particular public controversies in order to influence the resolution of the issues involved. In either event, they invite attention and comment."

Continuing this line of thought, the Court establishes two categories of "public figures":

> In some instances an individual may achieve such pervasive fame or notoriety that he becomes a public figure for *all purposes and in all contexts.* More commonly, an individual voluntarily injects himself or is

drawn into a particular controversy and thereby becomes a public figure *for a limited range of issues.* In either case such persons assume special prominence in the resolution of public questions. [Emphasis supplied.]

This test has led to some speculation that certain public figures are not such for all purposes, but instead are merely a kind of "limited" public figure. Particularly in the area of sport, there are many personal factors in an athlete's life which may affect his career but which may not be the proper subject of unlimited publication.

The Court specifically refused to extend the *New York Times* privilege to cases involving defamation of private individuals. The rationale behind that decision also explains the extending of the *New York Times* rule to public figures. As the Court explained, public officials and public figures traditionally have easier access to the channels of communication and can thereby more effectively counteract false statements than private individuals can, and the state is more interested in protecting the vulnerable private individual.

A second compelling consideration is that public figures, like public officials, generally expose themselves voluntarily to increased risk of injury from defamatory falsehood, and therefore the communications media are justified in assuming so.

Having laid the groundwork for the constitutional privilege of the *New York Times* rule as it applies both to public officials and public figures, let us now review the extensive litigation of that issue involving sports personalities.

§ 2.7(C). Public Figures — Position, Public Controversy, Public Interest or Public Official.

This section reviews cases where a court has considered the question of whether or not the defamation plaintiff was a public figure. This one issue appears to be the key to any defamation action in sport, since the designation of "public figure" increases substantially a plaintiff's burden of proof.

(1) *Position of Prominence.*

First to be reviewed are the cases where a court decided that the *New York Times* rule did provide privilege to the defamation defendant due to plaintiff's personal importance, which made him a public figure.

One of the first major sports-related defamation decisions following *Butts, supra,* was *Cepeda v. Cowles Magazines & Broadcasting, Inc.,* 392 F.2d 417 (9th Cir. 1968). Cepeda was a star baseball player for the San Francisco Giants; Look magazine published an article which quoted his employer's criticism of Cepeda's competence and popularity. The court affirmed the district court's judgment in favor of the defendant publisher, noting that, like the *Butts* decision, this libel action "cast important obstacles in Cepeda's path that he had not overcome," i.e., the burden of proving actual malice. The *Cepeda* court said: "Such figures include artists, athletes, business people, dilettantes, anyone who is famous, or infamous, because of who he is or what he has done."

Also decided under the controlling reasoning of *Butts* was *Grayson v. Curtis Publishing Co.,* 72 Wash. 2d 999, 436 P.2d 756 (1968). *Grayson* was the head basketball coach at the University of Washington; he brought a libel action against the Saturday Evening Post for a 1963 article entitled "Basketball's Bullies," which described violent outbreaks caused by Grayson who had allegedly whipped the fans into frenzies protesting the calls of the referee, Al Lightner. Grayson, the plaintiff, was named as an example of "explosive bench behavior" along with Bones McKinney of Wake Forest and others. The court stated that lack of good sportsmanship by Coach Grayson and its effect on others were of such character as to affect his competency to pursue his college coaching career, an occupation in which good sportsmanship is a particularly valuable qualification.

But the court also declared Grayson to be a public figure in which the public had a justified and important interest, and the case was remanded to be tried under the *New York Times* standards to determine whether the article had been published with actual malice.

In the case of *Chuy v. Philadelphia Eagles Football Club,* 595 F.2d 1265 (3rd Cir. 1979), the court found that professional athletes generally assume a position of public prominence. Plaintiff Chuy had been a starting player for the Eagles and had gained special prominence for being involved in a major and well-publicized trade. Accordingly, the court had no difficulty in concluding as a matter of law that Chuy was a public figure.

In the libel action of *Fitzgerald v. Minnesota Chiropractic Association, Inc.,* 294 N.W.2d 269 (Minn. 1980), the parties agreed that the plaintiff was a public figure. Fitzgerald was a widely-known amateur speed skater and winner of many awards, including an Olympic medal in 1948.

The decision in *Bilney v. Evening Star Newspaper Co.,* 406 A.2d 652 (Md. App. 1979), is also useful for its analysis of the public figure issue. This action was brought by six members of the University of Maryland basketball team against reporters and newspaper publishers for articles detailing the poor academic standing of these six players, thus putting them in danger of being declared ineligible to play. The court could find no evidence that the defendants had learned of the players' academic problems from confidential records or by any acts of invasion or intrusion, and therefore it boldly analyzed the issue of "public figure." College basketball, it declared, is a "big time" sport and generates a great deal of interest and excitement throughout the country. The court also acknowledged not only the large sums of money raised for the University and the Atlantic Coast Conference but also the sums illicitly wagered on college sporting events. Individual performers, the Court said, "achieved the status of public figures . . . by virtue of their membership on the University basketball team [and] . . . having sought . . . the limelight . . . will not be heard to complain.

A similar situation exists in the libel action brought by the executrix of Hamilton "Tex" Maule in *Maule v. NYM Corp.,* 429 N.E.2d 416 (N.Y. 1981). The court ruled that as a matter of law Tex Maule, who had been for nineteen years one of the best known writers at Sports Illustrated, was also a public figure. Maule testified to having written 28 books and having made many public appearances, both live and on TV, to speak on sports. Further, the court found that not only did Maule welcome publicity, but that "by his own purposeful activities he thrust himself into the public eye." As the court had ruled previously that Maule was not a public figure, the matter was remanded for a new trial to be considered under the *New York Times* standard.

A similar combination of definitions of public figure is found in the case of *Rood v. Finney*, 418 So. 2d 1 (La. App. 1982). Rood, the plaintiff, was a professional golfer who had been involved for over 20 years in unique and well-publicized golf activities. In one project called "highway golf," Rood had made cross-country tours to raise money for youth assistance by hitting golf balls across land and water. Publicity is, of course, essential to any such effort, and so Rood had employed public relations experts of all sorts.

This libel action was the result of an apparent misprint which stated that Rood was raising funds through highway golf in order to solve "his" personal drug problem, instead of "the" drug addiction problem, as it had been written originally by the defendant, Finney. The court declared Rood to be a public figure and that he would therefore have to prove "actual malice" before he could recover. Rood failed to do this, and the disposition of plaintiff's suit by summary judgment was affirmed.

The final case to be examined is *Vandenburg v. Newsweek, Inc.*, 507 F.2d 1024 (5th Cir. 1975). Vandenburg, the track coach at the University of Texas at El Paso, brought a libel action against *Newsweek* for an article entitled *The Angry Black Athlete.* In this article statements were made on the black power movement and its effect on college and university athletics, and Vandenburg took issue with two paragraphs:

> It is a mess that extends from Niagara to the University of California, from Michigan to the University of Texas at El Paso. Sometimes the racial issue is inflamed by a coach's get-tough policy. "I could give in to a lot of Negro demands," says one Southwestern track coach, "and keep my team intact. But someone has to hold the line against these people."
>
> At El Paso, track coach Wayne Vandenburg threatened to kick six athletes off the team if they joined the boycott . . . . Vandenburg won and the athletes competed. But two months later . . . the same athletes refused to enter a meet at Brigham Young University in Utah because of Mormon doctrines about blacks. Vandenburg promptly dropped champion long-jumper Bob Beamon and five others from the squad.

Based upon testimony of the plaintiff and of author Pete Axthelm, the court designated Vandenburg a public figure, "at least for a 'limited range of issues.'" The court carefully examined Axthelm's investigative efforts and decided that the plaintiff could not show actual malice as required under the *New York Times* rule.

Despite the outcome, however, lingering doubt remains as to the status of athletes and sports personalities, owing to the words a "limited range of issues." For example, at what point would a referee become a "public figure" and thus be required to fulfill the *New York Times* requirement in a defamation action? Two people who are both lawyers and basketball officials suggested using officiating levels ranging from "public figure" to "private individual." At one end, the professional sport official would probably qualify as a public figure. In the middle range would be college sport officials and semi-professionals. At the lowest level would be found high school officials to be known as "private individuals." According to Narol and Depoulas, in their article entitled "Defamation: A Guide to Referee's Rights" published in *Trial* No. 1 (January, 1980), factors to be considered when assessing such a possible defamation case would be: "(1) level of competition . . . (2) number of years . . . officiating; (3) whether the athletic event was broadcast on radio or television; and (4) the sport official's notoriety in the particular sport community."

(2) *Public Controversy.*

The case *Gertz v. Robert Welch, Inc.*, 418 U.S. 323 (1974), established that it is possible to become a public figure by injecting oneself or allowing oneself to be drawn into a public controversy, thereby becoming a public figure for at least a limited range of issues. The Court also found that some individuals classed as public figures "have thrust themselves to the forefront of particular public controversies in order to influence the resolution of the issues involved."

Illustrative of this method of achieving public figure status are three cases, the first of which is *Hoffman v. Washington Post Co.*, 433 F. Supp. 600 (D.D.C. 1977). In this case a weight-lifting coach who sold high-protein tablets brought a libel action against a newspaper for an article which questioned in harsh terms the value of the plaintiff's protein supplements. The article declared that weight lifters wasted their money on the plaintiff's supplements while he got rich and drove a Rolls Royce. The writer was Dr. Gabe Mirkin, a recognized expert in sports medicine. The court found the article to be defamatory; therefore, the question of privilege was confronted.

In applying the *Gertz* test, the court found a public interest in the need and value of protein supplements. The plaintiff, Dr. Mirkin, had achieved general fame throughout the United States by lecturing, making television and radio appearances and by writing. The court concluded that Hoffman had voluntarily injected himself into a public controversy which had been examined in the press, acted upon in Congress and discussed before the Federal Trade Commission. The plaintiff was therefore clearly a public figure for a limited range of issues — protein supplements and their value — and in order to recover he had to show actual malice. This the plaintiff could not do, and the court affirmed all judgments in favor of all defendants as a matter of law.

In the recent case of *Woy v. Turner*, 573 F. Supp. 35 (N.D. Ga. 1983), the court decided that the plaintiff was a public figure as a result of his thrusting himself into a public controversy over contract negotiations between William "Bucky" Woy, acting as agent for Bob Horner, and Bill Lucas, general manager of the Atlanta Braves National Baseball League Club. Before the dispute could be settled, Lucas died, whereupon the defendant and owner of the Braves, Ted Turner, told the press that Woy, the plaintiff, had made accusations regarding Lucas's character which had contributed to or caused his death.

The defendant contended that the *New York Times* standard applied to the case since Woy, due to his prominence in the case, was a public figure.

Evidence was presented that Woy used the media to promote himself as a sports agent, and also that he had co-authored an autobiographical book entitled *Sign Em Up, Bucky.* Despite this showing, the court was not convinced that Woy's position was one of special prominence.

The court did find, however, that Woy was indeed a public figure for other reasons: he had thrust himself into the much-publicized contractual dispute between Bob Horner and the Atlanta Braves, and he had made himself readily available to the media by soliciting them regarding the contract dispute and by holding press conferences on the matter. Woy would only be entitled to recover on his libel and slander claim if he could prove actual malice. Note that the court held, as indicated *supra,* the *New York Times* standard is applicable to a nonmedia defendant.

But public figures are not necessarily people, as we can see in the final case involving a public controversy, *Stop the Olympic Prison v. United States Olympic Committee,* 489 F. Supp. 1112 (S.D.N.Y. 1980). An organization which was opposed to the use of the Lake Placid Olympic Village as a prison after the games were over filed suit, declaring its first amendment right to print and distribute its own poster using part of the Olympic trademark. The Olympic Committee counterclaimed for defamation, trademark infringement and violation of other trademark-related New York law. Only the issues related to defamation are discussed here.

In addition to finding no libel in the poster, the court also found that in order to recover for the claimed libel the Olympic Committee would have to show actual malice within the *New York Times* standard. In so ruling the court declared the Olympic Committee to be a public figure, because, as the court pointed out, the Olympic Committee "exercises exclusive jurisdiction . . . over all matters pertaining to the participation of the United States in the Olympic Games and over the organization of the Olympic Games . . . when held in the United States. 36 U.S.C. § 374(1), (3) (as amended Nov. 8, 1978)." Thus, the Olympic Committee in fact is obliged to thrust itself and its views into any public controversy involving amateur athletics and "the organization of the Olympic Games when held in the United States." In addition, the court noted that the Olympic Committee has had "regular and continuing access to the media."

(3) *Public Interest.*

While the *Gertz* Court rejected the assumption that merely to be connected with a matter of public interest makes an individual a public figure for *New York Times* purposes, it does appear that a qualified privilege survives in matters of genuine public interest and fair comment.

In *Bon Air Hotel, Inc. v. Time, Inc.,* 426 F.2d 858 (5th Cir. 1970), Dan Jenkins, the well-known sports writer, wrote an article on the Masters Golf Tournament which appeared in the April 4, 1964 issue of Sports Illustrated. Jenkins had attended the Augusta, Georgia event for fourteen years; his article described the conditions under which the tournament was held, the accommodations available in Augusta for players and spectators and, specifically, conditions at the plaintiff's hotel, focusing on the "decline into dishevelment of the Bon Air Hotel" with unflattering descriptions of ancient waiters, sloping halls, tiny rooms, nonfunctional windows and late night departures via fire escapes.

The ruling of the court was that the *New York Times* rule applied in this instance because of the tremendous national public interest in the Masters. Publications concerning such a public interest were protected by the first amendment's necessary proof of actual malice.

Examination of Jenkins's careful, first-hand investigation convinced the court that the plaintiff could not show actual malice by the defendants. The summary judgment motion in favor of the defendants was affirmed.

In *Garfinkel v. Twenty-First Century Publishing Co.*, 291 N.Y.S.2d 735 (App. Div. 1968), an owner and publisher of a high school basketball scouting report complained of a magazine's references to him as a "flesh peddler" who did not like the NCAA. The court ruled that such remarks were not libelous *per se* and the plaintiff could not recover on his libel claim since he had not pled special damages. Moreover, the plaintiff would lose to the defendant's motion to dismiss, because Garfinkel had failed to plead malice or reckless disregard of the truth by the defendant. "Basketball and basketball scouting are matters of general public interest, particularly in light of the great attraction the game has for the public."

Sports Illustrated's publisher again found itself on the receiving end of a libel action in *Championship Sports, Inc. v. Time Inc.*, 71 Misc. 2d 887, 336 N.Y.S.2d 958 (1972). After the 1962 Patterson-Liston championship fight the magazine had published a story about the Internal Revenue agents who had seized all the receipts on the night of the fight in order to ensure the collection of the government's share of excise and corporate income tax. Apparently, the plaintiff promoter had failed to file a 1961 corporate income tax return and as a result had delinquency records. In support of its motion for summary judgment the defendant relied on the widespread publication of the incident and upon inquiries made by the defendant's representatives to the Internal Revenue Service, which resulted in a confirmation from the IRS. The court held that the test of "actual malice" was proper under these circumstances, to protect first amendment rights of free expression. Further, to demonstrate the absence of malice it is not necessary for a reporter to seek out the plaintiff's version of a dispute. Summary judgment was granted for the defendant.

The final libel case to be considered is also one of the most recent: *Fazekas v. Crain Consumer Group Division of Crain Communications, Inc.*, 583 F. Supp. 110 (S.D. Ind. 1984). Dale J. Fazekas, a two-time national champion race driver in the "showroom stock" category, brought a libel action against the publisher of Auto Week magazine for an article alleging illegal conduct by the plaintiff in performing certain modifications to race cars. Although there was substantial evidence that Fazekas was a public figure, the decision was based instead upon whether or not the article in question involved a matter of general or public interest.

While some of the reasoning in *Fazekas* appears to be in conflict with *Gertz* principles, the result is sound in view of the plaintiff's position and the community interest in the contested article. The subject of the article was racing rules and enforcement which were of general interest to racing enthusiasts — the very community at which the article was directed. Without a showing of actual malice, therefore, the plaintiff could not recover for alleged defamation in the very community most interested in the article.

(4) *Public Officials.*

Two cases within the past 10 years should be studied by coaches, athletic directors and any other sports-related employees of local or state governments, including high schools and even grade schools. As previously discussed, the United States Supreme Court in *Rosenblatt v. Baer* held that the *New York Times* rule applied in any slander or libel action brought by a public official, and the Court offered a two-part standard for determination of that status.

In *Johnston v. Corinthian Television Corp.,* 583 P.2d 1101 (Okla. 1978), the Oklahoma Supreme Court relied on the *Rosenblatt* test to determine that a grade school wrestling coach was a public official within the *New York Times* rule. A local television broadcaster gave newscasts of prepared scripts describing the ordeal of a sixth grader who tried to rejoin the grade school wrestling team and was made to submit to a whipping by his gym teacher and fellow students while naked with his legs tied and crawling through the legs of the other team members. The coach brought a defamation action against the television broadcaster.

In remanding the case to the trial court for determination of actual malice, the supreme court found that the plaintiff's position as wrestling coach was of sufficient importance in that public school's athletic program for the public to have "an independent interest in Johnston's method of disciplining a sixth grade boy in conjunction with the grade school wrestling team." Even though the plaintiff's grade school coaching duties were voluntary, he was still operating within the framework of the public school system, an obvious governmental function. The public's interest in the coach's performance went beyond a general interest, "as indicated by the number of withdrawals of students by parents from Johnston's physical education classes."

In the case of *Basarich v. Rodeghero,* 321 N.E.2d 739 (Ill. App. 1974), community high school athletic coaches and teachers brought a libel action against publishers of newsletters. The issue before the court was whether the plaintiffs (coaches and teachers in the community high school) were public officials or involved in matters of general interest, with the result that statements concerning their conduct in office or elsewhere would fall under the conditional privilege noted in *New York Times.* In answering that question affirmatively, the court reasoned that the "plaintiffs are public employees, hired by the school board and paid from public funds. As coaches and teachers in a local high school, they maintain highly responsible positions in the community." Education is a prime governmental responsibility, and "public school systems, their athletic programs, and those who run them are consistent subjects of intense public interest and substantial publicity." Therefore, the conduct and policies of public school coaches "are of as much concern to the community as are other 'public officials' and 'public figures.'"

(5) *Not a Public Figure.*

There are only two decisions in which a plaintiff was not required to satisfy the *New York Times* standard of proof. In *Wheeler v. Green,* 593 P.2d 777 (Or. 1979), the plaintiff, R.C. "Bucky" Wheeler, was a professional trainer of Appaloosa race horses. The court acknowledged that Wheeler was "well-known as a trainer" having been named "Trainer of the Year" by the Appaloosa Horse Club in 1972 and 1973, an award which resulted in a certain amount of publicity. The defendants had employed Wheeler on several occasions and later made disparaging remarks about his training, loyalty, honesty and alleged criminal activity. Defendants also sent two letters to the editor of The Appy, a newsletter, in which they described Wheeler's "dirty tricks, lack of ethics and sportsmanship connected with the Appaloosa horse business . . . extortion, bribery, forgery, intimidation, graft, corruption, fraud, income tax evasion . . . ."

These defendants contended that Wheeler was a public figure who could not recover for defamation because he had not met the *New York Times* standard of proving actual malice such as knowledge of falsity or reckless disregard of whether false or not. The court rejected this contention and found the plaintiff not to be a public figure according to the *New York Times* rule. Although the plaintiff's success as a trainer had made him well-known to the public that followed Appaloosa horse racing, and although a controversy existed among those engaged in the sport regarding the adequacy of governing rules, there was "no evidence that plaintiff had attempted in any way to influence that controversy or that he had taken any public part in it whatsoever." Therefore, Wheeler was entitled to whatever protection from defamation of reputation the state of Oregon awarded to private persons.

It is harder to understand the case of *From v. Tallahasee Democrat, Inc.,* 400 So. 2d 52 (Fla. App. 1981). A writer for a Tallahasee newspaper wrote a tennis column, claiming that a local country club's tennis program rose in prestige when a new head professional replaced the plaintiff. The court identified two statements in the article which could be considered as defamatory: "From, however, has an improving player's grand illusions, which contributed to his problems as a pro"; and "From, who knows tennis equipment well, did not fully understand his members' needs . . . ." Ultimately, the court affirmed the trial court's dismissal of the plaintiff's libel action because the article only contained statements of "pure opinion," a form of expression protected by the Constitution.

But, in spite of the outcome, the court did not find From a public figure. The defendants argued that the plaintiff had tried to gain publicity as a club tennis pro by organizing city-wide tournaments and working with various teams and that he had even contributed to the purchase of television commercials. The club had also advertised From. However, the court found that the plaintiff had never attempted to discuss the subject of the article with any media representative and thus could not be considered as thrusting himself into this public issue, nor did he attempt to influence the outcome. Therefore, he was not a public figure.

This reasoning seems somewhat contradictory. At one point the court ruled that From had not placed himself before the public in such a manner as to become a public figure, but at another had declared that there could be no actionable defamation, since From had invited attention of the public through self-promotion.

§ 2.7(D). Rule of Repose.

Once an athlete has attained public figure status in terms of the *New York Times* rule, can he lose that status merely through the passage of time, and so become a private individual entitled to the appropriate protection of his reputation? This question was anticipated by the Court in the case of *Rosenblatt v. Baer,* 383 U.S. 75 (1966): "To be sure, there may be cases where a person is so far removed from a former position of authority that comment on the manner in which he performed his responsibilities no longer has the interest necessary to justify the *New York Times* rule." The decisions on this issue strongly indicate, as stated in *Time, Inc. v. Johnston,* 448 F.2d 378 (4th Cir. 1971), that generally "no rule of repose exists to inhibit speech relating to the public career of a public figure so long as newsworthiness and public interest attach to events in such public career."

Neil Johnston, an outstanding professional basketball player for the Philadelphia Warriors, in *Time, Inc. v. Johnston,* 448 F.2d 378 (4th Cir. 1971), brought an action for libel against the publisher of Sports Illustrated for publishing an article in which the great coach Arnold "Red" Auerbach was quoted as saying: "Bill Russell (star center for the Boston Celtics) destroyed players. You take Neil Johnston — . . . Russell destroyed him. He destroyed him psychologically as well, so that he practically ran him out of organized basketball." Johnston's libel action ultimately resulted in the court's finding that Johnston was a public figure, just like the plaintiffs in the *Grayson* and *Cepeda* cases discussed above. By offering his services to the public as a paid performer Johnston had invited comments on his performance. "In a sense, he assumed the risk of publicity, good or bad, as the case might be, so far as it concerned his public performance."

Plaintiff Johnston did not seriously question his status as a public figure at the time of the events described in the article. However, he did state that these events had occurred twelve years prior to publication of the story and nine years after he had retired from professional basketball. He contended, therefore, that he had shed his character as a public figure, which made the *New York Times* standard inapplicable. The district court concurred, but the United States Court of Appeals declared this as error.

The appellate court observed that while Johnston had retired as a player nine years prior to publication he had, by his own affidavit, "remained in organized professional basketball" for eight more years. Furthermore, at the time of publication Johnston was still actively involved in basketball as a coach at Wake Forest University. In a neat piece of reasoning, the court found that the plaintiff had not lost his public figure status based on professional playing prominence, because his allegations of damages applied to his present stature as coach and the adverse effects on that position that defamatory remarks would cause as well as to injury to the public's recollection of his pro career. Consequently, the court found the defendant entitled to the protection of the *New York Times* standard for public figures and, therefore, that the article was not libelous and so ordered judgment for the defendant.

Of related interest is the guidance offered by the court on the subject of proper reporting. "So long as the press correctly quotes another's statement about a matter of legitimate public interest, does not truncate or distort it in any way, and properly identifies the source . . . it may properly claim the protection of *New York Times.*" Nor does *New York Times* in its application prohibit normal press hyperbole. "To deny to the press the right to use hyperbole, under the threat of removing the protecting mantle of *New York Times,* would condemn the press to an arid, desiccated recital of bare facts."

Reasoning similar to that in *Johnston* as to the effect the passage of time can have on public figure status is seen in *Brewer v. Memphis Publishing Co.,* 626 F.2d 1238 (5th Cir. 1980). Plaintiff John Brewer had been a member of the Ole Miss football team the year it was ranked number one in the nation. He was an outstanding college player and record holder. Brewer played professional football from 1960 until 1970. The allegedly libelous article appeared in 1972. At the trial on Brewer's libel action against the publisher of that article, he admitted that his football career had publicized his name to such an extent that business opportunities were open to him for the rest of his life. In fact, Brewer consistently capitalized on his athletic fame in business commercials, in obtaining speaking engagements and in campaign literature in his (unsuccessful) bid for election to the state legislature. Thus, the court concluded that Brewer had actively and vigorously sought the public's attention and had achieved pervasive fame or notoriety. The court concluded that Brewer remained a public figure.

It has been suggested that for future resolution of such problems as the passage of time in defamation actions three categories of cases might be developed: (1) the subject matter of the publication which gives rise to the action is the same as that which made the plaintiff a public figure; (2) the subject matter of the publication was related to that which made the plaintiff a public figure; (3) the subject matter of the publication was unrelated to that which made the plaintiff a public figure. In determining whether or not a defamation defendant was entitled to the protection of *New York Times,* the element of passage of time is irrelevant in a same issue case, of more importance in a related issue case, and could well be the controlling factor in an unrelated issue case. *Time, Inc. v. Johnston,* for instance, falls into the first category and was so decided.

An authority often cited in defamation cases which concern public figure status and passage-of-time is the case of *Cohen v. Marx,* 211 P.2d 320 (Cal. App. 1949). "Canvasback Cohen" began his professional boxing career in 1933 and ended it "losing decisions" in 1939. In 1949, Groucho Marx broadcast on his program "You Bet Your Life": "I once managed a prize-fighter, Canvasback Cohen. I brought him out here, he got knocked out, and I made him walk back to Cleveland." In holding that the plaintiff had no actionable claim, the court noted that the 10-year passage of time did not affect his status as a public personage in relation to his professional boxing career:

> He relinquished his right to privacy on matters pertaining to his professional activity, and he could not at his will and whim draw himself like a snail into his shell and hold others liable for commenting upon the

acts which had taken place when he had voluntarily exposed himself to the public eye.

The one decision where a court was swayed by the passage of time is *Dempsey v. Time Inc.,* 43 Misc. 2d 754, 252 N.Y.S.2d 186, *aff'd,* 254 N.Y.S.2d 80 (1964). The plaintiff, former champion heavyweight boxer Jack Dempsey, brought a libel action against *Time Magazine* for publishing a *Sports Illustrated* article entitled: "Dempsey's Gloves Were Loaded". The story was a fictionalized account supposedly by Jack "Doc" Kearns, Dempsey's manager, in which Kearns confesses that he put plaster-of-paris in a talcum container and after bandaging Dempsey's hands drenched them with water to keep them "cool" and sprinkled them generously with the substance in the talcum can. This episode allegedly occurred 45 years prior to publication. The defendant contended that it enjoyed a qualified privilege against any defamation claim due to plaintiff's status as a public figure and the public's legitimate interest in the matter. In response, the court held: "It is the opinion of this court that the reaching back forty-five years, as was done in the instant case, is not within the purview of even the suggested extension of the New York Times case, so as to cloak the described event with a veil of privilege." The court dismissed the defendant's motion to dismiss, allowing a jury to decide the libel action.

§ 2.7(E). Conclusion.

In this area, the courts tend to guard the freedom of speech and press by finding some privilege, whether fair comment, public interest or public figure status, as established under *New York Times, Butts* and the cases that followed. But recovery was often denied in these cases, if only because the burden of proof placed upon a public figure to show actual malice on the part of a publisher proved to be too difficult. And defamation plaintiffs continue to have difficulty in obtaining recoveries, in spite of the increased interest in sports of all kinds at all levels and the increased coverage given them with cable programming.

One chink in the armor of the *New York Times* constitutional privilege may develop under the *Gertz* reasoning, which made a distinction between a public figure for all purposes versus such a status for a limited range of issues. It remains to be seen whether courts will move toward a protection of the private lives of sports personalities while continuing at the same time to recognize the *New York Times* privilege for publications that show public activity on the part of the sports personality, which rendered him a public figure in the first place.

CHAPTER 3

COACHING ISSUES

§ 3.1. Employment of Coaches: Is the Right to Hire the Right to Fire?

By Herb Appenzeller

Coaches enjoy a unique position in today's society; they are highly visible and, perhaps more than most professionals, subject to extreme praise or criticism. For years they had little to fear from the courts since most people did not sue coaches, nor did coaches sue others. That has changed and employment issues involving coaches continue to reach the courts and appear to be one of the most highly litigated areas of law and sport. In fact, it seems that the majority of lawsuits involving coaches deal with some aspect of employment.

This section will consider court cases of coaches on both the secondary school and collegiate levels. It will review the issues placed before the court and the court's position toward them. It is important to examine the issues through actual case studies so that decision makers can obtain appropriate guidelines to facilitate decisions and policies that are educationally and legally sound.

§ 3.1(A). The Secondary School Coach.

Over the years state and federal courts have been reluctant to usurp the discretionary duties of local school boards as they relate to personnel. As a result, local school boards have considerable freedom in matters that pertain to employment, assignment, nonrenewal, suspension, transfer and dismissal of teachers and coaches. Courts basically require only that the school board exert reasonableness in its dealings with personnel.

Generally, coaches go to court to seek judicial redress in cases which pertain to contracts. They frequently go to court when they believe they have been the victim of discrimination based on racial or sexual bias. Coaches also go to court for alleged violation of their constitutional rights. It is important to review court cases that indicate the attitude of the court in the area of employment.

§ 3.1(B). Tenure and Dismissal.

Coaches in most instances in the public schools are hired on contracts that are separate from their teaching contract. As such, the school system can terminate a coaching contract at the end of an academic year for little or no reason. Many coaches insist that they are teachers and should be protected by teacher tenure acts. When they are fired they challenge the school official's authority to sever the contract, and the court frequently becomes the arbitrator. Situations that center around dismissal raise questions of due process and the legality of divisible contracts. A common allegation is that the coach failed to receive due process of the law and guarantees of the fourteenth amendment.

Several cases are indicative of the problem and the court's attitude in such cases. In *Hood v. Alabama State Tenure Commission,* 418 So. 2d 131 (Ala. App. 1982), David Hood had been employed as a teacher and coach for 10 years when he notified the school superintendent that he wanted to remain at the high school as a teacher but that he did not plan to coach. The school board hired a new teacher to coach and teach physical education for the remainder of the year. At the end of the year, Hood was informed that the school could not afford two teachers to do the job of one teacher and that he was being transferred to an elementary school position. He discovered that the job was to teach physical education in grades one through eight. Hood contended that he was only certified to teach physical education on the secondary level.

The school superintendent pointed out that it would be unsatisfactory to put the new coach in a school other than the one he would be coaching and directed Hood to accept the transfer.

Hood took his case before the school board and the Alabama Tenure Commission, and both ruled against him. He then appealed to the Alabama Court of Appeals. The court supported the school superintendent and declared that the Tenure Act did not specify that a board of education had to give preference to a tenured teacher over a nontenured one in transfer decisions. It upheld the previous judgment in favor of the school superintendent.

Larry White taught social studies, coached basketball and coached the cross-country team at Elizabethton High School in Tennessee. He received a supplement of $1700 for his coaching duties. In Tennessee there is no certification for coaching, but all coaches must hold a teaching certificate. After five years as a teacher and coach, the school board relieved him of his coaching duties, but retained him as a teacher in the high school. The superintendent did not oppose the action. White taught the following year, but did not coach or receive a supplement for coaching. He went to court seeking reinstatement as coach and reimbursement of the $1700 he lost in supplement money, claiming that the superintendent had not agreed with the decision to terminate his coaching. When the trial court dismissed his petition, he appealed to the Supreme Court of Tennessee.

The court, in *White v. Banks,* 614 S.W.2d 331 (Tenn. 1981), held that a teacher who coaches has two basic rights: "(1) [H]is position as a teacher is protected by tenure, assuming that he has acquired tenure status, and, (2) his position as a coach is protected by whatever contract he has with the board to perform coaching duties, but not by tenure."

It concluded that the superintendent had agreed with the board's action in relieving him of his coaching duties, which was not a suspension or dismissal but equivalent to a transfer within the school system. It upheld the lower court's decision in favor of the school district.

The following case raises some pertinent questions regarding coaches in dual positions who have tenure in teaching but not coaching positions. Two physical education teachers, one who also coached football for 26 years, the other who coached baseball for three years, were informed that they would be retained as physical education teachers but not as coaches. The United States Court of Appeals, Seventh Circuit, in *Smith v. Board of Education of Urbana School District No. 116 of Champaign County, Illinois,* 708 F.2d 258 (7th Cir. 1983), upheld the school board's decision and commented:

The Fourteenth Amendment due process clause does not guarantee a football or baseball coach a job at a public high school even if his teams win and his players idolize him. The ultimate decision who is the best man to coach a state high school athletic team rests with state school officials, not with federal courts.

The court added:

At most, the Fourteenth Amendment due process clause guarantees a state athletic coach the right to know why he is being dismissed and to convince school officials before they dismiss him that they are making a mistake, that their reasons for dismissing him are either not supported by facts or less compelling than they think.

This case raises some pertinent questions regarding coaches in dual positions who have tenure in their teaching positions but not in coaching.

The decision to fire a coach with teaching tenure presents a frustrating dilemma to school administrators. If the fired coach chooses to remain at the school to teach, school officials often lack a teaching position for the coach's replacement. As a result, they often are forced to hire a less qualified coach or resort to employing a part-time and often noncertified coach.

In a day when sports programs are at an unprecedented high, the need for qualified coaches is greater than ever. With increased sport-related litigation, the pressure is on the administrator to provide qualified coaches.

A questionnaire was sent to 50 states and the territory of Puerto Rico to determine the status of coaches with regard to tenure and due process. Eighty-eight percent responded to the 1984-1985 survey, and the results indicate the situation that confronts the typical coach. A summary of the survey is as follows:

1. Coaches can be granted tenure
   Yes   8 No   35
   (Two responded that it varies with the school district.)
2. If given tenure,
   1 to 5 years must be served on a probationary status.
3. Coaches who give up coaching for teaching only can keep their teaching position.
   Yes   35 No   4
   (Several responded that it depends on the contract.)
4. Coaches can be given formal hearings when relieved of their coaching duties.
   Yes   13 No   22
   (Several responded that it depends on the school district, if requested, or if the individual had tenure as a teacher.)

To meet the problem of the divisible teacher-coaching contract, many school districts require the individual to sign an indivisible contract. Loss of either position results in a loss of both positions.

An Oregon case illustrates the court's attitude when a school board revoked a coach's indivisible contract. Robert George coached football in a community that had little patience or tolerance for losing seasons and even less for losing coaches. After two dismal seasons, in which only two victories were recorded, the coach was informed that he could stay on and teach mathematics, but could no longer coach the football team. He accepted the decision until he learned that his salary would be cut by $2000. He contended that his contract called for a salary of $9300. The school board was just as adamant in its determination not to pay someone to do nothing. It ignored his protest and hired another person to replace him in the classroom and on the football field.

The plaintiff was out of a job except for occasional days when he could substitute teach. In *George v. School District No. 8R of Umatilla County,* 490 P.2d 1009 (Ore. App. 1971), he sued the school board for damages, and the Oregon court held that while the school board could replace him as coach it could not reduce his salary once it had contracted to pay him another amount. It awarded George $7300, which represented his loss of wages from the time he was released to the present.

§ 3.1(C). Racial Discrimination.

The question of alleged discrimination based on racial bias has been taken to court on many occasions. Three cases involving racial discrimination and an unusual one involving alleged reverse discrimination illustrate the complexity of these cases.

Carroll High School had won only seven games in three years, fan support was down, the coach resigned, and the school board was considering dropping football because of a lack of revenue. The school board decided to hire an experienced coach with an outstanding record in several high schools in Alabama to attempt to build a strong football program. The board did not want to lock the new coach in by retaining the entire staff of four assistant coaches, so it voted not to renew the contract of two assistants.

Anthony Lee, a black coach who was one of two assistants dropped, sued the school board, alleging racial discrimination for terminating his contract. (Lee was a nontenured teacher.) In Alabama a nontenured teacher may be released for "any reason or no reason." The exception to such a broad statement occurs when the nonrenewal is based on race.

The court, in *Lee v. Ozark City Board of Education,* 517 F. Supp. 686 (M.D. Ala. 1981), found that the new coach hired two assistants, one black, the other white, to replace the black and white coaches who were released. It did not find evidence of racial discrimination and thereby affirmed the decision of the lower court in favor of the school board.

A school system in Alabama was in the process of desegregating its school system. Mr. Alexander, a black football and basketball coach at the school that was eliminated in the process of consolidation, was not hired as head football coach at the main school, Etowah High School. He was given the basketball job, however, and the district court entered a consent decree that promised him that he would be given preference over any white coach for the position of head football coach or athletic director. The preference would be his as long as the other candidate's qualifications were equal or less than his.

A year later Etowah High School came under the jurisdiction of the Attalla City Board of Education. The football coach resigned, and approximately 10 to 12 candidates applied for the position. The board of education assumed the responsibility for the consent decree relating to Alexander. In *Lee v. Attalla City School System,* 588 F.2d 499 (5th Cir. 1979), the board appealed to the court of appeals to permit it to hire a coach it felt had superior qualifications to those of Alexander. The board stated that its criteria for the coaching position were as follows:

1. the educational background of the applicants;
2. the type of certificate possessed by each candidate;
3. the applicant's total experience in education;
4. the applicant's experience as a head football coach;
5. the win-loss record of the applicant;
6. the applicant's experience at the college level.

The board petitioned the court to allow it to hire Charles Randall Hearn rather than Alexander and cited Hearn's superior qualifications as the overriding factor. Alexander had a master's degree in educational administration, but Hearn had two master's degrees and 36 hours toward a doctorate. Alexander had 23 years' experience and a Class A certificate. Hearn, however, had 25 years' experience and a AA certificate which was the highest awarded by the state of Alabama. Hearn also had eight years' more experience as a coach than Alexander, had been selected to coach the Alabama All Stars and received "Coach of the Year" honors twice. In addition, Hearn had also coached on the college level, while Alexander's experience was at the secondary school level only.

The court recognized that Alexander's qualifications were acceptable, but concluded that Hearn's made him "exceptionally well qualified." It ruled that the Attalla City School System could employ Hearn since his qualifications were superior to those of Alexander and awarded the job of head football coach to Hearn.

Three black coaches, Rufus Harris, Jr., Bobby Minard and George C. Moore, sued the Birmingham Board of Education for employment discrimination by hiring them to head coach and assistant coach positions only in black schools. All three had served as assistant football coaches, and Moore had served as a head basketball coach. The plaintiffs brought their suit after receiving a "right to sue" letter from the Equal Employment Opportunity Commission (EEOC), which had investigated the situation and found a pattern of discrimination in the hiring of head coaches within the Birmingham school system.

The federal district court dismissed the plaintiffs' cases, giving no weight to the findings of the EEOC. All three plaintiffs appealed to the U.S. Court of Appeals for the Eleventh Circuit.

The Eleventh Circuit Court, in *Harris v. Birmingham Board of Education,* 712 F.2d 1377 (11th Cir. 1983), reviewed substantial evidence which revealed that the Birmingham Board of Education followed a consistent pattern of assigning black coaches at predominantly black schools and assigning white coaches at predominantly or historically white schools. The evidence further showed that the hiring procedure for coaches did not entail posting advertisements or any formal notification of job vacancies, and that coaches or prospective coaches had to hear of promotional opportunities, if at all, by person-to-person communication. The Eleventh Circuit found that selection criteria were neither uniform nor written.

The court upheld the dismissal of Harris's and Minard's claims, holding that there was no evidence to show that their transfers were racially motivated. However, the court upheld Moore's individual claim, holding that the lack of objective hiring standards contributed to his establishing a case and finding that, in addition to the discrepancies already noted, the Birmingham school system used principals' recommendations without objective criteria and had a history of racial discrimination in the employment and assignment of black teachers, and admitted that statistically it appeared that coaches had been assigned to schools according to the racial composition of the schools. The court noted that "with these findings, it is easy to hold that Moore has been the victim of employment discrimination." They remanded the case to the district court for further proceedings on its merits in Moore's case.

§ 3.1(D). Reverse Discrimination.

In an unusual case involving a claim of reverse discrimination Norman Jett, a former football coach at South Oak Cliff Hill High School in Dallas, Texas, was awarded $850,000 in damages. Jett, who was one of the most successful high school coaches in the history of the Dallas Independent School District, was fired as coach at a predominantly black high school.

During the trial, Jett testified that his principal, who was black, "continuously and systematically conducted a series of activities designed to harass and undermine his position as football coach." Jett, who was in his fourth year of a five year contract, was fired as athletic director and head football coach and transferred to the Business Management Center to teach social science.

The jury decided that the coach's right of due process had been violated and that he was fired because of his race. According to the *Dallas Times Herald* of Oct. 16, 1984, the jury added that Jett's "working conditions were intolerable and they forced him to resign." The jury awarded Jett $850,000: $650,000 in actual damages against the school district, $150,000 against the principal and $50,000 in punitive damages against the principal.

§ 3.1(E). Sex Bias.

Three cases in which sex bias was alleged reveal the different attitudes of the various courts and states.

Linda Burkey graduated from college in 1970 after participating on four different school athletic teams. In 1976 she received a master's degree in physical education. From July 1, 1970 she had been employed as a teacher by the Marshall County Board of Education and had achieved tenure as a teacher after completing a three year probationary period.

From 1971 to 1976 she coached girls' basketball at Moundsville Junior High School. In 1976 she was transferred to an elementary school and was not reappointed as a coach. Coaching appointments were made on a one school-year basis, and no teacher employed by the board achieved tenure as a coach.

Burkey was primarily responsible for forming interscholastic girls' basketball in Marshall County, West Virginia, and during the period of four school years her teams won 31 games, lost four, and forfeited one game. In 1975 her team won the county championship.

Prior to the filing of this lawsuit on April 6, 1978, Burkey had spent five years attempting to achieve equality for women as coaches and participants in Marshall County, West Virginia. It was proven that during the early and mid-70's, the county paid women at a salary level one-half that of male coaches of comparable or identical programs. Further, there were written "Governing Policies of Marshall County Junior High Athletic Programs" which clearly discriminated against female faculty members, both in terms of pay and opportunities to coach teams of the opposite sex as well as restrictions on numbers of games that could be played and how the coaches must operate.

As a part of her efforts, Burkey had totally exhausted her administrative remedies by filing complaints with the school system through administrative agencies of the state and federal government, including the Equal Employment Opportunity Commission, the Department of Health, Education and Welfare and the West Virginia Human Rights Commission.

Burkey's primary claim was that she was discriminated against on the basis of her sex, both in terms of payment and work opportunities, and that her transfer to a noncoaching position at another school was a retaliation for her efforts to achieve equality.

In *Burkey v. Marshall County Board of Education*, 513 F. Supp. 1084 (N.D.W. Va. 1981), the district court agreed with Burkey and ruled in her favor. The court found that the board had an unwritten policy that female teachers could not coach boys' sports, that female teachers were at a salary level one-half that of male coaches and that Burkey was qualified to coach basketball and track for both girls and boys and in fact had qualifications equal or superior to those of most of the males who coached in Marshall County, West Virginia.

The court found that the board's defenses, including "economy measures" and "personality conflicts," were merely pretextual and that the board indeed had retaliated against her when they transferred her. The court held that these various activities constituted illegal discrimination against Burkey on the basis of sex, operated to deny her rights and were an unlawful employment practice prohibited under Title VII. The court awarded her back pay and ordered the board to offer her the next available physical education teaching position and to offer her the head coach's position for girls' basketball at any school in the county. The court further permitted Burkey to file a motion to recover attorneys' fees, costs and expenses.

Two cases present diverse rulings by the court and cause school officials concern regarding hiring procedures when economic reasons are at issue.

Mary Shenefield applied for a teaching position in Wyoming, but the principal hired a man who could coach as well as teach. Shenefield submitted her case to the Wyoming Fair Employment Commission (hereafter referred to as commission), and it agreed that discrimination based on sex had taken place. The District Court of Sheridan County reversed the commission's decision, and the teacher appealed to the Supreme Court of Wyoming.

During the trial several factors that influenced the school's decision were revealed. The principal testified that the plaintiff changed jobs frequently because she followed her husband whenever he took a new job. He described her as a "pushy, demanding type of person" who could not coach interscholastic activities or intramurals. In addition, she would have required a substantially higher salary than the teacher they hired, because of her degree and years of experience. The principal said that the teacher he hired had worked in the school system as a student teacher and was the type of person who could get along with the faculty. The school could hire him for $2600 less per year than the plaintiff.

In *Shenefield v. Sheridan County School District No. 1*, 544 P.2d 870 (Wyo. 1976), the Supreme Court of Wyoming referred to previous cases that considered similar litigation and upheld the principle that the courts will not interfere with the judgment of a school board in the employment or reemployment of a teacher for any reason or for no reason at all. The Wyoming court then reasoned that a school board does not give up its freedom to choose the teacher (coach) it wants just because it advertises such a position. It then favored the school board's decision to hire the male teacher:

> If it turns out for reasons of economy, one applicant can fulfill the needs of a district at a cost substantially less than another applicant, even though the rejected applicant may on paper possess the greater qualifications, a selection of the less expensive teacher cannot be said by any board or court to have been the result of discrimination on the basis of sex.

It then concluded that a school board has the discretion of hiring a teacher who is able to perform additional duties such as coaching in the school's program. A school board must be able to select a teacher who is personally attractive to it without the threat of discrimination leveled against it.

An Arizona court, in *Civil Rights Division of Arizona Department of Law v. Amphitheater Unified School District No. 10*, 680 P.2d 517 (Ariz. App. 1983), however, took a completely different attitude to the decision and opinion in *Shenefield* and presented a dilemma for school districts which are compelled to economize on salaries by combining teaching and coaching positions.

Due to a combination of circumstances, the Amphitheater Unified School District Number 10 needed a biology teacher and a football coach. Accordingly, they coupled the two positions and advertised them as a single position, that is, a biology teacher who had the ability to coach football.

Eighty-five applications were reviewed for the biology teacher-football coach position. Fifty-four of the applicants were men and 31 were women. Out of the 85 applicants, 10 men made the "finals." None of the female applicants had indicated a background in or a willingness to coach football. Some of the men applicants did not make it to the "finals" because they also did not have football coaching experience.

Jillyn B. Smith, one of the female applicants, filed a lawsuit contending that this practice of coupling academic contracts with addendum contracts to coach football had a disparate impact on women applicants for academic teaching positions. The trial court ruled in favor of the school district on the theory that it had established the defense of business necessity in filling the positions in this manner.

On appeal the Arizona Court of Appeals reversed and held that this method of filling the dual teaching-coaching position had a disparate impact on females. The court held that the Amphitheater School District had not carried its burden of proving that a business necessity existed which required them to couple the contracts. The court then stated:

> It is important to note what is not being decided in this case. We do not hold that it is not possible for Amphitheater Unified School District to show business necessity in the practice of coupling addendum and academic contracts. We hold merely that they have in this instance failed to do so.

School officials in the State of Arizona are uncertain of the proper method for advertising for future teaching-coaching positions. It is clear from the decisions in *Shenefield* and *Civil Rights Division* that various states and courts view similar situations in different ways.

§ 3.1(F). Constitutional Rights.

When coaches are fired or transferred to other positions, they frequently seek judicial relief by complaining that their constitutional rights have been violated. Coaches most often charge school officials with violation of their freedom of expression guaranteed by the first amendment to the United States Constitution. A common allegation is the contention that school officials failed to provide due process procedures guaranteed by the fourteenth amendment.

The following cases are interesting and illustrative of alleged constitutional rights' violations.

Minoru Shimoyama taught biology and physical education at Chatsworth High School in Los Angeles, California. He also coached football from 1970 until 1978 and track for the 1979 season.

In June, 1978 Shimoyama met with his principal and assistant principal to discuss his unauthorized purchase of new football jerseys and the major change in team colors. The principal cited a lack of communication between the two and the fact that Shimoyama did not follow policy and procedures in ordering equipment.

Shimoyama responded with a letter that denounced the principal. He sent copies of the letter to the district superintendent, booster club president, the assistant football coach and two faculty members who were active in the United Teachers of Los Angeles. He blamed the principal for low morale at the school and accused him of failing to support the athletic program.

The principal replied that the letter was full of inaccurate statements that did little to improve communications between the two, and then informed Shimoyama that he could not work with him as coach. The parties agreed, however, that the coach would apologize and retract his adverse statements against the principal. In return the principal would permit him to coach the football team and reevaluate his performance and make a decision regarding his status as coach after the season was completed.

In November the principal informed Shimoyama that he would not be reassigned as football coach for the following reasons:

1. A lack of communication existed between them;
2. The coach used an ineligible player in a practice game;
3. The coach lost his temper and grabbed the face masks of players;
4. The coach used profanity;
5. The coach's conduct resulted in penalties by the officials;
6. The coach ordered materials without regard to school policy.

Shimoyama contended that he was dismissed as football coach because he exercised his right of free speech guaranteed by the first amendment and charged the principal with violating his right of due process.

The court in *Shimoyama v. Board of Education of Los Angeles Unified School District*, 174 Cal. Rptr. 748 (Cal. App. 1981), considered the testimony and made an interesting observation when it said: "Although discussions among the faculty of a high school no doubt permit a greater flexibility of expression than the para-military atmosphere of a police department, still the necessities of harmonious working relationships and employee discipline are the same."

It then found that the trial court made the right decision in denying the plaintiff's petition to be reinstated as coach by concluding:

> If attacks upon a superior such as we have here were given constitutional protection, it would require a hardy administrator indeed to maintain a working relationship and to risk criticizing a subordinate's performance, knowing that the subordinate was free with impunity to retaliate by broadcasting accusations implying that the administrator was a conspirator, a liar and a hypocrite.

This is a fascinating case that deals with the right of a teacher to speak on matters of public concern as guaranteed by the first amendment of the United States Constitution.

Terry Knapp was a high school teacher and coach who filed a lawsuit against the Peoria School District Number 150, the superintendent, principal, assistant principal and later the assistant superintendent. Knapp claimed that the defendants had "retaliated against him for exercising his First Amendment rights."

In 1980 the teachers in the Peoria School District were negotiating for collective bargaining, and a key issue was the grievance procedure. Knapp asked a member of the school board if he could discuss the grievance procedure, and she invited him to talk with several members of the board. The board was anxious to have input on the issue from teachers. Knapp discussed issues involving classroom assignments, curriculum, evaluations, liability insurance and mileage reimbursements. At no time did any administrator or board member tell Knapp that it was against policy for teachers to talk with board members.

In March, 1981 Knapp filed a grievance based on unequal mileage reimbursement for coaches and a lack of liability insurance for coaches who drove students to athletic events. Knapp's grievance was denied, and he tried to get a board member to sponsor him so he could meet with the entire board to explore the denial of his grievance.

In April, 1981 the superintendent pointed to a regulation in the superintendent's contract that required all communication to go to the board through him. The superintendent reprimanded Knapp, who replied that such a policy violated his right of free speech. The superintendent responded, "Your rights end where my nose begins." Knapp was then placed in "remediation category," which is one step above termination.

On June 16, 1981 Knapp was unwillingly replaced as coach, allegedly because of his phlebitis condition, and in the fall his paid study hall was taken away. At the end of the year he received a second negative evaluation and was transferred from the high school to a grade school.

A jury awarded Knapp over $500,000 in compensatory damages, and the defendants appealed. In *Knapp v. Whitaker,* 577 F. Supp. 1265 (C.D. Ill. 1983), the court observed that the policy of reporting to the board through the superintendent was unconstitutional. It commented that the plaintiff was never informed that his conduct violated school board policy. The court stated that the plaintiff's action was not compelled by personal interest alone, but a desire to discuss the issues on behalf of other teachers in the district. The court upheld the lower court's huge award by finding that the teacher's "criticism of the grievance procedure was protected speech."

John McGee, a teacher and junior and senior high school track coach, received a satisfactory evaluation from his principal and public praise from three school board members a month before his contract was to be considered for renewal. A public controversy developed when a divided school board voted to discontinue the junior high school track program. The decision became the key issue in a hotly contested school board election. Three board members insisted that McGee had recommended the elimination of the junior high school track program, an allegation the coach denied. Four days before the election McGee wrote a letter to the town newspaper outlining his reasons for keeping the junior high school track program. His letter created considerable controversy in the community.

Following the school board election McGee's contract for renewal was denied. McGee claimed that his dismissal was a result of the letter he wrote to the newspaper and a violation of his freedom of expression guaranteed by the first amendment to the United States Constitution. McGee testified that he received a letter from the superintendent stating that the "letter was an act of disloyalty and warranted his dismissal."

Three board members, who voted against the coach, cited their displeasure with his ability to "work with the athletic director, keep a tidy classroom, and his having bought track uniforms without asking the proper authorities." (McGee testified that he paid for the uniforms with his own money.) The other board members, who voted in favor of the retention of McGee, reportedly commented that they would now vote against him because he could not follow directions. The athletic director testified that McGee could not effectively work "within the school's bureaucracy."

A trial court jury found that the school board had violated the coach's rights as protected by 42 U.S.C. § 1983 and awarded him $10,000 in damages. The district court, however, granted the defendant's motion for a judgment *non obstante veredicto* (which overrules the jury's verdict). The United States Court of Appeals, Eighth Circuit, reviewed the testimony and, in *McGee v. South Pemiscot School District R-V,* 712 F.2d 339 (8th Cir. 1983), commented that the jury had the responsibility to decide whether McGee's letter created the dissension between the coach and his immediate superiors. It also said: "The record suggests that McGee is a good teacher. He organized a popular and successful track program from scratch. All the parties seem to agree that he is enthusiastic and committed to the welfare of his students."

The court of appeals reversed the district court's verdict of *non obstante veredicto* and "remanded it with instructions to enter judgment on the jury verdict," thus reinstating the $10,000 damages award to the coach.

One of the judges vigorously dissented and pointed out that the firing was the best thing that could have happened to McGee. He explained that McGee accepted a position in another district for a higher salary and was also employed as a full-time minister at a local church. The dissenting judge could not support McGee's contention that he had suffered "mental anguish and loss of reputation" in light of his new employment. The dissenting judge also emphasized that McGee only sought $7000 in damages, but the jury awarded him $10,000.

Bob Bowman was an assistant football coach and science teacher at Jacksonville Junior High School Northside in Jacksonville, Arkansas. James Mackey was a science teacher and assistant coach in both football and basketball. Each had an excellent record as a teacher and coach. On April 29, 1982 head football coach Jimmy Walker disciplined five students in his office by striking them across the buttocks and thighs with a paddle. The single lick given to each student was excessive as it raised welts and bruises on the backs of the students' thighs.

The Pulaski County Special School District permitted corporal punishment, but regulated the practice. One of the regulations required a second faculty member to witness the actual punishment, to listen as the student was informed of the reason for the disciplinary action and then fill out and sign a form reporting the incident.

On the day of the incident, Bowman and Mackey were in the office when the punishment started, though Mackey left the room about the time the first lick was struck. Coach Walker did not request either of them to act as a witness though he did explain to the students the reason for the punishment.

Bowman and Mackey offered assistance to the students, discussed the punishment with parents, made public statements about the unwarranted severity of the licks and expressed opinions on how Walker should be disciplined.

The parents of the students were upset over the incident and made Coach Walker's method of discipline on this and other occasions a matter of public debate. The incident drew a considerable amount of press coverage, caused some turmoil in the community and was blamed for dividing a previously harmonious faculty and student body. Coach Walker, after the effects of the punishment were known, asked Bowman to complete and sign a witness form. Bowman refused to sign.

Coach Walker was briefly suspended, and his authority to administer corporal punishment was curtailed. He also issued a public apology. Bowman and Mackey were involuntarily transferred to Scott Middle School, a recently reopened facility.

After exhausting available administrative remedies, Bowman and Mackey filed a lawsuit alleging violation of their civil rights. The trial court heard the case and rescinded the involuntary transfer, ordered the parties to make a good faith attempt to resolve the dispute among the coaching staff and stated that if such efforts were unavailing, then a transfer of Bowman and Mackey to a better or comparable school would be permitted. Thereafter, Coach Walker remained adamant in his refusal to work with either party.

Mackey was transferred to another school where he was assigned to coach football and basketball and asked to teach social studies rather than science. His total round-trip mileage to and from work increased from less than one mile to approximately 68 miles. Bowman was transferred to another school where he assumed the position of head coach for tenth grade football and was required to teach American history rather than science. His driving distance increased to approximately 100 miles to and from work, an increase over his earlier minimal amount of travel time.

Bowman and Mackey remained dissatisfied with their new positions and petitioned the district court for further relief. The district court denied the motion for further relief, and Bowman and Mackey appealed. As a part of the trial court action, the district court had awarded Bowman's and Mackey's attorneys $11,268.50 in attorneys' fees.

On appeal, in *Bowman v. Pulaski County Special School District,* 723 F.2d 640 (8th Cir. 1983), the United States Court of Appeals for the Eighth Circuit reversed the trial court's decision and ordered that Bowman and Mackey be restored to the positions they held at Jacksonville Junior High School Northside. The Eighth Circuit also affirmed the award of $11,268.50 in attorneys' fees.

The Eighth Circuit noted that a three-step analysis must be undertaken in first amendment cases. The court must determine: (1) whether the plaintiff has carried the burden of proving that he engaged in protective activity; (2) whether the protected activity was a substantial or motivating factor in the actions taken against the plaintiff; and (3) whether the defendant has defeated the plaintiff's claim by demonstrating that the same action would have been taken in the absence of the protected activity.

In ruling in favor of Bowman and Mackey the court noted that this incident had generated substantial public interest, that the time, manner and place of their speech was reasonable in that it followed the incident closely, was on school property and was restrained and moderate and that the speech arose in the context of discipline of students. The court stated:

> While we recognize and respect the importance of harmony and cohesion in any educational institution, we must conclude that the appellants' speech was protected by the First Amendment. In our mind the public's

need to know whether children are being mistreated in school outweighs the other legitimate concerns of the government.

The court pointed out that involuntary transfers could be as effective as discharges in chilling the exercise of first amendment rights.

Two cases illustrate the allegation by coaches that their right of due process was violated. They argued that the fourteenth amendment to the United States Constitution guaranteed them this right of due process.

A search committee for the Paris Union School Board visited a successful coach-athletic director with the intention of hiring him to build a winning program. The coach requested enough time to build a successful program at the school and discussed job security before he agreed to leave his present job. The board hired him as football coach and athletic director with the agreement that he would have two years to improve the program. After one year, however, the board terminated his position without giving him an explanation as to the reason for firing him and failed to provide a hearing for the coach. The coach challenged the board's decision, arguing that he was assured of two years in this position. The United States Court of Appeals, Seventh Circuit, in *Vail v. Board of Education of Paris Union School District No. 95,* 706 F.2d 1435 (7th Cir. 1983), upheld the judgment of the lower court and affirmed the award in damages of $19,850.99 for "unlawful termination."

Two physical education teachers, one who also coached football for 26 years, the other who coached baseball for three years, were informed that they would be retained as physical education teachers but not as coaches. The United States Court of Appeals, Seventh Circuit, in *Smith v. Board of Education of Urbana School District No. 116 of Champaign County, Illinois,* 708 F.2d 258 (7th Cir. 1983), upheld the school board's decision and commented that:

> The Fourteenth Amendment due process clause does not guarantee a football or baseball coach a job at a public high school even if his teams win and his players idolize him. The ultimate decision who is the best man to coach a state high school athletic team rests with state school officials, not with federal courts.

The court added:

> At most, the Fourteenth Amendment due process clause guarantees a state athletic coach the right to know why he is being dismissed and to convince school officials before they dismiss him that they are making a mistake, that their reasons for dismissing him are either not supported by facts or less compelling than they think.

This case raises some pertinent questions regarding coaches in dual positions who have tenure in their teaching positions but not in coaching.

§ 3.1(G). Employment Issues on the Collegiate Level.

In most colleges and universities athletic coaches are hired to coach one or more sports. In the vast majority of these instances, coaches are terminated when they experience losing seasons. Unlike the secondary school coach, most college coaches sign indivisible contracts when teaching accompanies their coaching responsibilities, or they sign contracts for coaching duties only.

A case that illustrates the charge of due process violation occurred in Florida. John Parker, a law student and part-time assistant for the Florida University Athletic Department, became embroiled in a campus-wide controversy that led to his dismissal. Parker became the spokesperson for a group of disgruntled athletes who formed an organization known as the League of Florida Athletes. The athletes tried to alter the athletic department's rules regarding dress and grooming.

Parker wrote several articles in the school paper criticizing the athletic department's rules. After the articles appeared in the school paper, Parker's supervisor recommended his dismissal. The assistant athletic director charged Parker with failure to enforce regulations concerning dress codes, grooming and quiet hours in the athletic dormitory. The athletic director met with Parker in the presence of a university official and dismissed him for conduct disloyal to the athletic program. He contended that Parker's personal views seriously conflicted with his assignment to the athletic department.

The controversy took place during a disappointing football season and increased tension among athletes and coaches alike. While some athletes supported the articles, others bitterly resented them and insisted that they did not reflect the views of all the athletes. In addition, the unfavorable publicity created by the articles caused prospective athletes to turn down visits to the campus and adversely affected the recruiting of prospective athletes.

Parker instituted a lawsuit claiming that he had been denied his right to free speech and expression as guaranteed by the first amendment. The United States District Court, in *Parker v. Graves,* 340 F. Supp. 586 (N.D. Fla. 1972), however, viewed the plaintiff's conduct as divisive. The court held that the plaintiff was disloyal to the athletic director by failing to carry out the responsibilities for which he had been employed. It did not believe that his right of free speech had been violated. It favored the defendants by concluding with a statement from the United States Supreme Court's decision in *Epperson v. Arkansas,* 393 U.S. 97 (1968), in which the High Court said: "Courts do not and cannot intervene in the resolution of conflicts which arise in the daily operation of school systems and which do not directly and sharply implicate basic constitutional values."

Most collegiate coaches go to court to contest contractual disputes. Several cases are important court decisions giving guidance to college administrators regarding contracts.

Wake Forest University had a history of success with its golf program. It had won both team and individual NCAA championships under Jesse Haddock, who had been golf coach for 17 years when he resigned in July, 1976 to become golf coach at Oral Roberts University.

Ron Roberts was hired under a verbal employment contract to replace Haddock as golf coach shortly after Haddock's departure. During Roberts's first year as coach he was the subject of substantial controversy. Though he had inherited an allegedly talented team, the team did not perform up to expectations. Roberts allegedly posted a pledge of loyalty to him and the university and required each player to sign it. In addition to performing poorly in tournaments, several players quit the team and left school. Roberts was accused of not attending tournaments, not requiring team members to exercise proper discipline or dress properly and of occasional lapses of temper, on one occasion throwing a trophy at Scott Hoch and cursing him.

In view of the golf program's deterioration, athletic director Gene Hooks wrote Roberts in July, 1977 and suggested he resign. Roberts refused. Thereafter, the athletic council voted to retain him as golf coach. In the last tournament of the fall of 1977 the team finished eleventh out of 16 teams.

On December 2, 1977 Ralph Scales, president of the university, announced that Jesse Haddock was rehired as golf coach and notified Roberts that he was relieved of his duties as golf coach and would be reassigned to new duties in the athletic program. Roberts refused the offered reassignment and President Scales terminated his employment on December 7, 1977.

Roberts sued Wake Forest University, for breach of the oral employment contract, and Gene Hooks and Jesse Haddock for interfering with the contract. Roberts claimed that it was intended that the contract was for at least six years and that traditionally golf coaches have very long tenures. He also claimed he was a permanent employee and could not be dismissed without cause. Finally, Roberts claimed that since the North Carolina Employment Security Commission ruled he was entitled to unemployment benefits, the courts must follow that ruling. All defendants denied the claims.

The trial court reviewed the entire file prior to trial and entered summary judgment for the defendants, thereby dismissing Roberts's claims. In *Roberts v. Wake Forest University,* 286 S.E.2d 120 (N.C. App. 1982), the court affirmed this holding.

The court noted that the terms of the contract were indefinite and that at best the parties hoped that the relationship would be for a long period. The court said "it is a settled rule of law in North Carolina and other jurisdictions that employment for an indefinite term is regarded as an employment at will which may be terminated at any time by either party." The court held it was not bound by the holding of the Employment Security Commission and that Roberts's discharge, with or without cause, was not a breach of contract.

Franklin "Pepper" Rodgers was fired as the Georgia Tech head football coach on December 18, 1979, although his contract extended through December 31, 1981. Rodgers insisted that his firing led to a tort claim for "humiliation and injury to feelings."

In *Rodgers v. Georgia Tech Athletic Association,* 303 S.E.2d 467 (Ga. App. 1983), Rodgers brought a breach of contract action against the Georgia Tech Athletic Association to recover the value of perquisites that were available to him as head football coach. The State Court of Fulton County, Georgia granted the defendant's motion for summary judgment, and Rodgers appealed. The court of appeals affirmed in part and reversed in part the lower court's judgment.

The court of appeals reasoned that Rodgers was relieved of his head football coaching duties, but that he remained on as an employee of the association even though he had no duties to perform. The court observed that certain perquisites no longer were appropriate for his job, such as "the services of a secretary, the services of an administrative assistant, and the cost of trips to football conventions, clinics, etc." The court listed the perquisites in two parts, those that were excluded and those that were questionable in the case and needed interpretation by the court. It denoted the excluded items by an asterisk.

A. benefits and perquisites received by Rodgers directly from the Georgia Tech Athletic Association:

    (1) gas, oil, maintenance, repairs, other automobile expenses;

    (2) automobile liability and collision insurance;

    (3) general expense money;

    (4) meals available at the Georgia Tech training table;

    (5) eight season tickets to Georgia Tech home football games during fall of 1980 and 1981;

    (6) two reserved booths, consisting of approximately forty seats at Georgia Tech home football games during the fall of 1980 and 1981;

    (7) five season tickets to Georgia Tech home basketball games for 1980 and 1981;

    (8) four season tickets to Atlanta Falcon home football games for 1980 and 1981;

    (9) four game tickets to each out-of-town Georgia Tech football game during fall of 1980 and 1981;

    (10) pocket money at each home football game during fall of 1980 and 1981;

    (11) pocket money at each out-of-town Georgia Tech football game during fall of 1980-1981;

    (12) parking privileges at all Georgia Tech home sporting events;

    *(13) the services of a secretary;

    *(14) the services of an administrative assistant;

    (15) the cost of admission to Georgia Tech home baseball games during the spring of 1980-1981;

    *(16) the cost of trips to football coaches' conventions, clinics, and meetings and to observe football practice sessions of professional and college football teams;

    (17) initiation fee, dues, monthly bills, and cost of membership at the Capital City Club;

    (18) initiation fee, dues, monthly bills, and cost of membership at the Cherokee Country Club;

    (19) initiation fee and dues at the East Lake Country Club.

B. benefits and perquisites received by Rodgers from sources other than the Georgia Tech Athletic Association by virtue of being head coach of football:

    (1) profits from Rodgers' television football show, "The Pepper Rodgers Show," on Station WSB-TV in Atlanta for the fall of 1980-1981;

    (2) profits from Rodgers' radio football show on Station WGST in Atlanta for the fall of 1980 and 1981;

    (3) use of a new Cadillac automobile during 1980-1981;

(4) profits from Rodgers' summer football camp, known as the "Pepper Rodgers Football School," for June 1980 and June 1981;

*(5) financial gifts from alumni and supporters of Georgia Tech for 1980-1981;

*(6) lodging at any of the Holiday Inns owned by Topeka Inn Management, Inc. of Topeka, Kansas, for the time period from December 18, 1979 through December 31, 1981;

*(7) the cost of membership in Terminus International Tennis Club in Atlanta for 1980 and 1981;

(8) individual game tickets to Hawks basketball and Braves baseball games during 1980-1981 seasons;

*(9) housing for Rodgers and his family in Atlanta for the period from December 18, 1979 through December 31, 1981;

*(10) the cost of premiums of a $400,000.00 policy on the life of Rodgers for the time period from December 18, 1979 through December 31, 1981.

The issue was resolved by an out-of-court settlement between Rodgers and the Georgia Tech Athletic Association.

A similar situation developed at the University of South Carolina when the trustees fired Jim Carlen as head football coach in 1981. As reported in *The Charlotte Observer* from May 6 to July 5, 1984, Carlen, whose contract extended to 1986, was guaranteed payment of his annual salary of $67,200 until the contract expired. Carlen, like Rodgers, sought to recover his perquisites that he claimed brought his salary to $150,000. These included: "Life insurance, two cars, meals, association dues, and income from his radio and television shows, football camp and speaking engagements." Carlen settled out of court for an undisclosed amount.

Richard Bell replaced Carlen as head football coach in 1982, with a contract for four years at $50,000 per year in salary. Bell's record his first year was four and seven, including a season-ending loss to arch rival Clemson. Athletic director Robert Marcum ordered Bell to fire his assistant coaches and when he refused to comply fired Bell after only one year as head coach.

Bell sued the University for the remaining years' salary of $150,000. In addition, he named Marcum in a one million dollar defamation of character suit. A key issue at the trial was the question of who is responsible for the firing of the assistant coaches.

Several outstanding football coaches testified in Bell's behalf. Grant Teaff (Baylor), Bill Curry (Georgia Tech) and Athletic Director Frank Broyles (Arkansas) testified that a successful Division IA coach could expect to earn $250,000 in salary and perquisites. They insisted that Bell, not Marcum, had the authority to fire the assistant coaches. Broyles stated: "Everyone familiar with football knows it is paramount that a head coach has total control over his staff. When it is violated, it destroys the abilities of any coach to be effective."

A United States District Judge dropped the suit against the athletic director, which meant that the jury could only consider the question of the remaining $150,000 of Bell's contract. The jury awarded Bell the $150,000 and added $21,217 in interest, commenting that the university could fire its coach for any reason whatsoever as long as it paid for the remaining years on the contract.

When the University of South Carolina hired Joe Morrison to replace Bell as its new head football coach, it reportedly reworded the contract to give its athletic director more authority in the hiring or firing of the assistant coaches.

Coaches are notorious in their practice of resigning a job when a more attractive one becomes available. It does not seem to matter how many years are left on the contract. Institutions, on the other hand, that fire a coach are bound to pay the coach's salary for the remainder of the contract period. At best, it is not a two-way street.

It appears that the First Circuit Court of Appeals was taking to task the increasing contract jumping so prevalent in collegiate and professional sports by attempting to reaffirm the proposition that people should be held responsible for what they obligate themselves to do.

The University of Colorado allegedly lured Chuck Fairbanks from his head coaching position with the New England Patriots. As a result the Patriots sought to enjoin the University of Colorado and its officials from contracting with its head coach while he was under contract as football coach of the Patriots. The District Court for the District of Massachusetts granted the Patriots an injunction preventing the University of Colorado from employing Fairbanks. The court explained that the fact that the university was a state university failed to protect it from acting in an unlawful and tortious manner.

The University of Colorado appealed the decision contending that they should not be restricted in their dealings with Fairbanks since they were not connected with professional football. The university also believed that the doctrine of "unclean hands" would bar the Patriots from any relief. They based this on the fact that the Patriots had lured Fairbanks from the University of Oklahoma in 1973.

The First Circuit Court of Appeals, in *New England Patriots Football Club, Inc. v. University of Colorado,* 592 F.2d 1196 (1st Cir. 1979), upheld the district court, however, and commented: "Both parties may have done the University of Oklahoma dirt, but that does not mean unclean hands with respect to this case." The court noted that Fairbanks's contract contained a provision that he could not provide services associated with football to any entity without the permission of the New England Patriots during his employment. The court made a significant statement when it declared:

> A contract is not avoided by crossed fingers behind one's back on signing, nor by unsupported, and at once inconsistently self-deprecating and self-serving protests that the breach was to the other party's benefit. Equally, we are not taken by Fairbanks' claim that because, when he told Sullivan that he was leaving by the end of the season and Sullivan responded that he was "suspended," it was Sullivan who broke the contract.

(William Sullivan is the owner of the New England Patriots.)

The court held that the Patriots had the right not to accept the services of an unfaithful servant and was within its right to suspend him. In this instance, the court refused to distinguish between an athlete and a coach.

§ 3.1(H). Conclusion.

Employment issues involving coaches are among the most highly litigated areas of sport law.

State and federal courts over the years have been reluctant to usurp the discretionary powers of local school boards as they relate to personnel matters. As a result, local school boards have considerable freedom in matters that pertain to the employment, assignment, nonrenewal, suspension, transfer and dismissal of coaches. Courts basically require only that school boards exert reasonableness in dealing with their personnel.

The typical coach signs a divisible contract which requires the coach to teach and assume responsibility to coach one or more sports. The coaching assignment is separate and apart from teaching and can be terminated for little or no reason. If a coach acquires tenure for teaching, he may be able to keep the teaching position although the coaching assignment has been terminated.

A 1984-1985 survey of the 50 states and the territory of Puerto Rico revealed that only seven states grant coaches tenure for coaching while 22 states refuse them due process when they are fired from their coaching duties. A majority of the 88% of the states responding reported that tenured teachers who are dismissed from coaching responsibilities can keep their teaching jobs.

Some school districts throughout the nation favor indivisible contracts which mean that individuals are hired on one contract to teach and coach. Termination of either duty leads to loss of both positions.

The courts favor coaches who can prove that school districts have discriminated against them on the basis of sex or race. When coaches can prove that their rights of due process or freedom of expression have been denied them, the courts consistently rule in their behalf. The recent cases of *Knapp, McGee* and *Bowman* point out the attitude of the courts regarding violation of rights. The rulings in these cases favoring the coaches offer a warning to school officials that the rights of coaches must be upheld.

On the collegiate level coaches can be fired for little or no reason. In most instances, however, the reason for termination is the result of a losing record. The courts have been consistent in ruling that coaches who are fired must be paid for the years that remain on their contract. The issue is not the remaining years of their contract but the value of the perquisites. In most cases, the perquisites greatly exceed the base salary, and coaches who are fired refuse to give them up. In several recent cases the school officials have arrived at a settlement for the perquisites of coaches who have been fired. This appears to be an issue that will continue to plague school officials until the court establishes guidelines by interpreting the law in future cases.

It seems clear that employment issues involving coaches will continue to be a problem that will go to the courts for judicial redress in the years to come. If enough judicial decisions are resolved, guidelines for coaches and school officials may finally help school officials in their role as decision makers.

§ 3.2. Certification of Coaches.

By Robert B. Turner

Litigation as a result of sports-related activities has been widely viewed as reaching the epidemic stage. Almost daily we read or hear of a sports-related case entering the judicial system. A review of legal literature reveals that many of those cases are a direct result of a coach requiring athletes to perform tasks beyond their capabilities or introducing game tactics which lead to injury. Because of those factors and others, the issue of certification of coaches is a major concern to many people in sport.

The certification of coaches is a highly controversial issue and leaves little, if any, room for a neutral stance. Arguments have been made for each side of the issue. For example, consider the comments received from a questionnaire about youth sports in North Carolina regarding certification:

Pro: No longer can youth be handed over to well-intentioned adults who make inadvertent errors that can have life-long effects on the child (e.g., errors in skill teaching, weeding out the poor players, turn youngsters away from fun and healthful activity, and cause serious physical and emotional problems).

Con: There is just not that much to know about being a coach. You see how they do it on television, or played when you were in school, and just pick up the rest as you go along. It is not necessary to do all of this extra preparation.

Similar feelings are found when reviewing the literature on certification of coaches. For example, Lynne Gaskin, a legal scholar at the University of North Carolina at Greensboro, wrote in 1981 that "there is an increasing, extensive national concern for the preparation of qualified coaches of interscholastic programs." She presented the following reasons as opposition to certification:

1. The present system is adequate.
2. It will create a hardship to current coaches in time and money if they are required to take additional course work.
3. Some sports will have to be cancelled.
4. Certification will not guarantee better coaches, as specific courses do not necessarily bring success in coaching.

The majority of thought in this area centers on the preparation of interscholastic coaches since, beyond youth sport, interscholastic sports are believed to have the largest number of participants and coaches, creating a higher probability for injury or violation of rights. A majority of coaches at the middle, junior and high school levels are certified to teach in a specific subject area. Unfortunately, many of those coaches have only their playing experience or an interest in a particular sport as qualification for coaching.

Rainer Martens, a youth sport leader, wrote in *Joy and Sadness in Children's Sports* that the idea that former players make qualified coaches is mythical. Martens states: "Two myths exist about coaching children's sports. One is that the only qualification needed is to have played the sport. The second is that the better a person played, the better coach he or she will be."

Even though Marten's comments appear to apply to coaching at the youth sport level, those myths appear to apply to interscholastic coaching as well. As evidence of the former-player myth consider Al Rosen, a former baseball great with the Cleveland Indians, who had his coaching qualifications questioned by his son. In reflection, Rosen stated: "The funny thing about it, he was right to wonder. I had played the game for twenty years, but I found out that I did not know anything about teaching it to beginners."

Conversely, Arthur Gallon, a professor at the University of California at Santa Barbara, wrote in *Coaching Ideas and Ideals* that a coach "by participating actively in a sport . . . will better understand the technical and emotional problems encountered by the athletes." There is merit to what Gallon says, and we cannot totally refute the value of experience gained by playing a sport as a qualification for being a coach. We can, however, question the validity of appointing people to coach by virtue of that playing experience alone, as there is more to coaching than designing X's and O's.

Coaching is a complex process as pointed out by C.A. Bucher, a well-known author of sport administration texts, who lists four qualifications for coaches:

> First, the coach is able to teach the fundamentals and strategies of the sport; he or she must be a good teacher. Second, the coach needs to understand the player: how a person functions at a particular level of development — with a full appreciation of skeletal growth, muscular development, and physical and emotional limitations. Third, the coach understands the game he or she coaches; thorough knowledge of techniques, rules, and similar information is basic. Fourth, the coach has a desirable personality and character. Patience, understanding right and wrong, courage, cheerfulness, affection, humor, energy, and enthusiasm are imperative.

To meet those qualifications, Gallon believes "a high school athletic coach should be a graduate of an approved college. His or her preparation for teaching should be the same as that for all teachers." Gallon also feels "the course of study followed by physical education majors . . . best prepares potential coaches." R.A. Postolesi and W.A. Sinclair feel that if "a coach is to be held responsible for the well-being of the participants in any athletic program it should be the responsibility of the specific school, district, or state to see that these individuals are properly prepared."

Larry Noble, professor of health and physical education at the University of Kansas, and Charles B. Corbin conducted a survey in 1978 on coaching certification and noted: "Forty-five states, Puerto Rico, and the District of Columbia have no specific certification requirements for coaching." This indicates that a majority of states (certifying agencies) are either unconcerned about the responsibility expressed by Postolesi and Sinclair, authorities in the administration of physical education programs, or that those states believe competency is fulfilled by being certified to teach any subject. This sentiment is supported by a 1980 survey of the 50 states and the District of Columbia by Noble and Garry Sigle, an instructor at Riley County High School in Riley, Kansas, which indicated that 32 certifying agencies require coaches to be certified to teach. That study also revealed that 12 states have no teacher certification requirement to coach and seven states require teacher certification for head coaching only.

The impetus for the Noble and Corbin study came from the Kansas legislature as it considered a bill that would make it legal for anyone to coach regardless of educational background. As reported by Noble and Corbin, "the bill's sponsor argued that this would allow local people (farmers, lawyers, and other non-professionals) with athletic backgrounds to coach and thus allow teachers more time to teach." They also reported that "the bill's sponsor had observed that coaches sometimes did a poor job of teaching because they spent so much time coaching. This bill would eliminate this problem."

It should be recognized that the sentiment of that legislator may be an isolated case. Even so, the thought of coaches not teacher-certified caused Noble and Sigle to state that "the use of community people who have no training as teachers or coaches other than sport participation is abhorrent." Gaskin concluded her survey of colleges and universities in North Carolina that offer programs related to coaching preparation in a similar way when she said "full-time faculty members should be assigned coaching responsibilities."

The preceding information indicates that coaches arrive at coaching positions through various routes. It is somewhat unsettling, however, to learn that some states lack any type of certification or training requirements for coaches. Conversely, some satisfaction is gained by knowing that a majority of states require coaches to be certified teachers. The disquieting aspect of that situation is: how well does certification in math, English or social science prepare a person to coach? Many people in physical education believe coaches should be a graduate of an approved college, following a course of study leading to a physical education degree or at the minimum an endorsement in coaching.

§ 3.2(A). Preparation of Coaches.

Gaskin, in her 1981 study, reported that the issue of coaching certification has been of concern to the American Alliance for Health, Physical Education, Recreation and Dance (A.A.H.P.E.R.D.) for 27 years. According to her, the Division of Men's Athletics of A.A.H.P.E.R.D. established a task force in 1967 to determine competencies for the certification of high school coaches. The work of that task force led the Division of Men's Athletics to publish minimum areas of professional preparation for high school coaches in 1971. Those recommendations, however, have not been universally accepted or adopted by the states.

Perhaps of greater significance, Gaskin found that 15 of 43 institutions of higher education in North Carolina have a program of instruction leading to a minor in coaching. In a related study conducted the same year, Robert Bunnell, a physical education professor at Purdue University in Indiana, found that 46% of 127 institutions of higher education from six geographical regions of the United States offered course work leading to a coaching endorsement.

The Bunnell report is of significance as the 127 responding institutions represent 40 (80%) of the 50 states. Coaching endorsements are offered by four or more colleges or universities in each of those 40 states. Geographically, Indiana and bordering states Kentucky, Illinois, Ohio and Michigan lead the way with 17 institutions providing courses for coaching endorsement. That region is followed by the Upper Midwest and Plains region that includes Wisconsin, Minnesota, Missouri, Iowa, Nebraska, North Dakota, South Dakota and Kansas with 12 institutions offering coaching endorsement programs. The Mid-Atlantic, South and Southeast region that includes Virginia, Maryland, North Carolina, South Carolina, Georgia, Alabama, Florida, Tennessee, Arkansas, Mississippi and Louisiana follows with 11 institutions having programs leading to a coaching endorsement.

One may conclude from the Bunnell report that almost half of the physical education departments in 80% of the colleges and universities across the United States are providing professional training for potential coaches. One may also conclude that those institutions having coaching minors, or courses leading to a coaching endorsement, offer those programs for a variety of reasons. There appears to be no indication that those programs are being offered primarily to meet state certification or endorsement requirements. For example, Gaskin reported that "certification of coaches in North Carolina is not anticipated in the near future." The Bunnell study did not indicate what courses compose the coaching minor or endorsement programs; therefore one must look elsewhere for that information.

According to Gallon, the A.A.H.P.E.R.D. task force recommended that a coaching minor should include the following courses and credit hours:

Medical Aspects of Athletic Coaching	3 sem. hrs.
Principles and Problems of Coaching	3 sem. hrs.
Theory and Techniques of Coaching	6 sem. hrs.
Kinesiological Foundations of Coaching	2 sem. hrs.
Physiological Foundations of Coaching	2 sem. hrs.
	16 sem. hrs.

Let us see how those recommendations have been applied.

According to the 1980 report "Minimum Requirements for Interscholastic Coaches" by Noble and Sigle "eight states have requirements for coaches in addition to teacher certification." Those states and minimum requirements follow (only courses are listed; for more detailed information the reader is urged to seek out the original source, Journal of Physical Education & Recreation (Nov./Dec. 1980).):

Arkansas:

Anatomy, physiology, or kinesiology.	3 sem. hrs.
Care of athletic injuries.	3 sem. hrs.
Organization and administration of athletics or physical education.	3 sem. hrs.
Coaching theory.	3 sem. hrs.

Iowa:

Human growth and development as it relates to physical activity.
Theory of coaching.
Care and prevention of athletic injuries.

Structure and function of the human body.
No semester or quarter hour requirements were listed.

Minnesota:
A minimum of 12 quarter hours in the following for head coaches in varsity sports:
First aid and prevention of athletic injuries.
Science of sports.
Theory and practice of sport techniques.
Psychology of sports.
At least 40 clock-hours of supervised field experience.

New York:
Nine semester-hour preservice or 120 clock-hour inservice program consisting of:
Philosophy, principles and organization of athletics.
Health services applied to coaching.
Theory and techniques of coaching in the sport being coached.

Oklahoma:
Head coaches and athletic directors:
Care and prevention of athletic injuries.   2 sem. hrs.
Four semester hours from one or more of the following:
Organization and administration of athletics.
Kinesiology, applied anatomy, human physiology and physiology of exercise.
Theory of athletic coaching.
Elective courses which include audiovisual education, physical education activities, officiating, principles and psychology of athletic coaching, athletic workshop, athletic training, athletic facilities, and equipment.
All other coaches must complete a two semester-hour course in the care and prevention of athletic injuries.

Oregon:
All coaches are required to complete an approved first aid course and verify coaching experience to the State Teachers Standards and Practices Commission.

South Dakota:
All coaches must have a minimum of eight semester hours of college credit in:
Coaching athletics, or
Health and physical education, including:
One course in prevention and care of injuries.
One course in coaching the sport assigned.

Wyoming:
No specific course work. Coaches must be certified to teach physical education or complete 12 semester hours in athletic coaching.

In addition to the above states, Ohio has recently adopted a rule regarding qualification for coaches. The guidelines require six hours in sports-related first aid for new coaches and three hours for experienced coaches. Also, in the Noble and Corbin study, "Professional Preparation," Nebraska was reported as requiring coaches to be certified to teach and have a coaching endorsement with a minimum of 12 hours in the following areas:

Organization and administration of athletics.
Treatment of injuries.
Coaching methods in at least three sports.

Of interest in the Nebraska requirement is that physical education majors are not exempted from completing the requirements.

Other examples of course work leading to certification of coaches are those used by the United States Wrestling Foundation (U.S.W.F.), National Coaches Certification Program and the training program adopted by the military as conducted by the National Youth Sport Coaches Association (N.Y.S.C.A.). The U.S.W.F. has three levels of accreditation — Bronze, Silver and Gold. Requirements for Bronze certification (entry level) include current membership, one year of coaching experience and successful completion of a written examination covering fifteen topics in seven different disciplines as follows:

Physiology
Psychology
Motor Learning
Sports Medicine
Officiating
Training Methods
Wrestling Techniques

According to Fred C. Engh, President, National Youth Sport Coaches Association (N.Y.S.C.A.), in his article "Youth Sports in the Military an Example Worth Emulating":

NYSCA believes that all individuals who volunteer to coach should receive basic training in the psychology of coaching youngsters, first aid and safety, preventing injuries through proper conditioning, how to organize fun and interesting practices, and finally, the techniques of playing each sport — *before* they are even permitted to step on the field as a youth sport coach.

Stephen J. Nathanson, author of "Athletic Coaching Competencies," recommends five focus areas containing 51 competencies perceived as necessary for coaching. Those five focus areas are:

medical/legal aspects of coaching.
sociological and psychological aspects of coaching.
theory and techniques of coaching.
kinesiological foundations of coaching.
physiological foundations of coaching.

He recommended that all athletic coaches be required to demonstrate competency in all 51 coaching competencies. A further recommendation of Nathanson's was that the state of New York should automatically certify coaches upon attainment of the 51 competencies.

Other perceptions such as those of E. James Kelley, Assistant Dean, Pennsylvania State University, and Shelby Brightwell, Professor of Physical Education, Southeastern Louisiana University, in "Should Interscholastic Coaches Be Certified?" and "Bridging the Gap from Student to Coach: Experienced Coaches Speak Out" by Becky L. Sisley, University of Oregon professor, indicate courses similar to those presented before. Kelley and Brightwell emphasize care and treatment of injuries, conditioning programs, diet, salt and water, heat stroke, heat exhaustion, athletic training principles, and duration, intensity and frequency of training and conditioning programs.

As a result of her interview with four past and present interscholastic coaches, Sisley put forth the following recommendations for prospective coaches:

1. Require prospective coaches to have at least two coaching practicums.
2. Have students in coaching classes complete structured observations of several different coaches during practices and games.
3. Plan role-playing experiences in athletic administration and/or coaching theory classes.
4. Require students in coaching classes to develop an annotated list of current references for the sport.
5. Require a core of courses which present a solid base of information essential for all coaches.
6. Expose students to avenues for increasing their in-depth knowledge of the sport.

Based on the preceding information, it appears that some of the recommendations of A.A.H.P.E.R.D. for potential coaches are perceived as necessary by at least 10 states and various physical education professionals. Furthermore, a majority of the recommendations form guidelines for certification of coaches in those states where it is required. Due to the increasing complexities of coaching, more specific recommendations are needed. The five focus areas presented by Nathanson, augmented by Sisley's recommendation of practicums, are worthy of consideration for adoption for both certifying agencies and physical education departments offering coaching programs.

Due to the rise of litigation in sport, those recommendations would become more meaningful by the addition of a course in legal aspects of sport as a requirement. It should be given consideration as a mandatory course not only in the certification of teachers and coaches but for all persons seeking a physical education degree.

§ 3.2(B). Legal Ramifications.

The threat of injury is an inherent possibility in any sports activity. Participants in sports are generally aware of that possibility and generally assume an element of risk because of voluntary participation. That fact alone does not relieve a coach or an educational institution from the responsibility of providing a safe environment for the sports participant.

Many factors are considered to be part of providing that safe environment. For example, Cym Lowell in "Liability for Injuries in Sports" perceives proper instruction in how to play the game and assurance that athletes are in proper physical condition as ways of fulfilling the duty of reasonable care. Others such as Andrew Grieve, author of *The Legal Aspects of Athletics,* believe that a coach's training and qualifications are of equal importance.

A majority of the states consider certification to teach, regardless of subject area, as qualification for a person to coach. The implication of that requirement is that the coach who is certified to teach is qualified to coach. A case involving such a situation, *Stehn v. Bernard McFadden Foundations, Inc.,* Civil Action 4398 U.S. Dist. Ct., M.D. Tenn., Nashville Div., 1969, indicates the fallacy of such reasoning.

Lowry Stehn was injured in a wrestling program supervised by a faculty member who had little wrestling and coaching experience. Allegedly the coach introduced a wrestling hold that he had learned in the Army. It was reported at the trial that the coach did not teach a method of escape from the hold nor a defense against it. In addition, the coach was attempting to supervise two matches simultaneously with his concentration directed toward the one in which Stehn was not wrestling. The plaintiff based his case on inadequate supervision and raised the question as to the qualification of the coach for coaching boys of Stehn's age in a wrestling program, plus several other pertinent questions concerning the wrestling hold. Stehn was awarded $385,000 in damages for his injury.

A recent decision reported by Dr. Samuel Adams, a legal expert at Washington University, in "Court Decision Hits Hard With New Liability Twists," has even greater impact on the issue of certification of coaches. According to Adams, it is not known to what extent the question of certification was used by the Seattle jury during its consideration and determination of that case. We can surmise, however, that it was of some importance as questions were raised as to how coaches are chosen, whether they are just teachers and how a coach is determined to be an expert. As a result of that consideration, Adams states that "administrators will have to provide viable answers as to questions of how coaches are chosen and how one is determined to be an expert." He also feels that certification of coaches may be a positive step in the prevention of future liability cases.

The *Seattle* case, reported by Adams, placed the blame for injury on the school district, indicating that what Grieve wrote in 1969 continues to be true: "The courts have tended to approach the coaching of athletics as a distinct phase of the educational program, even though it may be classified as extracurricular, and concluded a person must be trained in proper educational practices to be considered as a competent supervisor."

Without referring to a specific certification or training program for coaches, Grieve alludes to it when he states: "Individual judgment as to the qualifications of a competent supervisor for athletic activities may not be strictly comparable to that of the courts. If there is the least question as to such qualifications, the court may take a dim view in negligence cases."

In a similar manner, Lowell reasons that with respect to athletic activities, educational institutions have a general duty to exercise reasonable care to prevent reasonably foreseeable risks and, where such risks are foreseeable, to take sufficient precautions to protect the students in their custody. Lowell lists several specific obligations of that general duty, among them the obligation to provide adequate supervision for the various sports and to exercise due care in the selection of supervisors.

Adams believes that coaches have done outstanding jobs in regard to safety instruction in sports for many decades. He further believes that the decision in the *Seattle* case will cause coaches to put a greater emphasis on an awareness of the latest safety techniques in their particular sports. Adams speculates that coaches must become more specific in their instructions to athletes concerning safety procedures and the dangers involved in their sport.

The *Seattle* case delineated what Lawrence Graham in "New Look in Sports ... New Faces in Our Courts" called the new kid on the block, "failure to warn." That action further tightened an already strict view by the courts of assumption of risk. Most important, the allegations — failure to have coaches certified — is now a matter of judicial record. Regardless of its importance in rendering the *Seattle* decision, one may predict that because of that fact, the prevailing interpretation of assumption of risk and "failure to warn" considerations in sports liability cases by the courts, the certification of coaches will receive further legal attention. Eventually, we may see that allegation as the sole reason for bringing suit against an educational institution when a sports injury is involved.

It is clear that the responsibility for hiring qualified coaches rests with the educational institution. This is emphasized by Grieve, Lowell and others — yet many institutions do not establish certification criteria for coaches. That is done at the state level although school systems have input as to what constitutes proper training for their teachers. Due to the decision in the *Seattle* case, that input may become more forceful in the future since school systems cannot afford to pay damages of millions and continue to maintain programs.

§ 3.2(C). Conclusion.

It is significant that proponents for certification are many and vocal, perceiving certification as being the way for bringing about better coaching, reducing injuries and deemphasizing the win-at-all-costs attitude in inter-scholastic sports. On the other hand, the literature is empty of material from opponents of certification. That also is significant. Perhaps the opponents feel that no response is necessary, that things are fine as they are, that they know something the proponents do not know or that states (certifying agencies) lack responsibility for extracurricular activities such as sports.

The possibility of states universally requiring separate and distinct coaching certification requirements appears remote at this time. A possible reason is that while states are charged with the responsibility of providing an education for children, that responsibility does not include sports although sports have been held by the courts to be a distinct part of the educational program.

States establish certification requirements, but they do not employ nor release teachers or coaches. School systems have that responsibility plus ensuring that those employed are qualified, which may mean qualifications beyond those required for certification. Very simply, if school systems want to stay out of harm's way, they must provide qualified teachers, coaches and sponsors for extracurricular activities.

Since most school systems employ coaches on the basis of teacher certification, some form of additional training program is necessary to ensure that coaches are qualified. Whether that training is accomplished as preservice or inservice is immaterial. The minimum core of any such training program should focus on:

> Physical Conditioning.
> The Learning and Performance of Physical Skills.
> First Aid.
> Theory and Techniques of Coaching (to include psychosociological aspects).
> Legal Aspects of Coaching.

Additionally, persons should not be appointed to head coaching positions until they have gained a minimum of three years of experience in the sport they coach.

Each of the minimum core subjects should require completion of thirty contact hours of inservice training or three semester hours of academic credit with the exception of first aid, which should be twenty contact hours of inservice or two semester hours of academic credit. Because the need for a training program appears to center on judicial decisions, legal aspects of coaching should be a foundation course.

Developing and implementing training programs for coaches will not be an easy task for most school systems. Many people and organizations will be opposed to it and may point to their own programs as being sufficient. That opposition may be overcome by enlisting those opponents' support, input and cooperation. Should they choose not to assist, the school system must proceed with its program. The important thing to remember is that educational institutions are responsible for employing qualified supervisors. It is the school system, not a coaching or state athletic association or even a state, that must answer liability charges. Because of that fact the school system must have minimum qualification requirements and a training program that prepares coaches in those requirements.

---

§ 3.3. The Coach as Codefendant: Football in the 1980's.

By Richard A. Lester

During the 1970's everyone associated with organized football was made aware of the "football helmet crises." While the manufacturers of football helmets were involved in a struggle for survival as the result of an onslaught of lawsuits filed by participants who had sustained serious head and neck injuries, the football community chose to do little more than lend a sympathetic ear to the plight of the industry. Since it had been only the manufacturers who had been sued, the attitude had been that it was only the manufacturers' problem.

The 1980's may well be remembered as the decade during which the manufacturers' problem became the problem of the coaches, athletic directors, administrators and athletic associations as well. Several court decisions make it clear that the football community can no longer afford to view the crisis as one for the manufacturers alone to deal with.

In July, 1981 a jury in Portland, Oregon returned a verdict against the Oregon School Activities Association for $1,080,000 in a case filed by a former high school football player who was paralyzed during a practice session in 1976. In February, 1982, in a case involving a similar injury in Seattle, Washington, a jury returned a verdict against the Seattle School district for $6,400,000. As a result of the Seattle verdict, at least one school board member suggested that the district consider cancelling football and other "high risk" sports. Coaches, athletic directors, administrators or athletic associations are now being joined as defendants in many of the cases pending against manufacturers. The issue is no longer merely the survival of the helmet manufacturers. It is the survival of the sport.

§ 3.3(A). The Role of the Coach.

Today's football coach must both recognize and address this issue. He must ask himself what actions he can take to reduce the incidence of serious head or neck injury. He must also be concerned with the risk of exposure of both himself and his institution to liability, in the unfortunate event of serious injury to one of his players. There are a number of steps which a coach can take to reduce both the risk of injury and the risk of liability in the event of such an injury.

In those cases in which a coach, athletic director or school has been named as a defendant, one of the charges usually leveled is that the injured player received insufficient instruction and supervision. This was the basis for the Seattle verdict. Accordingly, the experience and qualifications of the coaching staff are usually questioned. In order to answer such a charge, the coach must be able to demonstrate that he is qualified by his education and experience, and that his knowledge of the football rules and accepted coaching techniques is current. A permanent record of the seminars, conferences and clinics attended by the coaching staff should be maintained in order to demonstrate a continuing desire to keep abreast of rule changes, techniques which have been identified as injury producing and improved methods of administering emergency treatment to the injured player.

A library should be maintained containing all books, periodicals and articles which the coaching staff has utilized in establishing their program. Such reference material may prove invaluable in both preventing injuries and in demonstrating the institution's concern for the safety of its players. For example, many articles have been written identifying the techniques of butt blocking, head tackling and spearing as the most significant causes of serious head and neck injury in football. As a result of rule changes in 1976 which outlawed the use of the head as the initial point of contact in blocking and tackling, the incidence of cervical fracture or dislocation injuries has been reduced by over 50%. Studies have been reported indicating that the majority of serious neck injuries are sustained by defensive backs and members of special teams while attempting to make tackles. Fatigue has been identified as a contributing factor in these injuries, with many of them occurring late in the second quarter or near the end of the game. By keeping abreast of the results of such studies, the coaching staff can more effectively address the issue of injury prevention, and in so doing reduce their risk of exposure to liability.

§ 3.3(B). Provide Quality Equipment.

Another claim typically advanced in these cases is that the school failed to provide adequate protective equipment or failed to properly fit and maintain the protective equipment. In order to defend itself against this charge, the school, through its purchasing agent and coaches, must have sufficient information on file to demonstrate a conscious effort on its part to provide the best protection available to its players. Equipment manufacturers' informational materials, such as sales catalogs and brochures, used in the selection process for protective equipment should be kept on file for reference in the event it becomes necessary at a later time to explain the selection process and the particular attributes of the equipment ultimately selected. The rules governing the sport at the high school, junior college and college level now require that each participant wear a helmet which meets the Standard Method of Impact Test and Performance Requirements for Football Helmets adopted by the National Operating Committee on Standards for Athletic Equipment (N.O.C.S.A.E.). Any helmets purchased prior to adoption of the N.O.C.S.A.E. standard in September, 1973, or any which fail to meet that standard should be discarded.

Virtually all equipment manufacturers provide fitting and maintenance instructions with their helmets at the time of purchase and will provide additional copies of these instructions on request. Coaches should read and follow these instructions, distribute copies to each player and maintain a copy on file for periodic reference. In order for any helmet to perform its protective function, it must be properly fitted.

§ 3.3(C). Maintenance of Equipment.

Few institutions are financially able to purchase new helmets each year. In order to ensure that their helmets are maintained in the condition necessary to perform efficiently, the manufacturers' recommended instructions for periodic inspection and maintenance must be followed and documented. A specific cycle for reconditioning, recertification to the N.O.C.S.A.E. standard and replacement should be adopted and the helmets individually serial numbered or otherwise permanently identified so that the maintenance history of any specific helmet can be recorded for future reference. Each year when the helmets are issued a listing should be made identifying the serial number of the helmet issued to each player, so that in the event of an injury the identity of the specific helmet worn at the time of the injury is known. By utilizing these procedures the coaching staff or school will always be able to identify the helmet involved and its history of maintenance if a case is ever filed as a result of an injury.

§ 3.3(D). Failure to Warn.

In many cases the injured player bases his claim against all defendants on a "failure to warn" theory. Although this claim can be asserted in many forms, the typical complaint alleges that the injured player was never warned of the danger of using his head as the initial point of contact or never warned that he could be paralyzed or killed while engaged in the sport. Although it would seem that anyone who is familiar with the game, particularly those who play it, could not help but recognize and appreciate that there is some risk involved, a jury in Franklin, Indiana awarded a player $5,800,000 in 1981 in a case based on the failure to warn theory. Accordingly, no matter how obvious the danger appears, it is in the best interest of the coach and school to take the necessary steps to ensure that the participants are advised of and acknowledge the risks involved in playing football.

In January, 1980, the N.O.C.S.A.E. Committee adopted the following warning language and recommended its use and distribution by all members of the organization:

> Do not use this helmet to butt, ram or spear an opposing player. This is in violation of the football rules, and such use can result in severe head or neck injury, paralysis or death to you and possible injury to your opponent. No helmet can prevent all head or neck injuries a player might receive while participating in football.

Shortly after its adoption helmet manufacturers and athletic equipment reconditioners began inserting this warning inside all new and reconditioned helmets. Other N.O.C.S.A.E. members, most notably the National Collegiate Athletic Association, the National Association of Intercollegiate Athletics and the National Federation of State High School Associations, began distributing the warning to their member institutions in pamphlet and poster form. In early 1982 N.O.C.S.A.E. funded the purchase of exterior warning labels to be distributed to all high schools by the N.F.S.H.S.A. This program was repeated in 1983, with the NCAA, N.A.I.A. and N.J.C.A.A. joining the N.F.S.H.S.A. in the distribution of exterior warning labels to their institutions. In January, 1983, in an effort to reinforce the effectiveness of the warning, N.O.C.S.A.E. revised the warning language to read as follows:

Warning

> Do not use this helmet to butt, ram or spear an opposing player. This is in violation of the football rules and can result in severe head, brain or neck injury, paralysis or death to you and possible injury to your opponent.

There is a risk these injuries may also occur as a result of accidental contact without intent to butt, ram or spear.
NO HELMET CAN PREVENT ALL SUCH INJURIES.

Although most helmets now exhibit this warning language and institutions have received it in numerous pamphlets and posters distributed by N.O.C.S.A.E. members, there is no guarantee that an injured player has read or will acknowledge having read its contents.

A more effective means of ensuring that the player and his parents are aware of the contents of the warning is available to the coaching staff and school administrators. Most high schools now require the execution of consent forms before a young man is allowed to participate in school-administered sporting events such as football. As a result of the Seattle verdict, a number of institutions both at the high school and college level have amended their consent forms to include the N.O.C.S.A.E. warning language and an acknowledgment that the player and his parents have read the warning and appreciate the risks involved in the sport. Both the player and his parents should be required to sign the form prior to his participation. At the college level, where the player has reached the age of majority, only the participant's signature would be required.

§ 3.3(E). Precautionary Steps.

Another means of communicating the risk of making initial contact with the head and the risk of serious head or neck injury is through the use of films which have been produced for the use of coaches and their institutions. In 1976, at the time major rule changes outlawing use of the head in initial contact became effective, the National Federation of State High School Associations produced "Football — Point of Contact," a film which graphically demonstrates the blocking and tackling techniques which have been found to cause head and neck injuries and those techniques which are illegal. Copies of this film were distributed to the federation's state affiliates and should be available to coaches, administrators and school districts through their state association or through the N.F.S.H.S.A. at their offices in Kansas City, Missouri. More recently, the Athletic Institute in North Palm Beach, Florida has produced two films which are available through their offices. "A Report On Serious Football Injuries" explains the risks of playing football, provides the latest statistics on the incidence of catastrophic injury, presents demonstrations of proper blocking and tackling techniques, and emphasizes the importance of observing key rules designed to lower the risk of injury. "Warning — It Could Happen To You" provides medical, biomechanical and statistical information on a full range of injuries from minor to catastrophic for all sports. These films are designed specifically for young athletes and their families and should be shown to the team with their parents prior to the start of practice each season. As in all steps taken by the coaching staff to prevent injury, a record of the date shown, title of the film and those in attendance should be retained.

In addition to exhibiting the films to the team prior to the start of drills, there are a number of other precautionary steps which the coaching staff should take before the season starts. Complete physical examinations should be required of all prospective players, with the additional requirement that any player with a history of head trauma undergo a CAT scan. Studies have shown that many players who sustain serious brain injury playing football have had a prior, less severe head injury. At the time equipment is distributed and fitted, each player should be instructed in the proper method of determining for himself whether the equipment continues to fit properly and in the recommended procedures for inspection and maintenance of the equipment. Players should be encouraged to immediately report any problem in this regard to the coaching staff. Most manufacturers provide wall charts for the coaching staff to post in the locker room as a continuing reminder to the players of the proper method of inspection and maintenance.

§ 3.3(F). Providing Adequate Insurance.

Recently a new issue has surfaced in at least two cases filed against school districts and municipalities in Massachusetts. Injured players in those cases sued the districts and municipalities for negligence in failing to procure adequate medical coverage for their participants prior to the start of the season. In both cases players sustained paralyzing neck injuries and, although medical insurance coverage had been obtained, its policy limits were exhausted early in the treatment of the injuries, leaving the players and their families with no coverage for present or future medical expenses. One of these cases was settled before a determination of the merits of this particular issue had been made. The second case is currently pending. Regardless of the ultimate decision in that particular case, that issue will continue to arise in future cases. School districts must now review their insurance programs to determine if medical insurance policies for their players are adequate, or face the consequences of litigation in the event of a catastrophic injury.

Once fall practice begins, coaches must structure their program to include a sufficient number of sessions for conditioning and strengthening drills prior to having the team engage in contact drills. In the case in Portland, the verdict was based on a claim that the Oregon School Activities Association (O.S.A.A.) failed to promulgate rules for the schools requiring such conditioning and strengthening drills at the start of fall practice. The injured player sustained his injury in a contact drill during the first week of fall practice. Another procedure which should be followed once practice begins is to arrange for the presence of appropriately trained medical personnel and equipment at all practices and games. In doing so the school may avoid a later charge that it failed to provide adequate emergency treatment on the field or enroute to a medical facility.

§ 3.3(G). Conclusion.

If the procedures suggested are closely adhered to, the coach and school will minimize the risk of serious injury to their players. Nevertheless, the very nature of the game suggests that, as in any contact sport, some injuries can and will continue to occur. The coaching staff must recognize this possibility and be prepared to take a number of steps to investigate the cause of injury and preserve evidence which may be crucial to its defense if a lawsuit is ever filed. Most important, the injured player's protective equipment should be kept, labeled and isolated. Under no circumstances should it be returned to the equipment room, reissued or released from the school's possession. Films of all games during the season up to the time of the injury, whether the injury occurred in a game or practice, should be preserved. If the injury occurred during a game, the impact resulting in the injury may be on the film. If not, the films of prior games provide excellent evidence of the techniques utilized by the team. Immediately locate and preserve the records of purchase, maintenance and reconditioning of the specific equipment worn at the time of injury. Obtain written statements from coaches, teammates and officials who witnessed the injury. And, finally, notify the state association and the National Football Head and Neck Injury Registry of the injury.

By exercising the precautionary steps discussed in this article, coaches and school administrators can effect a significant reduction in the incidence of severe head and neck injury to football players and at the same time enhance their ability to defend their football programs in the event they are included as defendants in litigation resulting from a catastrophic injury. Today's coaches and administrators can no longer afford to remain on the sidelines in the battle against litigation which threatens the survival of the sport.

CHAPTER 4

STUDENT-ATHLETE ISSUES

§ 4.1. Athletes' Rights: Fact or Fiction.

By C. Thomas Ross

What rights do athletes have? Some people state that athletes have no rights; they argue that sport participation is a privilege and so must be strictly governed by the authorities controlling sports programs. Others insist that athletes should have complete rights, even to the extent of forming labor unions that would bargain for increased educational and financial benefits. The answer to this question depends upon many factors and is somewhere between the two ends of the debate on the rights of an athlete.

The stand on the question is a compromise between the two extremes; it is a synthesis of applicable case law, statutory law, common sense and a respect for the practical as well as the theoretical. Litigation in the sports area has proliferated at such a rapid pace that courts are being asked to decide and define what rights, if any, athletes have. The courts have been asked to rule on matters ranging from suspension for violating training rules, to such important issues as sex and racial discrimination. Courts must deal with old problems in new ways, such as liability for injuries inflicted by participants in sporting contests, the question of whether sport is a property right, the ability of voluntary athletic associations to govern their members, payment by athletes of fees for participation in sports events, the status of athletes as public figures, as well as the position in law of the athletes with disabilities as participants.

§ 4.1(A). Are Athletes' Rights Legal?

Over the last two decades some of the answers have become self-evident and have come close to a consensus. Others are still being decided in different ways by different courts. Any analysis must consider any question in the context of whether athletes' rights are truly legal or whether the rights claimed also involve ethical or moral questions. We must acknowledge that an ethical or moral problem may not extend to the level of a legal right.

In the early years of the sports litigation explosion, most of the lawsuits were based on attempts to recover for injuries suffered in a game or practice session. Some other cases dealt with conduct, such as whether or not a player may be told how to wear his hair or may be married, or denied participation in sport because of violation of a training rule. Of the courts around the country, some favored school officials and some favored students; but these decisions were based only on the facts in a particular situation. Since there were no legitimate natural standards that could be applied in these decisions, each case rested on its own merits.

§ 4.1(B). A Landmark Case in Athletes' Rights.

Then in 1969, when the Supreme Court of the United States decided the case of *Tinker v. Des Moines Independent Community School District,* 393 U.S. 503 (1969), the court held that the wearing of black armbands by students to protest the Vietnam war was closely akin to pure speech and was therefore entitled to comprehensive protection under the first amendment of the United States Constitution. This was the first landmark case in the field of students' rights. A second landmark case, *Goss v. Lopez,* 419 U.S. 565 (1975), held that a student could not be suspended from public high school without a hearing, since this violated the due process clause of the fourteenth amendment to the United States Constitution.

After many years it was becoming apparent that predictions of a tremendous surge in the number of court cases involving students' rights were turning out to be true.

During this time, two other significant matters were being developed. In 1972 the United States Congress passed a law (Title IX, Public Law 92-318) to ensure equality and opportunity for women athletes. In 1973 Congress enacted the Rehabilitation Act and in 1975 it passed the Education for All Handicapped Children Act (Public Law 94-142), both attempting to ensure the opportunity to participate in sport for persons with disabilities.

These case decisions and statutory enactments were simply illustrative of our changing society. As our population increased, people became more litigious, while courts and legislatures were becoming more and more conscious of individual rights.

This brief historical review leads to the current question of what rights athletes actually have. It is clear that a student athlete will have the same rights as other students while he is a student. But it is less clear whether or not the rights of a student will carry over to the rights of an athlete. Most judicial decisions take the position that participation in sport, particularly at the scholastic level, is a privilege and not a right and that, therefore, the controls and restrictions which may be imposed are greater. The athlete, in exchange for the privilege of participating, surrenders certain areas of control.

§ 4.1(C). Categories of Athletes' Rights.

There are six arbitrary categories into which an athlete's rights may fall: (1) constitutional, (2) protective, (3) disciplinary and behavioral, (4) educational, (5) financial and (6) human and personal.

In the area of constitutional rights, it is clear that athletes are entitled to certain minimum due process requirements as well as to equal protection under the law. This also applies in cases of racial or sexual discrimination. At the scholastic level it is relatively clear that students do not have a property right to participate in sport, although they may have a property right in the educational process in general. (*Herbert v. Ventetuolo,* 638 F.2d 5 (1st Cir. 1981); *Pegram v. Nelson,* 469 F. Supp. 1134 (M.D.N.C. 1979).) The argument that expulsion from a team will cause loss of a potential scholarship to play in college has generally been dismissed as being too speculative. At the college level the courts seem to be saying that a scholarship athlete does have a property right in sport participation and, as a result, is entitled to higher due process requirements before sport participation can be terminated. (*Hall v. University of Minnesota*, 530 F. Supp. 104 (D. Minn. 1982); *Gulf South Conference v. Boyd*, 369 So. 2d 553 (Ala. 1979).)

In the matter of religious beliefs, courts have ruled that no student athlete's religious belief will be permitted to interfere with his sport participation or with reasonable rules dealing with training, practice and safety. (*Menora v. Illinois High School Association*, 683 F.2d 1030 (7th Cir. 1982); *Keller v. Gardner Community Consolidated Grade School District 72C*, 552 F. Supp. 512 (N.D. Ill. 1982).)

The next area concerns the question of an athlete's safety. Countless cases have established that an athlete is entitled not only to competent instruction and supervision and safe, properly maintained equipment, but also to adequate medical care, treatment and rehabilitation. (*Stineman v. Fontbonne College*, 664 F.2d 1082 (8th Cir. 1981).) Finally, case law states that an athlete is entitled to "freedom from injury by wilful and wanton acts of opposing players." *Hackbart v. Cincinnati Bengals, Inc.*, 601 F.2d 516 (10th Cir. 1979); *Nabozny v. Barnhill*, 334 N.E.2d 258 (Ill. App. 1975).

In discussing the rules of discipline and conduct, it is well to remember that these are subject not only to a variety of circumstances but also to varying interpretations by different courts. Generally speaking, rules which are related to safety in sport as a part of the educational process will be upheld unless a clear discriminatory intent is proven. My own belief is that an athlete is entitled to know the rules and to have them applied fairly. I also believe that an athlete is entitled to privacy and freedom of association, including the right to be married while participating.

Perhaps most important of all their rights, athletes are entitled to education without exploitation. In recent years, athletes are beginning to institute lawsuits when they feel they have been denied a proper education. Educators on both the scholastic and collegiate level are giving attention to this issue so that they can better meet the educational needs of their athletes.

An athlete at the collegiate level is entitled to a clear explanation of all scholarship rights as well as insurance coverage.

§ 4.1(D). Conclusion.

The question of whether there is also a right to free participation in sport has become an issue because of the increase in financial problems encountered by school systems throughout the nation. Several states have imposed fees on sport participation, and student athletes have gone to court to challenge their constitutionality. In *Hartzell v. Connell*, 186 Cal. Rptr. 852 (Cal. App. 1982), a California court ruled that such fees for sport participation are illegal. It is possible that the question of fees will become a controversial issue in the days ahead.

Debates over athletes' rights will continue; however, it is undeniable that today athletes enjoy more rights than ever before and that in all likelihood these rights will continue to increase.

It is inevitable that as sports litigation continues to increase, issues involving rights of athletes will be included. It is also predictable that more and more individuals and groups will become concerned with athletes' rights as a cause, thus focusing more attention on the questions raised in the public's debate. The athlete should benefit from this exchange of ideas and views.

---

§ 4.2. Educational Exploitation of Athletes.

By Herb Appenzeller

Curtis Jones is suing his high school coaches and the University of Michigan for $15 million for exploitation of his athletic ability. Jones, an ex-high school basketball star from Detroit, alleges that learning disabilities prevented him from keeping pace academically with his classmates. Although he was sent to a school where he could receive attention for his disability, word spread of his outstanding athletic skills, and from then on he was moved from school to school to capitalize on his basketball talent.

Because he was academically unprepared to attend the University of Michigan, Jones was sent to a junior college in North Dakota. When students at the junior college realized that Jones could not read or write, they reportedly subjected him to "thoughtless and unrelenting criticism, taunts and insults." Unable to cope with the humiliation and emotional pressure and suffering severe psychological illness, Jones has been in and out of hospitals since 1970 and today lives on a welfare disability check.

Maria Ironside, writing in the Athletes' Rights Bulletin, puts the blame on an educational system that allowed Jones to be exploited: "Coach after coach, teacher after teacher, school official after school official ignored Curtis Jones' educational needs and personal well-being in favor of advancing his basketball stardom." She concludes:

> If Curtis Jones had ever known just one school administrator, one advisor or coach, or anyone with the clearheadedness and courage to stand up and speak for his educational rights, he might have stood a chance for something better than what he got. He, and all of us, deserve better.

Eight athletes at California State University at Los Angeles sought $14 million for a series of alleged abuses they contend deprived them of a legitimate education. The athletes, admitted under a special program for minority students, claimed they wasted four to six years of their lives on courses such as backpacking — courses they contend were designed to keep them eligible for varsity basketball. Their attorney argued that the situation was a "classic kind of exploitation," but the university and its basketball coach characterize the charges as "180 degrees wrong." Seven of the former basketball players agreed to a settlement that provides them with $10,000 each and payment of the loans that range from $2100 to $6000. In addition, the university "agreed to issue a public statement expressing regret for what happened and guaranteeing that such a situation will not recur."

The University also instituted a scholarship fund for any of the plaintiffs who desire to continue their studies.

§ 4.2(A). Pressures Make It Difficult for Athletes to Get Good Education.

Mark Hall, an outstanding basketball player at the University of Minnesota, experienced a different problem. Hall passed 90 hours of work in the university's nondegree program. Under Big 10 Conference rules, he had to enter the degree program or lose his eligibility. The admission committee accepted him for the degree program on two occasions, but each time an administrative officer intervened and denied Hall's request.

Hall sought injunctive relief. In *Hall v. University of Minnesota,* 530 F. Supp. 104 (D. Minn. 1982), a district court judge made the following comments regarding athletics and academics on the collegiate level during the hearing:

> The defendant university's academic wing argues that if this court orders the plaintiff into a degree program, its academic standards and integrity would be undermined. The plaintiff and his fellow athletes were never recruited on the basis of scholarship and it was never envisioned they would be on the Dean's List. Consequently we must view with some skepticism the university's claim, regarding academic integrity.

The judge noted that athletes are capable of scholarship, but, because of the pressure to compete in sports, often find it difficult to obtain a good education. He granted an injunction which enabled Hall to participate in basketball when he reasoned: "If this situation causes harm to the university, it is because they have fostered it and the institution rather than the individual should suffer the consequences."

Dick Crum, the football coach at the University of North Carolina, deplores the lack of academic courses required for eligibility to college and declares that he once saw a transcript that gave credit for dry cleaning. Crum labels as a joke the current NCAA 2.0 admission standard and urges college presidents to repeal it. He proposes a standard that would require 11 core academic courses for admission; at the same time, he estimates that one fourth of all athletes on major college football squads (including his own) would not qualify under the core requirement.

Edward T. Foote, II, President of Miami University (Florida), believes that the culprit is not intercollegiate sports but a system that allows and fosters "endemic perversion of education." Foote is convinced that the solution is simple if we start in elementary school and require athletes to be students first, with the same requirements as other students. He observes:

> We do no favors to the fabled poor but coordinated child if we pass him along grade by grade through high school because he graces the playing fields, then slide him into college on the hopeless side of predictable academic success because he runs the 40-yard dash in 4.5 seconds, then avert our gaze as he flounders for two or three years before failing out.

Kevin Ross, a former Creighton University basketball star, agrees with the sentiments expressed by Foote. Ross is convinced that "social promotion" for athletes just does not pay. Ross wants to be a teacher and, with financial help from Creighton University, returned to the seventh grade to learn basic academic skills.

John Reeves, athletic director at Rochester University, suggests a new degree in "professional athletics." He notes that "borderline illiterates" could thereby obtain a college degree after putting in four years of work in athletics.

In *Strurrup v. Mahan,* 290 N.E.2d 64 (Ind. App. 1972), the court, in a case involving the question of high school recruitment, emphasized the importance of education when it declared:

> Schools are for education. There is no doubt that extracurricular athletic competition may add to the educational process, but the extracurricular activities should not take precedence over the curricular activities of the school. THE SIDESHOW MAY NOT CONSUME THE CIRCUS. The prevention of recruiting and school-jumping are both fitting and proper goals by which the IHSAA maintains the amateur standing of high school athletics. This we deem to be a compelling state interest.

The unprecedented interest in sports in recent years has been accompanied by a record number of sports-related lawsuits. The joint areas of concern have created a dilemma for the education profession: educational exploitation. Plaintiffs claim they fail to receive a proper education in return for their services to the athletic program, and they seek millions in damages for the alleged exploitation.

§ 4.2(B). Education Malpractice Becoming a Powerful Factor in the Profession.

With such educational exploitation lawsuits entering the courtroom, it is important to look at several cases involving educational malpractice. A number of cases have been decided in this area, and the two issues are very closely related from a legal standpoint. The decisions reveal the attitude of the courts.

Elizabeth Kurker-Stewart and David G. Carter, Sr., in the NOLPE School Law Journal, comment that while educational malpractice did not become an issue until the 1950's, it is now a powerful factor in today's education profession.

A recent case, *D.S.W. v. Fairbanks North Star Borough School District,* 628 P.2d 554 (Alaska 1981), is important for its conclusions. Two students suffering from dyslexia attended the Borough School District schools in Fairbanks, Alaska. Their condition went undetected for several years, and after diagnosing the problem and giving two special courses the school district discontinued help. The students sought financial restitution in court charging that the alleged negligence caused them to suffer "loss of education, loss of opportunity for employment, loss of opportunity to attend college or post high school studies, past and future mental anguish and loss of income and income earning ability."

The Alaska Supreme Court noted that while the issue represented "a claim for first impression in Alaska," two other jurisdictions addressed the question of "whether a claim may be maintained against a school for failing to discover learning disabilities or failing to provide an appropriate educational program once learning disabilities are discovered."

It referred to *Peter W. v. San Francisco Unified School District,* 131 Cal. Rptr. 854 (Cal. App. 1976), the earliest case of this type, in which the plaintiff charged that the school district failed to detect his reading disability and place him in an appropriate class. The California court considered whether "an actionable duty of care existed" by raising questions concerning:

> The foreseeability of harm of the plaintiff, the degree of certainty that the plaintiff suffered injury, the closeness of the connection between the defendant's conduct and the injury suffered, the moral blame attached to the defendant's conduct, the policy of preventing future harm, the extent of the burden to the defendant and consequences to the community of imposing a duty to exercise care with resulting liability for breach, and the availability, cost and prevalence of insurance for the risk involved.

The court declared that the case posed questions that were "highly problematical" in educational malpractice claims when it declared:

> Unlike the activity of the highway or the marketplace, classroom methodology affords no readily acceptable standards of care, or cause, or injury. The science of pedagogy itself is fraught with different and conflicting theories of how or what a child should be taught, and any layman might — and commonly does — have his own emphatic views on the subject. The "injury" claimed here is plaintiff's inability to read and write. Substantial professional authority attests that the achievement of literacy in the schools, or its failure, are influenced by a host of factors which affect the pupil subjectively, from outside the formal teaching process, and beyond the control of its ministers. They may be physical, neurological, emotional, cultural, environmental; they may be present but not perceived, recognized but not identified.

The court found no rule of care against which the defendant's alleged conduct might be measured within the law of negligence. It also reasoned that if such lawsuits were permitted, a flood of expensive litigation would result. It commented on the problems that would be added to the burdens of already beleaguered school systems when it said:

> Few of our institutions, if any, have aroused the controversies, or incurred the public dissatisfaction, which have attended the operation of the public schools during the last few decades. Rightly or wrongly, but widely, they are charged with outright failure in the achievement of their educational objectives; according to some critics, they bear responsibility for many of the social and moral problems of our society at large. Their public plight in these respects is attested in the daily media, in bitter governing board elections, in wholesale rejections of school bond proposals, and in survey upon survey. To hold them to an actionable "duty of

care," in the discharge of their academic functions, would expose them to the tort claims — real or imagined — of disaffected students and parents in countless numbers. They are already beset by social and financial problems which have gone to major litigation, but for which no permanent solution has yet appeared. The ultimate consequences, in terms of public time and money, would burden them — and society — beyond calculation.

§ 4.2(C). Judicial Interference Would Disrupt Administration of Schools.

The Alaska Supreme Court then referred to *Donohue v. Copiague Union Free School District,* 418 N.Y.S.2d 375 (N.Y. 1979), in which the facts of the case were similar to those in *Peter W.* The New York Court of Appeals was of the firm opinion that judicial interference would disrupt the administration of the schools when it declared: "Recognition in the courts of this cause of action would constitute blatant interference with the responsibility for the administration of the public school system lodged by Constitution and statute in school administrative agencies."

The Alaska Supreme Court also reviewed the highly publicized case of *Hoffman v. Board of Education of the City of New York,* 424 N.Y.S.2d 376 (N.Y. App. 1979), which presented a different problem. Hoffman, a student of normal intelligence, was placed, due to a faulty diagnosis, in classes for the mentally retarded for the majority of his schooling. A New York jury awarded him $750,000 in damages, and the appellate division affirmed the decision. The court of appeals, using *Donohue* as its guide, however, reversed the decision, denying any award.

After reviewing the previous cases involving claims of educational malpractice, the Alaska Supreme Court agreed with the decisions of the New York and California courts by making a timely observation:

> In particular we think that the remedy of money damages is inappropriate as a remedy for one who has been a victim of errors made during his or her education. The level of success which might have been achieved had the mistake not been made will, we believe, be necessarily incapable of assessment, rendering legal cause an imponderable which is beyond the ability of courts to deal with in a reasoned way.

The court made it clear that, while it did not favor damage suits for educational malpractice cases, it felt that parents who believe that their children have been placed or classified inappropriately do have recourse. It believed that a parent in such a situation can request:

> an independent examination and evaluation of the child, and for a hearing before a hearing officer in the event of a substantial discrepancy. Further, that section (AS 14.30.191 (C)) provides that, the proceedings so conducted are subject to the Administrative Procedure Act, which in turn expressly provides for judicial review.

The Alaska Supreme Court commented that such procedures for solving classification and placement disputes are best settled through provisions above rather than tort action for damages. It felt that administrative and judicial review handled promptly could correct previous errors, in time to enable a student to attain an appropriate education.

The court concluded: "Money damages, on the other hand, are a poor, and only tenuously related, substitute for a proper education."

§ 4.2(D). It Is Time to Meet the "Exploitation" Challenge.

A star fullback, who transferred from a large university known for its nationally ranked football team, was dismayed when he learned that he had failed all his courses. He indignantly questioned the commitment of the university to football and its desire to be a gridiron power, since a former university had given him passing grades in every course although he never attended class.

That was the 1940's, however, when many entrance requirements, transfer rules and academic standards were relaxed because of World War II. Athletes in the 1940's seldom questioned courses that were available to them, in order to maintain athletic eligibility. It is a whole new ball game today, as a number of athletes challenge their coaches and institutions in court, seeking damage awards in the millions.

Educational exploitation and malpractice lawsuits are an ever-increasing threat to the education profession. Although no appellate court has awarded damages to the plaintiffs, this fact has not prevented the increase in such litigation. As the court noted in *Peter W. v. San Francisco Unified School District,* 131 Cal. Rptr. 854 (Cal. App. 1976): "To hold them to an actionable duty of care, in the discharge of their academic functions, would expose them to the tort claims — real or imagined — of disaffected students and parents in countless numbers."

§ 4.2(E). Conclusion.

Many courts predict that if plaintiffs win these decisions, the burden in both time and money will be beyond calculation. Legal experts, however, predict that if "proximate cause" can be established in these cases, the plaintiffs will win and the education profession will be changed immeasurably.

Numerous legal experts predict the demise of sports as we know them if sports-related litigation continues with its enormous awards to plaintiffs. There are also those who take the opposite side of the controversy and contend that sports-related litigation — or the threat of it — has made sports safer than ever. They point out that the rights of athletes are protected as never before.

The new litigation is threatening athletics and the education profession in a serious way; the solution may lie somewhere between the two extremes. The threat of litigation may cause educators to correct many of the existing abuses that border on unfair educational exploitation. With the majority of programs educationally sound, such litigation may persuade others to join the ranks with positive programs.

At any rate, the education profession and athletics itself face a serious dilemma, and the time has come to recognize it and meet its challenge.

---

§ 4.3. The Athlete With Disabilities.

By Julian V. Stein

Three pieces of legislation enacted in the mid-1970's are important to every person with a disability who is engaged in a sports program. They are:

— The Education for All Handicapped Children Act (Public Law 94-142).
— Section 504 of the Rehabilitation Act (Public Law 93-112).
— Amateur Sports Act (Public Law 95-606).

The Education for All Handicapped Children Act guarantees a free appropriate public education for every child with a disability. In addition to physical education, extracurricular activities, including interscholastic sport, must be available to all students with disabilities up to and including 21 years of age. Some states have extended the age limit to 25.

Further than this, the Rehabilitation Act prohibits discrimination against any individual with a disability in any program sponsored by a recipient of federal funds.

The Amateur Sports Act placed responsibility for all United States participation in international sport competition on one organization. The Act includes participation in sport for individuals with disabilities and gives the United States Olympic Committee the responsibility for coordinating the activities.

The United States Olympic Committee has established the Committee on Sports for the Disabled, which includes two representatives from each of several associations including those for the blind and for the deaf athletes, for amputees and for the cerebral palsied.

One of each of these organizational representatives must be an athlete. By definition of the United States Olympic Committee, an athlete is an individual who has competed in sport within the last ten years. In this way, athletes with disabilities serve as their own advocates at the decision- and policy-making level.

These legislative mandates ensure equal opportunities in sports programs for participants of all ages, provide opportunities for special programs for individuals who are unable to participate in regular sports programs and explore ways to organize sports activities so as to integrate them in regular sport programs including both summer and winter olympic games.

As an example of achievements of these legal committees, a swimmer born with only one hand, whose right arm ends just below the elbow, finished second in an open 100-meter breaststroke race in Australia. He was disqualified because the rules state that a swimmer must simultaneously touch the wall at the end of the race with both hands. This rule is now abolished. Interpretations and applications of rules now emphasize equal opportunities, individual needs and nondiscrimination for all, both able-bodied and disabled.

§ 4.3(A). Legalized Discrimination.

Prior to legislation of the 1970's, both governance and sports rules traditionally discriminated against individuals with disabilities. For example:

— Many mentally retarded and learning disabled students could not participate in interscholastic activities, including sport, because scholastic eligibility rules required them to pass a number of class units or obtain a set number of Carnegie units. Since many of these students were in self-contained special education classes or resource programs, which were not organized or evaluated in terms of class or Carnegie units, it was impossible to meet eligibility requirements.
— While some states permitted students in special education classes to participate in any interscholastic activity except sport, other states permitted special education students to participate in sport at any level except at the varsity level.
— Individuals with artificial limbs were prohibited from participation in interscholastic football, soccer and wrestling.
— Individuals without vision could not participate in distance events in cross country, road races or track because rules prohibited assistance to runners in these events.
— Individuals with hearing impairments had been placed at disadvantages in sports such as track and swimming because no accommodations were made regarding starting these events.

Because of the three pieces of legislation enacted in the 1970's, changes have been made to accommodate athletes with disabilities. For example, rules in interscholastic football, soccer and wrestling now permit individuals with prosthetic devices to compete. In football and soccer, prosthetic devices must be approved by respective state high school athletic or activity associations. In wrestling, an individual who weighs in with a prosthetic device must compete using the device.

Provisions have also been made whereby a blind runner can receive various kinds of assistance from a partner, e.g, holding hands, touching elbows, talking with each other or using a short rope held by each runner.

§ 4.3(B). Problems Confronting Individuals With Disabilities.

Certain problems continue to frustrate individuals with disabilities despite recent legislation such as the Education for All Handicapped Children Act and the Rehabilitation Act. One problem is lack of understanding of the legislation:

It is essential, therefore, to examine the educational and legal issues associated with legislation as it applies to disabled individuals in the public schools, colleges and universities so that decision makers can obtain appropriate information to facilitate decisions and policies that are both educationally and legally sound.

Although § 504 of the Rehabilitation Act was in force, Columbia University denied participation in intercollegiate football to Joseph Wright because he had sight in only one eye. In *Wright v. Columbia University,* 520 F. Supp. 789 (E.D. Pa. 1981), Wright sued the university and was permitted by the court to go out for the football team.

Another example of ignorance of the law or a disregard for it took place in New Jersey. A high school student was denied the opportunity to participate in the wrestling program because he had only one kidney. After graduation from high school, the individual, in *Poole v. South Plainfield Board of Education,* 490 F. Supp. 948 (D.N.J. 1980), sued for damages under § 504 of the Rehabilitation Act. The New Jersey court found that the school's decision to prohibit participation in the wrestling program violated § 504 regulations.

Similar inconsistencies, misinterpretations and misapplications have been observed at both regional and national levels. In games of the National Wheelchair Athletic Association (N.W.A.A.) and the National Association of Sports for Cerebral Palsy (N.A.S.C.P.), competitors in wheelchair track events have been automatically disqualified for going out of their lanes. To be disqualified, an individual must gain an advantage or interfere with another competitor. The rules of N.W.A.A. and N.A.S.C.P. specify that the referee *may* disqualify an athlete who goes out of his or her lane. Consistency of rule interpretations and application is important and necessary in special sport programs.

§ 4.3(C). Progress in Sport for the Disabled.

Much progress has been made regarding sports participation for the disabled. Special sports associations have been established in some states for athletes with disabilities.

Few individuals or teams with athletes with disabilities are of school age or affiliated with schools or state high school athletic or activity associations. Many special sports groups therefore sponsor competitive activities on local, state, regional, national and international levels.

Adaptations of decathlon scoring have been used successfully to break down competitive barriers. For example, each competitor can be scored against a point system based on performances by individuals with similar conditions and classifications. This method enables athletes with different disabilities and both sexes to compete against each other. It also enables able-bodied and disabled athletes to compete on an equitable basis. This system has been used successfully by individuals with various degrees and levels of spinal cord injuries.

Several universities in the United States have recognized competition in wheelchair basketball or track and field as official teams of the university.

Two major steps toward the integration of athletes into regular and special sports programs were accomplished in 1984 during the Winter Olympics in Sarajevo, Yugoslavia and the Summer Olympics in Los Angeles, California. Thirty disabled skiers were selected on the basis of their performances during the 1984 Winter Games for the Disabled in Innsbruck, Austria and invited to participate in a giant downhill slalom race at the regular Winter Olympics in Sarajevo. In Los Angeles, two wheelchair track races were included as official exhibition events, complete with medals, an 800 meter wheelchair race for women and a 1500 meter wheelchair race for men. The International Olympic Committee has agreed to a full exhibition tournament for athletes with disabilities in the 1988 Olympic Games in Seoul, Korea.

Similar approaches for athletes with disabilities have been included in prestigious events in Canada for the past ten years. Disabled athletes compete in prestigious sport meets involving able-bodied athletes at subprovincial and provincial levels.

During the 1984 Texas Southern Relays in Houston, Texas, eight wheelchair athletes competed in 400 meter and 800 meter races. The Orange Bowl in Miami, Florida includes a wheelchair section for children in the Junior Orange Bowl Tournaments. Most marathons conducted in the United States now permit and encourage participation by athletes with disabilities.

Such events are becoming widespread and continue to receive official sanctions from regular and special sports governance organizations.

§ 4.3(D). A Look to the Future.

Sports teams representing regular or special schools must be offered programs of the same high quality as similar teams of able-bodied athletes. Such things as bus transportation to and from practice must be provided for students with disabilities, just as for the able-bodied. Without special transportation, most students with disabilities cannot participate in interscholastic sports programs. Qualified coaches and all other elements of interscholastic programs such as uniforms, equipment and supplies must be provided to ensure equal opportunities for individuals and teams consisting of athletes with disabilities.

Mutual understanding among governing groups must result in more opportunities for the student with disabilities. Coordination and cooperation among governing groups are necessary to ensure sports competition for all participants, able-bodied and disabled.

Attention must be given to sports rules to ensure equal opportunities for athletes with disabilities. Rules should be adopted that accommodate the starting of track and swimming events for deaf athletes.

Classification systems based on functional abilities of individuals rather than medical diagnosis or categorical conditions should be considered. Classification based on functional abilities has the potential to break down competitive barriers among the individual with disabilities and the nondisabled.

Changes are needed to improve rules related to use of prosthetic devices in various sports. Consideration should be given to materials of which prosthetic devices are made and not their location. Rule makers need to address these problems to ensure that the rules do not penalize the disabled as well as the able-bodied.

Organizations that train coaches should encourage and actively seek individuals with disabilities for coaching positions. Individuals with disabilities who are otherwise qualified cannot be denied the opportunity to participate in personnel preparation programs or denied coaching positions because of such conditions.

§ 4.3(E). Conclusion.

Performances based on individual ability, preparation and application are keys to success in the world of sport. Individuals in sport should be judged by what is accomplished.

Too often, individuals responsible for making decisions and governing sports programs continue to discriminate against individuals with disabilities. Discriminatory practices are often the rule rather than the exception. Legal mandates have caused individuals and organizations in sports programs to look closely at all aspects of their programs. While equal opportunities in sport are becoming more available, much remains to be done so that a sport for every person and a person for every sport becomes a reality.

---

§ 4.4. The College Participant: Student Athlete or Paid Professional?

By David K. Stotlar

Standing on the floor of the Nebraska legislature, dressed in a football helmet, jersey #71 and with a football under his arm, Senator Ernie Chambers introduced a bill (L.B. 211, 88th Legislature, 1st Sess., Neb., Feb. 13, 1983) that could dramatically change college athletics.

Chambers feels that college football players should be paid for their participation. He indicated that college football is not sport, it is business, and players contribute to the business of the university by performing "personal work." The only difference noted between a professional athlete's responsibilities and those of a college player is that the professional does not have to go to class.

This issue is receiving considerable attention with, a variety of coaches favoring the payment of college players, and other authorities feel that they are already paid. Exactly what is this thing called an "athletic scholarship"?

Even the most casual reader of the sports page in our nation's newspapers is aware of the significant role athletic scholarships play in amateur sport throughout the United States. According to E.J. Shea and E.E. Wieman in *Administrative Policies for Intercollegiate Athletics,* "the term scholarship has been applied loosely when associated with students who are also athletes and generally refers to financial aid awarded primarily for athletic prowess."

Since the proliferation of the practice of granting athletic scholarships in the early 1950's, there has been continuing controversy on the matter. Many authorities feel that the athletic scholarship should be eliminated as a source of educational assistance and that athletes should receive financial aid on the same basis and through the same sources as all other students attending the institution.

There are also authorities who believe that athletics violate the amateur status of college and university athletes and should therefore be eliminated. According to James Michener, author of *Sport In America,* Paul "Bear" Bryant, the former football coach at the University of Alabama, said that at the level of competition on which our major universities participate, the student athlete is no longer a student first and an athlete second, but quite the opposite.

§ 4.4(A). Athletic Scholarship Differs From Other Financial Aid.

Features which make the athletic scholarship different from other types of financial aid are: (1) the amount of aid is not dependent on need; (2) the scholarship may be withdrawn for nonacademic reasons; and (3) the recipients need no special academic qualifications (in most cases they must meet only minimum admission standards). In other words, "an athletic scholarship is payment for athletic performance."

In relation to the athletic scholarship, there is one major disagreement between the National Collegiate Athletic Association (NCAA) and the International Olympic Committee (I.O.C.) which states in its regulations that scholarships are permitted but that they must be "dependent upon the fulfillment of scholastic obligations and not athletic prowess." The NCAA, however, does permit the use of athletic ability as a determining factor in the granting of scholarship aid.

The I.O.C. states: "Individuals subsidized by governments, educational institutions, or business concerns because of their athletic ability, are not amateurs." Although this has been loosely applied and there has been considerable discussion surrounding the opening of the Olympics to professionals, the regulation does exist. If the athletic scholarship continues to be a part of our institutions of higher education, it will undoubtedly be increasingly affected by the litigation which has already begun to plague our colleges and universities.

In reviewing possible approaches to litigation involving the NCAA, one must examine the "doctrine of private associations," a term which describes any group of individuals who join together in a formalized structure to forward common purposes. In dealing with these associations, the courts have been guided by the principle that private associations need freedom from external intervention to achieve their purposes. Therefore, courts have been reluctant to hear disputes where individuals of an association claim to have been injured by the action of the association.

The courts usually refrain from intervening in disputes between the NCAA and its members or individual athletes, on condition that the association is private in nature and that the dispute is internal. The opposition, as a rule, argues that the NCAA is not a private organization because it is involved with public functions. This is supported by the contention that "when private individuals or groups are endowed by the state with powers or functions which are governmental in nature, they become agencies of the state."

The NCAA would clearly fall into this agreement because many members of the Association are public colleges and universities that pay membership fees from public funds, and since many of the activities of the Association take place in public facilities, the NCAA performs a state function. As an argument on the second stipulation, if it is put forward that the athlete himself is not a member of the Association, and therefore has none of the rights and privileges of the NCAA, it would therefore follow that the dispute would not be internal.

With these discrepancies in mind, the courts have adjudicated cases involving the NCAA and individual athletes. In these cases the primary motivation was the protection of the athletes' constitutional rights and the important interests of the athletes in participation in intercollegiate athletics. But the interest of the majority of the college athletes has been in the funding of their education, and that reason must not be overlooked, since it amounts to a property interest and should receive judicial protection. In short, if the two facts (of the state or public function and a property interest) can be shown to exist, then the rights of the athletes fall under the protection of the fourteenth amendment to the United States Constitution.

§ 4.4(B). Contractual Relationship of Athletic Scholarship.

With regard to the interpretation of the athletic scholarship, it has been said that a contractual relationship may exist. According to H. M. Cross, in an article published in *Law and Contemporary Problems* (1973) entitled "The College Athlete and the Law": "The rationale behind this approach is that college athletes contract by scholarship agreement to perform a job" and, as stated by J. L. Davis, in an article in 49 Oregon Law Review (1970) entitled "The Authority of a College Coach: A Legal Analysis," although an institution may grant financial aid to a student athlete in expectation of participation in intercollegiate athletics, it would not "condition the receipt of aid on participation." As discussed by Herb and Thomas Appenzeller in their book *Sports and the Courts,* there may be situations, however, when the student athlete's status would be that of an employee if "athletic service is exchanged for financial aid."

One argument contends that the scholarship athlete is expected to engage in almost daily practices or forfeit his financial aid, and this, it is said, clearly constitutes an employee status. The opposing argument states that employee status can exist only when the consideration is based on specific performance and when a binding contract exists. Two major cases have illustrated this point.

In February, 1967 Gregg Taylor and his father submitted an application to Wake Forest University for an Atlantic Coast Conference football grant-in-aid. Wake Forest is a member of the conference, and the conference is an allied member of the National Collegiate Athletic Association.

Taylor entered the university in the fall and participated in football. At the end of the first semester his grade point average was 1.60. The university required a 1.35 grade average. In order to try to improve his grades, Taylor did not report to spring practice. At the end of the second semester his average was above 1.9, and when he finished the third semester he had achieved 2.4. Taylor did not return to the football program while completing his education at the university.

In May of 1969, the Faculty Athletic Committee of Wake Forest University called Taylor for a hearing concerning the termination of his grant-in-aid. At the time of the agreement between Taylor and the university, the Association had stated that any such gradation or cancellation of aid is permissible only if: (1) such action is taken by the regular disciplinary or scholarship awards authorities of the institution, (2) the student had an opportunity for a hearing and (3) the action is based on institutional policy applicable to the general student body.

After graduation from Wake Forest University in 1971, in *Taylor v. Wake Forest University*, 191 S.E.2d 379 (N.C. App. 1972), Taylor sued the university for expenses incurred after the termination of his grant-in-aid. He was attempting to recover only the educational expenses involved in the completion of his education at Wake Forest. He argued that he had maintained his eligibility for the scholarship and that its withdrawal was a violation of the contract which existed between himself and Wake Forest University.

Judge Robert Campbell stated that the court did not agree with the position taken by the plaintiffs. The scholarship application filed by Gregg Taylor provided: "I agree to maintain eligibility for intercollegiate athletics under both Conference and Institutional rules. Training rules for intercollegiate athletics are considered rules of the Institution, and I agree to abide by them." Both Gregg Taylor and his father knew that the application was for a "football grant-in-aid or a scholarship," and that the scholarship was "awarded for academic and athletic achievement." It would be a strained construction of the contract that would enable the plaintiffs to determine the "reasonable academic progress" of Gregg Taylor. Gregg Taylor, in consideration of the scholarship award, agreed to maintain his athletic eligibility both physically and scholastically. As long as his grade average equaled or exceeded the requirements of Wake Forest, he was maintaining his scholastic eligibility for athletics. Participation in and attendance at practice were required to maintain his physical eligibility. When he refused to do so in the absence of any injury or reason other than his intention to devote more time to his studies, he was not complying with his contractual obligations.

The record disclosed that Wake Forest fully complied with its agreement and that Gregg Taylor failed to do so. There was no "genuine issue as to any material fact," and summary judgment in favor of the defendant was proper.

In another case involving an athletic scholarship, Mark Begley attempted to recover his educational expenses from Mercer University after it was discovered that the basketball scholarship had been awarded as a result of incorrect assumptions.

Begley was advised by an assistant basketball coach at Mercer University that his transcript from high school reported his grade point average as 2.9 and that such a GPA plus the score of 760 which Begley had attained on a scholastic aptitude test were sufficient to render him eligible for the scholarship or grant-in-aid involved. However, on July 17, 1972 it was discovered by admissions officers of Mercer that the high school based its grade point average on a maximum of 8.0 instead of the usual 4.0 system. This obviously reduced by one half Begley's previously considered high school grade point average. In a letter of August 2, 1972 the scholarship offer was withdrawn.

It was the obvious intention of Mercer University to extend financial aid to Begley in the stipulated amount for his use in working toward the completion of an undergraduate degree in exchange for his participation in its basketball program, provided that he abide by its regulations, keep its training rules, maintain satisfactory process toward graduation and a minimum GPA of 1.6 and abide by all rules and regulations of the NCAA. It was the obvious intention of Begley to participate in Mercer's basketball program, to abide by Mercer's regulations, to keep its training rules, to maintain satisfactory progress toward graduation and a minimum average of 1.6 and to abide by rules and regulations of the NCAA in exchange for the aforementioned financial aid toward his completion of an undergraduate degree.

Begley could not fulfill the requirements of the contract (abiding by NCAA regulations); therefore, on the principle that where one party is unable to perform his part of the contract, he cannot be entitled to the performance of the contract by the other party, the motion of the defendant was sustained and the plaintiff was denied all relief in *Begley v. Corporation of Mercer University,* 367 F. Supp. 908 (E.D. Tenn. 1973).

The basic issue concerns the interpretation of an athletic scholarship as a contract. In *Taylor,* although the court ruled in favor of the defendant, the scholarship was established as a contract since it contained an offer, an acceptance and consideration. Taylor had signed an agreement in which he had agreed to maintain his eligibility (which the court said included physically participating in practice). When he failed to fulfill the conditions of that agreement (or contract), such agreement would have been broken by him; therefore, he would not be allowed to recover expenses incurred due to the failure of the institution to fulfill its part of the contract. The interpretation of the scholarship as contract was not of paramount importance to the case. (The court could have reached the same conclusion if it had viewed the scholarship as an educational grant with conditions which Taylor had failed to fulfill.) But viewing the scholarship as a contract became a precedent, as proven by the cases which followed.

The most rigid interpretation of the scholarship-as-a-contract concept came in *Begley.* The basis for the court's denial of damages was the fact that Begley was unable to perform his role in the contract and that, as a result, when one party could not perform, the contract became void. As a result of this decision and others that involved it, a historical base and solid precedents were established for the scholarship as a contract.

The same rationale has surfaced in a recent case concerning the withdrawal of a scholarship offer. Jeff Fishel sued Northeast Missouri State University for breach of contract when a promised scholarship for football was not granted. According to N. Yance in an article published in the February 1, 1984 issue of Chronicle of Higher Education entitled "Athlete Wins Lawsuit Against University That Withdrew Its Scholarship Offer," in its award to the plaintiff of $8600, the court indicated that in the future "college coaches should be cautious in making offers of sports scholarships."

Superficially, these rulings placed the student athlete in the position of being able to hold the institution to the contract only if he maintained his eligibility. The courts did not consider the possibility of a university preventing a student from leaving the institution. This problem had yet to surface, but the complications could be severe. If an institution contracted with a student athlete for his athletic abilities in exchange for financial assistance, and if the student subsequently decided not to attend the institution or withdrew from it, the institution could then file suit for breach of contract and ask for damages as a result of the athlete's absence from the team. This ability on the part of the institution to keep a student from leaving would further prevent the student athlete from being considered as a part of the "normal" student body.

Following the reasoning that a contractual relationship between an athlete and an institution can result in an employee status for the student-athlete, several cases have attempted to gain relief for injured athletes under workers' compensation legislation.

§ 4.4(C). Workers' Compensation.

In an early case involving workers' compensation, *University of Denver v. Nemeth,* 257 P.2d 423 (Cal. 1953), Ernest Nemeth alleged that he was an employee of the University of Denver, claiming compensation benefits arising from an accidental injury which, as the evidence shows, he suffered while playing football on the University of Denver grounds. Nemeth was a student regularly enrolled in the college of business administration of the university. In April, 1950, while engaging in spring football practice, Nemeth suffered an injury to his back which prevented his participation in further football practices. At the time, he was receiving $50 a month from the University of Denver for certain work in and about the campus tennis courts. The college deducted $10 a month from this amount in payment of three meals a day that Nemeth ate at the student cafeteria.

In lieu of cash payment for rental of a room on the campus, Nemeth serviced the furnace and cleaned the sidewalks of these premises. Nemeth maintained that he was employed to play football at the university and that his injury arose out of and in the course of that employment. It was at this point that the university brought suit in order to prevent the award of damages by the Industrial Commission.

A student who augments the funds necessary for his maintenance while attending the university may be considered to be an employee and therefore, irrespective of the amount of his earnings, subject to and entitled to the benefits of the workers' compensation law. When a stipulated monthly amount is paid for a particular service rendered by a student, it cannot be said that the University is merely "assisting" the student to obtain an education or that the student, if injured in the course of his employment, cannot be allowed the benefits of the compensation law. The defendant, therefore, may recover damages due to his injury as an employee of the university.

Edward G. Van Horn was a member of California State Polytechnic College's football team. He was killed in a plane crash while returning from a regularly scheduled football game in Ohio. In *Van Horn v. Industrial Accident Commission,* 33 Cal. Rptr. 169 (Cal. Dist. App. 1963), Van Horn's wife sought relief and death benefits through the workers' compensation statutes of California. The sole question was whether or not the defendant was an employee of the college within the meaning of the Workers' Compensation Act.

It cannot be said as a matter of law that every student who receives an "athletic scholarship" and plays on the school athletic team is an employee of the school. To do so would thrust upon such a student an employee status to which he has never consented and deprive him of the valuable right to sue for damages. Only when the evidence establishes a contract of employment is the student an employee. The evidence did not establish a contract of hire-to-play-football and consequently did not support a finding of an employee-employer relationship.

A college football player at Fort Lewis A. & M. College received a head injury during the opening play of a football game. This injury later resulted in the player's death. This player had been employed as a service station attendant before he was asked to join the football team, but the hours when he was working at his job would have prevented his practicing with the team, so he asked the coach whether employment could be found for him at a different time. The coach arranged for the athlete to be offered a job on campus with hours that would not conflict with football practice. The player was also provided with an athletic scholarship in the form of a tuition waiver. After his death, the player's widow filed suit, in *State Compensation Insurance Fund v. Industrial Commission*, 314 P.2d 288 (Colo. 1957), for death benefits under the workers' compensation laws of the state.

The court denied benefits to the widow on the grounds that his campus employment was not dependent upon his participation in the college's athletic program. It also ruled that, since the student was previously enrolled in the college, the arrangements made by the coach did not constitute an inducement; therefore no employee relationship could have resulted.

Fred Rensing was a varsity football player who injured his neck while working on punt coverage. Rensing made a "very hard hit" on the receiver and was rendered a quadriplegic through a fractured dislocation of the cervical spine. At the time of the injury Rensing and the university had entered into a financial aid agreement. This agreement provided that in exchange for participation in football, Rensing would receive "free tuition, room, board, laboratory fees, a book allowance, tutoring, and a limited number of football tickets." The agreement provided that in the event of an injury during supervised play, which would make it medically inadvisable to continue to participate, the aid would continue. It was also noted that if such an event were to occur, the university could ask him to "assist in the conduct of the athletic program within the limits of physical capabilities." Rensing, claiming he was an employee of the university, had filed a claim with the Industrial Board under the Workers' Compensation Act, and appealed its denial of benefits.

After a transfer from the court of appeals of Indiana, the supreme court, in *Rensing v. Indiana State University Board of Trustees*, 444 N.E.2d 1170 (Ind. 1983), entered judgment in favor of the defendant university, affirming the findings of the Industrial Board. The primary basis for the finding was an examination of "intent." Under the workers' compensation statute, "employee" was defined as "every person, including a minor, in the service of another, under any contract of hire . . . except one whose employment is . . . not in the usual course of trade, business, occupation, or profession of the employee." The court reasoned that it was not the intent of either Rensing or the university to enter into a contract for hire, because to do so for pay would violate NCAA regulations. Therefore, lacking that intent, no contract existed, which precludes recovery under workers' compensation.

Workers' compensation statutes were established to protect employees from job-related injuries which would affect their employment. The statutes indicate that injuries are compensable when they arise out of and occur during employment; therefore, in applying this principle to athletics, an athlete who was found to be an employee of the university and who was injured on the job (athletics) should be entitled to the benefits of workers' compensation. A reexamination of the NCAA regulations shows that the award of athletically related financial aid cannot be made for a period longer than one year. Therefore, if an athlete was injured in the athletic program, the athlete's scholarship could not be renewed for the remainder of his career. Although most colleges and universities do not cancel scholarships of injured athletes, the enforcement of the practice of withdrawing financial aid would not be without a legal base.

Precisely this point was raised in *Coleman v. Western Michigan University*, 336 N.W.2d 224 (Mich. App. 1983). Although similar to the *Rensing* case, in that the court denied recovery under workers' compensation, the facts of the case differed. After his injury which precluded his participation in football, Coleman's scholarship was reduced.

The court found in *Van Horn* that the payments which had been termed an "athletic scholarship" were, in fact, payment for participation in athletics. The contractual relationship and the employee status were substantiated by the fact that the compensation which Van Horn received was not required to be used for educational expenses. The court did report that not all athletes who received a scholarship would have an employee status, but that such a status was possible.

In general, an employee status would be found only when the payment to the athlete was directly related to his performance as an athlete. The provision of a tuition waiver would not be as likely to mean an employee relationship as would the payment of cash, the use of which was not restricted by the institution.

In the case *State Compensation Insurance Fund v. Industrial Commission*, 314 P.2d 288 (Colo. 1957), the relationship was more typical. Where the student athlete was the recipient of an athletic scholarship and also worked on campus, it was ruled that the work had no relation to either the granting of the scholarship or to the athletic activities of the student athlete. The student athlete did enjoy an employee status with the university, but the injury did not occur as a result of the job which gave him that status.

Most workers' compensation laws demand that two criteria be met by a person before benefits can be recovered: "First, he must qualify as an 'employee' and second, he must suffer a 'personal injury by an accident arising out of and in course of employment.'"

The most important question is the determination of the employee status. (This discussion will concern only the typical athletic scholarship and not associated work-study relationships.)

Because workers' compensation status differs in different states, there cannot be one set of standards which apply to all of them. Four factors are used in recognizing a contract for hire with its resultant employee-employer relationship: (1) the employer's right to control the employee's duties, (2) the employer's right to fire or discipline the employee, (3) the payment of wages to the employee on which the employee is dependent for daily living and (4) when the work of the employee is an integral part of the employer's business. *Askew v. Macomber,* 247 N.W.2d 288 (Mich. 1976).

Regarding the first of these, a university operating under the bylaws of the NCAA is required to regulate and control the student athlete's employment during the season, any contractual relationships with other sport-related enterprises, such as advertising and professional teams, and other eligibility requirements.

Regarding the second factor, the NCAA's guidelines operate in reducing or changing the scholarship during its period of award.

For the third factor, the payment may be anything of value, not necessarily money. Also, since the NCAA prohibits a student from working during the year (or reduces the aid proportionately), the athlete must rely on the scholarship for his living expenses. Although Rensing acknowledged that he had not considered his scholarship as pay, that point is arguable.

In light of the earlier court's decision granting Rensing benefits, Mark Hemphill of Southern Illinois University, Carbondale, filed a similar suit, contending that he "viewed himself more as an employee than as a student."

The fourth factor, which concerns the "integral part" of the employer's business has yet to prevail in court. The courts have failed to rule that athletics fall within the scope of "integral part" of the employer's business. The *Rensing* court did, however, state that "Rensing's participation in football may well have benefited the University in a general way." On the other hand, the legislation introduced in Nebraska states that "maintaining a winning football team is an important aspect of the university's overall business or occupation as an institution."

§ 4.4(D). Taxation of Athletic Scholarship.

If an employee status can be demonstrated, what effect will this have on the taxation of the scholarship? In the area of taxation of athletic scholarships, there is an analogy to teaching assistantships. The tax court has had little trouble in holding that teaching assistants must pay taxes on the monies which they receive for their educational expenses. Similarly, medical interns cannot avoid taxation on the stipends received during their internships. This situation is not dissimilar to that of the scholarship athlete.

The Internal Revenue Board states that an athletic scholarship is not taxable so long as it does not "exceed expenses for tuition, fees, room, board, and necessary supplies, awarded to the students by a university that expects, but does not require the student to participate in a particular sport."

Two important cases have been litigated in this area. James Heidel was a football player at the University of Mississippi; after completing his eligibility, he signed a professional football contract with the St. Louis Cardinals, which earned him a large bonus. Then, because he wanted to follow the income averaging rules so as to reduce his federal income tax liability, he maintained that the averaging rules were applicable because of the athletic scholarship he had received in college-constituted support.

But Heidel could not have it both ways. If he accepted the premise that the grant-in-aid was given him as support in return for his services as a football player, then the money must be considered as income. On the other hand, if the grant-in-aid was to qualify as a scholarship and therefore not considered as income, it must have been furnished by the university solely as a "no strings" education grant.

The court, in *Heidel v. Internal Revenue Service,* 56 T.C. 95 (1971), therefore concluded that since Heidel had not provided at least 50% of his support, he was not eligible for income averaging. The petition was denied.

In another case, *Frost v. Internal Revenue Service,* 61 T.C. 488 (1973), William Frost received an athletic scholarship to play baseball at the University of California at Berkeley. At the end of his senior year, he was drafted, and signed a professional baseball contract with the San Francisco Giants. Frost received a large cash bonus for signing, and attempted to reduce his federal income tax by applying the income averaging rules of the IRS.

Although the athletic scholarship is based on athletic ability and the promise to participate, the purpose of the funds is to defray educational expenses, not for playing a specified sport. Therefore, in this particular case the funds cannot be considered as payment for employment, and the petition was denied.

This issue of the athletic scholarship as a contract is an important one. The courts have consistently ruled that the athletic scholarship is indeed a contract, as distinct from an educational grant. A contract requires an offer, an acceptance and considered agreement. The athletic scholarship meets these requirements.

But, as the courts have applied contract law, they have placed considerable emphasis on the offer and acceptance and less on the consideration. The plaintiffs, on the other hand, have stressed the consideration aspect so as to gain due process protection when a scholarship is in dispute — when, for example, the scholarship was threatened by revocation or was denied.

A situation could occur in which a coach decides to keep an athlete from playing in a game for disciplinary reasons. If the game were nationally televised, the athlete could file suit against the coach on the basis of a denied property interest. The fact that the courts have ruled that participation in itself is not a property right is therefore extremely important.

In the matter of cancellation and nonrenewal of a contract, contract law has made a distinction between them which has not been thoroughly understood by student athletes. Nor do coaches seem to have understood the principle of nonrenewal. The experienced coach realizes that not every player awarded a scholarship will become a star, and, if necessary, the scholarship or "contract" will not be renewed.

The athlete, on the other hand, thinks only of success and believes that as long as he tries his best the scholarship will remain. This has resulted in a very real problem. If the player's scholarship is not renewed, was the scholarship a grant or a loan?

Coaches can use — and often have used — the nonrenewal of the scholarship as a threat to get a better performance from the players, and the court could use this fact to point up a "play for pay" situation. In this contractual relationship, the institution is required to provide the aid for the period of the award if the athlete has maintained both physical and academic eligibility, and the athlete is required to maintain eligibility in order to keep the award from being cancelled.

The question of whether the income received from the scholarship gives the athlete an employee status is not so clearly answered by the courts. In some cases, the NCAA clearly puts the student athlete in the same category as other members of the student body, so that he cannot be considered as an employee. But the courts have also found that it is possible to establish an employee relationship in the guise of athletically related financial aid. And, in some other cases the court was farsighted enough to state that not all athletic scholarships create such a relationship.

There remains the question of taxation on the income received by athletes with scholarships. In answer, the Internal Revenue Code has said that these funds are taxable. The Internal Revenue Service has said nothing. The United States tax courts have said that the funds are not taxable. In this instance we must follow the tax court.

§ 4.4(E). Conclusion.

The following guidelines may help both parties:

1. The athletic scholarship is awarded as an educational grant. The conditions of receiving and maintaining the grant are those set forth by the constitution and bylaws of the NCAA on the maintenance of eligibility of the student athlete, which is measured by both academic standing as evaluated by the institution and by physical condition as judged by performance at practice sessions.
2. An athletic scholarship is given to assist a regular member of the student body with the expenses of an education in return for participation in the athletic program. It does not establish an employee-employer relationship between student and institution.
3. Any aid administered through the financial aid office (which is not an athletically related educational grant) should be so identified, and it entitles the recipient to the same benefits and protections as the regular student body receives.
4. The gradation and cancellation of the athletic scholarship is regulated by the rules of the NCAA only during the period of the award. The renewal or nonrenewal of the scholarship award is therefore the responsibility of the head coach of the specific sport. In the event of nonrenewal, a written statement must accompany the notification and is retained in the athletic director's file. This information is available to the student athlete in case of an official hearing.
5. When a scholarship is revoked for whatever reason, the student athlete must be given the opportunity for a hearing. The hearing includes a written notice of the action, with specific time and place, and a presentation of statements from both parties. Formal hearings allowing cross-examination of witnesses and the right to legal counsel may be advisable.

6. The "Rights of the Scholarship Athlete" are read to each potential student athlete prior to signing either a National Letter of Intent or a financial aid agreement (the specifics of which can be found under guidelines for the scholarship which follow).

SAMPLE FINANCIAL AID AGREEMENT

Name _____   Sport _____

This agreement is an acknowledgement of the receipt of a conditional educational grant from the department of athletics. The conditions of this agreement are that I maintain eligibility as outlined by the Constitution and Bylaws of the NCAA.

I understand that this grant can be cancelled for the following reasons:

A. If I render myself ineligible for competition.

B. If I file a fraudulent application for admission or letter of intent.

C. If I am involved in serious misconduct which warrants disciplinary action by the institution.

Cancellation shall mean the termination of the grant during the period of its award.

I understand that the award of the educational grant is for a period of one year initially and for a maximum of one year thereafter. The minimum period of award (after the initial year) may be from term to term.

I understand that the option of renewing the scholarship following each period of award shall be at the discretion of the institution. The reasons for nonrenewal may include:

A. Voluntary withdrawal from participation in the sport for which the grant was awarded.

B. The evaluation of my athletic ability and potential to contribute to the success of the team.

C. My inability to participate because of an injury (the athletic department may indicate that its general policy is to extend the grant for athletes who are injured, but they are not legally bound to that extension).

I understand that I am expected to participate in athletics as a condition of this grant, but that such participation is not required. This stipulation affirms the scholarship as an educational grant and subsequently does not affect my status as an amateur athlete, assures that the grant is not taxable by the Internal Revenue Service, and voids any employee relationship which might be construed between myself and the institution.

I understand that my financial aid for this term (Fall ____ Winter ____ Spring ____) 19 ____ is accepted in the following amounts:

Tuition: $ _____   Board and Room: $ _____

Books (on loan): $ _____   Non-Athletically

Related Work: $ _____

In addition to accepting the conditional education grant, I agree to report campus and off-campus employment to the Director of Athletics.

_____   _____

Date   Athlete

_____   _____

Coach Administering   Director, Financial Aid
Agreement

---

§ 4.5. The Athletic Scholarship as Contractual Basis for a Property Interest in Eligibility.

By Brian Porto

In recent years, no question in intercollegiate athletics policy has been the subject of more litigation or more law review commentaries than whether or not the college athlete possesses a constitutionally based property right to athletic participation which protects him against being declared ineligible without the benefit of due process. However, both the litigation and the commentaries have largely been limited to instances of ineligibility resulting from nonacademic violations and to petitions seeking merely the traditional due process guarantees, notably an on-campus hearing. Neither the lawsuits nor the scholarly writings have attempted to assess the likely limits of the asserted property right or to identify the benefits to which such a right would entitle the athlete. Similarly, neither instrument has endeavored to weigh the likely implications of this right for the universities' academic expectations of their athletes. Most important, no practitioner or scholar of the law has asked: if such a property interest in athletic participation were recognized, could it be used, by basing the property right upon the economic interest in pursuing a professional sports career, to exempt the athlete from academic requirements?

§ 4.5(A). Property Right.

Although this question has not yet been directly addressed, it has certainly been raised by several recent commentaries which have asserted the property right to participation in college athletics as well as by four court decisions which have recognized that right. Indeed, two authors have argued that the college athlete possesses a constitutionally protected property interest in intercollegiate participation which derives from his economic interest in pursuing a career in professional athletics. Moreover, in *Hall v. University of Minnesota,* 530 F. Supp. 104 (D. Minn. 1982), a University of Minnesota basketball player who had been declared academically ineligible for athletics argued successfully that his property interest in regaining full-time student status lay not in the opportunity to prepare for a career in business or one of the professions, but rather in the chance to demonstrate his basketball talents. If successful in that regard, he might be selected in an early round of the 1982 National Basketball Association draft and rewarded with a lucrative "no-cut" contract. In Mark Hall's view, the University of Minnesota was training him for a career in professional basketball, hence was no more justified in denying him access to that training without due process than it would have been in suspending a student of law, medicine or journalism from classes without a suitable hearing.

Under these circumstances, it is not only appropriate but necessary to examine the various rationales which have been presented in court and scholarly publications in support of a constitutional right to participation in intercollegiate athletics. Although the college athlete occupies a precarious legal status vis à vis his university and the National Collegiate Athletic Association (NCAA), which would seem to underscore the need for such a right, it is imperative that that right not be based upon a rationale whose academic implications have not been analyzed. Unfortunately, the justification which has been accepted in three cases wherein the right has been recognized seems to disregard its academic implications, which include a designation of the athlete as a "student" of preprofessional athletics. Should this rationale gain widespread judicial acceptance, the time when an athletic scholarship confers freedom from unwanted academic burdens will not be far away.

Thus, if college athletes are to be protected against arbitrary and capricious decisions by their institutions and the NCAA, but not at the price of blurring the remaining distinctions between themselves and their professional brethren, serious thought must be given to finding a method for simultaneously fostering due process and academic integrity. In this way, the judiciary would be able to respond appropriately to a serious legal problem in higher education while leaving the larger issue of whether or not athletes must fulfill academic requirements to be determined by educators. The purpose of this section is to identify a practicable method for the simultaneous achievement of due process and academic integrity in intercollegiate athletics.

As indicated earlier, there has been no dearth of suits in recent years asserting that college athletes possess a property interest in athletic participation. At the same time, there has been no consensus among the federal judges who have ruled in these cases regarding the existence of such a right.

§ 4.5(B). State Action.

However, the judges have been virtually unanimous in the conclusion that NCAA regulations constitute "state action" which will be subject to due process requirements in the event of a finding that the asserted property interest indeed exists. (The only exception has been *McDonald v. National Collegiate Athletic Association,* 370 F. Supp. 625 (C.D. Cal. 1974).) In determining that NCAA activities are state actions and hence potentially subject to fourteenth amendment strictures, the courts have employed two distinct rationales, "public function analysis" and the "entanglement theory." The former argues that since the NCAA's role as coordinator of intercollegiate athletics causes it to perform legislative, administrative and adjudicative tasks of a "traditionally governmental" nature, the Association is clearly engaged in a "public function" which would otherwise be performed by government. As one court noted, in *Parish v. National Collegiate Athletic Association,* 506 F.2d 1028 (5th Cir. 1975), if the NCAA were to disappear tomorrow, it would be necessary for government to step in and fill the void left by the Association's departure.

The latter rationale, the entanglement theory, is best explained by the words of the court of appeals for the District of Columbia in *Howard University v. National Collegiate Athletic Association,* 510 F.2d 213 (D.C. Cir. 1975). The court said the "N.C.A.A. and its member public instrumentalities are joined in a mutually beneficial relationship, and in fact may be fairly said to form the type of symbiotic relationship between public and private entities which triggers constitutional scrutiny." Hence, the realities that approximately one half of the NCAA's member schools are state-supported, that these public institutions provide the vast majority of the Association's revenues and that such schools are a dominant force in the determination of, as well as major beneficiaries of, Association policies have convinced the District of Columbia Court of Appeals and other federal courts that NCAA action is state action within the meaning of the fourteenth amendment.

To date, only one federal court, in *McDonald,* has ruled that NCAA activities are not state action. That court concluded that such activities are the work of a "voluntary, unincorporated association which, unlike state high school athletic associations, . . . has an existence separate and apart from the educational system of any state." In this view, the voluntary nature of NCAA membership and the private status of the Association prevent it from being a "sovereign equivalent" whose actions are subject to due process requirements. However, this argument recognizes a state-supported public university as a "sovereign equivalent" which can be required to afford athletes a hearing before imposing ineligibility upon them.

Although athletes have had no substantial difficulty in convincing the federal judiciary that NCAA activities are state action, they have been significantly less successful at persuading the courts of the existence of a constitutionally protectable property interest in intercollegiate participation. In part this has been a result of the unwillingness of some courts to view the athletic scholarship as creating for the college athlete a property interest which the high school athlete cannot claim. These courts have extended the ruling of *Albach v. Odle,* 531 F.2d 983 (10th Cir. 1976), that participation in interscholastic athletics is not a constitutionally protected civil right, to the collegiate context. This has occurred despite the plaintiffs' claims that the presence in college of financial aid in return for athletic participation means that the collegiate athlete possesses a contract which confers upon him an "entitlement" to his scholarship benefits and to freedom from the arbitrary and capricious revocation of those benefits. In *Colorado Seminary (University of Denver) v. National Collegiate Athletic Association,* 417 F. Supp. 885 (D. Colo. 1976), the court held that an athletic scholarship may give an athlete a "unilateral expectation" of a certain set of benefits, but it does not accord him the legal entitlement, derivative of a source other than his own expectations, necessary to create a property right.

The courts which have rejected the contractual argument for a property right to intercollegiate participation have also rejected the contention that such a right derives from the college athlete's economic interest in pursuing a career in professional sports. In both the *Colorado Seminary* decision and in *Parish,* they concluded that because so few former college athletes ever sign a professional sports contract, the college athlete's economic interest in professional sports opportunities is "speculative and not of constitutional dimensions." Although the courts acknowledged that participation in college athletics is a customary and even necessary precursor to a career in professional athletics, they determined that the slim likelihood of a collegiate career ever being parlayed into a professional career precludes the assertion of a property right in intercollegiate participation. According to this view, then, the college athlete preparing for professional athletics does not merit, in the event of a declaration of ineligibility, the due process protections which would be provided to a business student accused of abusing a college fund under his control or a medical student charged with employing dangerous clinical techniques.

In two other cases in which a property right to intercollegiate participation has been asserted, courts have sidestepped the constitutional issue, while deciding that sufficient due process was provided in that particular instance. In one of those, *Howard University v. National Collegiate Athletic Association,* 510 F.2d 213 (D.C. Cir. 1975), the court expressed "substantial doubts" whether the plaintiffs possessed any recognizable property interest which warranted the imposition of due process protections, but went on to say that even if they did possess such an interest, these plaintiffs had in no way been deprived of due process.

As noted earlier, there have to date been four instances in which a court has recognized a property right to participation in intercollegiate athletics. The only one of these cases which was not decided in the District of Minnesota and the only one in which the plaintiff was denied relief despite the constitutional decision is *Hunt v. National Collegiate Athletic Association,* G 76-370 C.A. (W.D. Mich. 1976). The *Hunt* court ruled that the plaintiffs, Michigan State University football players, satisfied the "entitlement" requirement for a property interest. Their athletic scholarships constituted contracts with the university which clearly, and with the support of university authorities, conferred upon the plaintiffs a readily identifiable package of benefits. Quoting an opinion of the United State Supreme Court, *Perry v. Sinderman,* 408 U.S. 593 (1972), concerning the concept of a property interest, the *Hunt* court observed: "A person's interest in a benefit is a property interest if there are rules or mutually explicit understandings that support his claim of entitlement to the benefit and that he may invoke at a hearing."

Notably, although the court recognized a property interest in intercollegiate athletic participation derivative of the scholarship contract, it rejected the notion that that contract necessarily entitles the athlete to the full trappings of due process, namely, a formal judicial hearing with the athlete represented by counsel rather than by university officials. Rather, the *Hunt* court ruled that the informal meetings with Michigan State officials, in which the athletes had participated prior to the Infractions Committee's hearings and at which they were notified of the charges against them and given an opportunity to confront their accusers, had afforded the athletes sufficient due process. However, it should be noted that the reasons for the court's conclusion that these meetings afforded adequate due process were that (1) the meetings had been held prior to the Infractions Committee's declaration of ineligibility and (2) the university's decision to declare the plaintiffs ineligible was appealable to the NCAA's Subcommittee on Eligibility Appeals. According to the court, had the athletes' only opportunity to present their case been at meetings with Michigan State officials after the university had been ordered by the NCAA to declare them ineligible, a due process violation would have occurred. Said the court: "The University, when faced with the choice of declaring a student ineligible or risking sanctions including expulsion from N.C.A.A. membership, has a direct, substantial pecuniary interest in ruling against the student regardless of whether it believes such a decision to be justified."

Thus, although *Hunt* acknowledged a property right to participate in college athletics, it ruled that that right does not necessitate a formal judicial proceeding in the event of ineligibility, at least where a campus hearing precedes NCAA hearings and where an opportunity for appeal to the NCAA exists. Representation of athletes at NCAA hearings by school officials is sufficient. In two other decisions recognizing the property right, the rationale was two-fold. In both *Behagen v. Intercollegiate Conference of Faculty Representatives,* 346 F. Supp. 602 (D. Minn. 1972), and *Regents of the University of Minnesota v. National Collegiate Athletic Association,* 560 F.2d 352 (8th Cir. 1977) (hereinafter referred to as *Regents*), the courts reasoned that the property right derived, on the one hand, from the athlete's economic interest in pursuing a professional sports career and, on the other, from the intimate association between the opportunity to participate in college athletics and the constitutionally protected right to pursue an education. Regarding the economic interest, the *Behagen* court observed that

> the opportunity to participate in intercollegiate athletics is of substantial economic value to many students. In these days when juniors in college are able to suspend their formal educational training in exchange for multi-million dollar contracts to turn professional, this Court takes judicial notice of the fact that, to many, the chance to display their athletic prowess in college stadiums and arenas throughout the country is worth more in economic terms than the chance to get a college education.

Moreover, the court argued that since it has long been recognized that the opportunity to receive an education is so essential to professional and economic success in later life that it cannot be impaired without due process, and since intercollegiate athletics are an integral component of higher education, the college athlete has a substantial interest in continued participation. Whether they parlay their collegiate athletic accomplishments into professional sports contracts or use the lessons of the arena (discipline, perseverence, self-control) and the classroom to pursue careers in business or the professions, college athletes, said Judge Earl Larson in *Behagen,* have a property interest "in participating in activities which have the potential to bring them great economic rewards."

Four years later, in *Regents,* U.S. District Judge Edward Devitt, using the same reasoning which his Minnesota colleague, Judge Earl Larson, had employed in *Behagen,* also granted relief to ineligible athletes on the grounds that they had been denied their property right to intercollegiate participation without benefit of due process. Six more years would pass before U.S. District Judge Miles W. Lord, also of Minnesota, would rule in favor of a college athlete's claimed property right to participation. That ruling, in the case of *Hall v. University of Minnesota,* 530 F. Supp. 104 (D. Minn. 1982), possesses monumental implications for the future of college athletics. As a result, it will be the point of departure for our analysis of the educational consequences of a property right which is based upon the athlete's economic interest in pursuing a career in professional sports.

The *Hall* case involved the efforts of one student athlete at the University of Minnesota to recover his rights to matriculate at the university and to participate in intercollegiate basketball competition, which he had lost because he was unable to gain admission to any degree-granting program at the university. That forfeiture resulted from the requirement of the Big Ten athletic conference, of which Minnesota is a member, that student athletes at its member institutions must be enrolled as candidates for degrees in order to remain eligible for intercollegiate competition. The plaintiff claimed that his two applications to Minnesota's "University Without Walls," a degree-granting program, were evaluated in an arbitrary and capricious manner which denied him the due process of law to which he was entitled under the fourteenth amendment. In finding for the plaintiff, the court agreed with Hall that he had been singled out by two successive directors of the University Without Walls for unusually harsh reviews of his applications without ever having been informed of the allegations which precipitated such unprecedented measures or having been afforded an opportunity to rebut the charges against him. In the view of the court, Hall had clearly been denied a property right, namely, his interest in attending the University of Minnesota, without the benefit of due process. Like his Minnesota colleagues in *Behagen* and *Regents of the University of Minnesota,* Judge Miles Lord acknowledged that the athlete's property interest was "ostensibly academic," but primarily oriented toward improving "the plaintiff's ability to obtain a 'no-cut' contract with the National Basketball Association." Once again, a property right to intercollegiate athletic participation based upon the athlete's interest in securing a professional contract was recognized in a federal district court in Minnesota.

Judge Lord's ruling resolved the immediate issue of Mark Hall's athletic eligibility, but it has not assured the legitimacy of the economic rationale which Hall used to support his claimed property right. As Mark Hall saw his property interest, it was not in obtaining an undergraduate degree, but was instead in showcasing his athletic talents as a member of the University of Minnesota's basketball team in order that he might be selected in an early round of the 1982 National Basketball Association draft and generously rewarded for those talents.

Hall's peculiar interpretation of a property interest in attending a university begs the question: in the absence of due process violations such as those suffered by Mark Hall, is a potential professional contract an interest which a college athlete can legitimately assert in court against a university which seeks to bar him from athletic competition because of his failure to satisfy its academic requirements? More specifically, can an athlete whose eligibility has been revoked for academic reasons successfully sue a university on the grounds that since he was recruited primarily to participate in its athletic program, in hopes of one day becoming a professional athlete, his progress toward a professional contract should not be impeded by academic requirements which are tangential to his career goals and about which he was not adequately informed during the recruiting process? That is, could a university's suspension of an athlete from competition because of a subpar academic record, after it had recruited him despite an unimpressive high school transcript, reasonably be construed as the denial of a property right (the pursuit of a professional contract) without due process, namely, adequate notice of the academic requirements for athletic eligibility? Moreover, even if athletes are sufficiently informed of their academic responsibilities, can they realistically be expected to fulfill those responsibilities in the face of their often woefully inadequate preparation and motivation for college-level studies and the time demands of their sport? Ultimately, would it be possible for an academically ineligible athlete to take Mark Hall's economic rationale to its logical conclusion by asserting that part of the process to which he is due by virtue of his property right to intercollegiate participation is freedom from academic requirements?

Certainly, the ostensible concern in this case was the validity of Mark Hall's claim that his two applications to the University of Minnesota's "University Without Walls" were treated in a fashion which denied him due process. However, the real significance of the case derives not from its disposition, but rather from the fact that it raises complex and troubling legal questions regarding the relationships which should exist between the academic purposes and the athletic programs of our universities and between those same universities and the professional sports leagues whose players typically are products of intercollegiate athletic programs. Without a doubt, *Hall* brought out of the shadows and into clear focus the antagonism which exists between those academic purposes and athletic programs, casting doubt in the process upon the veracity of any suggestion that intercollegiate athletics are an integral component of the process of education. Moreover, in light of the demonstrated reluctance of most university authorities to clearly define the relationships which shall exist between academics and athletics at their institutions, *Hall v. University of Minnesota* may well be a portent of things to come. It has opened a Pandora's box of vexing issues which, unless resolved by educators, are likely to be brought to court in the near future.

Given that prospect, it is appropriate to examine carefully each of the rationales which might be presented in support of a college athlete's property right claim, toward the end of identifying one which is sensitive to both the athlete's need for due process protection and the colleges' interest in promoting academic integrity in intercollegiate athletics.

§ 4.5(C). A "Liberty" Interest.

Prior to discussing the four property right rationales which have, at one time or another, been presented in the federal courts, it is appropriate to point out that the ineligible athlete could choose instead to base his due process claim upon an alleged denial of a "liberty" interest. That is, rather than argue that a declaration of ineligibility denied him property without due process, the plaintiff might contend that the penalty violated his liberty interest in avoiding reputational damage as well as substantial restrictions upon future employment and educational opportunities. If he can show that the declaration of ineligibility has resulted from disciplinary allegations against him which can reasonably be regarded as stigmatizing or defamatory, and which could prevent him from demonstrating his skills to professional scouts, the student athlete could conceivably persuade a court that his reputational damage rises to the level of a liberty interest.

It should be noted, however, that this interest has been asserted successfully in only one instance, largely because the United States Supreme Court has erected formidable hurdles which have prevented regular success. The student athlete who claims a liberty interest in continued athletic eligibility must show that (1) he has indeed been defamed, (2) his ineligibility significantly alters his legal status (i.e., he has suffered not only reputational damage but a separate loss, such as a job, playing eligibility or the opportunity to pursue an education), (3) the defamation rather than the resulting penalties have caused his legal injury and (4) the NCAA has publicized his violations.

If those barriers are not sufficiently daunting, two others exist which are likely to prevent the frequent assertion or judicial acceptance of the stigmatized reputation rationale. One is that NCAA rules identify a wide variety of activities which are punishable by a declaration of ineligibility for intercollegiate competition, including some which are arguably quite innocuous. As a result, any test of a liberty interest which is based upon the stigmatized reputation rationale would be highly subjective and difficult to implement. Courts would regularly have to decide whether ineligibility resulting from the acceptance of a few meals and concert tickets from a university athletic booster who has befriended the athlete would pass the reputational damage test right along with ineligibility stemming from betting on one's games.

The other reason why this rationale is unlikely to be asserted often is that it may be unnecessary to the successful assertion of a constitutionally protectable interest. If the plaintiff can show that the loss of athletic eligibility represents a significant change in his legal status, he may be able to prove that he has been denied a property right (i.e., benefits to which he was legally entitled), thereby making the liberty claim superfluous. In light of the fact that lower legal hurdles typically face the athlete who asserts a property as opposed to a liberty interest, the property claim is more frequently made. The athlete who makes a property claim has available to him four distinct lines of reasoning.

One such line of reasoning suggests that the athlete's property interest lies in the opportunity which intercollegiate athletics afford him to train for a potentially lucrative career in professional athletics. In this view, it is a mistake to conclude that that interest is too speculative to merit constitutional protection because it lies not in having a career in professional sports, but rather in having the opportunity to pursue such a career. The extraordinary odds against the attainment of a professional athletic career are irrelevant to the student athlete's right to pursue it. Moreover, since participation in intercollegiate competition has become a necessary precursor to a professional career in football and basketball and is increasingly leading to professional careers in baseball and hockey, college-level competition has become all but synonymous with the opportunity to pursue a professional sports contract.

According to one recent scholarly commentary, in 10 Stetson Law Review 483-505 (Spring 1981), participation in college athletics is not only career preparation but education. Its authors, R.G. Riegel, Jr., and M.A. Hanley, argue that the courts have erroneously viewed athletics as merely a "component" of the educational process when, in fact, it is frequently the only education which the college athlete receives. Given this reality, the authors maintain, the athlete should be afforded the opportunity to develop his skills free from the interference of "arbitrarily imposed disciplinary measures" which interrupt his education and hinder his preparation for a career in professional sports. In the estimation of these commentators: "Intercollegiate athletics should be viewed as a process by which the specialized qualifications for a profession are obtained, rather than a component of the educational experience." As a result, "where the N.C.A.A. disciplines an athlete without due process of law, it interferes with that athlete's property interest in pursuing his or her occupation."

A second rationale which can be employed in support of the claimed property right is that intercollegiate athletics are an integral part of the educational process; therefore, to deprive a student athlete of eligibility for sports competition without due process is tantamount to depriving him of educational opportunity without due process. Since the courts have mandated that due process be provided to those who have been denied the chance to pursue an education, they should provide equivalent protection for athletes who face ineligibility.

These sentiments were clearly expressed by U.S. District Judge Edward Devitt in his decision in *Regents.* Judge Devitt wrote that

> the opportunity to participate in an athletic program is a very important part of each student-athlete's education. The concepts of winning, losing, and doing your best, while made somewhat trite by modern media, are nonetheless important to everyone's development. In the athletic experience, all these concepts are intensely focused into brief periods of competition, either with oneself or another. Because an education is such a necessary ingredient of economic success in later life, a student must be afforded due process rights before the right to it, or any substantial element of it, can be adversely affected.

This argument, in tandem with the economic or career preparation rationale, has produced decisions recognizing a property right to intercollegiate athletic participation not only in the *Regents* decision, but also in *Behagen* and *Hall.*

A third property right rationale available to the plaintiff views the loss of an athletic scholarship, resulting from a declaration of ineligibility, as the denial of a protectable property interest in intercollegiate competition. According to this argument, by losing his scholarship, the athlete is likely to incur financial hardship and may be deprived of the opportunity to continue attending college and to complete his education. As a result, in being deprived of the scholarship, the student athlete is also being deprived of benefits to which he was entitled under the terms of the award; the continued receipt of those benefits is a property interest which cannot be denied without due process.

Thus far, this argument has not been successful in court and it is not likely to be in the near future. The reason for this is that, to date, the courts have concluded that since no school has revoked a student athlete's scholarship because he has been declared ineligible, no plaintiff has been deprived of any benefits which rise to the level of a property interest. Moreover, since NCAA rules permit but do not require a university to revoke an athlete's scholarship if he renders himself ineligible, it is likely that courts will continue to rule that no benefits to which the athlete was entitled have been taken from him. By rendering himself ineligible, the player would have forfeited any legal entitlement he might have had to those benefits. Finally, it is worth noting that all athletic scholarships are annually renewable and that the university possesses a great deal of discretion regarding decisions to renew or not to renew a player's scholarship. Under these circumstances, it is likely that a school could revoke the scholarship of an ineligible player at the conclusion of an academic year, ostensibly because of poor performances or insubordination during the previous season, but in reality because he is ineligible for the upcoming season. Hence, it appears that even if an institution were to revoke the scholarship of an ineligible player, the NCAA's system of annual renewal and its failure to require the continuation of scholarships for ineligible players would enable the school to successfully defend the revocation against a court challenge that it violated the player's property interest.

§ 4.5(D). Legal Contract.

Last but certainly not least, an ineligible athlete could base his claimed property right to intercollegiate participation upon the contention that his athletic scholarship is a binding legal contract which has conferred upon him certain benefits, including the right to participation in intercollegiate athletics, which cannot be denied to him without due process. In this view, then, the contractual nature of the athletic scholarship creates for the recipient a property interest in continued eligibility.

This argument has met with mixed reviews in court. In *Colorado Seminary v. National Collegiate Athletic Association,* 417 F. Supp. 885 (D. Colo. 1976), the court ruled that, although the athletic scholarship agreement is a contract, it does not confer upon the recipient the legal "entitlement" to its benefits which is necessary to generate a property interest. In finding that no such entitlement was created by the scholarship, the court reasoned that the scholarship athlete had a "unilateral expectation" of participation in intercollegiate athletics rather than a "right" to play. Indeed, the court argued: "The athlete on scholarship has no more 'right' to play than the athlete who 'walks on'."

On the other hand, in *Hunt,* the court accepted the contractual rationale, concluding that the plaintiffs possessed a property interest derivative of the contracts which they had signed with Michigan State University, wherein each had been granted a package of benefits constituting a "football scholarship." Since those benefits had been conferred according to established NCAA rules and procedures and were understood by the athletes and their schools to bestow certain benefits upon the players, the court determined that the Michigan State athletes had satisfied the entitlement requirement for a protectable property interest. Unlike the *Colorado Seminary* court, which saw no difference between the athletic scholarship recipient and the "walk-on," or nonscholarship athlete, for purposes of recognizing a property interest in intercollegiate participation, the *Hunt* court viewed the scholarship recipient as not merely expecting to participate, but rather as being "entitled" to participate.

The discussion just concluded has outlined the arguments that ineligible college athletes are likely to make in court in support of their claims to a constitutionally protectable interest in participating in college athletics. That which follows will endeavor to assess the strengths and weaknesses of each argument in hopes of identifying one or a combination which would best serve the twin goals of due process and academic integrity in collegiate sport.

Three of the rationales which have been presented possess serious weaknesses which make it unlikely that they will ever command a substantial measure of judicial respect. Certainly, a liberty interest predicated upon a stigmatized reputation is one of these. The reasons for this argument's likely failure in court were discussed at length earlier and need not be repeated in full here. Nevertheless, it bears reiterating that a stigmatized reputation test requires the plaintiff to show that he has been defamed, publicly charged with specific violations and deprived of a tangible benefit which has altered his legal status and legally injured him. Even if this test were considerably easier to satisfy, courts would likely be cool to the difficulties associated with its administration. How are the courts to readily and realistically determine when a declaration of ineligibility has stigmatized a student athlete's reputation and when it has not? Is a reputation likely to be as adversely affected by charges of selling one's allotted game tickets at highly inflated prices as by allegations of accepting occasional small gifts from an athletic booster? More important, what criteria can a court possibly use to answer such a question? Finally, since a student athlete can also argue that his loss of athletic eligibility has deprived him of a property interest, he would be wise to follow that course, for it features fewer and less formidable obstacles than does the path of the liberty interest.

Nevertheless, two of the property right rationales are also plagued by serious weaknesses. The argument that a student athlete possesses a property interest in intercollegiate competition derivative of the fact that athletics are an integral component of an undergraduate education blithely ignores the realities of big-time college sports. To say, as did Judge Edward Devitt in *Regents,* that "[t]he concepts of winning, losing, and doing your best, while made somewhat trite by modern media, are nonetheless important to everyone's development" is to view the undergraduate experience as merely a socialization mechanism. This ignores its at least equally important role as an instrument of intellectual growth. Hence, while participation in intercollegiate athletics is arguably a significant component of an important socialization experience offered by the undergraduate years, it would be difficult to argue that intercollegiate athletic competition is an essential ingredient of the undergraduate's intellectual development. Thus, to assert that athletic participation is an integral component of a college education is to define a college education in an unduly narrow fashion.

Moreover, it is a well-established fact that participation in big-time intercollegiate athletics requires such a substantial proportion of the student athlete's time and energy that he often has very little of either to devote to his studies. Under these circumstances, not only is participation in college athletics not an integral component of an undergraduate education, but rather it is frequently a major detriment to the completion of an undergraduate program. Thus, to argue that a plaintiff's property interest in continued eligibility derives from the intimate relationship which exists between intercollegiate athletics and the aims of higher education is to badly misread the realities of collegiate sport and the aims of higher education.

Furthermore, to argue for such a property interest is to misread the decision of the United States Supreme Court in *Goss v. Lopez,* 419 U.S. 565 (1975). As one recent commentary has pointed out, when *Goss* recognized a property interest in education which entitled a student who had been suspended from school for ten days or less to notice and a hearing, it based that recognition upon the requirement by Ohio law that local authorities provide free elementary and secondary education to all residents between ages 5 and 21 and that all residents between ages 5 and 18 attend school for at least 32 weeks each year. In the Court's view, those regulations conferred upon Ohio public school students an "entitlement" to an education, based in state law, which in turn created a property interest in continued attendance protectable by the fourteenth amendment's due process clause. Said Mr. Justice White, in writing for the Court: "Having chosen to extend the right to an education to people of appellees' class generally, Ohio may not withdraw that right on grounds of misconduct, absent fundamentally fair procedures to determine whether the misconduct has occurred."

The commentary cited above also argues that it is a mistake to conclude, as Judge Devitt did in *Regents v. University of Minnesota,* that the property interest in an education announced in *Goss* can be extended to the collegiate context and used to protect athletes who have been declared ineligible for intercollegiate athletics. While the high school student may possess a property interest in education which derives from state requirements that localities provide free public education to all children and that all children must attend school, colleges and college students are bound by no such requirements, hence no equivalent entitlement accrues to the student.

Any test, then, which endeavors to base a property interest in intercollegiate athletic participation upon an asserted nexus between athletics and education misconstrues both big-time college sports and the *Goss* decision.

The two remaining rationales which an athlete might use in court to support a property right to intercollegiate participation appear to have greater potential for success than those cited above, for they lack the doctrinal weaknesses, flawed assumptions and adverse administrative consequences associated with the arguments already presented. However, of the latter two, one is clearly preferable in the view of this commentary, for it is likely that the other will foster due process for college athletes at the expense of academic integrity.

The rejected rationale asserts that a property interest in intercollegiate athletic participation derives from the college athlete's economic stake in pursuing a career in professional sports. At first blush, this argument may appear to be sound, for it certainly is realistic in recognizing that big-time intercollegiate athletics have a much closer relationship to professional athletics than to higher education. However, realism and wisdom are not synonymous, and the widespread judicial acceptance of this rationale would be most unwise.

To accept this argument is, in effect, to accord constitutional protection to the "professionalized" conception of intercollegiate athletics to which many athletes and university athletic departments subscribe. That is, the long-held but unofficial view that the college athlete is not a student engaged in an extracurricular activity, but rather an apprentice entertainer training to be a professional entertainer, would not only be officially recognized but constitutionally sanctioned through the recognition of a career-based property right. Under these circumstances, it is likely that an athlete who has been declared academically ineligible for competition would challenge that declaration on due process grounds, either substantive or procedural.

A substantive due process challenge would argue that university or NCAA academic regulations pertaining to athletes are unrelated to any reasonable or legitimate educational purpose. Certainly, such challenges are not often successful. Moreover, this one could be answered by an argument that as long as college athletes are amateurs and full-time, if not enthusiastic, students, it is reasonable for universities and the NCAA to impose upon them academic requirements for continued matriculation and for continued eligibility in specific extracurricular activities.

However, it is not so unlikely that a court which accepted the career-based property interest would also accept the suggestion that academic regulations which were reasonable when applied to students of business, philosophy or biology were quite unreasonable when extended to a young linebacker preparing for a career in professional football.

Even if a substantive due process challenge were unsuccessful, the athlete could sue on procedural due process grounds with a greater likelihood of success. Certainly, it is not unusual for universities to recruit promising athletes despite their substandard high school transcripts and lack of basic academic skills and to encourage the athletes' "professionalized" conception of intercollegiate athletics. Therefore, it is quite likely that an athlete who had been recruited in this fashion and was subsequently declared academically ineligible for athletics could argue that he had been deprived of his property interest in intercollegiate competition without due process, namely, firm notice during recruitment of university and NCAA academic requirements.

Hence, the best argument against the notion of a property interest based on the opportunity to pursue a professional sports career is not that that interest is too speculative because the odds against such a career are astronomical. As one authority, in Arizona State Law Journal No. 1 at 109-31 (1982), has pointed out, the protectable interest involved here is not in having such a career, but rather in having the chance to pursue that career; the odds against the player's success in the pro ranks are irrelevent to the constitutional issue. Rather, the best argument against the career-based property interest is that it would potentially expand "due process" in academic ineligibility cases to a point where many athletes could be exempted from academic requirements. While such exemptions may ultimately prove desirable in order for big-time intercollegiate athletics to operate honestly, the choice of whether or not to abandon the concept of the "student athlete" is a major policy determination which should be made directly by educators, rather than indirectly by judges. It must be appreciated that to abandon the "student athlete" notion is to announce that the training of people for careers in professional athletics has joined teaching, research and community service as a major mission of our universities. Most assuredly, that announcement, if and when it comes, should be made by educational, not judicial, policymakers.

In this commentator's view, only one rationale can ensure due process in college athletics without further blurring the distinction between amateur and professional athletes or forcing judges to make educational policy. That argument bases a property interest in college competition upon the notion that an athletic scholarship is a "contract" which confers upon the recipient "entitlement" to a package of benefits in return for fulfilling his obligation to participate in intercollegiate athletics for his university. This contractual rationale is distinguishable from that which views the property interest as directly derivative of the scholarship proceeds, because according to the contractual notion the college athlete's property interest includes not just money but also the expectation that, if sufficiently healthy and skillful, he will be permitted to participate in intercollegiate competition.

Indeed, the athletic scholarship recipient does not merely expect to play, but rather he is obligated by the terms of the scholarship agreement to play. As a result, the opinion of the court in *Colorado Seminary,* that the scholarship athlete is no more entitled to participate in college sports than the athlete who tries out for a team without benefit of a scholarship, is erroneous. Clearly, the nonscholarship player, or "walk-on," possesses merely a "unilateral expectation of a benefit," namely, the hope of participation; hence, he can claim no property interest in eligibility. The scholarship player, on the other hand, possesses a contractual obligation to participate; the expectation of his participation is not unilateral, but rather is shared by the athlete and his institution. If he chooses not to compete, he most likely loses the scholarship. This contractual arrangement then, represents for the athlete not just an "abstract need or desire" for or a "unilateral expectation" of eligibility, but rather a "legitimate claim of entitlement to it," thereby creating a property interest in the maintenance of that eligibility. The words of a recent law review commentary are instructive on this point:

> The possession of an athletic scholarship ensures the student-athlete of a place on the team and of a right to compete for a position on the first string. The walk-on has no rights: the coach may prohibit him from trying out altogether and cut him from the team any time thereafter. The position of a walk-on thus is in no way analogous to that of a matriculated recruit.

Although the contractual rationale has been successfully asserted in support of a property right to athletic eligibility only in *Hunt,* the notion that an athletic scholarship creates contractual obligations for both the athlete and the institution has been accepted by courts on several occasions. The clearest statements of this view were made in *Taylor v. Wake Forest University,* 191 S.E.2d 379 (N.C. App. 1972), and *Begley v. Mercer University,* 367 F. Supp. 908 (E.D. Tenn. 1973). In *Taylor,* a football player who had been declared academically ineligible during his freshman year refused to play even after he had improved his grades sufficiently to regain eligibility, but sought nonetheless to recover the benefits which he had forfeited by refusing to compete. The court observed that by signing a scholarship agreement with Wake Forest, Taylor had agreed to maintain his athletic eligibility both academically and physically. As long as his grade point average equalled or exceeded the university's requirements, he was scholastically eligible and was required to participate in practice sessions unless injured, in order to satisfy the physical eligibility standards of the scholarship agreement. By refusing to practice after his freshman season, Taylor failed to satisfy physical eligibility standards, thereby breaching his contractual obligations with Wake Forest University. The court rejected the argument of Gregg Taylor and his father that they had an oral agreement with Wake Forest which provided that Gregg could cease playing football if necessary in order to assure "reasonable academic progress." Reasoning that the Taylors and Wake Forest had signed a contract which the school had lived up to but the plaintiffs had reneged on, the court concluded: "It would be a strained construction of the contract that would enable the plaintiffs to determine the 'reasonable academic progress' of Gregg Taylor."

In *Begley,* a prospective scholarship athlete sued Mercer University for breach of contract after the school revoked the award which he had been given by mistake for the coming school year. The revocation resulted from a discovery that Begley's 2.9 high school grade point average was based on an 8.0 scale rather than the customary 4.0 scale, which placed his average below the minimum necessary for freshman athletic eligibility under NCAA rules. The court accepted the plaintiff's assertion that he had signed a contract with Mercer, but concluded that since he was unable to perform his duties under that contract he could not expect Mercer to perform its duties under the agreement; ineligibility, of course, would prevent Begley from fulfilling his contractual obligation to participate in intercollegiate athletics. Said the court:

> Because Mercer is unable to secure the consent of the N.C.A.A. to violate the latter's regulations, and because of the nature of the agreement between Mercer and Mr. Begley, the indication is inescapable that Mercer did not assume the risk in contracting with Mr. Begley that N.C.A.A.'s consent would be forthcoming. It is Mr. Begley who seeks damages from Mercer because of its inability to perform its promise; but, under the circumstances presented, Mercer is excused from liability for its inability to perform its promise to Mr. Begley.

Clearly, the *Taylor* and *Begley* decisions suggest that, under ordinary circumstances, an athletic scholarship is a contract which confers upon the recipient a right to participate in intercollegiate athletics and a corresponding duty to maintain his physical as well as academic eligibility for athletic competition. To proceed from this position to the point of recognizing a contractually based property interest in intercollegiate athletic participation is by no means to make a great intellectual leap.

Finally, the contractual rationale is not only a logical extension of prior decisions in the case law of intercollegiate athletics, but also the most effective argument available for promoting due process without diminishing academic integrity in college sports. It is not plagued by the formidable judicially imposed barriers to success which accompany the "stigmatized reputation" argument. It is not based upon the dubious notion that college athletics, despite their present form, are intimately related to the larger purpose of higher education. It cannot be dismissed just because an ineligible plaintiff's scholarship has not been revoked or because the annual renewal of scholarships permits the revocation of a grant-in-aid in the academic year following a declaration of ineligibility. Last and certainly not least, it cannot be interpreted in such a way as to absolve athletes of responsibility for meeting academic requirements for continued eligibility.

Thus far, this section has accepted, without criticism or qualification, the view that a rationale must be found which will promote not only academic integrity but also due process in college athletics. However, while the discussion has described some of the academic attitudes and practices which threaten to destroy any remaining distinctions between college and professional athletics, it has not identified the attitudes and practices which threaten to deny fundamental fairness to the athlete who, for whatever reason, has been declared ineligible for intercollegiate competition. Hence, a discussion of the need for higher standards of fairness toward the athlete is our next, and last, order of business.

§ 4.5(E). Enforcement Procedures.

Present NCAA enforcement procedures fail to satisfy even minimal standards of due process. The Association refuses to permit the athlete's interest (restoration of eligibility) to be presented independently of his school's interest (regaining access to television appearances and postseason competition by paying the penalty imposed) during regulatory proceedings. For example, at the hearing conducted by the Infractions Committee to present the findings of the investigators and the arguments of the school, the athlete may appear only as a representative of his university. Because the process assumes that the interests of the athlete and the schools are identical, the former is not entitled to cross-examine witnesses against him or be represented by counsel. Once the Infractions Committee has found the athlete culpable and has recommended to the school that he be declared ineligible, the athlete is entitled to an on-campus hearing but that hearing must result in a declaration of ineligibility or the university will be penalized by the NCAA. Even where hearings are held prior to NCAA hearings, as in *Hunt,* a school's decision not to declare a player ineligible will quickly be rendered meaningless by an NCAA ruling of ineligibility. In other words, the Association's conception of due process includes hearings with predetermined results. Hence, the conclusion in *Hunt,* that the plaintiffs had received due process because Michigan State's decision to declare them ineligible was reviewable by the NCAA and because the university held hearings prior to those of the Infractions Committee, is naive and misguided.

At the same time, the NCAA completely controls big-time college sports and may profoundly influence a student athlete's eligibility for future scholarships essential for the completion of a college education. The athlete is powerless to alter association policies and procedures which shape his life on campus. In 10 J. of College and Univ. L. No. 2 at 167-80 (Fall 1983), J.C. Weistart has written:

> A significant portion of NCAA regulatory activity affects student-athletes who neither participate directly in the group's rulemaking nor have an opportunity to select representatives to act on their behalf. The consequences for the athletes can nonetheless be quite significant. Issues ranging from whether one's education will be affordable to whether the athlete will be able to transfer from an unpleasant school environment to whether he or she will be allowed to participate in athletics at all will be greatly affected by deliberations in which the athlete has no role.

To make matters worse, the NCAA's investigating and adjudicative processes give to the Committee on Infractions the roles of fact finder, judge and jury. The committee aids the investigative staff in the conduct of its unofficial inquiry, reviews the investigation's findings, helps to determine whether an official inquiry is justified and presides over the hearing which is accorded to schools which are the subjects of official inquiries. As a result, it has been charged that while the ostensible purpose of the hearing is to furnish due process to athletes and their schools, the real aim is to aid the Committee on Infractions in determining appropriate penalties for the guilt which has already been established by the committee. Certainly, these types of procedures are not in keeping with customary due process requirements, which include the opportunity (for both athletes and their schools) to confront and cross-examine opposition witnesses before an impartial tribunal and, of course, the separation of investigative and adjudicative functions and personnel.

Finally, the aforementioned procedures are often used to enforce rules which are buried in the nooks and crannies of the NCAA's massive structure of regulations, are couched in convoluted language not readily comprehensible to a nonlawyer and confer upon coaches and athletic directors, who typically are not lawyers, responsibility for their application.

Under these circumstances, it is not difficult to see why the college athlete who has been declared ineligible for competition is in need of judicially mandated due process protection. Clearly, such protection is not likely to be forthcoming from the NCAA.

Admittedly, a judge need not believe that the Constitution contains a property right to participation in intercollegiate athletics in order to justify scrutinizing NCAA disciplinary processes to ensure fairness. He might simply admonish the Association that, in light of its exclusive control over big-time college sports and of the student athlete's vulnerability to its disciplinary edicts, it must permit on-campus hearings to reach whatever results they will, allow athletes to appear before its enforcement hearings represented by counsel who can confront and cross-examine witnesses, and recodify its rules in order to foster simplicity and clarity.

Given the demonstrated soundness of the contractual rationale and powerlessness of the student athlete, courts will be remiss if they do not soon accept the most effective means of ensuring procedural fairness, namely, a constitutionally protectable property right to intercollegiate competition which is based upon that rationale.

§ 4.5(F). Conclusion.

Clearly, this section has assigned to judges an important role in fostering procedural fairness by the NCAA in its relations with athletes and their institutions. Yet, in doing so, the essay has nonetheless confined judicial power to a sphere with which it is familiar and in which its expertise is well-established, namely, the identification of rights and suitable procedures for enforcing them. Hence, it is recognized here that the ultimate responsibility for ensuring that humanistic values such as procedural fairness and academic integrity influence the regulation of college sports rests neither with judges nor the staff of the NCAA. That responsibility rests with educators, who must begin to assume substantially greater control over the governance of intercollegiate athletic programs. A recent law review commentary by B.F. Brody, in Ariz. L.J. 1982 No. 1 (1982) at 109-31, made this point eloquently:

> If a reduced level of athletic success is the price of educational credibility, then educators are the ones who must pay that price. We cannot expect athletes, coaches, athletic administrators, and N.C.A.A. employees to pay it. And if educators are not willing to take the steps and make the sacrifices necessary to preserve educational values, higher education will surely get the N.C.A.A. enforcement it deserves.

All who are concerned with the future of college athletics should heed these words.

CHAPTER 5

SPORTS MEDICINE ISSUES

§ 5.1. The Legal Status of the Athletic Trainer.

By Boyd B. Baker and Phillip B. Parry

The unique predicament into which the athletic trainer is thrust appears, at times, to be a definite "no-win" situation. Several states in the country have, over the past decade, enacted athletic training statutes which have had the effect of "legalizing" the activity of the athletic trainer particularly as it relates to the use of modalities more commonly associated with the profession of physical therapy.

§ 5.1(A). States Require Licensure for Physical Therapists.

All 50 states have licensure statutes for physical therapists. These laws define very precisely what acts physical therapists may legally perform. The use of physical therapy modalities by physical therapists is allowed in every state. These statutes also define what others, if any, are allowed to use such modalities and under what circumstances. Such statutory provisions are of vital importance to the athletic trainer and to the athletic trainer's employer.

A decade ago only Texas had licensure of athletic trainers. Today, ten additional states enjoy such licensure, and passage of similar statutes is imminent in several other states. These statutes have "legalized" the use of physical therapy modalities by athletic trainers by carefully outlining the circumstances under which such use is authorized. It is obvious, however, that until such time as all 50 states enjoy licensure of athletic trainers, the athletic trainer must be absolutely conversant with the understanding of the therapy statute in effect in his state.

Prior to a categorization of existing physical therapy statutes and their implications for the practice of athletic training, a look at the wording of such a statute is warranted. The Kansas statute reads as follows:

> As used in this act, the term "physical therapy" means the treatment of any disability, injury, disease, or other conditions of health of human beings, or the prevention of such disability, injury, disease, or other conditions of health and rehabilitation as related thereto by the use of the physical, chemical, and other properties of air, cold, heat, electricity, exercise, massage, radiant energy, including ultraviolet, visible and infrared rays, ultrasound, water, and apparatus and equipment used in the application of the foregoing or related thereto. The use of roentgen rays and radium for diagnostic and therapeutic purposes, and the use of electricity for surgical purposes, including cauterization, are not authorized or included under the terms "physical therapy" as used in this act.

Kan. Stat. Ann. § 65-2901.

In earlier research by B.B. Baker and C.A. Rode in the Athletic Training J. 209 (Dec. 1975), the various states were classified into four categories according to the provisions of their respective physical therapy laws. That categorization scheme is as follows:

§ 5.1(B). Categories Regarding Physical Therapy Laws.

Type I. *States limiting the practice of physical therapy to those licensed to do so in that particular state.* Basically, this restricts the use of physical therapy to those who are registered or licensed physical therapists. Athletic trainers in states with this particular type of law would not be allowed to use physical therapy. An example of this law is taken from the Connecticut statutes:

> No person who is not licensed by the department of health services as a Physical Therapist shall practice or hold himself out as authorized to practice physical therapy as defined in section 20-66, or represent himself as being so registered or licensed or use in connection with his name the term "Registered Physical Therapist," "Licensed Physical Therapist," or "Physical Therapist" or the letters "R.P.T.," "L.P.T." or any other letters, words, or insignia indicating or implying that he is a licensed physical therapist in this state. The treatment of human ailments by physical therapy shall only be performed by a person licensed under the provisions of this chapter as a Physical Therapist upon the oral or written referral of a person licensed in this state, or in a bordering state having licensing requirements meeting the approval of the appropriate examining board in this state to practice medicine and surgery, osteopathy, podiatry, natureopathy, chiropractic, or dentistry.

Conn. Gen. Stat. Ann. § 20-73.

Under Connecticut law, only registered or licensed physical therapists are allowed to use physical therapy. Connecticut does require the physical therapist to have oral or written referral from a physician.

Type II. *States which require licensure to practice physical therapy or hold oneself out as a physical therapist, but do not limit any person licensed or registered in the state under another law from engaging in the practice for which he or she is licensed or registered.* This type of law again limits the use of physical therapy to just those registered or licensed as physical therapists. It does allow those professions which have stated in their licensure laws that they may use physical therapy to do so. Athletic trainers who have state licensure in a state with a Type II law are completely legal in using physical therapy under the provisions of the athletic trainer licensure laws. The athletic trainers who are in a state without licensure for them and who are under Type II laws would not be allowed to use physical therapy. An example of a Type II law is taken from the Minnesota statutes:

> "No Person Shall:
>   a) Use the title of Physical Therapist without a certificate of registration as a Physical Therapist issued to him pursuant to the provisions of sections 148.65 to 148.78.

b) In any manner represent himself as a Physical Therapist, or use in connection with his name the words or letters Physical Therapist, Physiotherapist, Physical Therapy Technician, Registered Physical Therapist, Licensed Physical Therapist, P.T., P.T.T., R.P.T., L.P.T., or any letters, words, abbreviations or insignia indicating or implying that he is a Physical Therapist, without a certificate of registration as a Physical Therapist issued to him pursuant to the provisions of sections 148.65 to 148.78.

c) Employ fraud or deception in applying for or serving a certificate of registration as a Physical Therapist.

Nothing contained in sections 148.65 to 148.78 shall prohibit any person licensed or registered in this state under another law from carrying out the therapy or practice for which he is duly licensed or registered.

Minn. Stat. Ann. § 148.76.

Type III. *States which require licensure to practice physical therapy or hold oneself out as a physical therapist, which do not limit any person licensed or registered in the state under another law from engaging in the practice for which he or she is licensed or registered, and which permit the use of physical therapy as previously defined, by unlicensed personnel under the supervision of someone who is licensed.* This type of law is the same as Type II except it allows the use of physical therapy by unlicensed persons under the supervision of doctors and physical therapists. An athletic trainer working under the direction of a team physician could easily fall into the category of unlicensed personnel in states which do not have athletic trainer licensure laws. Athletic trainers in states with athletic trainer licensure and Type III physical therapy laws would still be legally able to use physical therapy as in Type II states. An example of Type III law is taken from the Tennessee Statutes:

a) From and after July 1, 1976, no person shall practice physical therapy or act as a physical therapist's assistant, nor hold himself out as being able to practice physical therapy or act as a physical therapist's assistant, unless he holds a license and otherwise complies with the provisions of this chapter and the rules and regulations adopted by the board.

b) Nothing in this chapter, however, shall prohibit any person licensed to practice any of the other health-related professions in this state under any other law from engaging in the practice for which he is licensed; nor shall it prohibit persons employed as subsidiary workers in approved hospitals, nursing homes, physician's offices and medical and rehabilitation clinics who do not represent themselves to be licensed physical therapists or physical therapist's assistants from assisting in the physical therapy care of patients under the direction and supervision of a licensed physician, dentist, osteopath, or physical therapist.

Tenn. Code Ann. § 63-13-105.

Type IV. *States placing no licensure requirements as to practice of physical therapy as defined, so long as one does not hold oneself out to be a physical therapist.* With a Type IV law, almost all persons can use physical therapy as long as they do not try to represent themselves as physical therapists. An athletic trainer in such a state could easily use physical therapy as long as he or she did not refer to its use as such. Baker and Rode suggested the following in their article:

> It would be best to eliminate the words "physical therapy" from the training staff vocabulary and records. Physical therapy modalities could be referred to as treatment modalities. The term "rehabilitation" should be eliminated because of its close relationship to the field of physical therapy and replaced with "injury reconditioning."

§ 5.1(C). Statutory Requirements by States.

Following is a categorization of statutory requirements in the fifty states into either Type I, Type II, Type III or Type IV statutes:

Type I (11 states):
Alaska (§ 08:84.150), Connecticut (§ 20-73), Hawaii (§ 321-13), Michigan (§ 14:15 17820), New Hampshire (§ 328-A), New Jersey (§ 45:9-37:1), New York (§ 6730), Rhode Island (§ 5-40-9), South Carolina (§ 40-45-100), Texas (§ 4512e), Virginia (§ 54-274).

Type II (26 states):
Alabama (§ 34-24-190), Arizona (§ 32-3001), Arkansas (§ 72-1330), California (§ 2630), Colorado (§ 12-41-120), District of Columbia (§ 2-1703.3) Florida (§ 486-161), Georgia (§ 84-3011), Illinois (§ 91-22.2), Indiana (§ 25-27-1-2), Kentucky (§ 327.020), Maine (§ 32-3113), Maryland (§ 13-102), Massachusetts (§ 112-23A) Minnesota (§ 148.76) Nebraska (§ 71-2800), Nevada (§ 640.169), New Mexico (§ 61-12), Oklahoma (§ 59.887), Pennsylvania (§ 63-1301), Utah (§ 58-24-5), Vermont (§ 26-2082), Washington (§ 18:74.125), West Virginia (§ 30-20-3), Wisconsin (§ 448.09), Wyoming (§ 33-25-102).

Type III (6 states):
Delaware (§ 24-2606), Idaho (§ 54.2204), Louisiana (§ 37:2410), North Carolina (§ 90:270.24), Ohio (§ 47.55.40), Tennessee (§ 63-13.105).

Type IV (7 states):
Iowa (§ 148A.3), Kansas (§ 65-2913), Mississippi (§ 73-23), Missouri (§ 334:500), Montana (§ 37-11-10), North Dakota (§ 43-26-12), Oregon (§ 688:030).

§ 5.1(D). Conclusion.

It can be plainly seen that the majority of states have physical therapy statutes which are reasonably strict in that they restrict the number and types of individuals who can legally engage in the practice of physical therapy and who may legally use physical therapy modalities.

It should also be noted that of the 11 states which presently have licensure statutes for athletic trainers, all require that the athletic trainer function either under the direction and supervision of a licensed physician or have written authorization from a physician to use physical therapy techniques and modalities. Such may not necessarily hold true for physical therapists.

Athletic training as a profession needs to continue to strive for licensure in each state as its top priority. Until the lofty goal is achieved, the profession needs to attempt to ensure that the day-to-day functions and activities of its members fall completely within the legal parameters for such activity in each state where licensure is not yet a reality.

§ 5.2. Drug Testing in Sports.

By Kenneth S. Clarke

Drug testing for performance-enhancing drugs (i.e., drugs taken by athletes with the expectation or at least hope to increase their athletic prowess) came into the editorial forefront at the 1983 Pan American Games in Caracas, Venezuela. A number of athletes were detected through laboratory analysis to have banned substances in their urine and, as a result, lost their eligibility and medals earned. A number of other athletes decided to return home before competing, claiming among reasons given confusion as to what was banned and how long innocent use of a banned substance (e.g., in Dristan, Allerest, Nyquil, etc.) would remain detectable in the urine. A number of other athletes stayed, yet allegedly performed below their true capability to avoid being selected, as all top medalists were, for drug testing.

Exacerbating the highly publicized situation were complaints that the world championships in track and field in Helsinki, Finland a few weeks before also included drug testing; and while according to one journalist a number of athletes allegedly were found positive for a banned substance (such findings were vehemently denied the next day by the meet's officials), no official positives emerged from their drug testing program.

It was understandable that confusion, rumor, sensationalism, face-saving, hyperbole and frustration permeated the media's investigative pursuit of clarity. It was also understandable that the United States Olympic Committee (U.S.O.C.) wanted clarity as to the problem and the solution and, by the conclusion of the Pan Am Games, created a Drug Control Task Force to create a protocol for a professional, credible and practical drug testing program that would protect the athlete's rights as well as detect users. The key missing ingredient that had kept the U.S.O.C. from entering into this earlier was a lab with true proficiency in detecting anabolic steroids and testosterone. Dr. Manfred Donike, a member of the International Olympic Committee (I.O.C.) Medical Commission, who with his staff from Cologne had been retained for the Pan American Games and had demonstrated the proficiency that enabled the "drug problem" to emerge into the open, offered to the United States the services of his lab until the University of California at Los Angeles (U.C.L.A.) Laboratory (Pharmacology and Toxicology) was evaluated and found proficient by the I.O.C.

In explanation, the saying goes: "Any lab can find a negative." The challenge is not only to declare a positive for an anabolic steroid, especially one that typically is in the urine of an athlete who had tried various means to disguise such, but also to document without legal or professional question that this indeed was that particular substance. As we learned in the fall of 1983 while attempting to find a backup lab in the United States to U.C.L.A., a number of laboratory directors offered that they "would be ready in a few weeks," whereas U.C.L.A. trained their staff for about a year before seeking the certification exam. There simply has been no call in our society for any proficiency in the detection of anabolic steroids and exogenous testosterone except in the Olympic movement, and it is not easy to attain.

With that as preface, the resulting U.S.O.C. Drug Control Protocol was eventually drafted, reviewed by physicians and athletes (and attorneys) and adopted as policy by the U.S.O.C. Executive Board in November, 1983 with provision both for formal testing (leading to punitive action if positive) and informal testing (leading to the education of athlete and the sport's leadership with the individuals' findings kept confidential) up to the Olympic trials, and with the new policy that all Olympic-bound athletes shall be drug-tested at the Olympic trials and at least disqualified from joining the Olympic team if found positive.

Following are the legal considerations within the protocol:

1. the banned list
2. informed consent
3. prevention of a false positive
4. prevention of a false negative
5. confidentiality
6. accurate information
7. appeal

§ 5.2(A). The Banned List.

The U.S.O.C. adopted the List of Banned Drugs issued by the International Olympic Committee. This list is what is invoked at the sites of the Olympics and other international occasions, and consequently is utilized verbatim for U.S. purposes as well. It may be that in the future an expert committee in the United States can and will be formed to examine that list and cause changes, but until then any challenge of a banned substance must be directed to the I.O.C., not U.S.O.C., for it is the I.O.C.'s list against which our athletes' urine contents will be evaluated.

§ 5.2(B). Informed Consent.

Prior to any occasion at which formal testing is to be conducted, the athlete is notified prior to registration of that fact and that the athlete who does not comply or has a positive finding will be subject to disqualification and loss of eligibility. Registration for competition then constitutes informed consent to accept this responsibility of compliance if selected at the event.

For informal testing, the sponsoring National Governing Body (N.G.B.) for that sport may require compliance (to ensure interpretable aggregate data) or simply have it an opportunity for interested athletes. Whichever it may be, if it is not purely voluntary the athlete must be informed at or prior to registration for that event of the opportunities, confidentiality and obligations associated with the drug test.

§ 5.2(C). Prevention of a False Positive.

Nothing is of more concern than labeling an innocent athlete guilty of using a banned substance. Whether it be tampering or lab error, the following procedures are used to negate this possibility.

When the athlete is notified of being selected for drug testing (typically, immediately after his event), the athlete is escorted personally to the drug testing station, and information is obtained to be sure that the person about to be tested is the athlete selected for testing.

At the drug testing station, every conceivable measure is taken to prevent an athlete from being "set up." The athlete selects a code number from a list of code numbers. The athlete selects a beaker that is sealed in plastic from a bin of such beakers. The athlete is then observed directly as he provides a specimen in the beaker. The athlete then carries the specimen back to the desk, selecting a pair of bottles sealed in plastic from a bin of such paired bottles. The athlete pours the urine into both bottles (Specimen A and Specimen B) and observes the crew member first plug, cap and seal the bottle (turning it upside-down to demonstrate the seal) and then apply the athlete's code number to the two bottles (by diamond stylus, currently) and place the two bottles in a special shipping case. The athlete then signs a form attesting that all these procedures were followed. These "Athlete Signature Forms," the only documents that combine name and code number, comprise the confidential "master code." They are sent to the U.S.O.C. Executive Director by the physician Crew Chief under formal (confidential) conditions and kept solely by the physician Crew Chief if informal.

The specifically designed shipping case (e.g., no external hinges) is eventually closed and sealed (with a manifest listing all code numbers inside) and sent to the lab by a special freight-carrier service that requires a chain-of-custody series of signatures as the case passes from person to person attesting acceptance and delivery from point to point with the case's seal intact. The last person in this chain is at the laboratory.

When opened at the lab, the personnel examine each bottle and record that the respective seals are intact (if so) and analyze Specimen A. A "standard" or known drug is included in the analysis to permit the laboratory to verify that the machine was functioning properly. If a positive is found in a formal test, the Lab Director notifies the U.S.O.C. Sports Medicine Division Director of the code number, who in turn informs the Executive Director, who in turn breaks the master code and informs the athlete by overnight/signature-required confidential letter (and phone call if available) that Specimen A was positive and Specimen B thereby will be analyzed. The athlete is given the right to be present or be represented when this occurs (to verify the code number and examine Specimen B for evidence of tampering). Further, Specimen B is analyzed by a lab person other than the one who analyzed Specimen A. The results of Specimen B constitutes the final official result. Documentation of a positive is enabled by mass spectrometry that clearly identifies the banned compound by its actual molecular structure.

§ 5.2(D). Prevention of a False Negative.

It is far easier to know that a positive is a true positive than it is to know a negative is a true negative. All innocent athletes want to be assured, however, that an opponent who is not innocent stands the least possible chance of beating the system. Many of the procedures used to protect from false positives also serve to prevent false negatives: e.g., athletic identification, continuous observation of the athlete from selection to delivery of the specimen, direct scrutiny of the urine delivery process.

In addition, the acidic level of the urine is checked (from the residual in the beaker after the two bottles are sealed) to see if an alkalizing agent was taken to confuse the analysis. If so, the athlete is detained until an acidic urine is provided. Diluted urine also is cause for detaining the athlete for a normal specimen, to preclude use of diuretics that dilute the urine and thereby lessen the chance of revealing a banned substance.

Other methods are employed to get at patterns of use as they are learned.

§ 5.2(E). Confidentiality.

For formal or informal tests, the athlete is known by name only by the person maintaining the master code. For formal purposes, this is U.S.O.C.'s Executive Director; for informal purposes, it is the physician serving as Crew Chief for that occasion. All other communications deal with the four-digit number selected by the athlete at the time he provides a urine specimen from a list of four-digit numbers. For informal tests, the physician shares the result confidentially with the athlete and offers assistance if the athlete wishes assistance with a problem associated with that drug's use. The sports administrators involved receive a summary report with the aggregate data for that occasion (e.g., "of the 24 athletes tested, two were positive for ephedrine, and the Crew Chief is in contact with them").

In formal testing, the U.S.O.C. Executive Director informs only the athlete (see § 5.2(C)) that Specimen A is positive. Until Specimen B confirms that the athlete had used a banned substance, no one else is informed.

§ 5.2(F). Accurate Information.

Of major concern to all athletes is the list of banned drugs. The I.O.C. identifies five categories: psychomotor stimulants, miscellaneous central nervous system stimulants, sympathomimetic amines, narcotic analgesics and anabolic steroids. At the end of each is the catch-all phrase "and related compounds." This is done because of the plethora of compounds emerging in different countries having similar characteristics, but it poses a need for accurate awareness of the status of a given drug or medication because numerous banned substances are found in medications that are commonly used by athletes for maladies they may experience (e.g., sinus congestion, cough) who had no intent nor knowledge that banned substance was being taken. Because laboratory machines cannot read motive, innocent use (and prescribed use) is no defense against disqualification.

Consequently, the U.S.O.C. puts great emphasis on the availability of its Hotline for athletes and their physicians to call to check out *any* medication the athlete may take or be given to see if it contains a banned substance. The U.S.O.C.'s Chief Medical Officer not only oversees this Hotline but also informs the U.S.O.C. Sports Medicine Division Director if the status of a particular drug or medication is unclear. A telex is then sent to the I.O.C. Medical Commission with a documented response returned typically within 48 hours.

Informal testing periodically identifies a few athletes from various sports who still haven't gotten this message. At least punitive action is not a result under these conditions, and the grapevine sensitizes the others to take this threat of inadvertent use seriously. As the risk of certain adverse effects must accompany the desired effects of a given drug, the potential for penalizing inadvertent use of a banned substance must accompany the deterrence, via credible drug testing, of the purposeful use of that drug.

§ 5.2(G). Appeal.

The athlete who faces punitive action by the U.S.O.C. via a positive Specimen B has the privilege of appeal by expressing on paper to the U.S.O.C. Executive Director the basis for the appeal. If that basis reveals a possible breach in the protection of the athlete from a possible false positive, this possibility will be pursued by appropriate experts at the request of the Executive Director. The facts found by this pursuit will determine the course of action on the appeal.

§ 5.2(H). Conclusion.

Drug testing is not merely the collection of urine and its laboratory analysis. Every one of the many steps in the process, from the athlete's awareness of what drugs are banned (including medications that contain banned drugs) to the athlete's right for appeal if grounds exist, must be treated as the most critical component of these linked steps. Short of that, it is difficult to have positives from users substantiated under scrutiny and to have those with negatives be accepted in society as other than false negatives.

---

§ 5.3. Emergency Medical Services for Large Crowds.

By Chester Lloyd

§ 5.3(A). Introduction.

As the football crowd grows anxious during the end of the second half of the season's last game, a middle-aged spectator clutches his chest, moans and falls backward into his seat. His wife and friends attempt to revive him, but he does not respond — heartbeat and breathing have ceased. If he is to have a chance at surviving the heart attack, trained help must arrive shortly.

When incidents such as this occur at home, we pick up the phone and dial our local emergency medical service. But when life-threatening emergencies occur in a crowd, the public is often at the mercy of the facility for providing a planned, organized and rapid response to its emergency medical needs.

§ 5.3(B). Duty to Provide an Emergency Medical Capability.

Numerous studies have shown that medical emergencies occur with some frequency at large gatherings. One such study, published in volume 30 of J. of American College Health Ass'n at 145-47 (Dec. 1981), reviewed injury and illness data collected over four football seasons at a stadium with a capacity of 75,000. The results showed that an average of 5.23 patients (2.83-8.00 patient range) were seen by stadium emergency medical teams per 10,000 spectators during a four-hour game. Using this data, the facility could foresee from 21-60 medical or traumatic incidents per game. In addition, the stadium or arena environment may foster more medical emergencies than those expected in the general population, because many spectators gulp down "tailgate dinners," imbibe alcoholic beverages and then rush up 100 steps to their seats. For some, this type of activity is the ultimate stress test which increases the risk of cardiac problems.

Facility managers have a legal duty to protect and warn spectators of foreseeable hazards and harms. If medical emergencies and injuries which are foreseen in large crowd situations are not handled properly through an organized emergency medical response system, the spectator may suffer additional harm. Harm results from improper emergency management causing aggravation of the acute illness or injury.

§ 5.3(C). Standards and Guidelines Specify the Scope of Treatments.

The American Heart Association (AHA) sponsored a conference in 1979 to update standards for emergency cardiac care that were originally developed in 1973 by the AHA and the National Academy of Sciences — National Research Council. Based upon medical research and reports during the 1970's, special recommendations were made for facilities where large crowds are regularly present or can reasonably be anticipated. In such facilities, the recommendations call for a basic cardiac life support capability to be available in 60 seconds or less and an advanced cardiac life support capability within ten minutes, preferably less.

Basic cardiac life support prevents circulatory and respiratory arrest via prompt recognition and intervention in cardiac and respiratory emergencies. This level of emergency cardiac care also provides for mouth-to-mouth breathing and chest compression (Cardiopulmonary Resuscitation — (CPR)) should breathing and heart stop. This procedure keeps the vital organs alive since the rescuer acts as the victim's heart and lungs. This procedure can be learned in 4 to 12 hours.

Advanced cardiac life support includes basic life support and elements of cardiac care that require more specialized training. Doctors, nurses and paramedics may provide this type of care which consists of administration of lifesaving drugs and defibrillation of the heart in an attempt to stimulate the heart back into action.

When basic cardiac care is initiated and followed quickly by advanced cardiac care, 80% of those spectators who suffer respiratory and circulatory arrest (sudden death) may survive. This is the basis for the special recommendations. If CPR is not provided to a pulseless and non-breathing patient, after four minutes, irreversible brain death starts to occur. When CPR is provided rapidly but advanced cardiac care is delayed, survivability will be low. The 1979 American Heart Association Standards and Guidelines go on to state that "failure of a facility to provide such a readily achievable lifesaving capability (following the special recommendations) may be found to represent legally actionable negligence." It is known that standards distributed by professional societies, such as the American Heart Association, are likely to be viewed as evidence of the accepted standard of medical care by the courts.

During the AHA conference, much attention was given to "cardiac care." While fractures and other acute injuries and illnesses are important, heart disease is the number one killer in this country. More than half of these deaths occur outside the hospital and many could be prevented through a rapid emergency medical response. If the facility can respond appropriately to a "sudden cardiac death" emergency, other emergencies, many of them not as urgent, will be handled effectively as well. It is important to note that those capable of specialized training in advanced cardiac care usually have the capability to treat other medical and trauma emergencies.

§ 5.3(D). Other Facilities and State Laws May Dictate Level of Care.

Many facilities which attract large crowds have programs that provide emergency medical systems. Other facilities may be judged by the standards set by such facilities.

Some states have laws relating to emergency medical care at mass gatherings. These laws address numbers of personnel, training, length and type of the event, equipment, and crowd size. Some laws seem impractical because they do not ensure basic and advanced cardiac care according to Heart Association Standards. For example, Connecticut law requires that any gathering of 3,000 persons or more lasting for 18 consecutive hours must provide one physician per 1,000 people. In addition, stadiums, athletic fields, arenas, auditoriums, coliseums or other permanently established places of assembly are exempt from this law. The law is probably never used with the exception of a state fair or outdoor music festival. On the rare occasion the law is applied, the physician requirement is not practical and is expensive.

It is important to note that whether a state law addresses emergency medical responses or not, a facility may still be held to other standards of medical care. These standards include the Heart Association's standards and those set by other large-capacity facilities nationally.

§ 5.3(E). The Emergency Medical System in Action.

Returning to the football game, the following scenario will suggest how a fictitious large-capacity stadium would likely handle medical emergencies.

After the victim's wife shook him with no response, she had to summon aid. She remembered reading the notice which came with her season ticket and which was announced over the loudspeaker at each event. "In case of medical emergency, please notify the nearest usher, police officer or emergency medical team." She had her friend run to the nearest usher to request medical aid.

The usher's orange vest made him clearly visible to the crowd. In addition, he was trained to concentrate on the crowd and not the game. When notified of the emergency, he knew how to react. His facility's emergency medical system had provided him with CPR training, written guidelines and practice in approaching medical emergencies.

On his portable radio, he notified the central communications center of a medical emergency in section L, row 25. He approached the victim and after a quick assessment notified the communications booth that he had a spectator who was not breathing and had no pulse. As he had learned from frequent drills, he positioned the victim across the bench with the help of another usher and provided CPR.

Central communications immediately dispatched a team of emergency medical technicians (EMTs) covering that sector of the crowd. The technicians had taken an 80 to 120 hour course covering the management of medical and trauma emergencies which was used as the ambulance training program for the state. This facility provided experienced EMTs to stabilize and then evacuate victims of medical trauma emergencies from the spectator area.

The communications center also notified the physician and both nurses in the emergency life-support station closest to that area of the stadium. While one nurse readied the station for receiving the patient, the physician and other nurse responded to the incident with advanced cardiac care equipment via a golf cart modified to serve as a "mini" ambulance.

Through the communications center other ushers and public safety personnel (police, security, etc.) were alerted for crowd control. Since all radio messages were coordinated through one central point, all facility public-safety and medical personnel were notified of the emergency and acted as per a planned, clear and concise protocol. Some responded to the incident, others filled in areas left vacant by those responding to the victim and the remaining public safety staff were alerted that resources for a particular area were busy and to be prepared to provide coverage to other areas as well as their own. The emergency medical-system coordinator, the security chief, the head usher and other administrative personnel were present in the center to help coordinate the response.

Shortly after the ushers started CPR, the team of two EMTs arrived with oxygen and a special patient litter to facilitate safe evacuation. The team continued CPR but provided ventilation to the victim now using the much-needed oxygen. The team prepared the victim for transportation to the waiting golf cart just outside the section L entrance.

In order for the patient to receive advanced cardiac care as soon as possible, the physician and nurse, both proficient in emergency medicine, met the EMTs with the cart and administered the initial steps of advanced cardiac care. Basic cardiac care, now supplemented by advanced cardiac care, was continued enroute to the life-support station.

At the station, which offered a more controlled environment and an additional complement of life-saving drugs and equipment, the patient's heart resumed beating after a few rounds of treatment. The physician-in-charge relayed the details of the patient's condition and treatment to the local hospital via the telephone so they could prepare to receive the patient. After the victim's condition stabilized, he was transferred to the local hospital by one of the three ambulances stationed at the stadium. One ambulance was on the playing field solely for the participants, the other two were parked outside the life-support units on each side of the stadium for spectator emergencies. By having an ambulance near a station, the risk of hitting spectators on crowded walks and drives was lessened considerably.

The entire incident, from the initial call for help to hospital admission, was thoroughly documented by written reports. The EMTs, being licensed and responsible for basic cardiac care, documented their treatment which also specified that ushers were doing resuscitation. This report and the physician's documentation of advanced care were kept on file for legal purposes and follow-up evaluation.

In summary, a heart attack victim was given a second chance at life because the facility's emergency medical system was planned and organized around the goal of rapid basic (within 60 seconds) and advanced (in less than 10 minutes) cardiac care. Coordination through experienced leadership and interagency cooperation was responsible for meeting this goal.

§ 5.3(F). Planning for Emergency Medical Response.

Plan an on-site, emergency medical response system, by structuring the system around the following elements:

1. *Public Access to Emergency Medical Aid.*
   a. Provide and train public safety officers, ushers, vendors and other facility personnel who know how to promptly summon medical aid.
   b. Place emergency medical teams strategically throughout the crowd (coverage in parking areas before/after events).
   c. Clearly mark emergency life support units (medical aid stations) and place them in highly visible locations.
   d. Use printed programs and season-ticket package inserts to identify locations of emergency life-support units (so those with minor ailments know where to seek aid) and briefly describe how

to summon help (for medical and trauma emergencies requiring evacuation by emergency medical teams).

e. Use public address announcements such as: "In the case of emergency, notify your nearest usher, police officer or emergency medical team."

f. Install public emergency phones or video monitors on exit ramps, stairways or other hard-to-monitor areas of the facility.

g. Provide emergency signs, done professionally, and targeted to the facility and crowd characteristics.

2. *Personnel and Training.*

a. Provide all nonmedical personnel with guidelines on how to react in medical emergencies.

b. Train nonmedical personnel (ushers and security) in basic cardiac life support (CPR).

c. Staff emergency medical teams with emergency medical technicians.

d. Staff emergency life support units with personnel capable of providing advanced cardiac life support (paramedics, nurses or physicians).

e. Provide an adequate number of public safety personnel based upon the size of the crowd, crowd make-up, facility lay-out, environment, event-type, general vs. reserved admission and past injury and illness experience.

f. Arrange for ambulance transportation by a competent service after patient stabilization in the emergency life-support unit; if outside ambulance service provides on-site ambulances, get proof that personnel are properly trained.

g. Utilize periodic drills to test the effectiveness of the emergency medical system and update the skills of facility personnel.

3. *Central Communications Center.*

a. Coordinate all public-safety communications (medical, security, crowd control, etc.) through a central post allowing for rapid relay of emergency messages.

b. Link emergency medical teams to each other and a central post via portable radios or other means.

c. Develop the capability of nonmedical personnel to notify the central post (via radio, intercom or phone) to request emergency medical assistance.

d. Place supervisory public safety and administrative personnel in center to troubleshoot problems.

e. Locate the center preferably in press box or other location which allows view of as much of the facility as possible.

4. *Written Protocols and Guidelines.*

a. Make certain that all nonmedical personnel understand written guidelines defining their specific roles in medical emergencies (i.e., who to call or what actions to take before medical teams arrive).

b. Provide the medical staff with written treatment protocols signed by the physician medical director covering all phases of patient treatment in the facility.

c. Develop plans that address actions to be taken when heavy patient load or simultaneous emergencies occur.

d. Coordinate mutual aid agreements and disaster plans with outside public safety agencies in case of heavy patient load or catastrophe.

e. Provide written protocols to demonstrate that the facility and its staff are prepared for medical and trauma emergencies should litigation arise.

5. *Record-Keeping.*

a. Document all emergency treatment rendered at the facility in writing.

b. Include in the record: The patient's name, sex, age, address, next-of-kin; nature of the illness or injuries and a description or the mechanism of how the injuries occurred; location and how the patient was found (i.e., lying face down, sitting, etc.); the chief complaint or signs and symptoms displayed by the patient; vital signs; patient's past medical history, current medications and known allergies to any medications; all treatment rendered by facility personnel (treatment rendered by other persons prior to medical team arrival should be noted, too); how the victim was transported to the emergency life support unit (stretcher, walked, etc.); disposition of the patient (to hospital via ambulance, referred to private physician, etc.); and data such as time call received, date, names of team members and who made the initial call for help.

c. If possible, obtain a signed refusal of medical treatment from any sick or injured person refusing medical assistance.

d. At the emergency life support station keep a log of all patients seen by name, injury or illness complaint and time.

e. Utilize complete records to prevent or defend charges of negligence.

f. Review records retrospectively to prevent future injuries by identifying hazards as well as crowds and events at high risk for problems.

g. Review records to assess emergency medical program effectiveness.

6. *Equipment.*

a. Provide adequate communications devices which permit clear signal reception in all areas of the facility.

b. Equip emergency medical teams (comprised of EMTs) with oxygen and other "tools of their trade."

c. Provide specialized patient litters for safe evacuation from the spectator area and provide a wheeled cart or other device for transport to the emergency life support unit.

    d. Provide emergency life support units with state-of-the-art equipment for advanced cardiac life support and other medical and trauma emergencies.

    e. Provide on-site ambulances properly equipped as per state and local laws.

7. *Physician Medical Director.*

    a. Responsible for all medical treatment given by a facility's emergency medical personnel.

    b. Experienced in emergency medicine.

8. *Administrative Coordinator.*

    a. Responsible for the overall operation and management of the emergency medical response system.

    b. Prepares written protocols and guidelines with the medical director as well as mutual aid and disaster plans with outside public safety agencies.

    c. Experienced in emergency medical operations.

    d. Probably the most important person in determining the success and cost-effectiveness of the facility's emergency medical program.

These eight elements are guidelines that will help assess present methods for handling medical emergencies or in constructing a new emergency medical system. Pay particular attention to items 7 and 8. The coordinator and medical director should oversee the entire program. Specifically, the coordinator serves as the link between all agencies and should be available during events in the communications center. Whether the coordinator's position is full-time, part-time or assigned to an existing staff member, depends on the facility size and event traffic.

A consultant knowledgeable in emergency medical operations at large gatherings may be used to evaluate and prepare an emergency medical system for a facility. In preparing a system, the consultant may identify community resources (personnel, equipment, etc.), evaluate local and state laws, develop training programs, review facility insurance coverage (relating to the emergency medical program), and give advice on crowd management and facility safety. A consultant can also instruct a facility manager in emergency medical-program maintenance and can be available for future planning. Using a consultant to develop a program to fit a facility may save time and reduces the chance for costly error.

A coordinator or consultant should select a physician medical director with knowledge of emergency medical response. This physician should underwrite all medical protocol and treatment given by the facility medical staff. To illustrate, a facility may request a physician from the local medical center's emergency department to serve as the director. If he agrees, for a stipend or as a service of the medical center, he and the coordinator would draw up treatment procedures addressing the scope of medical care provided in the facility. Only treatment provided for in writing, signed by this physician, may be given. Even if aspirins are dispensed by facility nurses, written protocol, signed by the physician should specifically define under what conditions and to whom aspirin should be provided. Whether the medical director attends each event or not, all medical treatment is carried out under his initial written protocol. The medical director, in cooperation with the coordinator, will want to certify that all medical personnel are competent. Should litigation arise, treatment protocol shows the courts that medical treatment provided at the facility followed the accepted standard for medical care and was given under the direction of the facility's physician medical director.

In planning a system, facility managers should use caution if they depend on outside agencies for on-site emergency medical needs. In a true account, while city ambulances and paramedics sped away from a stadium of 50,000 spectators to respond to a serious auto accident, a spectator with a medical emergency was without transportation to the hospital. Finally, a station-wagon-type vehicle was used because no ambulances would be available for some time. Fortunately, the facility had an on-site emergency medical system which attended to the victim. In this case, it would have been prudent for the facility to require that the ambulance contractor commit the ambulances to the facility from one hour before to one hour after the game.

If hospitals or ambulances are next door, the emergency medical response system should still be planned as if the facility were across town. Remember that the rescue vehicles may be out on other calls and a hospital's emergency-department staff usually is not available to come to the facility. Consider too that ambulance crews stationed outside the entrance may have long response times trying to get through the crowds. Only with the emergency medical personnel and the emergency life-support station(s) placed strategically throughout the crowd and the facility, along with other facility personnel knowing their roles in emergencies, can the public be assured of rapid access to emergency medical help. The days of the simple first-aid station are gone. Today, having enough people on hand under one roof or in a confined area to populate a small city is quite a responsibility.

Liability insurance covering the facility should be reviewed when implementing the emergency medical program. Since the type of coverage depends upon the individual facility and insurance company, facility administrators should seek advice from their insurer or consultant.

Emergency medical technicians, paramedics, nurses and physicians are all state-licensed health professionals. Even though they may have liability insurance, a facility should have its own liability insurance policy. Ushers, security and other ancillary personnel who are trained in CPR or first aid will usually be covered under the facility's general-liability policy which may include an incidental malpractice clause covering personnel in the event they assist the medical teams with CPR or other basic procedure. Since it is not their specific duty to provide medical treatment at the facility, and provided they are not licensed health professionals, they do not need medical malpractice insurance.

In regard to outside ambulance companies contracted to provide transportation to the hospital or additional personnel, the facility should be named as an additional insured on the ambulance company's insurance policies. The facility should also check on the limits of such policies. All ambulance staff and vehicles should be checked to make sure they comply with state and local laws.

The argument has been made that having personnel with little or no training may be "safer" than having licensed professionals. This is not a valid argument because in court the facility with the documented and functioning emergency medical system in place will be better able to defend charges of negligence. The only loss may be that of the lawyer's fees. But without an emergency medical program, loss in the form of claims may be more because of damage done to a victim by inexperienced and untrained rescuers in an environment that called for trained professionals. Even the "Good Samaritan laws" are being challenged because victims need protection too.

In summary, plan your program around the eight guidelines to achieve a "tiered" emergency medical response; provide basic cardiac care initially using ushers or security personnel and continue with teams of emergency medical technicians who transfer the patient to an on-site life support station where advanced cardiac care may be provided under the direction of a physician.

§ 5.3(G). Program Complexity.

Every facility, large or small, should have a plan of action for medical emergencies and the capability of rendering basic cardiac care. The question of program complexity deals primarily with the provision of advanced cardiac care. The responsibility to provide advanced cardiac care is not clear-cut when dealing with facilities which attract moderate-sized crowds (1-10,000 spectators). Whether advanced care should be provided at these facilities or events may depend upon: event length and type (rock concert vs. musical), crowd type (age, emotion, etc.), a facility's or event's past illness and injury record, weather (i.e., warm weather often results in more medical incidents), and medical (personnel, equipment, etc.) and financial resources.

The special recommendations from the Heart Association do not define an absolute crowd size when dealing with the provision of advanced cardiac care for a "large gathering." If a facility attracts 40,000 per event, advanced cardiac care should be made available without reservation. But in planning a system for a facility with 7,000 (for example) in regular attendance, the decision to provide advanced care on-site may weigh on a facility audit addressing the factors listed above and other considerations which may surface during the investigation.

To illustrate, New York State's Mass Gathering Law requires a physician-on-site at any public function with 25,000 or more in attendance. If a facility in New York was expecting 7,000 "60-and-over folks" for a "senior olympics," a reasonable and prudent facility manager would do well to exceed the law and provide advanced cardiac care. If a person suffered a heart attack and was unable to be revived with basic cardiac care alone, considering the event and the type of crowd, a lawyer might argue that medical emergencies were foreseeable and the facility should have followed the Heart Association's recommendations.

As a distant alternative to on-site advanced care personnel in small facilities, a "life-support kit" carrying some essential resuscitation equipment may be kept and maintained at the facility in the event that physicians in the crowd are willing to help. The kit would have to be checked and restocked periodically with a physician's order. Facilities should take care and make sure those who offer to provide treatment with the kit are licensed physicians.

§ 5.3(H). Conclusion — Program Benefits.

Although there is initial expense for such a program, costs can be kept low depending upon existing facility and community resources. At a university, volunteer student EMTs may supplement a paid local staff. Equipment may be borrowed from university agencies or local service groups, such as the Red Cross or the local disaster agency. Having all agencies sit down after events to critique and improve public safety is not expensive. A facility's emergency response capabilities can be improved greatly through education, coordination and interagency cooperation.

At facilities hosting sporting events, a spectator emergency medical system will benefit athletes by making available to them the most up-to-date emergency treatment procedures. In certain facilities across the nation, spectators receive much more advanced emergency treatment than athletes simply because the athletic field is often the trainers' and coaches' domain and, except in extreme situations, off-limits to facility emergency medical teams. An experienced emergency medical technician or emergency physician should serve not to replace the trainer or team physician, but could offer valuable advice in handling emergencies on the field. After witnessing players being removed from the playing fields with unstable fractures which did not receive immobilization, or upon reading about a marathoner who was unable to find emergency medical aid when suffering heat exhaustion during her twentieth mile, it is evident that athletes would gain advantages in spectator emergency medical plans.

Through rapid detection and prompt intervention of medical emergencies, the emergency medical system helps manage crowd confusion and promotes good public relations. In addition, facility safety hazards may be decreased by thorough review of well-documented injury reports. Most important, state-of-the-art emergency medical treatment, delivered by a trained staff, in a well-organized and controlled emergency medical system, will save lives and reduce risk and the chances for liability.

CHAPTER 6

OFFICIALS AND SPECTATOR ISSUES

§ 6.1. Violence in Sport.

By Teri Engler

The game started out all right, but before long it got rather bloody. This is when both my English visitors started asking questions.

"Is the object of the game to injure as many players on the other team as possible?" the husband asked.

"No, that is not the object of the game," I said.

The wife said, "Do you get more points for breaking a man's leg or his neck?"

"You don't get points for breaking either his leg or neck. You get penalized for it."

"Oh," said the husband. "What is the penalty?"

"Your team is penalized 15 yards."

"Do you mean to say that if you break an opponent's leg, you only get 15 yards against you?"

"What do you think he should get?" I said, trying to hold my temper.

"In England, I believe it's three years in prison," the wife replied.

"It's a game!" I said. "The men who play expect to have their legs broken. That's what makes it so exciting."

"How civilized," the wife said.

I couldn't keep my temper any longer. "What do you think we are — barbarians?"

"Quite," the husband said.

Art Buchwald, "Beginners Watching Football," *Atlanta Journal and Constitution* (Oct. 23, 1977).

Americans turning to the newspaper's sports section or tuning in to television news are likely to run across enthusiastic accounts of violence on playing fields and rinks around the world. The images are enough to make a tender-hearted nonathlete (and even some seasoned jocks) squirm with discomfort: football players ramming their helmets into their opponents' bodies or batting them with their taped-up forearms . . . hockey players maiming each other with their sticks . . . baseball players sliding into base with their spikes intentionally aimed at the infielders . . . fans streaming out of the stands for mass assaults on officials, players or other fans. Most of these incidents take place in the professional arena, but school and amateur sports have become increasingly violent, too. Violence, some contend, is becoming a part of the game, just as it is becoming a part of our everyday life.

§ 6.1(A). Is Winning Everything?

Sports used to be appropriately rugged, but now they've slid over to being too violent. Why? Although several social and psychological theories have

179

been advanced, most commentators agree on at least two factors: (1) a greater emphasis on winning than on sportsmanship and (2) a surge in spectators' demands for brute force.

Our society values winning because it represents a reward for skill, work and commitment. But that is a far cry from the "winning is everything" attitude that has become prevalent in sports. How many times have you heard well-known and respected sport figures touting the need to win at all costs? "Winning isn't everything; it's the only thing." "Defeat is worse than death because you have to live with defeat." "Nice guys finish last." Sound familiar? Most of us were raised on questionable sports truisms like these, and many of us have probably repeated them to others — children, students, colleagues — at some point in time. The late Vince Lombardi, revered coach of the Green Bay Packers football team (and known as the "high priest of competition"), is often quoted as having said: "To play this game you have to have fire in you, and there is nothing that stokes that fire like hate." Jerry Kramer, one of Lombardi's best players, had a football fantasy that is a good case in point: "I see myself breaking (my opponent's) leg or knocking him unconscious, and then I see myself knocking out a couple of other guys, and then I see us scoring a touchdown . . . ."

Coaches and parents play a big part in inculcating the "winning is everything" attitude that can ultimately lead to brutality in sports. "Violence is learned," says Professor Henschon, psychologist and associate professor of health at the University of Utah. "Kids don't come into this world violent. They learn it from you and me. And we reward that violence in many subtle ways." Henschon believes, for instance, that coaches and parents often show youngsters that they care more about the product — winning — than the process of learning about a sport and developing the skills necessary to play and enjoy it to the fullest.

Part of the problem is the reverence coaches and parents have for extreme competitiveness. Their rationale is generally that competitiveness goes hand in hand with other "positive" personality traits, but as Thomas Tutko and William Bruns trenchantly observed in *Winning Isn't Everything and Other American Myths:*

> One of the strange beliefs that underlie competition is the assumption that if a person is competitive, he also possesses other positive character-istics. The athlete can throw a racquet, start fights, use "gamesmanship" to disrupt his opponent, throw tantrums, deliberately roughhouse a player or curse the officials, and it's dismissed because "He's a hell of a competitor. He wants to win." The athlete can be immature or childish or destructive, but because he "wants to win," this excuses his behavior. We surely wouldn't give the same consideration to a bank robber who beat up a teller and three customers, if his legal defense was: "He's a hell of a competitor. He really wanted to rob that bank. He's the number-three ranked bank robber in Colorado.

Henschon claims that a new set of sport heroes should replace the "anti-heroes" currently highly visible as a result of slanted media coverage. Fierce professional athletes like Jack (They Call Me Assassin) Tatum get too much attention for being violent. This, says Henschon, elevates their status in the eyes of young sports fans who are likely to follow the examples their "heroes" set.

§ 6.1(B). The Chicken or the Egg?

Though it is the focus of renewed attention, spectator violence is hardly new. As far back as 70 A.D., spectators at the games in Pompeii broke into wild sword fights which resulted in many deaths. The Roman Senate responded by banning all gladiator events for a decade. Five centuries later, thousands of people were killed when rival chariot-racing groups set off a series of riots that nearly destroyed Constantinople. In the early 1900's, a soccer match between the Scottish Football Association's Glasgow Rangers and the Glasgow Celtics became mayhem when the game ended in a draw and officials refused to allow any overtime. Clubhouse buildings were set afire by rampaging fans, who then cut the hoses as firemen attempted to fight the blazes. Fifty-eight policemen and hundreds of others were injured. In 1985 a riot broke out in Brussels, Belgium during the final soccer match of the Cup championship involving teams from Italy and England. British fans stormed into the Italian section and, in one of the worst acts of violence in the history of sports, 40 people were killed and 267 were injured.

Some observers suspect a link between violence on the field and that in the stands, though there is no hard evidence to support a causal connection. It also remains unclear in which direction the relationship between spectator and player violence runs — does spectator violence promote hand-to-hand combat among players, or is fan rowdiness fueled by player violence?

Michael Smith of New York University in Toronto has written extensively on the sociological aspects of sports violence. In a study he conducted of some 3000 issues of the Toronto Globe and Mail between 1963 and 1973, Smith found 100 incidents of sport violence reported. Twenty-seven of those incidents were fan violence, most of which were sparked by player violence, according to Smith.

But Smith and others are quick to point out that many other factors can play a part in spectator violence at sport events. Says Dr. Stanley Cheren of the Boston University School of Medicine: "An angry, drunken sport fan, aggravated by the difficulty of getting to the event, parking, dealing with crowds, stirred up by a support group of pals, is easily provoked to violence by the very presence of other violent behavior, namely that on the field." Although psychologists once thought that spectators could release their own aggressive urges simply by watching contact sports, some research shows just the opposite. Cheren, in an article entitled "The Psychiatric Perspective: Psychological Aspects of Violence in Sports" published in the *Journal of Sport and Social Issues* (Feb. 1981), says: "As people become experienced with violence the need grows for more extreme violence to satisfy the wish for violent stimulation."

§ 6.1(C). Courts as Referees.

Whatever its cause, sport violence — like so many other modern issues — have collided head-on with the law. Because of more and more dramatic instances of this growing violence, people are asking whether that law should intervene on the playing field. Consider, for example, the devastating case of the New England Patriots' young Darryl Stingley, who was permanently paralyzed as a result of a hit by Jack Tatum of the Oakland Raiders. Tatum has been quoted as saying that "intimidating" receivers by knocking them senseless is a legitimate part of the game of football. Should he have been criminally prosecuted? Should the courts be used to make a public declaration that this kind of savagery will not be tolerated in our society?

State criminal laws (assault and battery, disorderly conduct) generally prohibit spectator violence to other spectators, coaches and game officials. As for violence among the participants, a few states have specific laws covering attacks at sport events. In Oklahoma in 1980 an assistant baseball coach was convicted of "assault on a sports officiary." In that case the home plate umpire had just finished calling a ball game and was preparing to change his uniform for a second game when several players from the losing team surrounded him in the parking lot. Their assistant coach joined them and began exchanging words with the umpire, then suddenly struck the umpire in the jaw with his fist.

The coach was found guilty under a statute which provides:

> Every person who commits any assault and battery upon the person of a referee, umpire, timekeeper, coach, player, participant, official, sports reporter or any person having authority in connection with any amateur or professional athletic contest is punishable by imprisonment in the county jail not exceeding six months or by a fine not exceeding $500, or both such fine and imprisonment.

The case was affirmed on appeal and the coach was sentenced to pay $425 and court costs (*Carroll v. State,* 620 P.2d 416 (Okla. Crim. App. 1980)).

Criminal prosecutions against athletes for violence during the games are something else, though. They are hard to prove and thus are rarely undertaken. Before a person can be convicted of a crime, the prosecution must show that he or she not only committed the act, but also consciously intended to do it. This is extremely difficult to prove. In sports like football, hockey, soccer and basketball, there inevitably is hard contact between players without any specific intent to injure. Most of the time players are acting purely reflexively. Since the standard of proof in criminal cases is "guilty beyond a reasonable doubt," the prosecutor has a nearly impossible job.

But, says Harvard University Professor Arthur Miller, "possibly the greatest impediment to a criminal prosecutor is the reluctance of a jury to stigmatize a player with a criminal conviction, let alone a jail term. We are so accustomed to roughness on the field that the player who engages in it is seen as merely doing his job. A jury might hesitate to make him a scapegoat for the entire system — especially if he's a hometown hero."

Two cases show just how hard it is to get a conviction for on-field violence. In one of the earliest recorded cases of this type (*Regina v. Bradshaw,* 1978), an English soccer player was charged with manslaughter for the death of an opposing player. A soccer player was dribbling the ball toward his opponent's goal, and when an opposing player appeared in his path he kicked the ball out of the opposing player's reach. Meanwhile, during this action the side-stepped opponent charged, jumped into the air and struck the first player in the stomach with his knees. The blow ruptured the player's intestines and he died the next day.

The court identified the main issue as intent. It said:

> if a man is playing according to the rules and practice of the game and not going beyond it, it may be reasonable to infer that he is not actuated by any malicious motive or intention, and that he is not acting in a manner which he knows will be likely to be productive of death or injury.

That would imply that there has been no crime as long as there has been no violation of the rules. But, the court went on, if,

> independent of the rules, [the athlete causing the injury] intended to cause serious hurt to the deceased, or if he knew that, in charging as he did, he might produce serious injury and was indifferent and reckless as to whether he would produce serious injury or not, the act will be unlawful.

In this case, there was not enough evidence to show that the player intended to do harm. Because it was unclear whether the action took place before or after the deceased player had kicked the ball away, the court ruled that the accused player should be acquitted.

More recently, during a 1975 professional hockey game between the Boston Bruins and the Minnesota North Stars, Dave Forbes (of the Bruins) attacked Henry Boucha (of the North Stars), and both were assessed a first period penalty. Later, Forbes pounded on Boucha from behind, pummeling him with his fists and hockey stick. A local state's attorney who witnessed the incident from the crowd took the case to a grand jury and got an indictment against Forbes for aggravated assault with a deadly weapon. As it turned out, though, the jury could not agree upon a verdict and a mistrial was declared.

§ 6.1(D). Enforcing Civility.

Of course, civil actions for sports injuries may be brought regardless of the success of criminal actions. Civil suits are, in fact, brought far more frequently and have a greater chance of success, since the "preponderance of the evidence" standard of proof of a civil case is easier for plaintiffs to meet than the "beyond a reasonable doubt" standard in criminal actions. In the Forbes-Boucha incident, for example, after the jury failed to reach a verdict in the criminal case, Boucha filed a $3.5 million suit against Forbes, the Bruins and the National Hockey League. The suit was ultimately settled out of court.

Many other civil lawsuits on violence in sports events have gone to trial, and so far the message from the juries has been crystal clear: extreme violence in sports is unacceptable.

In 1979, a federal court jury awarded Houston Rockets basketball player Rudy Tomjanovich $3.3 million in actual and punitive damages for disfiguring injuries he sustained from a punch thrown by Kermit Washington (then of the Los Angeles Lakers) during a 1977 NBA game. (The suit was brought

against California Sports, Inc., the owner of the Lakers.) The jury found that
Washington had acted as an employee of the Lakers and that the team had
failed to train him adequately to avoid such violence. Knowing of his
"dangerous tendencies," the club did nothing to prevent the violence which
occurred. The jury deemed Washington's acts to be battery and a reckless
disregard for the safety of another person.

Similarly, a federal jury awarded $850,000 in 1984 to Dennis Polonich,
formerly of the Detroit Red Wings, who suffered a broken nose, a concussion
and several cuts when Wilf Paiement, then of the Colorado Rockies, struck
him with his hockey stick in October, 1978. The decision marked the first civil
penalty ever levied against a hockey player for violence on the ice, and the
jury of five women and one man took only three hours to hand down the
verdict (which included $350,000 of exemplary damages). The most alarming
part of the judgment to some observers is that the Rockies' insurance coverage
may only provide $500,000. If the appeals are unsuccessful, Paiement could
therefore be personally liable for the rest. Bill Waters of Toronto, the agent for
Paiement, says: "You can't buy personal liability insurance for an athlete.
There is not adequate coverage for an athlete. It's going to change the game."

§ 6.1(E). How Much Risk to Assume.

In many suits involving sports violence, the primary defense is "assumption
of risk." This defense is not unique to sports. It is an old defense, derived from
the common law, which may be used by defendants in any negligence suit who
claim that the plaintiff knew about the danger and yet voluntarily exposed
himself to it. If you know I am a terrible driver and nonetheless ride with me,
then you have assumed the risk of an accident and probably cannot collect if
one occurs. The underlying rationale is that no one should be held liable for
injuries that another essentially consented to.

But how can we apply this old principle to contact sports? For one thing, the
player does not assume all risks. Courts have ruled, for example, that a person
does not assume the risk of being hurt as a result of flagrant and intentional
violations of safety rules. Consequently, a base runner who purposely ran five
feet outside of the baseline to smash into the second baseman found himself on
the losing side of a court case (*Bourque v. Duplechin,* 331 So. 2d 40 (La. App.
1976)).

A federal appellate court reached an analogous conclusion in the now
famous case of *Hackbart v. Cincinnati Bengals, Inc.* (435 F. Supp. 352 (D.
Colo. 1977), *reversed,* 601 F.2d 516 (10th Cir. 1979)). The plaintiff in the case,
Dale Hackbart of the Denver Broncos, was a veteran defensive back in the
NFL. Just before Hackbart was injured, Charles "Booby" Clark, a rookie
running back, had run a pass pattern on the right side of the Broncos' end
zone. The pass was intercepted by Billy Thompson, a Denver free safety, who
returned it to midfield. Hackbart's injury occurred in the aftermath of this
pass play.

Because of the interception, the roles of Hackbart and Clark suddenly
changed. Hackbart, who had been defending, instantaneously became an
offensive player, and Clark had to try to make the tackle. Acting as an

offensive player, Hackbart attempted to block Clark by throwing his body in front of him. Afterwards, he remained on the ground and turned, with one knee on the ground, to watch the rest of the play. The summary of facts from the court case on the incident tells what happened next. Booby Clark, "acting out of anger and frustration but without specific intent to injure," stepped forward and struck the back of Hackbart's head and neck with his right forearm. The force of the blow caused both men to fall forward to the ground. Both players, without complaining to the officials or to one another, returned to the sidelines since the ball had changed hands, and new offensive and defensive teams took the field.

Since the officials did not see the incident, no foul was called. However, the game film showed very clearly what had happened. Hackbart did not report the incident to his coaches or to anyone else during the game. Next day, he felt so much pain that he could not play golf. He did not seek medical attention, but the continued pain caused him to report the injury and the incident to the Bronco trainer, who gave him treatment. Although Hackbart played the next two games, his usefulness was limited, and he was then released on waivers. He sought medical help, and only then was it discovered that he had a serious neck injury. Hackbart felt the blow shortened his career, as well as causing him pain and suffering, so he sued Clark and the Bengals.

Though Clark admitted that the blow had not been accidental, the trial court ruled as a matter of law that the game of professional football is basically a business which is violent in nature and that the available sanctions are imposition of penalties and expulsion from the game. The court recognized that many fouls are overlooked, that the game is played in an emotional and noisy environment and that incidents such as the one in this case are not unusual. Indeed, said the court, the very character of professional football suggests that a player's conduct cannot be judged by standards of reasonableness.

The court also said it was wrong to apply personal injury law to professional football, noting the unfairness of holding that one player has a duty of care for the safety of others. According to the court, the concepts of assumption of risk and contributory fault applied because, as a professional football player, Hackbart had been trained to disregard injury to himself and opposing players. Hackbart had in effect accepted the risk that he would be injured by an opposing player during an emotional outburst.

Finally, the court ruled that earlier cases which had imposed liability did not apply because, since they involved injuries in amateur contests, their theory of recovery depended on the notion that players had a duty to each other, and thus an objective standard of conduct could be derived, based on what a hypothetically reasonable and prudent person would do in a given situation. This was not applicable in professional football since training does not include regard for safety of others. The court held that professional football must regulate itself.

On appeal the Tenth Circuit reversed, holding that tort principles are not suspended simply because an injury takes place during a game, even a professional football game. The court looked to recklessness rather than assault and battery as the proper basis for liability.

Although acts of violence might be common in other professional games, the court added, this was irrelevant to the present inquiry. Noting that the trial court went beyond the evidence in determining "that as a matter of social policy the game was so violent and unlawful that valid lines could not be drawn," the appellate court took the view that this was not a proper issue for determination and that "the plaintiff was entitled to have the case tried on an assessment of his rights and whether they had been violated."

Though the appellate court sent the case down for a retrial, it never came to court again. The Bengals and Hackbart agreed on a settlement.

§ 6.1(F). "I Didn't Mean It."

A new trend is also emerging for nonintentional injuries that athletes cause by failing to act reasonably in a given situation. Away from the sports arena, the key to liability is usually how foreseeable the risk of injury was. If it was a pretty clear possibility and you did nothing to forestall it, then you may be liable. So if you did not shovel snow off your sidewalk and someone falls, watch out; but if a piece of the roof blows off without warning and hurts someone, you may be in the clear.

This standard means that if the player who commits the action that led to an injury should have foreseen that someone would be hurt, he may be liable. The same question, pretty much, is pertinent on the other side. How foreseeable was the injury from the injured player's perspective? Sports are inherently risky anyhow, and courts recognize that opponents may not always adhere to the rules. The idea is that since it is reasonably foreseeable that in the heat of action some procedural and safety rules will be broken, players effectively consent to the risk of injuries caused by rule infractions.

A much publicized Illinois decision has apparently put a kink in these traditional concepts, and courts sometimes refer to this case to express their opposition to sports violence. The case, *Nabozny v. Barnhill,* 334 N.E.2d 258 (Ill. App. 1975), began when two amateur soccer teams of high school boys squared off one afternoon. Julian Nabozny, the goalkeeper of a Winnetka, Illinois soccer team, was severely injured when a forward from the opposing team rushed towards him while he was crouched in the penalty area hugging the ball to his chest. The forward did not turn away and accidentally kicked Nabozny in the head, causing a fractured skull and permanent brain damage.

The appellate court ruled for Nabozny on the theory that players have a legal duty to every other player on the field to refrain from conduct that is forbidden by safety rules as long as (1) all teams involved in an athletic competition are trained and coached by knowledgeable personnel, (2) a recognized set of rules governs the conduct of the competition and (3) safety rules are included which are essentially designed to protect players from serious injury (e.g., in *Nabozny,* the Federation Internationale de Football's rule prohibiting any contact with the goalkeeper in the penalty area). Thus athletic participants will be liable for injuries they cause if their conduct is either "deliberate, wilful or with a reckless disregard for the safety of another player." Nabozny and its progeny (see, e.g., *Oswald v. Township High School District No. 214,* 406 N.E.2d 157 (Ill. App. 1980)) are important because they point out that even though players assume the normal risks of the sport, they do not assume the risks of unintentional but negligent conduct.

§ 6.1(G). Statutory Control.

Despite these well publicized cases, there is more and more violence in sports, and it does not seem to be deterred by court actions. Some influential people think that the federal government should intervene.

The most interesting of their suggestions came in 1980 in the form of a proposed bill to Congress co-authored by attorney Richard Horrow, chairman of the A.B.A. Task Force on Sports Violence, and Representative Ronald Mottl (D-Ohio). Basically, the "Sports Violence Act of 1980" would have barred excessive violence during professional sports events and imposed penalties of a $5,000 fine and/or one year in jail for violations. "This bill seeks to draw a line between the kinds of natural physical contact that are a normal part of any rugged physical sport, and the kinds of vicious, dangerous contact that a civilized society should brand as criminal, whether it occurs inside or outside the sports arena," said Mottl. "You can play rough and hard, but you cannot play to deliberately or recklessly hurt someone."

The bill would have made a player liable only if the alleged act fit six criteria:

1. It is inflicted in circumstances that showed a definite resolve to harm another, or negligent, reckless, deliberate or willful disregard for the safety of another;
2. It is in violation of a safety rule of the game designed to protect players from injury;
3. It occurs either after play is stopped or occurs without any reasonable relationship to the competitive goals of the sport;
4. It is unreasonably and excessively violent, and beyond the generally accepted nuances and customs of the particular sport;
5. It could not have been reasonably foreseen by the victim as a part of the normal risk in playing the sport; and
6. It results in contact that causes a significant risk of serious injury to the victim.

Some of the most publicized sports violence acts might not fit all these criteria, Horrow has noted, and prosecution might occur only once or twice a year, if at all. However, he favors the "symbolic effect" that would follow if the federal government took a strong stand on the issue. "It will make the game safer for everyone," he said. "This defines unnecessary violence, while the present law is confusing."

Horrow contends that athletes, former athletes, player representatives and player associations would benefit from a statute that would symbolically criminalize the most repugnant conduct. He also points out that society as a whole would benefit because young athletes and sports fans who look to professionals for examples "must be taught that repugnant violence is intolerable and illegal." No segment of society, says Horrow, can be licensed to break the law with impunity. As he puts it: "The operation of the law does not stop at the ticket gates of any sporting event."

Despite all the publicity it gained, the bill never left the House Judiciary Committee's subcommittee on crime. Several congressmen complained that in light of important pending legislation the proposed Sports Violence Act was totally frivolous. Others rejected it as an unnecessary expansion of federal criminal jurisdiction into an area that could adequately be handled by state laws.

In addition, NFL Commissioner Pete Rozelle, NHL President John Ziegler, NBA Deputy Commissioner Simon Gourdine, North American Soccer League Commissioner Philip Woosnam and James Reynolds of the Justice Department all spoke in opposition to the bill. The commissioners and Baltimore Orioles General Manager Hank Peters, representing Baseball Commissioner Bowie Kuhn, were unanimous in their view that each sport has the means within its rule to police violence.

§ 6.1(H). Conclusion.

As with all socio-legal problems, the legal questions related to sports violence are easy to identify but difficult to address. Few would disagree that violence in sport is bad, but how can the problem be solved? Whether we devise new approaches to train young athletes, develop stricter game rules against excessively rough conduct or continue to rely on the law to deal with violence in sport, the games and everyone involved in them will lose out unless something is done about excessive violence.

---

§ 6.2. Officials and the Law: Rights and Liabilities.

By Melvin S. Narol

Addressing a group of attorneys in the spring of 1984, the Princeton University basketball coach Pete Carril said: "I spent most of yesterday thinking about the relationship between basketball and the law, and calling upon all the experience and education I have garnered here in the Ivy League, I have found the answer. There is none!"

Twenty years ago, Coach Carril would have been correct. Little time was spent on the relationship of the law to sport, but this is no longer the case. In spite of his "tongue in cheek" comment, Coach Carril knew that a knowledge of the law is essential to anyone involved in sport, be it high school, college or professional. One need only read the daily newspaper sports section in any part of the country to realize that the law has permeated our sport-conscious society. Whether it is a baseball players' strike, the purchase and relocation of a National Football League team or a challenge by a female athlete to participate in a traditionally male sport, our legal system is on the path to assuming the role of football's legendary twelfth man.

Ten years ago, the relationship of the law to sports officials was rarely considered; today, sports officials not only frequently consult their bible — the rule book — but also their attorneys. In the last decade, court decisions have established a new set of legal principles. And, as a result, sports officials and their associations have found their way into the courts to assert their legal rights and protect themselves against liability.

§ 6.2(A). Recovery for Injuries.

Violence at all levels of athletic competition has spiralled, and the sports official has not escaped. The more than 250,000 men and women officiating various sports have often been subjected to assaults by frustrated players, coaches and fans in an atmosphere tense with economic pressure and the increasing necessity to succeed.

§ 6.2(B). Intentional Injuries.

A sports official may bring suit seeking damages for an injury intentionally inflicted while officiating. In these assault and battery cases, the major questions are whether or not the official has consented to the physical contact inherent in the sport and whether or not it occurred as "part of the game."

Any assertion by the attacker that the official involved has given his consent by implication is absurd; clearly, no official starts a game by telling the players that they may strike him if they believe that he has made an incorrect call.

The *Restatement of Torts (Second)*, § 50, Comment 6 delineates the ways in which consent may be an effective defense with regard to a player's participation in a game:

> Taking part in a game manifests a willingness to submit to such bodily contacts or restrictions of liberty as are permitted by its rules or usages. Participating in such a game does not manifest consent to contacts which are prohibited by rules or usages of the game if such rules or usages are designed to protect the participants and not merely to secure the better playing of the game as a test of skill.

Like a player, a sports official consents by implication only to those intentional acts that are "part of the game." A football official understands that he might be in the path of a player who may run into and injure him during the course of a play. When a player or coach becomes upset and shoves or strikes an official, clearly that behavior is not "part of the game"; in this case recovery is possible.

A sports official may also seek redress in the criminal courts for an intentional attack; the charge is then assault and battery. Oklahoma has made a special effort to deter violence against sport officials by passing this law:

> Every person who, without justifiable or excusable cause and with intent to do bodily harm, commits any assault, battery, assault and battery upon the person of a referee, umpire, timekeeper, coach, player, participant, official, sports reporter or any person having authority in connection with any amateur or professional athletic contest is punishable by imprisonment in the county jail not exceeding six (6) months or by a fine not exceeding five hundred dollars ($500.00), or by both such fine and imprisonment.

There is one reported court decision involving this statute. An umpire had just finished officiating in a ball game and was preparing to change his uniform for a second game when several players from the losing team surrounded him in the parking lot. Their assistant coach joined them and began exchanging words with the umpire, when suddenly the coach struck the umpire in the jaw.

The District Court, Oklahoma County found the coach guilty of assault upon a sports official and fined him $425. The coach appealed the decision. The coach claimed that the statute under which he was convicted was "vague and indefinite." In *Carroll v. State,* 620 P.2d 416 (Okla. Crim. App. 1980), the Oklahoma Court of Criminal Appeals upheld the coach's conviction, holding that the statute clearly informed the coach and the public of the particular conduct which would be punishable by law.

§ 6.2(C). Negligent Injuries.

Sports officials have a difficult time recovering damages for injuries that are judged to be the result of an inherent risk in an activity. The doctrine of assumption of risk usually prevents the official from recovering damages, since the court assumes that the official was aware of the risk and engaged in the activity with the knowledge that he could be injured.

In *McGee v. Board of Education of City of New York,* 226 N.Y.S.2d 329 (App. Div. 1962), the New York Supreme Court stated that "players, coaches, managers, referees and others who, in one way or another, voluntarily participate must accept the risks to which their roles expose them." And it added that

> this is not to say that actionable negligence can never be committed on a playing field. Considering the skill of the players, the rules, and nature of the particular game, and risks which normally attend it, a participant's conduct may amount to such careless disregard for the safety of others as to create risks not fairly assumed.

In *Dillard v. Little League Baseball, Inc.,* 390 N.Y.S.2d 735 (App. Div. 1977), the same court became the first to apply this general rule to a sports official. Umpire Dillard was working behind the plate in a Little League baseball game; the pitcher threw a ball that went past the catcher and out of play. The umpire called time out and looked away; at the same time, the pitcher threw another ball which hit home plate, bounced upward and struck Dillard, injuring him. Dillard sued the young pitcher for negligence in failing to heed the time-out call and for pitching the ball when the umpire's attention was not on the pitcher. At the trial, testimony revealed that the coach had instructed the pitcher not to pitch when an umpire signals time out.

Although the court acknowledged the principle that a player can be held responsible for negligent acts that result in injury to an official, it held that Dillard had assumed the risk because he was aware of the erratic play of Little Leaguers and knew that the incident was "fully to be expected during the heat of a game from so young a player."

Recovery by a sports official for an injury sustained as a result of the negligent act of a player during an athletic contest may seem to be a difficult burden. It must be emphasized, however, that the court's decision in the

Dillard case was based upon the youth and inexperience of the player. In a situation involving an older player, of greater skill and experience, the outcome may well be different; but it is important to remember that what the scorekeeper may record as an error is not, in law, the equivalent of negligence.

Another important yet open question is whether an arena or educational institution is responsible for providing reasonable security and a safe place to work for sports officials. A New Jersey court has unfortunately decided that a public entity, such as a school district or governmental arena or stadium, is immune from suit, according to the state's Tort Claims Act.

In this case, *McHugh v. Hackensack Public Schools,* D. No. L-2542-81 N.J. Super. Ct., Mercer County (Jan. 28, 1983), the issue was both important and novel. It posed the question of whether a high school basketball referee who was attacked and injured on the court by an unknown fan should be denied the opportunity to recover. The attack occurred in a crowded gymnasium where the fans streamed onto the court from the bleachers without restraint by the police or assigned teachers. The host school and competing schools, who were defendants, claimed immunity from suit because, according to the law, a "dangerous condition" did not exist.

In 1981, the New Jersey State Interscholastic Athletic Association held a high school basketball state tournament in which two schools participated hosted by a third. Referee Larry McHugh of Princeton, New Jersey was attacked by an unknown student when, at the end of the game, he attempted to leave the floor of the gymnasium to go to the dressing room. As a result, McHugh sustained serious injuries to his head, neck and back and was under psychiatric treatment for several months.

In the gymnasium ropes were available, hung on the walls, to use in keeping the fans off the floor. The teachers and police stationed near the court failed to do so at the end of the game. Responsibility for crowd control during the game is set by the N.J.S.I.A.A. on both teams when the game is played at a neutral site; the responsibility after the game is on the host school.

McHugh alleged in this lawsuit that the host and participating schools had a duty to provide (1) a safe place to work, (2) safe entry and exit before and after the game and (3) proper supervision of the crowd.

The Superior Court of New Jersey granted all the schools' motions for summary judgment and dismissed the complaint, stating that the school was immune from suit.

An appeal was filed with the Superior Court of New Jersey, Appellate Division, which in 1984 affirmed the trial court's decision. The court held, based upon a narrow interpretation of the statute, that no "dangerous condition" existed because McHugh was not injured by a "condition of the property," e.g., a loose floor board. The appellate division concluded:

> The alleged failure of the defendant to take affirmative action to prevent or discourage assaults by spectators in the gymnasium does not create a "dangerous condition" within the meaning of N.J.S.A. 59:2-7 so as to make such conduct actionable and deprive the public entity of the immunity conferred by that statute.

McHugh sought review by the Supreme Court of New Jersey, but his petition for certiorari was denied.

The bringing together of two opposing teams in the final series of games of the season which would culminate in a championship for one team certainly created a "dangerous condition" affecting the safety of the officials who would necessarily make calls adverse to one team or the other. Anyone who has attended such tournaments knows that fans often run onto the court after a game and that officials are often viewed with contempt by fans who blame them for their team's loss. The McHugh incident was not only reasonably forseeable; it should be expected in a crowded public arena, and measures taken to prevent it. The school's failure to provide adequate protection by placement of ropes or other protective devices around the court and by the failure of the officers and school personnel to keep the fans off the court until McHugh and the players safely exited the court constituted a "condition of the property." This certainly created a substantial risk of injury and a "dangerous condition."

The appellate division's interpretation of "dangerous condition" will leave the sports officials of New Jersey and perhaps other states without legal remedy when they are attacked by an unknown (which is more often than not the case) assailant while participating in, attending or officiating athletic events. Hundreds of thousands of people of all ages will be affected. Further, there will be a substantial chilling effect upon sports officials from continuing to officiate and other persons from becoming involved in officiating and a concomitant effect on amateur athletics. Sports officials may reconsider whether the small game fee received is worth the risk of serious injury without the right of recovery. Such public entities now, at least in New Jersey, have no obligation to provide security to those who participate in or attend athletic events. Yet, they are better able to bear the risk of loss by purchasing additional insurance coverage. If the New Jersey court's interpretation of "dangerous condition" is adopted by other states' courts, not only will the sports official have no recourse after sustaining injuries inflicted by disappointed fans or players, neither will the fans or players.

When a team's coach or manager attempts to rouse the crowd to hostility toward a sports official, the official may have a claim. In 1964, in *Toone v. Adams,* 137 S.E.2d 132 (N.C. 1964), the Supreme Court of North Carolina dealt with this question. An umpire alleged that he was assaulted after a minor league baseball game because he had ejected the home team's manager from the game in the ninth inning. The spectators verbally abused the umpire and challenged him to fight. The umpire was being escorted from the field by two policemen and a fellow umpire when a fan pushed through these guards and hit the umpire on the head. The umpire sued the baseball team, the manager and the spectator who struck him, arguing that he was entitled to recover for the injuries he had sustained. To prove his point he referred to the rules and regulations that governed professional baseball:

1. The home team shall provide police protection sufficient to preserve order at a game.

2. The umpire may remove managers, players, spectators, or employees from the game or field for a violation of the rules or unsportsmanlike conduct.

3. An umpire's decisions which "involve judgment" shall be final and players or managers shall not object thereto.

The Supreme Court of North Carolina considered the plaintiff's claim that the home team officials failed to perform their duty in protecting him from irate fans who were irritated at the manager's ejection. The court aptly commented:

> For present day fans, a goodly part of the sport in a baseball game is goading and denouncing the umpire when they do not concur in his decisions, and most feel that, without one or more rhubarbs, they have not received their money's worth . . . however, an umpire garners only vituperation — not fisticuffs. Fortified by the knowledge of his infallibility in all judgment decisions, he is able to shed billingsgate like water off the proverbial duck's back.

The court dismissed the umpire's claim because it found no causal connection between the actual assault by the angry spectator and the action of the manager. The court concluded: "It would be an intolerable burden upon managers of baseball teams to saddle them with responsibilities for the actions of every emotionally unstable person who might arrive at the game spoiling for a fight and become enraged over an umpire's call which the manager had protested."

In a case where a direct cause can be proved, a coach or manager may be liable if he incites hostility in the fans toward the officials which leads to an assault. The proof, however, would be difficult.

§ 6.2(D). Workers' Compensation.

When a sports official is injured by the negligence of another person or entity or merely sustains an accidental injury, he may seek recovery by way of a workers' compensation claim, although such recovery is rarely permitted; in fact, only one such court decision is reported. The sports official is an independent contractor, never an employee of the officials' association nor of the educational institution at which he or she officiates. Therefore, the workers' compensation laws, which are designed for employees, do not generally cover the sports official.

State workers' compensation laws compensate employees for injuries whether or not the employer is at fault. The employee need only prove that the injury "arose out of" and "in the course of" employment. The decisive test is whether the employer has the right to control and direct the worker in the manner in which the work is done.

Umpire Donald Gale confronted the general rule when he tried to recover in a case against his local association. In a softball game Gale was umpiring, a player became enraged by a call that he thought was bad and hit Gale on the neck, hip and leg with a baseball bat.

Gale claimed that his injuries arose out of and in the course of his employment as a member of the Greater Washington, D.C. Softball Umpires'

Association, which had assigned him the game. He therefore filed a claim for workers' compensation. The Maryland court, in *Gale v. Greater Washington Softball Umpires Association,* 311 A.2d 816 (Md. App. 1973), found that he was not an employee of the association but an "independent contractor," a status which did not allow him recovery under workers' compensation. As an official he was not obligated to accept game assignments from the association and was solely in control of the same.

Nor will a sports official be able to obtain a workers' compensation recovery against an educational institution at which he or she officiates unless there is a written employment contract with its officials. In *Ehehalt v. Livingston Board of Education,* 371 A.2d 752 (N.J. Super. App. Div. 1977), the Appellate Division of the New Jersey Superior Court denied basketball official Calvin Ehehalt's claim against the local school board. He sustained an injury to his teeth when he struck himself in the mouth as he raised his hand to prevent being hit by the ball. Ehehalt was regularly employed as a fireman, and officiated at some 30 games each season for various schools through direct contracts; he was therefore found to be an independent contractor and so responsible for his own accidents.

The one court decision that was decided contrary to the general rule involved a workers' compensation claim by a sports official against a school district in which he officiated. This Idaho Supreme Court case, *Ford v. Bonner County School District,* 612 P.2d 557 (Idaho 1980), was brought by Charles Ford, a high school football official and a member of the North Idaho Officials' Association. On October 25, 1974 Ford officiated in a game between Lewiston and Sandpoint High Schools for which he was paid by the Bonner County School District. Ford became trapped in a play and was accidently struck by a moving player, sustaining an injury to his knee which disabled him for 13 weeks.

The court found Ford to be an employee of the school district, thereby entitling him to a workers' compensation award:

> Claimant was assigned to officiate in a particular game several weeks in advance and could not refuse an assignment unless he had good cause. Assignments were determined by the commissioner for high schools . . . and the commissioner was paid by the member schools themselves. A school which accepted the claimant as an official for one of its games paid him in advance and often paid his travel expenses as well. If a school did not desire the claimant as a referee the local coach had the right . . . to reject the claimant for that school.

This decision does not contain sound reasoning. It is incorrect that the school district had the right to "control and direct the activities of the claimant" merely because the coach *could have* rejected Ford as an official and he would not have officiated the game. This is not the control test envisioned by states' workers' compensation laws. That control is control of how the employee performs the work. In the context of sports officiating, no one can control how a sport official works a game. To do so would be the antithesis of a sports official. Once armored with the rules of the sport, the sports official must then use reasoned judgment in the application of the rules to the players' action. It is also very interesting that the Idaho Supreme Court failed to cite any of the previously discussed court decisions, all of which had been decided prior to *Ford* and all of which found that a sports official is an independent contractor.

The dissenting opinion by Judge McFadden, however, sides with prior precedent and states what is, and should be, the general rule. Judge McFadden commented:

> Once the game began, the district had no control over the manner in which the referee carried out his duties, although they did set the time of the game. *The very essence of the position of a referee requires that the referee be free from control by the district. To hold otherwise would subject the referee to the position of being influenced in his decisions by his "employer's" desires. He must remain neutral . . . .* The right to control, not the actual control, is the deciding factor and during the game the district had no right to interfere at all . . . . [I]n the instant case, at no time during the football game did the school district have the right to "inspect" or review the referee's decisions, or to alter or change them if the district believed they were not in conformance with the "specifications" (the rules of play for high school football games).

(Emphasis added.)
Judge McFadden further commented:

> In addition, there are other factors present in this case that this court has held to be indicative of a principal-independent contractor relationship. The district could not conditionally fire the employee while they could give him a low rating which would probably keep him from coming to their school. However, he would still be a member of the association and able to officiate other games in the conference and even likely to officiate other games involving the Bonner County district schools when they were not the home team.
>
> . . . .
>
> The district negotiated the price per game with the association, not with the individual referee. The payment was made prior to the game. The referee was not on the payroll. No deductions were taken from his pay for taxes or social security. He was not given the benefits which other district employees were given. He brought his own uniform, shoes, hat and whistle. From all these factors it is evident that the respondent was an independent contractor and not an employee.

Judge McFadden's reasoning was adopted, and this decision was overruled by legislative action in 1981 to bring Iowa into line with the other states which have dealt with this issue.

There is only one situation in which a sports official might be entitled to a workers' compensation recovery. That is where the sports official is asked to officiate in a game which is part of the recreational activities of his full-time employer.

In 1970, a member of the Umpires Association of Colorado was struck in the eye by a softball while he was umpiring a company intramural league game.

In *Daniels v. Gates Rubber Co.*, 479 P.2d 983 (Colo. App. 1970), the Colorado Court of Appeals denied his workers' compensation claim on the ground that he was not an employee of the company. But Daniels had been hired by the athletic director of Gates Rubber Company to officiate at games held by the employees of Gates. He was paid by the Gates Fire Brigade, an employee recreation group. The game was played on a field owned by Gates. The Gates recreation director arranged with the Umpires Association of Colorado to provide umpires for the games.

The workers' compensation judge found that Daniels was therefore an employee for workers' compensation purposes and made an award. This decision was overturned by the workers' compensation commission, a decision which was affirmed by the court. In holding that the workers' compensation judge was in error, the court looked to the following factors:

1. Gates exercised no control over the umpire nor did it have a contract with him.
2. The games were not part of Gates' regular business.
3. The employment was not pursuant to any regular schedule but depended upon the times an umpire's service was required.

The court held that, at the time of his injury, Daniels was only a casual employee and was therefore not covered by workers' compensation.

However, in 1982 the Court of Appeals of Oklahoma, in *Warthen v. Southeast Oklahoma State University*, 641 P.2d 1125 (Okla. App. 1981), found quite the opposite in a case in which a drama professor who was also a licensed basketball referee was asked by a dean to referee an interfraternity game. The professor did so and died of an injury while officiating the game.

The court found an employer-employee relationship based upon the following:

1. Professors at the university were encouraged and expected to participate in extracurricular activities.
2. Warthen was specifically requested by the dean of men to officiate at the game as part of his participation in extracurricular activities, and without additional pay.
3. The university provided the facilities for the game, including the fieldhouse, lighting and equipment.
4. The university benefited by such extracurricular sports activities.

While only Colorado, Idaho, Maryland, New Jersey and Oklahoma have dealt judicially with the issue of whether a sport official is an employee or an independent contractor, the general rule now clearly regards the sports official as an independent contractor who has no right to workers' compensation recovery. California has legislatively dealt with the issue by an amendment to the California Labor Code S3352 (j), which provides that an amateur sports official is not an employee for purposes of the workers' compensation law.

§ 6.2(E). Liability for Player Injuries.

American League Umpire Dale Ford wears a T-shirt on which is printed: "Once I thought I was wrong, but I was mistaken." Unfortunately, a sports official can be wrong by not acting as a reasonably prudent official should under the circumstances.

Only a decade ago, few sports officials would have believed themselves liable for an injury to a player, nor would plaintiffs' attorneys have attempted to prove such an argument. There was no such legal precedent, nor was there a "deep pocket."

Today, however, courts are taking an increasingly active role in determining the rights and liabilities of sports officials. Meanwhile, sports officials' associations throughout the country have obtained or are in the process of obtaining professional liability insurance. N.A.S.O., the National Association of Sports Officials, is an organization made up of more than 10,000 officials, at all competitive levels in any sport, which provides liability insurance to its members.

At one time, under common law it was generally believed that the law did not apply to anything that happened in a sporting event. Gradually, however, courts overcame their reluctance to become involved in questions of liability in athletic contests, and in sport-related lawsuits there began to emerge a pattern of legal theories beginning with cases in which one player sued another player for an injury sustained during a contest.

Although most of these player-versus-player cases have arisen from incidents on the amateur level, at least one professional athlete has sued an opponent for injuries he sustained during a game. In that case, *Hackbart v. Cincinnati Bengals, Inc.,* 435 F. Supp. 352 (D. Colo. 1977), Charles "Booby" Clark, of the Cincinnati Bengals, apparently acting out of anger and frustration and with no specific intent to injure, stepped forward and struck a blow to the back of Dale Hackbart's head. Federal district court Judge Matsch concluded that there could be no liability for such an occurrence, stating that players in the National Football League are not bound by the "restraints of civilization" while on the field.

Judge Matsch ruled:

> My conclusion that the civil courts cannot be expected to control the violence in professional football is limited by the facts of the case before me. I have considered only a claim for an injury resulting from a blow, without weaponry, delivered emotionally without a specific intent to injure, in the course of regular play in a league-approved game involving adult, contract players. Football as a commercial enterprise is something quite different from athletics as an extension of the academic experience and what I have said there may have no applicability in other areas of physical competition.

On appeal to the United States Court of Appeals for the Tenth Circuit, 601 F.2d 516 (1979), this decision was reversed. The appeals tribunal ruled that professional football games are indeed governed by our law and the mores of society. Therefore, a professional player who intentionally strikes an opposing player during a game in a manner not condoned by the rules may be held liable in tort for reckless misconduct. The United States Supreme Court declined to hear the matter, 444 U.S. 931 (1979), and the case was remanded to the district court and finally resolved.

The newest category of sport lawsuits is that in which the sports official is the defendant. Cases are appearing on court dockets alleging that a sports official has failed to supervise or control an athletic contest, resulting in injury to a player. To date, no court has found a sports official liable for such negligence.

Damages can be very substantial, particularly in professional athletics. The following sections discuss potential liability of the sports official. Bear in mind, however, that the sports official's association is generally joined as a defendant based upon a claim of failure to properly train its members. Therefore, the discussion which follows also applies to these associations.

§ 6.2(F). Before the Game.

(1) *Playing Conditions.*

Before an athletic contest begins, it is the responsibility of the sports officials to determine that the physical conditions for playing are safe. In baseball the umpires must check for visible hazards, e.g., holes in the field, large rocks on the field, loose game equipment or a base not properly fastened in place. Rule 10-2-3 of the National Federation of State High School Associations (N.F.S.H.S.A.) baseball rules, which govern most interscholastic baseball in the United States, states that it is the umpire-in-chief's duty to inspect the field conditions.

In basketball these rules provide that the referees make sure that there are no loose balls around the gym on which a player might trip, that the backboard has padding around it and that the court and surrounding area are clear for the players.

(2) *Weather Conditions.*

In deciding whether to begin play when the weather is bad the officials must first inspect the condition of the playing surface. On one occasion in New Jersey, high school football officials were sued for permitting a game to be played on a field that was allegedly extremely muddy after a heavy rain and therefore unsafe. As a player attempted to make a tackle, he fractured two vertebrae, resulting in partial paralysis from the neck down. The player not only sued his coach and school for failure to provide proper training and safe headgear, but also named as defendants the game officials, alleging the condition of the field contributed to his injury. The case was eventually dismissed against the officials, and a settlement reached with the other defendants for approximately one million dollars. Other cases involving this same issue are now pending in Wisconsin and Ontario, Canada.

(3) *Failure to Enforce Rules.*

Many specific rules not only relate to the playing of the game, but also are safety rules which relate to the players' equipment and condition of the playing area. In baseball one rule requires "each batter, runner and the catcher to wear a head protector," a description of which is included. A recent amendment includes the on-deck batter. The same rule provides a list of equipment which must be worn by the catcher. Also, a rule prohibits a player from wearing any exposed jewelry, such as a watch or ring. It is important to note further that this rule also provides that "any equipment judged by the umpire to be potentially dangerous is illegal."

In softball the Amateur Softball Association (A.S.A.) makes it illegal to wear shoes "with rounded metal spikes", while in youth play "no metal spikes are allowed in any division at any level of play." It is also mandatory for catchers in fast pitch softball to wear masks. The use of donuts or any attachment to a bat for warm-up purposes are also prohibited.

In slow pitch softball a catcher is not required to wear a mask. This, however, in *Nash v. Borough of Wildwood Crest,* Docket No. L-6624-77 N.J. Superior Court, Cape May County (1983), did not prevent softball player Nash from filing a lawsuit against a softball umpire. Nash was struck in the eye by a softball while catching without a mask during a municipal league game in New Jersey and suffered partial loss of vision. He alleged that the umpire should have given him his mask and then officiated from a position behind the pitcher rather than behind home plate. The case was settled prior to trial in 1984 with Nash receiving $24,000.

In college football the NCAA rules include certain safety rules. If a sports official fails to enforce these and if a player sustains an injury caused by that failure, liability may result.

The rules provide:

> *Soft flexible four-sided pylons* 4″ x 4″, with an overall height of 18 inches, which may include a two-inch space between the bottom of the pylon and the ground, are required. They shall be red or orange in color and placed at the inside corners of the eight intersections of the sidelines with the goal lines and end lines and at the intersections of the end lines and in-bounds lines extended.

If other than the prescribed pylons are used and a player falls on them, sustaining injury, the game officials would probably be responsible.

In NCAA football rules it is the responsibility of the officials to be sure the game is played with proper equipment:

> *Article 4.* All players *shall* wear head protectors which carry the manufacturer's or reconditioner's certification indicating satisfaction of NOCSAE test standards. All such reconditioned helmets *shall* show recertification to indicate satisfaction with the NOCSAE test standard.
> *Article 5.* No player wearing illegal equipment shall be permitted to play. Any question as to the legality of a player's equipment shall be decided by the umpire. Illegal equipment includes:
> a. Any equipment worn by a player which, *in the opinion of the umpire,* would confuse his opponents or any equipment including artificial limbs which would endanger other players.

> b. No hard, abrasive or unyielding substances on the hand, wrists, forearm or elbow of any player, no matter how covered or padded.

(Emphasis added.)

The N.F.S.H.S.A. basketball rules also place an obligation upon the officials to be sure that the game is not played with any dangerous equipment. They provide that:

> The referee shall not permit any player to wear equipment which, in his or her judgment, is dangerous to other players. Elbow, hand, finger, wrist, forearm guard, case or brace made of hard and unyielding leather, plastic, metal, or any other hard substance, even though covered with soft padding, shall always be declared illegal. Head decorations, headware or jewelry are illegal.

The A.S.A. softball rules contain a similar provision.

§ 6.2(G). During-the-Game Inspection.

(1) *Playing Conditions.*

The same principles apply as set forth in the previous section dealing with physical playing conditions before the game.

(2) *Weather Conditions.*

The tradition of trying to play a certain sport in inclement weather if it is at all possible is in jeopardy since sports officials are now being sued for not postponing or suspending a game. Reasonable judgment is the key. The rules of sport give the official the power to so act — the question is when to exercise this power. Rule 10, § 8 of the A.S.A. softball rules provides umpires with the authority to "suspend play when, in his/her judgment, conditions justify such an action." The N.F.S.H.S.A. baseball rules similarly state that the umpires are "the sole judges, as to whether conditions are fit to play."

(3) *Failure to Properly Supervise or Control Game.*

A sports official may be liable for injuries to a participant by failing to observe that the participant is seriously injured or in danger of being seriously injured and not stopping the athletic contest. This is especially true in the strong contact sports of boxing, wrestling and football. Other liabilities may include negligent supervision and failure to control the contest.

An example of this may be the case of boxer Willie Classen, who died of brain injuries several days after being knocked out in the tenth round by Wilfred Scypion. The New York Athletic Commission investigated this incident and made 23 recommendations in a 37-page report on the fight; one of these recommendations was that referees and ringside physicians should be trained to recognize head injuries. *Sports Illustrated* carried the following paragraph in its December 10, 1979 issue:

> Classen had been taken unconscious from the ring at Madison Square Garden's Felt Forum after he was knocked out 12 seconds into the 10th and final round. Many observers, Scypion among them, felt that referee

Lew Eskin should have stopped the fight right after Classen was knocked down in the 9th round. And some ringside onlookers were surprised that Classen's young and somewhat inexperienced manager, Marco Minuto, and the State Athletic Commissioner's attending physician, Dr. Richard Izquierdo, allowed him to answer the bell for the 10th round. Classen was way behind in scoring and so dazed he remained seated on his stool several seconds after the bell rang.

A New Jersey case, *Pantalone v. Lenape Valley Regional High School,* Docket No. L-40828-26 N.J. Superior Ct., Sussex County, involved a high school wrestling referee who allegedly permitted a participant to continue an illegal hold on his opponent. As a result, the opponent became a quadriplegic. The case was settled before the trial for a substantial amount of money. The plaintiff cited failure on the part of the referee to supervise and control the match adequately and, in particular, failure to stop an athletic contest when a player appeared to be in danger of serious injury.

The most important negligence case and trial to date, *Smith v. National Football League,* No. 74-418 Civ. T-K U.S. Dist. Ct., Florida, involving a sports official and a claim of failure to properly supervise, was concluded in 1978 with the jury finding no liability. On August 26, 1972, the Baltimore Colts and the Pittsburgh Steelers played a preseason game in Tampa, Florida. The NFL provided the officiating crew for the game, but the people handling the down chain markers were local residents. Edward Marion was the head linesman that day; Robert Lastra attended one of the down markers. Playing defensive end for the Colts was Bubba Smith, who at 27 years of age had just been named All-Pro and NFL Lineman of the Year.

Late in the game, Smith's teammate Rick Volk intercepted a Terry Bradshaw pass and returned the ball upfield. As Volk was running toward and along the sideline where Marion and Lastra were positioned, Smith was running at full speed trying to block for Volk. As the play reached the sideline, Smith claimed he leaped over fallen players and struck the aluminum down marker, which he claimed was still stuck in the ground. In his $2.5 million negligence suit against the NFL, the Tampa Sports Authority, Edward Marion and Robert Lastra, Smith alleged that the collision with the marker caused a serious knee injury that cut short his career.

The basic contentions of the lawsuit were, first, that the equipment was dangerous and, second, that the chain holders were negligent in not moving the marker out of the way.

The major problem, however, was imputing any negligence of Lastra to the League. The plaintiff's attorney attempted to resolve this problem by first imputing negligence of Lastra to Marion, on the theory that Lastra was under the control of Marion, who was in turn under the control of the NFL.

Since Lastra had not been directly hired by the NFL, Smith's attorney argued that Lastra was a borrowed servant. Under the borrowed servant doctrine if one person lends his servant to another for a particular employment, the servant is treated for purposes of that employment as the servant of the one to whom he has been lent, although he remains the general servant of the person who lent him. The trial judge agreed with Smith's theory and permitted the case to go to the jury.

The case was tried twice. The first trial ended in a mistrial with the jury deadlocked 5-1 for the defendants. The second trial ended with the jury returning a verdict in favor of the defendants.

This case is significant despite the verdict, because the judge allowed the case to go to the jury, establishing for the first time that a sports official could possibly be found liable for negligence during an athletic contest.

A Washington case, *Carabba v. Anacortes School District No. 103,* 435 P.2d 936 (Wash. 1967), arising out of a high school wrestler becoming paralyzed, almost resulted in a finding of negligence against the referee of the match. Roger Anderson and Steve Carabba were wrestling near a corner of the mat when the referee spotted a separation in the mat and tried to close it. He took his eyes off the competitors long enough to fix the mats. During this split second, Anderson apparently put a full nelson on Carabba, and the match drew to a close. Anderson then lunged when the buzzer sounded and broke the hold on Carabba. As a result, Carabba sustained crippling injuries that left him paralyzed from the neck down.

Carabba sought recovery for his injuries on the ground that the school district was negligent through its agent, the referee, on the following counts:

1. failing to supervise the contestants in an adequate manner;
2. permitting his attention to be diverted from the action;
3. allowing an illegal and dangerous hold to be used by one of the participants;
4. allowing the hold to be applied for a substantial period of time.

The trial court jury favored the school district. The Supreme Court of Washington, however, denied the school district's contention that the referee was not its agent and ruled that as a matter of law he was. A new trial was ordered, but the case was settled without any finding of negligent supervision by the referee.

§ 6.2(H). Liability for Game Rulings.

Consider the following hypothetical situation. In January, 1987 the Dallas Cowboys file a lawsuit in the federal district court in Texas against the National Football League and game officials. The suit alleges that an improper call cost them a touchdown and victory in their playoff game with the Los Angeles Rams, thereby depriving their players of substantial bonuses and the team of millions of dollars in revenue. The key evidence upon which the Cowboys will rely to prove their case are videotape replays from cameras operated by the television networks and the NFL.

Such a situation might become far from unusual with the increasing economic stake at all levels of sports. Whether it is bonuses to professional athletes or possible college scholarships to high school athletes, the pressure upon sports officials has steadily increased. As a result, decisions by sports officials are being questioned not only on the court but in court.

Every court that has dealt with the issue of whether a cause of action exists against a sports official, either for an honest judgmental error or for misapplication of a rule of the game, has found that such a claim does not present a judicial controversy recognized in our courts. These courts have held that judicial review will not be exercised by courts for such claims. The only exception is when bad faith or corruption can be demonstrated the courts will intercede to protect the integrity of sport. One such case is *Wellington v. Monroe Trotting Park Co.,* 38 A. 543 (Me. 1897). More and more cases, however, are being filed by disgruntled teams and fans.

The basis for the courts' view finds its genesis in *Shapiro v. Queens County Jockey Club,* 53 N.Y.S.2d 135 (N.Y. Misc. 1945). In that case the New York City municipal court clearly enunciated the rule and its rationale:

> [I]t has been found of great practical importance to have umpires, referees, timekeepers and other officials . . . who are experienced, mentally alert, fair and otherwise well-qualified to make immediate decisions and whose decisions must be final and binding. In more than one sense, such officials are truly judges of facts, since they are closer to the actual situation and characters involved, at the time, as well as, when, and under the circumstances in which the events occurred. Surely their immediate reactions and decisions of the questions which arose during the conduct of the sport should receive greater credence and consideration than possibly the remote, subsequent matter-of-fact observation by a court in litigation . . . .

Every other reported court decision has followed this principle. In 1953, the Supreme Court of New York, in *Tilelli v. Christenberry,* 120 N.Y.S.2d 697 (N.Y. Misc. 1953), upheld the decision of a boxing referee and a ringside judge. The match lasted the scheduled ten rounds. The referee and one judge cast their votes for boxer Giadella; the third judge voted for boxer Graham. As a result of this 2-1 vote, boxer Giardella was declared the winner. However, the New York State Athletic Commission, which had two members in attendance, changed the voting card of the judge who had voted for Giardella, because of a suspicion that he was involved in a betting scheme, and awarded the decision to boxer Graham. The court held that the suspicion of such an illegality was not sufficient for a court to substitute its judgment for that of the assigned boxing judge. And in *State ex rel. Durando v. State Athletic Commission,* 75 N.W.2d 451 (Wis. 1956), the court upheld the Commission's decision that under its rules it had no authority to reverse a boxing referee's alleged failure to properly administer the "knock-down" rule.

The principal of nonreviewability was affirmed in 1981 by the Supreme Court of Georgia in a situation where a football referee misapplied a rule. In *Georgia High School Association v. Waddell,* 285 S.E.2d 7 (Ga. 1981), the court ruled that it does not possess authority to review the call of a high school football referee.

On October 23, 1981 in a state football play-off game between Osborne and Lithia Springs High Schools, the score was 7-6 in favor of Osborne with seven minutes remaining to be played. Osborne had the ball. With fourth down and 21 yards to go for a first down, Osborne punted, but a roughing-the-kicker penalty was called on Lithia Springs. The referee assessed a 15-yard penalty and declared it was again fourth down, with six yards to go for a first down. But the referee misapplied the rule since, according to high school football rules, Osborne should also have been awarded an automatic first down. Osborne punted again, and Lithia Springs drove down the field to score a field goal, putting them in the lead 9-7. Later in the game, Lithia Springs scored again and won the game 16-7.

Upon application to the superior court, Osborne succeeded in overturning the referee's ruling. The trial court ruled that the school had a property right in the game of football being played according to the rules, and that the referee denied it this right. The court ordered the game to be replayed from the moment of the referee's error.

The Supreme Court of Georgia reversed this decision, reiterating the general rule and refusing to exercise judicial review of the referee's call, even though the referee made an error regarding a rule and not merely a judgmental decision. The court stated: "We now go further and hold that courts of equity in this state are without authority to review decisions of football referees because those decisions do not present judicial controversies."

In March, 1982, the Boone County, Missouri Circuit Court dismissed a lawsuit filed by the Wellsville-Middletown School District for failure to state a claim. The suit was brought against the Missouri State High School Activities Association and an official scorer who had challenged the accuracy of the score in a state tournament basketball game with Glasgow High School.

During the third quarter, the scorebooks of both teams and the scoreboard showed Wellsville-Middletown leading 38-34. The official scorebook kept by the official scorer showed the score tied 36-36. After consultation, the referees stated that 36-36 was the correct score, since it was the score recorded by the official scorer.

N.F.S.H.S.A. Rule 2-11 provides:

> The scorebook of the home team shall be the official book, unless the referee rules otherwise .... The scorers shall compare their records after each goal, each foul and each charged time-out, notifying the referee at once of any discrepancy. *If the error cannot be found, the referee shall accept the record of the official book, unless he or she has knowledge which permits her or him to decide otherwise.* If the discrepancy is in the score and the error is not resolved, the referee shall accept the progressive team totals of the official scorebook.

(Emphasis added.) Pursuant to this rule, the officials declared the score to be tied. The game continued, and ended with the score tied at 54-54, and with Wellsville-Middletown claiming it had won 56-52. Glasgow won the game in overtime.

This lawsuit challenged the decision of the referees and the score of the official scorer. Wellsville-Middletown sought injunctive relief naming it the victor so that it could advance to the next round of the state tournament. A companion case against the referee was filed by three Wellsville-Middletown players who alleged that the referee failed to follow the proper procedure and, by failing to do so, cost their team the game. The players alleged that this had denied their team the opportunity to advance to the next round of the state tournament, thereby "substantially reducing their chances of obtaining a college scholarship." The three players sought $30,000 each, the claimed value of the scholarships. The players voluntarily dropped the case after the court had dismissed the first lawsuit.

In the most recent case, *Bain v. Gillispie,* Docket No. 47143 Iowa District Ct., Johnson City (1982), Big 10 basketball referee Jim Bain filed suit for injunctive relief and damages against the defendants, who produced T-shirts imprinted with his likeness surrounded by a noose. The defendants produced wearing apparel and related novelty items with the Iowa University logo on them. When Bain made a judgment call near the end of the 1982 Iowa-Purdue basketball game resulting in free throws and victory, the Gillispies produced the T-shirt. Injunctive relief was granted to Bain.

Following this segment of the case, the Gillispies filed a counterclaim alleging damage to their business due to Bain's call, which allegedly prevented Iowa from winning the game and progressing toward the NCAA championship. This, they alleged, deprived them of the opportunity to produce and sell more Iowa products. The Gillispies were strangers, and neither the teams nor the officials intended that they should benefit by the victory of one team or the other.

The trial judge dismissed the counterclaim on Bain's motion. He aptly stated:

> Heaven knows what uncharted morass a court would find itself in if it were to hold that an athletic official subjects himself to liability every time he might make a questionable call. The possibilities are mind boggling. If there is liability to a merchandiser like the Gillispies, why not to the thousands upon thousands of Iowa fans who bleed Hawkeye black and gold every time the whistle blows? It is bad enough when Iowa loses without transforming a loss into a litigation field day for "Monday Morning Quarterbacks."

In 1984, 357 N.W.2d 47, the Iowa Court of Appeals affirmed the dismissal. The court noted:

> It is beyond credulity that Bain, while refereeing a game, must make his calls at all times perceiving that a wrong call will injure Gillispies' business or one similarly situated and subject him to liability. The range of apprehension, while imaginable, does not extend to Gillispies' business interests. Referees are in the business of applying rules for the carrying out of athletic contests, not in the work of creating a marketplace for others. In this instance, the trial court properly ruled that Bain owed no duty. Gillispies have cited no authority, nor have we found any, which recognizes an independent tort for "referee malpractice." Absent corruption or bad faith, which is not alleged, we hold no such tort exists.

The Supreme Court of Iowa denied the Gillispies' application for further review when it held that:

It is therefore clear that courts will not review the claim that a sports official has made an honest judgmental error or even misapplied a game rule. Such a claim does not present a judicial controversy recognized by a court. Only when bad faith or corruption can be demonstrated will the courts intercede. Such mistakes are similar to a football player dropping a pass in the end zone in the final seconds of a game which would have resulted in his team winning. To permit sports officials to be sued in the absence of strong evidence of fraud or corruption would seriously impair the ability of a sports official to perform his task in an independent, professional and competent manner; it would also threaten the integrity of all levels of athletic competition.

§ 6.2(I). Conclusion.

Sport officials should, and will, continue to assert their legal rights and protect themselves against potential liability through the judicial process. As sport continues to play an increasingly larger role in our society, the members of the striped-shirt profession will be increasingly the targets of lawsuits. There is an important relationship between sport and the law in general, and between sports officials and the law in particular. As professionalism within the officiating community grows, so too will awareness of applicable legal principles.

---

§ 6.3. Spectators, Too, Sue.

By Betty van der Smissen

While cases do date back to the early 1900's, there has been increasing concern in the 1970's and 1980's of management for injuries to spectators when in attendance at nonprofessional sports events. Baseball and ice hockey have the most cases, then football and golf. A variety of sports have a few cases each, including basketball, polo, jai alai and bowling. Situations which give rise to lawsuits related to spectators include participatory risks, crowd control and safe premises.

§ 6.3(A). Participatory Risks.

Participatory risks are those risks which arise from the act of spectating. At issue is what risks are inherent in the game for spectators and thus assumed by the spectators. Also, can spectators waive certain rights, and what constitutes contributory negligence by spectators? In contrast, what is the duty of the owner/sponsor to warn the spectators regarding the nature of the game and to protect against certain participatory risks?

(1) *Baseball.*

Since the turn of the century spectators have sued for injuries sustained while at a baseball game when hit by a batted ball, but few have won any damages. The court stated back in 1913, in *Wells v. Minneapolis Baseball & Athletic Association,* 142 N.W. 706 (Minn. 1913), that baseball is the national game and the rules governing it, the manner in which it is played and the risks and dangers incident thereto are matters of common knowledge. It makes no difference if the spectator has not played baseball nor attended a baseball game before, and a knowledge of rules is not necessary. As a general rule, the spectator assumes the risks. The courts have held that the management is not an ensurer of safety and that it is required only to exercise ordinary care to protect patrons against such injuries by providing screened seats for those portions (behind home plate) of the stands that are most frequently subject to hazards of foul balls and for as many spectators as may be reasonably expected to call for them on any ordinary occasion. The spectator should voluntarily occupy the seat. There is a duty to provide seat locations for the spectators with a choice of screened seats for all who may wish them only for the most dangerous part of the grandstand. Assumption of an inherent risk extends only to seating of the usual custom and balls which are batted and thrown in the normal progress of the game or pregame activity. There is no duty to warn by signs or otherwise if the spectator is aware of the danger or it is so obvious that a person of ordinary intelligence would readily sense it and take measures to avert it. However, there is a duty to maintain protected areas in a manner such that the spectator is protected. This means that screening must be of appropriate size and in good condition (no holes for the balls to go through).

A 1982 case, *Falkner v. John E. Fetzer, Inc.*, 317 N.W.2d 337 (Mich. App. 1982), took a slightly different approach to the duty of the management and assumption of risk by the spectator. The plaintiff acknowledged that generally there is no duty to warn, but alleged that this particular area of the stands represented an unexpected high risk of a magnitude much greater than was common, and thus the management owed a duty to warn. (Area of location not specified in opinion.) The defendant countered that even if there was a duty to warn, such duty was fulfilled by the disclaimer printed on the back of each ticket and the announcement at the beginning of the game. The court stated that such disclaimers did not fulfill an owner's duty to warn of unexpectedly high risk; however, it held for the defendant on the basis that the plaintiff failed to show any evidence that if a proper warning had been given she would have taken precautions to prevent the injury; that is, she presented no evidence to show that failure to warn was the proximate cause of her injury.

Whereas a ball batted in baseball into the spectators is inherent and natural to the sport of baseball/softball, this is not necessarily true of other projectiles emanating from player participants, such as bats slipping from the hands of the batter or broken bats. The liability is totally situation-dependent. The basic criteria for assumption of risk must be met, and contributory negligence on the part of the spectator also may be a factor.

(2) *Ice Hockey.*

The courts have consistently found that it is the duty of the management to exercise ordinary care for the safety of spectators at hockey games. In most of these cases the plaintiff is given judgment. In some cases, however, spectators at a hockey game know the incidental dangers and so assume the risk of being injured. In a case in which the spectator was injured when a flying hockey puck struck her in the eye, *Kennedy v. Providence Hockey Club, Inc.*, 376 A.2d 329 (R.I. 1977), the court contrasted knowingly encountered danger with negligently encountered risk. In the former the plaintiff consents to the possibility of harm, whereas in the latter situation the plaintiff fails to assess accurately the possible results of his own action.

The court said further that contributory negligence and assumption of risk do not overlap and that the key difference between them is exercise of one's free will in encountering risk. Assumption of risk is not a variant of contributory fault. In this case the spectator was knowledgeable about the game of ice hockey and was aware that there was a risk that a puck might take flight and possibly injure her. Therefore no recovery was awarded.

In a 1981 case, *Riley v. Chicago Cougars Hockey Club,* 427 N.E.2d 290 (Ill. App. 1981), the plaintiff was seated in the first row of the balcony near one of the goals. During the third period, the puck deflected off a player's stick and struck the plaintiff on the left side of his head. An Illinois jury awarded the plaintiff $90,000 in damages when it concluded that the "team owed spectator a duty to exercise reasonable care for his protection."

In an Iowa case, *Parsons v. National Dairy Cattle Congress,* 277 N.W.2d 620 (Iowa 1979), the plaintiff was struck by a hockey puck while returning to her seat after intermission. She alleged that the defendants failed to erect barriers to protect her from errant hockey pucks and thereby provide her a safe place from which to watch the game. The defendants stated that the plaintiff was a hockey fan and based their defense on assumption of risk and contributory negligence. The trial court granted the defendants summary judgment, but the appellate court reversed and remanded the decision.

In another case, *Kennedy, supra,* the plaintiff was seated in the fourth row up from the arena floor. Protection for spectators consisted of a wooden wall 18 to 24 inches high topped by a five-foot sheet of half-inch thick plexiglass. However, this shield protected only the spectators in the first three rows. The puck was lofted from the ice and struck the plaintiff in the left eye. The plaintiff had attended 30 to 40 games at this arena and had seen many games on television; consequently she was aware of the risks. The court held that the plaintiff voluntarily and knowingly encountered the risk and favored the defendants.

In an early case, *Rich v. Madison Square Garden Corp.,* 266 N.Y.S. 288 (N.Y. Sup. Ct. 1933), a hockey stick flew out of the hand of a player when he collided with another player and hit a spectator; there was no liability. However, when the hockey puck went outside the seating area, liability was found.

(3) *Football.*

When spectators choose to sit or stand next to a football field they assume the obvious risks incidental to the game of football.

In a New York case, *Cadieux v. Board of Education of City School District of City of Schenectady, N.Y.,* 266 N.Y.S.2d 895 (N.Y. App. Div. 1966), a 17-year-old student was injured when the players in a football game which she was watching from the sidelines left the marked field during the course of play. She was aware that players occasionally left the field of play, and she also knew that seats were available in adjacent bleachers. No recovery; the plaintiff assumed the risks.

In a Washington case, *Perry v. Seattle School District #1,* 405 P.2d 589 (Wash. 1965), at about the same time, involving a 67-year-old grandmother, a similar result was reached. Although the court said that the school district could have roped off an area some yards back from the boundary to make safer the place to stand or could have provided seats, it found the school not negligent and that the plaintiff had a duty to protect herself from dangers incidental to the game even if she did not have actual knowledge of them. Judgment was for the defendant on the basis of contributory negligence by the plaintiff. Moreover, the court indicated that there is a higher degree of care required for spectators in games with large crowds than is needed for informal third-team games or contests attended for the most part by friends and relatives and where no admission is charged. Risks apparent to an "ordinary and prudent" person are assumed, as in this case.

An early case, *Ingerson v. Shattuck School,* 239 N.W. 667 (Minn. 1931), was quite similar. The spectator plaintiff was standing two to five feet outside a chalk line which had been laid around the field boundaries; bleachers were available but not used. Two players rolled out of bounds and against the plaintiff, fracturing one of her legs. Plaintiff alleged negligence by the defendants in not fencing or otherwise protecting the playing field and in not warning the spectators to stand further back. The court found the defendants not negligent.

A fourth case, *Colclough v. Orleans Parish School Board,* 166 So. 2d 647 (La. App. 1964), involved an informal football game. The court stated that, due to extensive viewing of football on television, it is common knowledge that players frequently run out of bounds. In this Louisiana case the injured person was a man who was watching his son play in a local public high school football team scrimmage. He was also a former football player and should have been well aware of the dangers.

(4) *Golf.*

While most of the injuries from golf balls are suffered by another player, there are a few cases of spectator injuries. In an Illinois case, *Duffy v. Midlothian Country Club,* 415 N.E.2d 1099 (Ill. App. 1980), the plaintiff went to her first golf tournament. She stopped at a roped-off concession stand set up between two fairways. As she watched an unidentified golfer hit a ball, she was struck. She sued the player who hit the ball, the country club on whose course the tournament was being held and the golf association which was sponsoring the tournament. The court said that the owner of a business premise is responsible for dangerous conditions on the premises and for giving sufficient warning to avoid harm. The court further stated that in raising the defense of assumption of risk the defendants had to prove that the spectator appreciated the danger of being struck by a golf ball while she was in a presumed area of safety, at the concession stand on the golf course. In another case, *Fink v. Klein,* 348 P.2d 620 (Kan. 1960), the plaintiff was on the golf course as a member of the rules committee for the junior tournament; further, she had instructed the junior player whose golf ball hit her and was aware of the type of golf he played. The court held that the plaintiff was contributorily negligent.

§ 6.3(B). Crowd Control.

What is the duty owed to a spectator to protect him from injury by another spectator? The nature of the duty appears to relate to the act and its foreseeability, for example, whether the act by the spectator who injured the plaintiff arose from his own exuberance or from rowdyism and lack of discipline or from allegations of intoxication or from an intent to injure, and the reasonableness of the measures taken to protect against such acts. It is clear, however, that management does owe a duty to protect a spectator from unreasonable risk of harm from other spectators. What is an unreasonable risk, of course, is defined by the particular situation.

In a North Carolina case, *Aaser v. City of Charlotte,* 144 S.E.2d 610 (N.C. 1965), a spectator sustained a broken ankle while walking along a corridor in a public building. He was hit by an ice hockey puck. A group of boys were playing with sticks and pucks in the corridor. The management knew that boys played in the hallways, but were not aware that they played dangerously. The plaintiff failed to show negligence in this case.

In still another case, *Jung v. Tulane University of Louisiana,* 300 So. 2d 542 (La. App. 1974), the plaintiff was knocked down by two unknown juveniles who were running through the crowd at a professional football game. The professional team rented and had allowed automobiles to park inside the stadium fences and block certain exits. The crowd objected and became unruly. The court held that a cause of action existed, and it was for the jury to determine negligence.

In *Bacon v. Harris,* 352 P.2d 472 (Ore. 1960), at a basketball game the plaintiff went for refreshment at halftime, and fell downstairs from the top of a landing. There were no handrails; she alleged that there should have been supervision to control running and jostling by the crowd on the stairway. The court held that there was no negligence. In *Klish v. Alaskan Amusement Co.,* 109 P.2d 75 (Kan. 1941), another concession-related case at an ice hockey game, the aisle was overcrowded and the concessionaire circulating in the crowd lost his balance and fell on the plaintiff. The court held for the defendant, saying that to permit crowding is not in itself negligence.

The number of attendants, guards or ushers is sometimes the issue. In trying to remove a disorderly spectator, a police officer bumped into the plaintiff, knocking him backwards across the edge of the chair he had been sitting in. The trial court in *C & M. Promotions v. Ryland,* 158 S.E.2d 132 (Va. 1967), ruled that the police officer was not in the employ of the defendant and therefore was not individually responsible for any negligence on the part of the proprietor. The plaintiff alleged both that the defendant should have erected a barrier between the ring and the front seats and that the number of ushers, guards or attendants was inadequate. But the court found no evidence that an increase in the number would have prevented the accident. Judgment was given for the defendant. Judgment was also for the defendant in a baseball case, *Shtekla v. Topping,* 258 N.Y.S.2d 982 (N.Y. App. Div. 1965). A spectator was injured when a fight broke out; the plaintiff alleged that there had been an insufficient number of guards who had arrived too late. The court held that reasonable care requires intervention only when more than ordinary rudeness and jostling takes place.

A different result was reached in a Florida case, *Nance v. Ball,* 134 So. 2d 35 (Fla. App. 1961), when the defendant had notice that the patron who assaulted the plaintiff during a bowling match had a tendency to assault others while engaged in competitive bowling.

In a 1980 case, *Gill v. Chicago Park District*, 407 N.E.2d 671 (Ill. App. 1980), against the Chicago Park District, the defendant obtained summary judgment. The district owned the stadium and football club. The plaintiff was assaulted and robbed. There was no evidence of prior incidents of violence showing that attack was reasonably foreseeable and consequently defendant owed no duty to protect spectator from such unforeseeable violence. In another Illinois case, *McDonald v. Chicago Stadium Corp.*, 83 N.E.2d 616 (Ill. App. 1949), the defendant also prevailed on the basis of the assault not being foreseeable. The plaintiff was assaulted by another spectator at an ice hockey game over the right to a seat. An early Illinois case, *Shayne v. Coliseum Building Corp.*, 270 Ill. App. 547 (1933), held that the stadium proprietor (boxing) was not an ensurer of spectator safety. In this situation the plaintiff was going on a ramp to the restroom when assaulted by an unidentified man who struck the plaintiff with a heavy metal object.

§ 6.3(C). Safe Premises.

(1) *Bleachers.*

Most of the lawsuits involving bleachers have been held in favor of the plaintiff due to negligent construction. There is a high standard of care in regard to inspection and appropriate repair. Most cases turn on notice of the defect. Inspections must be thorough; several cases especially mention the importance of inspection. The spectator is entitled to assume that the premises are in a safe condition; the duty to inspect is the proprietor's.

Spectator injuries have been caused by: temporary seats giving way when constructed with improper nails and insufficient bracing; collapse of bleachers due to their general construction; loose planks that move when the spectators stand up; overloading with people; unsatisfactory selection of site; bracing removed by mischievous boys; inadequate bracing; makeshift seats; cadence swaying of exuberant fans; crowd standing up in excitement.

Spectators are sometimes injured in the bleachers for some other reason than their collapse. The accidents include falling on an unlighted concrete ramp, which resulted in a fatal injury; falling on the stairs; slipping between the footboards and falling 15 feet; and falling off a grandstand when a railing broke. In another accident a spectator was killed when a pile of cement blocks fell on him while he waited in his seat for a baseball game to begin.

(2) *Walkways and Steps.*

A spectator has the right to safe egress and ingress at an event, and the proprietor has the responsibility for proper care of walkways, including holes, litter, condition of surface and lighting.

Holes must be given attention by maintenance. In *Buck v. Clauson's Inn at Coonamessett, Inc.*, 211 N.E.2d 349 (Mass. 1965), one plaintiff was with her husband at a professional golf match. She saw the ball coming toward her and was injured when she fell into a hole in the "rough," an area of higher grass near the fairway. The hole was about three feet across and three feet deep, lined with rocks and stones. The golf club corporation was liable for the condition of the premises. In another golf case, *Thompson v. Sunset Country*

Club, 227 S.W.2d 523 (Mo. App. 1950), a spectator following a tournament tripped on a rock which was concealed by tall grass. The court held that while reasonable care must be taken for the safety of the spectator, the proprietor is not an ensurer of safety, and that the burden of showing that the proprietor knew of, or should have known of, such danger rests on the plaintiff.

Obstructions must be removed. A spectator passing through a corridor, while waiting for a friend at the ticket window, fell over the projecting legs of a sawhorse used for making a temporary aisle. The court, in *Brown v. Reorganization Investment Co.,* 166 S.W.2d 476 (Mo. 1942), stated that it was the lessee's duty to exercise ordinary care to protect spectators. In *Douglas v. Lang,* 124 S.W.2d 642 (Mo. App. 1939), the plaintiff, on her way to a wrestling exhibition, fell over a stake protruding a few inches above the ground and was injured. The court held the manager responsible for safe grounds.

The surface of walkways and steps must be in safe condition, but the courts give a reasonable length of time for weather-caused conditions. For example, in a baseball case, *Lappin v. St. Louis National League Baseball Club,* 33 S.W.2d 1025 (Mo. App. 1931), the spectator slipped on steps filled with puddles of water. The court held that there was no negligence on the part of the club for failing to remove the pools of water so soon after the game was called on account of rain.

Lighting can be to blame for falls on steps and walkways. In one case, *Shannon v. Addison Trail High School, District No. 88,* 339 N.E.2d 372 (Ill. App. 1975), a man going to his son's high school wrestling match broke his wrist when he took a dimly lit shortcut at the side of the school. Since there were alternative paved surfaces to reach the school, the court held that the plaintiff was contributorily negligent.

In general, safety on the walkways and corridors is the responsibility of management. In a hockey case, *Lemoine v. Springfield Hockey Association,* 29 N.E.2d 716 (Mass. 1940), a spectator walking on the promenade to the restroom was struck by a puck. And in another case, *Jones v. Three Rivers Management Corp.,* 380 A.2d 387 (Pa. Super. 1977), the court again held for the plaintiff, who was struck in the eye during batting practice. She had been watching the playing field through an opening in an interior walkway and had been struck in the eye. The question was whether this was a "common, frequent and expected" inherent risk assumed by the spectator. Safety of patrons in a parking lot was an issue in *Bearman v. University of Notre Dame,* 453 N.E. 1196 (Ind. App. 1983). A woman returning from the stadium to her car after a football game was knocked down by someone who had been drinking and fighting. The court held that the university was aware that alcoholic beverages were consumed at tailgate parties in the parking areas and that some people became intoxicated and posed a general threat to the safety of other patrons. Therefore it was under a duty to take reasonable precautions to protect spectators from injury caused by the acts of third persons.

§ 6.3(D). Conclusion.

Injuries to spectators at nonprofessional sport events have increased, and concern on the part of management has increased accordingly. Since the

1980's the court has mandated that management has the responsibility to warn spectators of dangers from high risk areas.

The courts have said that contributory negligence and assumption of risk do not overlap and that the key difference between them is the exercise of one's free will in encountering risk. Assumption of risk is not a variant of contributory negligence.

The courts have indicated that a higher degree of care is required for spectators when large crowds are present than at informal games where no admission is charged. The owner of a business premise is responsible for dangerous conditions on the premises and has the responsibility to adequately warn the user. Risks apparent to an "ordinary and prudent" person are generally assumed.

Management has been found to owe a duty to protect a spectator from unreasonable risk of harm from other spectators. Unreasonable risk is defined by the particular situation. The court has held that reasonable care in crowd control requires intervention only when more than ordinary rudeness or jostling takes place.

The courts consistently favor the plaintiff in lawsuits involving injuries relating to defective bleachers. A high standard of care for spectators using bleachers is required, and emphasis is placed on inspection and repair. The duty to inspect is the proprietor's. Spectators have the right to safe egress and ingress at events, and the proprietor is responsible for safe walkways, holes, litter, condition of surfaces and lighting.

CHAPTER 7

EQUIPMENT AND FACILITIES ISSUES

§ 7.1. Product Liability: A Legal Dilemma.

By Maria Dennison

Lawsuits for damages arising out of the use of products are not a new development. What is new is that "fault" in the sense of negligence is not a prerequisite for recovery of damages. The development of tort law over the past ten years, according to Washington lawyer Victor Schwartz, frequently referred to as the "father of product liability reform," has produced a system that hurts manufacturers, product sellers and consumers.

Schwartz cites instances where:

> some judges have tried to turn product liability law into a compensation system that makes manufacturers insurers of their products; placing liability on them for harms that they were unable to prevent, or in some instances, did not even cause. On the other hand, some courts have restricted the rights of injured claimants to recover for a product-related harm, leaving the injured party with nothing.

To compound this confusion, manufacturers doing business in an interstate market have no way to predict which legal standards apply to them, since they are governed by 50 different product liability laws, interpretations or philosophies. Senator Robert Kasten (R-Wis.), the chief sponsor of a federal product liability bill, illustrated the confusion this way:

> In Illinois, if you drive your crane into a power line you can collect injuries from the crane maker. FMC paid $2.6 million learning this lesson. But in Minnesota or New Mexico, the courts say anyone who drives his crane into a power line is a fool and shouldn't collect anything.

He added that "if a manufacturer improves his product in California, New York, or Alaska, he's admitting that his old product was unsafe." This legal interpretation deters many sporting goods manufacturers from introducing new or technologically refined products into the marketplace. Anything that is different from that which is already in the marketplace invites product liability suits, based on the current interpretation of strict liability or liability without fault.

A *U.S. News and World Report* article indicates that the United States has more than 600,000 lawyers, which is two thirds of the world's total. Litigation now accounts for two percent of our gross national product, and the adversary system costs $320 million in taxpayers monies in addition to what litigants paid or spent in the courts in 1980.

Jury trials, which make up the bulk of product liability suits, can cost the court an average of $9000 in some state jurisdictions and up to $15,000 in a U.S. district court, according to the Institute for Civil Justice, a research group within the Rand Corporation. The consequence of our litigiousness goes beyond its expense, however, and is reflected in the price of goods, insurance rates and taxes, along with the availability of goods and the productivity of American industry and its workers.

Currently lawyers receive 41 cents from every dollar the plaintiff receives, while defense clients pay 58 cents per dollar received. Litigation and judgment against business becomes part of the cost of a product. It also costs jobs. Product liability costs of the United States sporting goods industry represents 4.2% of sales; in Japan it is only 0.5%, which gives that nation's products a substantial advantage in the world market.

In 1965 there were 50,000 product liability suits on file. Today there are more than one million, involving all different industries.

The expense associated with product liability incurred by sporting goods manufacturers is not limited to blockbuster suits. Many manufacturers are named as defendants in lawsuits alleging damages for which they are in no way responsible. They must respond to the allegations to avoid the possibility of default judgments, and many agree to pay something to relieve themselves of litigation burdens that can extend from 2 to 10 years. While the largest payouts have been to injured football players, as product claim filings continue to accelerate, multimillion dollar verdicts can be expected of baseball, boxing, soccer, camping, gymnastics and other sports unless a solution to the present product liability crisis is developed. Persons injured through no fault of their own should be recompensed, and manufacturers with inferior products should be made to pay. But the existing tort liability system does not always work that way.

Usually the firms being sued are reputable companies whose only real fault is being large enough to have sufficient insurance to be a target. Many people do not realize that huge awards cost everybody in the end. The doctrines of entitlement and strict liability have come full circle to pose a serious problem for the consumer.

§ 7.1(A). Liability for Design Defects and Failure to Warn.

Two areas of current liability law that have been a gold mine for the trial bar are standards for assigning liability for design defects and failure to warn.

In the case of design standards what one state emphasizes as the crucial test for liability another state rejects as irrelevant. What is an issue for the jury in one state becomes an issue exclusively for the judge in the next. And an issue for the plaintiff to prove in one state becomes an issue for the defendant to disprove in the next.

In the past, a plaintiff's lawyer alleged that the football helmet was defective because it would not attenuate the energy from blows that were foreseeable. This theory often failed because the plaintiff's counsel could not find a helmet anywhere that could have prevented a player's injury. Helmets are not, and cannot be, designed to protect the cervical spine while still allowing the game to be played as we know it.

A more recent approach used by plaintiffs is to claim that the helmet is defective because it does not contain a warning label advising the player that he could suffer catastrophic head or neck injury when wearing it. Today every football helmet is required to have a sticker on it that reads as follows:

Do not use this helmet to butt, ram or spear an opposing player. This is in violation of the football rules, and can result in severe head, brain, or neck injury, paralysis or death to you and possible injury to your opponent. There is a risk these injuries may occur as a result of accidental contact without intent to butt, ram or spear. No helmet can prevent all such injuries.

Despite these safety measures and the substantial reduction of injuries because of rule changes, the product liability crisis for sporting goods manufacturers continues to escalate. Plaintiffs' attorneys have now discovered that it is easier to attack school districts, athletic directors, coaches and league officials on the "failure to warn" issue than the manufacturers of equipment.

Under the law in some states, including New York, Pennsylvania and New Jersey, if someone suffers a head injury while wearing a football helmet, the manufacturer can be held strictly liable whether the helmet was made last year or even 40 years ago.

Dan Patterson, a California attorney who represents three football helmet manufacturers, estimates that there are 50-80 cases pending against schools, coaches and helmet manufacturers in which head and neck injuries were sustained with the football helmet.

The first case, tried in Florida eleven years ago, resulted in a verdict for the plaintiff of $5.3 million, settled on appeal for over $3 million.

Patterson also cites a more recent case in which the plaintiff sued for an injury suffered eight years earlier in a church-sponsored football game. The young man, now a quadriplegic, argued that the helmet was unable to withstand the blows received in the game and that the manufacturer should have warned potential users of this fact. The jury returned a verdict of $5.8 million. This case involved three tiers of trial, with exorbitant costs to the public and participants.

In 1982 a $6.3 million judgment against the Seattle School District was won by a student athlete for an injury that occurred in 1975. The district was insured for only $5.5 million.

The primary allegations of negligence were in two areas: (1) failure to properly instruct and (2) failure to warn sufficiently.

Dr. Samuel Adams, Associate Professor of Physical Education at Washington State University, discussed the allegations and their meaning to school administrators and coaches extensively in a May, 1982 article for Athletic Business.

The allegations directed toward the Seattle school district included:

1. failure to have coaches certified;
2. failure to adopt rules which would prohibit a ball carrier from using the top of his helmet as an initial point of contact with another player;
3. failure to adopt training rules such that players would avoid using their helmet as an initial point of contact;
4. failure to adopt a program for conditioning such players to avoid using their helmet as an additional point of contact;

5. failure to communicate to the coaches the medical, scientific and statistical knowledge concerning the use of the head as a battering ram;

6. failure to have a policy relating to instruction of matters concerned with safety for football coaches;

7. failure of the school district to make mandatory injury prevention techniques taught by coaches to football players;

8. failure of the school district to provide information to the players and the parents of players concerning the physical risks to students participating in varsity football programs; and

9. failure to have a person in the Seattle school district central administration who had the responsibility for identifying risks to students participating in the Seattle school district's varsity football program.

Adams noted that many of these contentions were not presented with the intent to be proven by the plaintiffs, but

> were presented as an attempt to frame a total picture of neglect by the school district. For example, in the State of Washington, coaches are not required to be certified. The question was used to raise doubts in the minds of the jury that every safety precaution was taken for preventing injury.

Football is the financial backbone of many intercollegiate and interscholastic sports programs, often providing up to 70% of the funding for all school sports activities.

Throughout the years the public has accepted the fact that playing contact sports such as football can cause injury. Although the incidence of such circumstances has been so minute, considering the large number of participants, we may be litigating football into extinction. This is grossly unfair to both the manufacturer and others in the commercial chain, as well as the injured player himself. For example, of 11 cases tried in 1981 the injured player prevailed five times obtaining verdicts of $19.8 million, while six permanently paralyzed players received nothing. Some 11 players settled their cases for a total in excess of $3 million.

Insurers for helmet manufacturers have paid over $18.3 million during this period alone, and the insurance industry simply will not stand for the resulting loss ratio.

Industry estimates are that the total premium paid by the helmet manufacturers is approximately $2.5 million per year. The cost of defending the suits, disregarding the judgments and settlements, consumes the premium.

Unfortunately, the solution is not safer protective equipment. According to Dr. Voight Hodgson, Wayne State University researcher, football injuries are down 55% this last decade. The problem is not that there are more accidents causing injury; the dilemma is that the awards for injury have escalated so dramatically. Attacks on entire industries will continue to rise until solutions are found. Success breeds success, and plaintiff attorneys are enriched and encouraged not only by victories in court but by outright capitulation by the defense in an astounding number of out-of-court settlements.

In the eyes of the sporting goods industry, there are no triable issues of fact in failure to warn cases. A manufacturer has a "duty to warn" of inherent dangers in a product where the risks are not obvious to the consumer. Sporting goods products are not inherently dangerous; that is the Catch-22. Failure to warn is a scam perpetrated by the trial bar to give itself a full-employment plan.

§ 7.1(B). Historical Efforts to Address the Problem.

In the mid-1970's the Sporting Goods Manufacturers Association spearheaded a coalition of more than 100 national trade associations to deal with the product liability crisis. It focused on rising insurance costs which resulted from increased litigation. Sporting goods companies were defending themselves in as many as 40 to 50 cases a year, and at times were cut off from insurance even when paying exorbitant premiums.

In 1976 the federal government responded to these concerns and created a Federal Agency Taskforce on Product Liability within the Department of Commerce. In 1978, following the Taskforce's report outlining options that the federal government should take in addressing the causes of the product liability problem, Congress passed the Risk Retention Act. The Risk Retention Act resolved the problem of overly subjective rate-making procedures by allowing businesses to form self-insurance cooperatives as well as purchase groups to bargain collectively for lower commercial liability insurance premiums. The latter encouraged commercial insurers to offer product liability insurance at competitive rates and to set accurate premiums. What the Risk Retention Act did not do was resolve the second major underlying cause of the product liability problem — the uncertainties in the product liability tort litigation system and the costs expended by all parties in determining the responsibilities of manufacturers and product sellers and the rights of consumers.

For sporting goods manufacturers the Risk Retention Act failed to address the inability to spread the risk.

Self-insurance considerations for sporting goods manufacturers were economically unsound, and possibly suicidal with one unfavorable jury action.

For the sporting goods industry the problem was not strictly an insurance problem. It was found that the majority of the total cost to insurance companies went to the legal community, with lawyer contingency fees running as high as $2 million dollars per individual case.

The only viable solution for sporting goods manufacturers was federal legislation which could establish uniform guidelines to treat the injured fairly and equally, guilty firmly but equitably and leave the innocent parties alone.

§ 7.1(C). Tort Reforms at the State Level.

Sporting goods manufacturers worked hard to bring about the introduction of model legislation in each of the 50 states. By joining with other groups there were some successes. Three states enacted tort reform measures in 1977, and 13 states followed their example in 1978. Six states passed similar bills in 1979, and by 1983 eight more states had enacted some form of product liability statute. But no state adopted the model act in full. The overwhelming majority only enacted statutes of repose; they did not deal with key issues of product liability law, thereby creating a maze of conflicting rules set by judges rather than by statute and creating incentives to constantly broaden the bases of liability. In having to research and brief every issue in every product liability case, millions of dollars have been expended in legal and production costs.

As Secretary of Commerce Malcolm Baldridge noted: "State action has not reduced uncertainties." State courts have proceeded in a multiplicity of directions on fundamental issues of product liability law. They have different views on whether a plaintiff must show the defendant manufactured the product in question. They also differ as to whether claimants can introduce evidence of post-manufacture improvements in product safety to establish that the product in question was defective.

And they also differ as to whether product sellers can utilize tort law, as compared to commercial law, for proving harm that is purely economic in nature. The net result of this helter-skelter state action is that an individual state cannot address the product liability problem in a meaningful way.

According to the Product Liability Alliance, a coalition of 200 corporations and trade associations, including the Sporting Goods Manufacturers Association, that are committed to federal tort reform:

> The wide variation among state product liability laws threatens insurers' efforts to accurately predict the potential liability of the manufacturers they insure and limits the ability of manufacturers to make informed decisions regarding the design of products for nationwide distribution and sale. Some state courts have expanded the strict liability concept (liability without fault) to include product design cases. Manufacturers have little incentive to improve the design or safety of their products where their actions may be judged without regard to whether they were at fault. Consumers ultimately pay the costs of this uncertainty in higher product prices.

The application of strict liability has been a particular bone of contention for sporting goods manufacturers and threatens the development of sports protective equipment which can reduce the possibility of serious injury.

Who is the villain? Certainly not the paraplegic doomed to a life of pain who would trade a multimillion dollar settlement in a second for yesterday's body. Certainly not an innocent company which has done nothing more than to have its product in the wrong place at the wrong time. Certainly not the school board that did not even know a baseball game was being played that Saturday. Certainly not the judge or jury who, with their limited visibility, are doing what they believe to be right. We could make the case that the attorney who serves his financial needs rather than those of society is the villain. But really, he is not. It is the system that is to blame.

§ 7.1(D). Federal Product Liability Reform: What It Would Accomplish.

A federal statute setting uniform standards for application by state courts in product liability actions would stabilize what has become a serious burden on interstate commerce. Conflicting product liability rules have made it extremely difficult for consumers to know their rights and product sellers to know their obligations.

Today the question is no longer whose fault it is, but rather, who can pay?

The situation with regard to injuries suffered on the football field repeats itself in many different scenarios, whether it be a baseball injury, an eye injury from a batted tennis ball or a head injury sustained from diving into shallow water.

The Senate Commerce Committee's Report on the proposed Federal Product Liability Act states:

> Judges and juries have expanded the doctrine of product liability beyond legal justification. Because manufacturers and product sellers are assumed to be in a better position than claimants to pay and distribute the risks of liability, they should be liable. This approach to liability makes the manufacturer the insurer of accidents, and damages for harms caused by a product are paid, not because of wrongful or negligent conduct by defendants, but because of a social policy judgment about which party should bear the loss.

To correct these imbalances a legislative solution is needed that would:

1. establish national rules to be applied uniformly by courts throughout the country in judging product liability claims;
2. lower consumer prices by eliminating unnecessary litigation, thereby lowering legal defense and product insurance costs;
3. protect consumers by holding manufacturers strictly liable for construction defects and misrepresentations;
4. hold manufacturers liable for failure to utilize a safe design or for failure to provide a warning about a dangerous aspect of a product, so that manufacturers would have to live up to the standard that "society requires for the protection of its own interests and the interests of others";
5. allow claimants to bring actions involving a product within two years from the date they discover both injury and cause, regardless of the number of years that have elapsed since the manufacturer made the product;
6. allow claimants to recover damages even if they were partially responsible for their own injury;
7. require manufacturers to pay damages in proportion to their responsibility for the claimants' injury;
8. encourage safety by prohibiting any improvements from being offered as evidence that the prior product was defective;
9. judge manufacturers along the same or stronger standards as everyone else — doctors, lawyers, engineers, drivers of cars — that is, by whether they have acted reasonably and prudently;

10. provide funding through damage awards for public purposes which further the national interest in health, safety, education or the environment;

11. establish an expert review panel to study whether additional changes in product liability law, such as no-fault compensation, are necessary;

12. not undermine existing rules on design and warnings in the overwhelming majority of states;

13. not undermine contract and commercial law;

14. not reduce the recovery of employees injured in the workplace;

15. not shield wholesalers, distributors, retailers and other product sellers who are not manufacturers from liability, so that they, too, would be liable for harms caused by failure to use reasonable care, by misrepresentations and in cases where the plaintiff is unable to sue the manufacturer; and

16. not remove the threat of punitive damages as an incentive to product safety. Very substantial damages could still be assessed against manufacturers for each different allegation that they recklessly disregarded the safety of others. Because judges would know there was only one punishment, as there is in criminal law, they would assure that the punishment was a sufficient and appropriate deterrent to wrongdoing.

§ 7.1(E). The Search for a Federal Legislative Solution.

Each year since 1976 various factions for and against product liability reform have formed lobbies to wage battle on the product liability issue. Each year the battle has ended in a stalemate.

On one side stands the business community, which agrees that a limited federal bill with uniform rules of liability would bring stability to both the litigation process and product liability insurance rates. On the other side, the legal community and consumer groups contend that product liability problems are not caused by fluctuating legal rules applied in the courts, but by insurance rate-making practices and unsafe products.

In the middle is Congress, primarily the Senate Commerce Committee, which at the instigation of Senator Robert Kasten (R-Wis.) developed a federal bill that codifies the various state product liability laws into clear and balanced standards that will freeze-frame the law as practiced in the majority of jurisdictions in the country and remedy some of the more unfair aspects by restoring fault as a consideration.

However, any legal action to change the present procedures appears to help some people and hurt others. While the Senate over the past ten years has worked diligently to develop a fair bill, differences of opinion still exist as to whether federal legislation would be a force for positive or negative change.

§ 7.1(F). Federal Preemption of State Law.

While most parties agree that uniform guidelines are needed to create a system of product liability litigation rules understood by everyone, the Trial

Lawyers of America vehemently disagree. They argue that federal tort reform "which codifies products law and pre-empts all state common law is a clear and present danger . . . and that it is the 'death knell' for tort practice in every field."

Although tort law is traditionally an area of state law into which the federal government should not intrude, blind adherence to the "federalism" argument, according to the business community, ignores the need for a workable solution to the product liability problem and the inability of states to develop that solution.

Only uniformity can improve the present climate of uncertainty caused by the application of nonuniform standards in various states.

Under the guise of "helping consumers," the trial bar benefits from contingency fees earned as a result of current product liability law in jurisdictions which make the plaintiff's case easy to win and the defendant's position difficult to defend.

Uniformity in the tort litigation system is necessary to facilitate trade and commerce, to prevent speculation in product liability insurance rates, to ensure that interstate commerce is not impeded by confusing requirements, to clarify grounds for lawsuits and to cut legal costs which result from the chaos generated by fifty different state laws.

The issue is simple — which will provide greater uniformity: courts attempting to interpret a single federal statute and faithfully applying federal decisions interpreting it, or courts with no statutory guidelines or unifying principles or with widely different statutes? The answer is evident.

§ 7.1(G). Standard of Liability for Design and Failure to Warn.

The real issue in the product liability debate is the standard of liability that should govern product design and warning cases.

The federal bill currently before the United States Senate proposes that manufacturers pay for injuries caused by construction defects or breach of warranty. It would adopt a negligence or fault-based standard for design defect and failure to warn cases.

By holding design defects to a negligence standard, the bill would eliminate departures from fault-based principles and some courts' reliance on arguments that (1) strict liability encourages the development of safer products and (2) the costs of product liability judgments can best be handled by distributing the costs through product prices. First, as a commentator on the application of strict liability noted: "Strict liability cannot be an incentive to increased research and development if the manufacturer knows that, despite whatever care is exercised in its design choice, liability will still be imposed." Second, if the risk distribution argument were to be accepted as a justification for departing from a negligence standard, a manufacturer would be liable for every harm caused by a product design simply because the manufacturer is assumed to be in the best position to distribute the risk and costs of such liability.

The Senate Commerce Committee noted that "if this result is desired, the tort litigation system is not the most-efficient mechanism to use. The more efficient mechanism would be a no-fault, limited damage compensation system, similar to the workers' compensation system."

In answer to the charge of some consumer groups that the proposed Federal Product Liability Act would require that the claimant prove something more than that the product was defective, the Product Liability Alliance notes:

> True strict liability does not work in design cases. One cannot look at the product and find the defect as one can with a manufacturing flaw. The "wrong" on the part of the manufacturer can only be found by looking at the decision he made, the judgment he used and what society required for safety.

Despite these arguments for a negligence standard on design and failure to warn cases, opponents of federal tort reform maintain that elimination of a strict liability standard in these cases frustrates the ability of injured parties to recover damages, because they might not be able to overcome the obstacles to proving negligence.

It is the conduct of the manufacturer that is at issue in a design case, not the product. Recovery for damages is not barred if it can be proved that a manufacturer knew or — based on knowledge in the scientific, technological or medical community — should have known about the danger in the design of a product that caused a claimant's harm. While a manufacturer has a continuing duty to discover product dangers, it is unfair to hold a manufacturer responsible for a design that could not have been improved given the state of the art at the time the product was made.

The lack of warning specifically directed to any hazard that results in an accident or injury has been sufficient ground for courts and juries to find the manufacturer liable. Thus the overwhelming majority of product liability actions against manufacturers and school districts are based on failure to warn.

Senator Kasten's bill provides standards that manufacturers must conform to in instructing a product user or third party about risks associated with the product or its use, while also providing that a product is not unreasonably dangerous for lack of warnings regarding (1) dangers that are obvious, (2) the consequences of product misuse and (3) the consequences of product alterations or modifications.

§ 7.1(H). Who Is Responsible in a Product Liability Action?

In some states rules totally bar an injured victim from recovering if he caused or contributed to his own injury in any degree, while other states totally bar recovery if the claimant caused half or more of his own injury.

Senate Bill 100 adopts the doctrine of "pure" comparative negligence, which apportions liability in direct proportion to fault. The bill not only describes how to determine the percentage of responsibility, but provides that misuse and alteration of a product by a person is a consideration in allocating responsibility for the claimant's harm. This provision is especially important to the sports community.

An advantage of the concept is that jurors would give weight to improper use or maintenance of a product, rather than be faced with the difficult decision of whether a person's improper or injudicious use of a product was the sole proximate cause of the accident.

In cases involving paralyzing bodily injuries juries are often influenced in their decision by sympathy for the injured party. This often leads to inequitable results; comparative negligence might reduce such inequities.

Misuse is defined in the legislation as occurring when a product is used for a purpose or in a manner that is "not consistent with the reasonably anticipated conduct of users, that is conduct that is not consistent with conduct 'which is expected, ordinary, and familiar to the class of persons likely to use or be exposed to the product.'"

In addition, "misuse" may include "use that is inconsistent with adequate warning or instructions regarding the product." An alteration or modification of a product includes changes or removal of warnings or safety instructions. Alteration or modification of a product does not include ordinary wear and tear or a product change in accordance with the instructions, specification or express consent of the manufacturer or product seller. The manufacturer or product seller in this latter instance bears responsibility for the consequences.

While "pure" comparative negligence may reduce damages awarded, it does not totally bar recovery as it would in many states under current law.

The opposition of the Conference of State Legislatures, the American Bar Association and the Consumer Federation of America to these proposed standards lies in the bill's language providing that the manufacturer is not liable unless the claimant's conduct is "reasonably anticipated conduct." The bill is accused of being biased towards the business community in that the balance of proof has been shifted from the manufacturer to the claimant.

Under current law the test for establishing whether a claimant's conduct should bar recovery is based on whether the claimant's use of the product was "foreseeable," not "expected" or "familiar." The manufacturing community maintains that it is totally unreasonable to require a manufacturer to warn against every conceivable use or misuse of a product.

The issue for the sports community is whether it should be held responsible for preventing injuries from all possible accidents or whether assumption of risk should be a factor.

Sports equipment can be misused in an unlimited number of ways, from hitting someone over the head with a baseball bat to using a helmet as a battering ram. In retrospect, any kind of product misuse can be foreseeable. The problem is that the plaintiff always is able to use hindsight, while the manufacturer must always use foresight.

§ 7.1(I). Punitive Damages.

Many legal scholars often refer to the doctrine of punitive damages as a "legal dinosaur that has evaded extinction." In the 1970's sporting goods manufacturers suggested that punitive damage awards be eliminated in product liability actions as unlimited exposure to punitive damages placed companies into a bankruptcy position. Moreover, they believed that the concept was contrary to modern jurisprudence, where the purpose of civil law has been to provide compensation, not penal retribution.

However, consumer groups and trial lawyers oppose any proposal to limit damage awards in the legislative arena.

To accommodate those who favor the use of punitive damages, the Senate Commerce Committee drafted procedures within the federal liability bill for assessing punitive damages, based on procedures followed in states allowing compensation beyond actual injury. More than twenty states do not permit punitive damages.

The bill as originally drafted would have allowed a claimant to recover punitive damages if he could establish by clear and convincing evidence, rather than just a preponderance of evidence, the defendant's "reckless disregard" for the safety of product users who might be harmed by the product. Also, to protect manufacturers from multiple jeopardy, only the first victim settling with a manufacturer of a defective product could collect punitive damages, with a judge rather than a jury responsible for determining the amount.

Major consumer groups and the bar lobbied hard against these limitations, citing that a claimant's "right to seek" and the "ability to recover" would be curtailed if not eliminated altogether. They argued that a manufacturer, in only having to settle with the first injured victim, had no incentive to correct a defective product.

Since Senator Ernest Hollings (D-S.C.) maintained a strident attitude on this issue and had some political clout that could table a bill, an effort was made to soften the bar on a claimant's ability to recover punitive damages. Senator Paul Trible (D-Va.) designed an amendment intended to deter a defendant from future outrageous conduct, but not to provide a windfall to the claimant. It allowed a manufacturer to be held liable more than once if new evidence in a later product liability action proved the same allegation or other allegations of reckless conduct by the manufacturer that had not been proved in the previous case. Trible's amendment also mandates that a portion of the punitive damage award be contributed to an appropriate public institution that promotes health and safety.

Although the bill was reported favorably out of committee with this amendment, unfortunately the displeasure with the punitive damages provision has not dissipated. The Federal Product Liability Act reintroduced in the 99th Congress deletes the Trible amendment.

The sporting goods industry believes the current proposal would be an effective instrument for creating product safety. Industry realizes that legislatively it is impossible to restrict punitive damages totally. The feeling, however, among members of the industry is that the law should not be designed to create inequities which outweigh any possible benefits. One of the biggest problems facing the sporting goods industry is the plaintiff's ability to compel a manufacturer to settle sometimes meritless cases because of the well-founded fear that a jury will return an outrageously large punitive award. As one court has perceptively observed: "It is difficult to understand why, when the sufferer by a tort has been fully compensated for his suffering, he should recover anything more."

§ 7.1(J). Where Do We Go From Here?

Senate Bill 100, the Federal Product Liability Act, represents a blend of the best law from our 50 states, yet it has repeatedly failed to get to the Senate floor for a vote. In the 97th and the 98th Congress the bill fell victim to a Senate calendar clogged with must-do legislation, and the threat of a filibuster led by Senators Ernest Hollings (D-S.C.) and Alan Cranston (D-Cal.).

Some observers have suggested that federal tort reform is dead for 1985, that Congress is tired of dealing with the issue and that the suspicions the business community, consumer groups and legal profession hold for each other will never be settled in the construction of a bill designed to be the engine of product safety.

Memoranda from the Product Liability Alliance suggest that the business community has no intention of dropping this legislative priority. They are championing corporations and trade associations to advance the cause and secure enactment in 1985.

There are a few considerations that challenge the optimistic forecast presented by the Product Liability Alliance, namely:

(1) Can businesses' grass roots continue to be mobilized in the fight for tort reform? Trade association leadership may have greater difficulty in convincing their corporate members that enactment can happen.

(2) Will the 99th Congress be more sympathetic to the business community or to consumer groups and the legal profession?

(3) Will business remain satisfied with tort reform legislation as drafted? Thus far, diverse industries have joined together to develop legislation in consensus. After expending thousands of dollars and still not making headway, will they continue to maintain a united front, or lobby for their own remedy specific to their own company interest?

(4) How hard will the White House support the legislation with members of Congress?

§ 7.1(K). Conclusion.

If the product liability challenge is not met successfully by the sports community, two scenarios will be played out. One is that the demand for gigantic damages for real or imagined injury will force United States manufacturers out of business, whereby consumers will have to depend on a foreign company to satisfy demand, or worse, depend on a person manufacturing out of a garage with none of the built-in safety innovations that companies have spent years and millions researching and developing; or that sports in America will no longer be basic to the education or recreation process as we know it. It will become an activity for the elite, for those who can afford to pay the high price of equipment.

While risks in sport cannot be eliminated, they can be minimized. This can be accomplished by product sellers maintaining good loss prevention programs and school districts and youth sports organizations implementing sports safety programs.

The product liability problem is not an isolated problem. It affects manufacturers, retailers, schools, leagues, athletes and the like. Increasing insurance costs, litigation and the threat of litigation are a detriment to sports programs and activities throughout the country.

Product liability law today is a moving target. Federal tort reform would create a national body of products liability case law that would set "standards that are understandable by manufacturers, equitable to product sellers and users, and uniformly interpreted by courts and juries nationwide."

If the sports community will join together in a united front with industry joining hands with professional sport and amateur and school sport, no greater coalition of interests could be devised to bring about federal product liability reform. The question is: will the sports community meet the challenge to ensure the continued viability of sport in America or will it be bested by the challenge?

We in sport have the unique ability to focus attention on the present costly product liability system. Since everyone can identify with sport and sporting goods products, we have the instruments of action with which we can help change the climate of civil justice in this country. Our task is to not only lobby for changes in law in the Congress, but to take this pocketbook issue to the media, which mold grass-roots public opinion. Once Americans understand how the present system is hurting them, their voices will ring the message for reform in the halls of Congress.

---

§ 7.2. Effective Design and Upkeep of Gymnastic Facilities.

By Marc Rabinoff

Glenn Sundly, editor of The Modern Gymnast, wrote in 1957: "For endless hours of fun and health, whether in school, camp, or at home, the trampoline has tremendous appeal, and it is a wonderful American contribution to the ageless sport of gymnastics."

Today, almost thirty years later, we seldom hear of trampolining either in print or in competition. What was once a great gymnastic activity is now banned in many school districts and eliminated as a competitive sport in high school or college. It is a major factor in numerous multimillion-dollar lawsuits throughout the nation.

In the 1950's there were many clubs and camps along with schools that used trampolines for their activity programs. Trampolines became very popular, and "jump centers" utilizing them became an activity accepted by the general public. The trampoline and trampolining lost much of their popularity because the general public did not understand the dynamics of the equipment. This led to a proliferation of serious injuries and the closing of these "jump centers." Although schools still use trampolines, a recommendation by the American Academy of Pediatrics to ban them caused many schools to discontinue their use. Because of public pressure, physical educators and coaches reevaluated the place of the trampoline in the school curriculum. In 1974 and 1977 the American Society for Testing Materials (A.S.T.M.) came up with standards for usage accompanied by appropriate warnings. In 1977 the American Alliance for Health, Physical Education, Recreation and Dance (A.A.H.P.E.R.D.) issued guidelines for use in formal physical education classes. Many schools that could not meet the guidelines eliminated the trampoline from their programs, while others faced the risk of an expensive lawsuit when things went wrong.

§ 7.2(A). Growth of Gymnastics.

At the same time trampolining was being de-emphasized, the sport of gymnastics was growing at an unprecedented rate. The United States Gymnastic Federation (U.S.G.F.) was established in the early 1970's, and gymnastic teams were formed for men and women. Today gymnastics is one of the premier sports events at the Olympics, and our athletes rank among the best in the world.

Now that times have changed, gymnastics may experience the problems that trampolining faced unless standards are set by the profession, not the courts. Physical educators, coaches and athletes must realize their limitations as well as expectations. Manufacturers of gymnastic equipment must test and retest new equipment and facilities to meet the needs of the participants. The prime consideration must involve safety and effective designs of gymnastic facilities. It is imperative that only the best equipment is utilized in gymnastics. The sport involves six olympic events for men: floor exercise, pommel horse, horizontal bar, parallel bars, still rings and the long horse vault. For women there are four olympic events: uneven parallel bars, balance beam, floor exercise and side horse vault. Since equipment is the basis of the sport, the standards of quality must be met to allow the gymnast to reach full potential in a safe environment. For this reason, new "spring" or "rebound" floors, better padded beams, more flexible bars, more responsive take-off boards and spotting rigs with the newest innovation of "pits" are available. These pits are foam-filled and deep, to absorb falls and misses, and are often built into the floor under the apparatus.

§ 7.2(B). Attempt by Equipment Manufacturers to Follow Standards.

Equipment manufacturers are expanding and upgrading apparatus and attempting to follow standards. These standards are set by the International Federation of Gymnastics (F.I.G.), located in Europe. The National Collegiate Athletic Association (NCAA) and the National Federation of State High School Associations (N.F.S.H.A.) have adopted these standards, but only the dimensions — i.e., height, length and maximum mats in competition — and construction of "high quality materials that provide a maximum amount of protection for the gymnast."

Today there are only two American companies recognized by the F.I.G. to meet its standards for gymnastic apparatus. They are the AMF and Nissen corporations. Although there are other companies that make an excellent product, the International Federation does not recognize them at this time. The question then becomes: "What standards should be followed?" The answer lies in two places: the U.S. manufacturers' testing programs and the gymnastic community's commitment to the education of coaches and teachers to follow proper progressions in learning gymnastic movements.

It is the manufacturer that should know if its new take-off board with five springs instead of two or three springs is better and why it is better. A manufacturer with a better or bigger spring under its rebound floor must test its responsiveness and reliability so that the entire floor is equal in dynamics.

Once tests are completed, the manufacturer has a responsibility to educate the purchaser on the new dynamics of the apparatus. When one learns how to do a back salto (flip) on the floor on a regular mat, that is one thing; however, when one learns to do a back salto on a rebound floor, the extra springs under the floor do aid in height gains. This is beneficial, but it can also be detrimental if the gymnast is relying solely on springs and not good technique in executing this movement. Further, since spring floors are not required in competition, a gymnast can practice on one, travel to another gym that does not own one and be in a dangerous situation if the progressions or techniques are not learned well and the participant relies on the floor for assistance. This same concept follows for new multi-spring take-off boards in the vault event, sometimes referred to as "super boards." Research (USGF Technical Journal, Oct. 81) reveals that more knee and ankle injuries occur from improper landings in vaulting than in any other event; therefore, the height of the after-flight caused by these super boards can be a problem on a poor landing if proper progressions and techniques are not followed when using a much springier board.

This issue of equipment standards is even more confusing since there are no specifications other than dimensions available for construction. This is especially true for spring boards. Because of this, several questions are raised. Are the other companies required to meet F.I.G. standards or not? If the U.S.G.F. adopts the F.I.G. specifications which were met by the two American companies, should other companies comply? It seems that there may not be any specifications to springiness, for example, so how can other companies comply? If this is the case, then what is the standard? None.

Today anyone can build his own spring floor with whatever wood, metal and fabric he desires and never test it for reliability or responsiveness, but use it in competition or practice.

Although it was not uncommon to build one's own gymnastics equipment in the past, it is not good practice today due to the multiple salto. The increased level of skill and abilities of our youth as well as improved coaching techniques make these movements more dangerous than in the past where poorly performed. This coupled with faultily constructed equipment provides less than adequate environments for the sport of gymnastics.

According to Jerry Todd, writing in International Gymnast:

> The equipment should be of the highest quality available. The coach and administrator should check the equipment regularly for wear and tear and for structural weaknesses. If the equipment becomes outdated it should be replaced. Proper markings warning of the equipment's danger should be placed on the apparatuses. Coaches should never improvise with make-shift equipment. To do so would endanger the gymnasts.

Improvising with such things as mats and landing pits does not improve the chances for the gymnast's success, but rather increases the chance for serious injury.

Furthermore, Todd, a highly respected expert in gymnastics, commented on landing pits when he said:

"The Pit" is the new method of teaching many skills involving flips. If constructed and used properly it can be an excellent aid. It should be enclosed on the four sides and have a uniform level of foam throughout. The foam must be of proper size and depth to both cushion and support the gymnast's body. The pit must be sufficiently long and wide so that the athlete does not risk striking the sides. The pit does not remove, however, the coach's responsibility to cover all phases of the learning process. There are no short cuts to safety in gymnastics.

Dr. Allan J. Ryan, editor in chief of Physician and Sports Medicine magazine, stated in his editorial entitled "Dismounting to Injury":

Safety measures should not play a part in the outcome of the event. Yet they can. For example, regulations require landing mats over the basic mats in the landing areas around all apparatus except the pommel horse. The thicker the cushioning, however, the more difficult it is for the gymnast to maintain the landing position . . ., without stepping or falling and losing points . . . . Technical developments and skill improvements due to a greater number of competitors and better coaching have forced changes, and rules organizations such as the U.S. Gymnastics Safety Association now deal with safety questions more than any other problems.

Equipment companies such as Spieth Anderson from Canada do significant research utilizing a computer such as an "Anthropomophic Humanoid (dummy) for precise, scientific simulation of potential injury during gymnastics" (Spieth Anderson Catalog, 1983, at 4). This research has resulted in what Spieth Anderson calls their "Anderson Ortho-Air Free x Floor." It "combines innovative orthopedic qualities to help absorb such impacts and minimize injury while giving great, responsive life — the ultimate in a free exercise floor suface." Similarly, AMF states in its 1982 products catalog: "The American Reflex 1200 is the only spring floor system approved by the FIG, and was selected as the official floor for the 20th World Gymnastic championships. From a performance view point, the Reflex 1200 is specially engineered, designed and tested to provide excellent shock-absorbency while allowing for the proper amount of resiliency." These companies reflect research and modern design ideas which have been tested.

§ 7.2(C). Recommendations for Upkeep of Gymnastic Equipment.

The same concepts apply to the pieces of apparatus for other events. The floor attachments and cables must be of steel and properly installed to give the gymnast the most efficient and safe environment in which to perform. With the environment in mind, both the performer and coach should do the following concerning the upkeep of gymnastics equipment.

1. *Locate apparatus safely,* taking into consideration required space for mats and travel or flow of users.
2. *Check all equipment daily or prior to usage.* This includes cables, floor plates, fastenings, hooks and turnbuckles and all other pieces of hardware used.
3. *Always examine settings to fit individual performers.* Some apparatus is adjustable within the rules.
4. *Use as much mat protection as needed.*
5. *Replace worn or defective parts immediately* and do not use makeshift parts nor interchange parts from one company to another. *They do not fit.*
6. *Know the limitations and dynamics of each piece of apparatus* in setting them up and using them.

These six items are only a few recommendations for keeping gymnastic equipment safety operational. The AMF company notes:

The best gymnasts in the world are extremely safety conscious; they know how dangerous it is to use equipment without supervision. Be intelligent; recognize not only your limitations (as gymnast or supervisor), but also the limitations of the equipment. One thing more, always check the apparatus carefully before using it.

In a 1982 report submitted to the F.I.G., Jackie Fie, Project Coordinator, illustrates the need for standards and testing of our gymnastic equipment. She stated:

Wood vaulting boards do not provide the most essential characteristics required of a piece of gymnastic apparatus, i.e. — first, that the apparatus be safe and durable, therefore, dependable, second, that the apparatus provides skill performance facilitation, and third, that composite type vaulting boards, (those made of synthetic materials, such as fiberglass, steels, aluminums, plastics, and other such materials) will be superior in both criterias. Therefore, composite boards should be the only apparatus allowed to be used in world class gymnastics competition.

Although the report is geared for world-class athletics, it can be applied to a novice performer. The report is complete and supports the above tested hypothesis. Furthermore, the summary stated: "Gymnastics apparatus has undergone comprehensive modification over the past two decades in order to stay abreast with the demands inherent in complex development." Notable examples include:

1. fiberglass uneven bars, parallel bars and rings;
2. smaller and rounder rail size;
3. mat and landing mat modifications;
4. springier, more elastic floor systems;
5. carpet on floors and vaulting boards;
6. padded beams;
7. aluminum beams; and
8. use of new stronger, lighter and more durable materials.

The primary purposes of such equipment modifications are:

1. to increase the safety and safety features of the equipment, thus reducing injuries; and
2. to facilitate skill performance, whereas the equipment should never be a limiting factor for the gymnast.

§ 7.2(D). Conclusion.

Mike Jackie, executive director of the U.S.G.F., in his editorial comments which appeared in *USA Gymnastics* (the official magazine of the U.S.G.F.) stated: "It has been said that an ounce of prevention is worth a pound of cure. In gymnastics terms, it means taking that extra moment to pull in the extra motion of your warm-up to prevent a possible ankle sprain." Jackie then reflects on the responsibilities of manufacturers by stating: "There are the companies that make the equipment meet the specifications and the demands placed upon it during athletic performance. The companies continually try to grade and improve their products. Their knowledge and expertise in contribution cannot be overlooked."

The gymnastic facility must be kept safe and updated. The fitness facility must be considered in this same light as millions of Americans become familiar with fitness and sport, because they deserve the best and highest standards from our professionals and product manufacturers, or the demise of the trampoline will look like nothing compared to the demise of fitness and gymnastics.

---

§ 7.3. Ski Area Liability for Downhill Skiers.

By John K. Fagen

The young man stood on the cornice overlooking the steep couloir. He hesitated, then pushed himself over the edge, dropping 15 feet before landing in the waist-deep powder. He bounded effortlessly through the deep snow and stopped about one quarter of the way down the tree lined chute. Looking around, he noticed there were no other skiers or patrolmen on the run. With this, he ducked under the rope and into the shade of the well spaced trees. Here the snow was fresher and virtually untracked because it was off the ski area. He was out of bounds. This in itself made the experience more exciting; the risk intrigued him.

He picked his line through the trees, then started down the steep grade. He moved slowly at first, bouncing rhythmically as the snow exploded into his face with each turn. Soon he gathered speed, as the slope fell away. The snow seemed bottomless. But the sensation changed. The snow cleared, and the bottom had dropped out from beneath him. He had skied off a small cliff and was suspended in mid-air just a second before slamming into a large Douglas fir.

Further down the mountain, a beginner was losing the struggle with her ski equipment. Sometime later she reached the top of the bunny hill, and proceeded down the gentle slope in an awkward but deliberate fashion. On her second run, she noted that the snow was deeper and fresher in the shade of the trees along the edge of the run. She made careful snowplow turns through the light snow and soon gained a little speed. But the shade stopped at the tree line, and the sun-exposed snow was wet and mushy. The abrupt transition caused her to lose her balance and fall, severely injuring herself.

These two hypotheticals provide examples of the varying degrees of danger involved in the sport of skiing and the extent to which some skiers accept or seek these dangers more than others.

The recent boom in both cross-country and downhill skiing has unfortunately brought an increase in injuries. The increase in injuries combined with the litigious nature of this society has brought an avalanche of suits for recovery for downhill skiing injuries. Traditionally these actions have been barred because the skier assumes the risks which inhere in the sport insofar as they are obvious and necessary.

Recently, however, one court, in *Sunday v. Stratton Corp.*, 390 A.2d 398 (Vt. 1978), refused to invoke this standard and allowed a skier to recover damages when he was injured after catching his ski on a snow-covered piece of brush. This court imposed liability based on the unprecedented theory that ski areas must protect skiers from such hazards because they are not inherent risks in the sport. This holding not only undermines settled doctrines for determining liability for downhill ski injuries, but also increases the likelihood of recovery for ski injuries which otherwise would have been barred. Due to the lack of well-defined duties and risks in recent ski injury litigation, many state legislatures have attempted to clarify the grounds for liability in these cases.

This section first examines the history of ski injury liability and defines the different standards imposed to determine negligence. It then discusses *Sunday v. Stratton Corp.*, its implications and the legislative response to it. The section concludes with a suggested method for determining responsibility for most skiing injuries and a review of recent court decisions on the issue.

§ 7.3(A). Historical Development of Ski Area Liability for Downhill Injuries.

(1) *Legal Relationship Between Ski Area Operators and Skiers.*

Skiers are business invitees of ski area operators. As such, the operator owes the skier the duty to exercise reasonable care to keep premises in a safe and suitable condition so skiers are not unnecessarily or unreasonably exposed to danger. According to the *Sunday* court, the operator not only owes a duty to protect the skier from known dangers, but is also required to exercise reasonable care in locating unknown dangers which pose potential threats to skiers. Whether the duty to exercise reasonable care has been discharged has become a key issue in recent ski injury litigation.

(2) *Assumption of Risk: The Traditional Defense.*

The issue of reasonable care is often never reached in ski injury suits because the skier is held to assume the risk inherent in the sport. For a skier to have assumed the risks the defendant must show the plaintiff knew of the risks, appreciated the extent of these risks and accepted them voluntarily.

Two distinct categories of assumption of risk have recently evolved that are of special consequence in ski injury litigation — primary and secondary assumption of risk. Primary assumption of risk arises when the plaintiff reasonably and voluntarily assumes a known risk in a situation where the defendant owes no duty or has discharged its duty to the plaintiff. Secondary assumption of risk is invoked as an affirmative defense to an established breach of duty by the defendant. With secondary assumption of risk, the question is whether the plaintiff acted reasonably in encountering the known risk. If the plaintiff acted reasonably and thus was free from negligence, there is no assumption of risk in the secondary sense. If, however, the plaintiff did not act reasonably, secondary assumption of risk may be asserted to bar recovery. Essentially, secondary assumption of risk is just a phase of contributory negligence because the plaintiff fails to exercise reasonable care for his or her own safety.

The distinction between primary and secondary assumption of risk was not crucial when contributory negligence also provided an absolute bar to recovery. However, adoption of comparative negligence necessitated finding relative fault, and thus the distinction became crucial. In theory, primary assumption of risk should coexist with contributory negligence because there is no duty or breach of duty and thus no negligence. On the other hand, secondary assumption of risk is subsumed within the framework of comparative negligence since it is merely an aspect of contributory negligence.

Wright v. Mt. Mansfield Lift, Inc., 96 F. Supp. 786 (D. Vt. 1951), is one of the earliest cases applying primary assumption of risk as a bar to recovery for a downhill skiing injury. This action arose when Florine Wright, an intermediate skier, broke her leg in a fall after hitting a snow-covered, five-inch tree stump.

The trial court found Mrs. Wright was an invitee of both defendants, the lift company and hotel company. As such, they owed a duty to advise her of any dangers which reasonable prudence would have foreseen and corrected. The court observed:

> Skiing is a sport; a sport that entices thousands of people; a sport that requires an ability on the part of the skier to handle himself or herself under various circumstances of grade, boundary, mid-trail obstructions, corners and varied conditions of the snow. Secondly, it requires good judgment on the part of the skier and recognition of the existing circumstances and conditions. Only the skier knows his own ability to cope with a certain piece of trail. Snow, ranging from powder to ice, can be of infinite kinds. Breakable crust may be encountered where soft snow is expected. Roots and rocks may be hidden under a thin cover. A single thin stubble of cut brush can trip a skier in the middle of a turn. Sticky snow may follow a fast running surface without warning. Skiing conditions may change quickly. What was, a short time before, a perfect surface with a soft cover on all bumps may fairly rapidly become filled with ruts, worn spots and other manner of skier created hazards.

The court applied the doctrine of assumption of risk and held that one who takes part in skiing or any such sport accepts the dangers that inhere in it so far as they are obvious and necessary. Noting there was no evidence of any existing danger which reasonable prudence would have foreseen and corrected, the court held that the ski area discharged its duty. It made clear the danger of hitting snow-covered stumps is one which inheres in the sport:

> To hold that the terrain of a ski trail down a mighty mountain, with fluctuation in weather and snow conditions that constantly change its appearance and slipperiness, should be kept level and smooth, free from holes or depressions, equally safe for the adult or the child, would be to demand the impossible. It cannot be that there is any duty imposed on the owner and operator of a ski slope that charges it with the knowledge of these mutations of nature and requires it to warn the public against such.

Citing *Murphy v. Steeplechase Amusement Co.,* 166 N.E. 173 (N.Y. 1929), the court directed a verdict for the defendants and quoted Chief Justice Cardozo in that case:

> One who takes part in such a sport accepts the dangers that inhere in it so far as they are obvious and necessary . . . . The plaintiff was not seeking a retreat for meditation . . . . He took the chance . . . with whatever damage to his body might ensue from such a fall. The timorous may stay at home.
>
> A different case would be here if the dangers inherent in the sport were obscure or unobserved . . . . Nothing happened to the plaintiff except what common experience tells us may happen at any time as the consequence of a sudden fall. Many a skater or a horseman can rehearse a tale of equal woe.

The doctrine established in *Wright* has since been applied in a variety of ways to bar recovery for skiing injuries. In many cases the defense was applied without distinction between primary and secondary assumption of risk. The difference between the two doctrines was not important until the adoption of comparative negligence, when secondary assumption of risk no longer acted as an absolute bar to recovery. As a result, case law provided no standards for the determination of duties and risks inherent in the sport. Nevertheless, many courts continued to apply the doctrine without distinction to prohibit recovery.

§ 7.3(B). Attacks on Assumption of Risk as a Defense.

The imprecise use of the doctrine of assumption of risk as a bar to recovery of damages for ski injuries inevitably led to attacks on its application. One particular ground of attack is that ski areas have changed the nature of the sport through improved slope grooming, maintenance and policing techniques. With such improvements, the argument goes, it is questionable whether many of the hazards encountered by skiers are obvious and necessary to the sport, and therefore they are not inherent in the sport.

(1) *Sunday v. Stratton Corporation.*

The above argument was adopted by the Vermont Supreme Court in the case of *Sunday v. Stratton Corp.,* a controversial case which undermines the traditional basis of the defense of assumption of risk in skiing injury cases.

The cause of action arose when James Sunday, a 21-year-old college student, was injured after his ski caught on a snow-covered piece of brush; he fell and hit a boulder. The collision with the boulder left Sunday a quadriplegic.

At trial the plaintiff alleged that the defendant ski area had negligently maintained its slopes by allowing the brush to exist and by failing to give notice of the hidden danger.

The ski area defended by maintaining that the assumption of risk doctrine survived the adoption of the state's comparative negligence statute, Vermont Stat. Ann. tit. 12, § 1036, and therefore was an absolute bar to recovery. Moreover, the ski area asserted that even if it owed the plaintiff a duty, that duty was discharged due to the elaborate grooming methods the defendant employed. And further, the defendant attempted to prove these grooming methods made the existence of such growth impossible. The jury found the defendant's negligence to be wholly the cause of the plaintiff's injuries and awarded the plaintiff $1.5 million, $250,000 over the amount the plaintiff requested.

On appeal to the Vermont Supreme Court, the defendant sought reversal on several grounds. Three are of interest here.

The first concerned the trial court's refusal to grant a directed verdict on the ground that the inherent nature of the sport precluded recovery under the circumstances. In refusing to grant the directed verdict, the trial court ruled that Vermont's comparative negligence statute precluded assumption of risk as a defense. The defendant objected to this ruling, claiming the issue was not one of the defendant's negligence, but one of the plaintiff's assumption of risk in the primary sense. Conversely, the defendant owed no duty to protect plaintiff from the vegetation:

> Some forms of vegetation in the trail belong as a matter of law in the category of things for which the ski area has no liability. Stated differently, a person who ventures forth to ski down the side of a mountain assumes the risk, as a matter of law, that he may come into contact with the ubiquitous vegetation on the mountain and may fall and be injured as a result. As a matter of law, any skier assumes the risk in the primary sense that he may fall should his ski catch on a lump of ice, hardened snow crust, a bare spot, or minor vegetation.

Thus the comparative negligence statute did not preclude application of the doctrine of assumption of risk in the primary sense; the issue was not one of the defendant's negligence.

The Vermont Supreme Court agreed that there was no conflict between primary assumption of risk and the comparative negligence statute, but held that primary assumption of risk did not apply in view of the evidence advanced. In reaching this conclusion, the court noted that Mr. Sunday was a novice slowly skiing one of the best-groomed novice trails when he became entangled in the concealed vegetation. Stratton's advertisements stressed grooming to attract novices, and Sunday had a right to rely on these in assuming the trail would be safe, aside from obvious dangers.

More generally, the court held that *Wright* did not apply to the circumstances of this case because the brush was not an inherent danger. This conclusion was based on the defendant's unchallenged testimony that its modern methods of grooming made such vegetation impossible. It observed:

> It is clear from the evidence that the passage of time has greatly changed the nature of the ski industry. Unlike those participants eloquently described by Chief Judge Cardozo in *Murphy v. Steeplechase Amusement Co.* ... heavily relied upon in *Wright,* the timorous no longer need stay at home. There is concerted effort to attack their patronage and to provide novice trails suitable for their use. This is the state of the evidence in the case tried below; none of it was calculated to show the brush to be a danger inherent in the use of a novice slope as laid out and maintained by the defendants.

The court found that the plaintiff was a business invitee and that the defendant's duty was governed by the case of *Garafano v. Neshobe Beach Club, Inc.,* 238 A.2d 70 (Vt. 1967):

> In the discharge of its duty, [defendant] was bound to use reasonable care to keep its premises in a safe and suitable condition so that plaintiff would not be unnecessarily or unreasonably exposed to danger. If a hidden danger existed, known to the defendant, but unknown and not reasonably apparent to the plaintiff, it was [defendant's] duty to give warning of it to the latter. In those circumstances he had a right to assume that the premises, aside from obvious dangers, were reasonably safe for the purpose for which he was upon them, and that proper precaution had been taken to make them so.

Although the plaintiff assumed the risks inherent in the sport, he did not assume the dangers of improperly maintained slopes. Where there has been an assumption of a duty and its breach, the risk created by the breach is not assumed by the plaintiff. The plaintiff did not assume the risk of injury, but the use of reasonable care on the part of the defendant. Therefore, the court reasoned, the motions for a directed verdict and judgment n.o.v. were properly denied.

Second, the defendant claimed the trial court erred in failing to adequately charge the jury separately on the issues of primary assumption of risk and contributory negligence. After reviewing the instructions the court denied this claim. In reaching this conclusion the court noted that the jury was instructed that liability had to be based upon fault, the reasonableness of protective measures taken and the need for determining what precautions were commensurate with the duty of due care. The instructions stressed that skiers accepted dangers inherent in the sport insofar as they were obvious and necessary, and that negligence in trail maintenance or in warning of dangers was a prerequisite to recovery. Thus primary assumption of risk did not apply, since the jury found the area had owed a duty to the skier and that duty had been breached.

The defendant also claimed the trial court erred in failing to charge the jury on secondary assumption of risk as an aspect of comparative negligence. The court also rejected this claim. It noted that secondary assumption of risk is only a phase of contributory negligence and that use of distinguishing language is confusing in a jury instruction on comparative negligence. Since the plaintiff had no prior knowledge of the existence of the vegetation before running into it, the doctrine did not apply.

(2) *Critique of* Sunday v. Stratton Corporation.

The main problem with the Vermont Supreme Court's holding in *Sunday* is that it imposes too great a burden on the ski area operator in fulfilling the duty owed to the skier. Since concealed natural obstacles are no longer considered inherent risks in the sport, the area operator has the duty to protect the skier from such dangers.

This precedent is dangerous because it exposes ski area operators to liability for injuries caused by unobserved natural obstacles. Even though advanced grooming and maintenance techniques have changed the nature of the sport, many hazards are beyond the reasonable control of an area operator. These obstructions — such as brush, roots, rocks and other mountain debris — are often so pervasive or indistinct on a mountain or hill that they are inherent in the setting. Because all of these hazards cannot be eliminated, they are necessary, and this fact should make their existence obvious to the skier. Thus the court was mistaken when it applied the following rule from *Garafano:*

> By also urging that the plaintiff assumed the risks inherent with the sport the defendant has mistakenly associated the injury with the playing of the sport itself whereas it is not. Rather, it is the condition of the recreation field provided for the game that was the cause of the injury.

The injury in that case resulted when the plaintiff stepped in a hole on the defendant's softball field. Yet the court failed to recognize the vast differences between the two sports when it applied this standard. Not only is the area greater in skiing; the rugged natural setting is an integral part and major attraction of the sport. Concealed natural obstacles are merely an inherent consequence of the necessary size and setting of the area of participation.

In this respect it is arguable that the defendant discharged its duty to the plaintiff by employing advanced grooming and maintenance techniques. They did everything within reason to extinguish the danger of natural obstacles, but it was simply impossible to eliminate all such hazards.

The court in *Marietta v. Cliffs Ridge, Inc.,* 189 N.W.2d 208 (Mich. 1971), also affirmed that the defendant was negligent for failing to extinguish or warn the plaintiff of the danger. However, it never found the defendant had actual knowledge of the hazard. By imputing such knowledge the court did not even adhere to the standard of care it set down: "If a hidden danger existed, known to the defendant, but unknown and not reasonably apparent to the plaintiff, it was [defendant's] duty to give warning of it to the latter."

The real issue is whether it was reasonable for the ski area to have knowledge of the hazard. The reasonableness of such knowledge depends on several general factors. For example, was the hazard man-made or natural, obvious or concealed, new or old? Specifics — such as the size of the mountain, the number of runs patrolled and groomed, the geologic and vegetative makeup of the mountain or hill and the number of skiers on the area — should also be considered. In general, it is more reasonable that knowledge of the possibility of such hazards be imposed on the skier, not on the ski area, because the skier exercises the ultimate control over his actions and must use caution and judgment in light of his skills.

Also, imputing knowledge to the ski area where no actual knowledge of a danger exists makes the areas insurers of their skiers' safety. In spite of specific instructions to the contrary, this is the effect of the court's affirmation.

It is also apparent that the trial court committed a reversible error by not adequately instructing the jury on the issue of primary assumption of risk as distinct from secondary assumption of risk. By failing to acknowledge the existence of the doctrine under Vermont's comparative negligence statute, Vermont Stat. Ann. tit. 12, § 1036, the trial court precluded the possibility of a proper charge on the question of the plaintiff's primary assumption of risk.

A proper charge would have highlighted the fact that the plaintiff assumes risks in the primary sense if he has knowledge of the general risks and he accepts them voluntarily and reasonably. This should be distinguished from the plaintiff's assumption of risk in the secondary sense, when he has knowledge of the specific risks created by defendant's breach, but nevertheless accepts them voluntarily although unreasonably. The distinction between reasonably assuming the general risks and unreasonably assuming the specific risks is crucial in determining whether the primary or secondary assumption of risk doctrine is applicable. The charge in *Sunday* was not sufficient to allow the jury to consider these differences and therefore provided grounds for reversal.

This verdict for the plaintiff in *Sunday* was more based on an understandable sympathy for him than grounded on sound legal reasoning. Reaching for the "deep pockets" is the ultimate justification for shifting the burden of this tragic accident from young Jim Sunday to the large ski area and ultimately its insurance company.

The obvious problem with the result in *Sunday* is that it upsets well-founded legal standards which guided ski areas in exercising reasonable care within feasible limits. Now it is no longer clear which risks were inherent in the sport and which are obvious and necessary.

(3) *Responses to* Sunday v. Stratton Corporation.

(a) *Insurance Rates.*

The initial repercussions of the decision in *Sunday* were not limited to Vermont. Throughout the nation ski areas and their insurers shared fears of seemingly boundless liability due to the broad holding of the case.

Some industry spokesmen felt this decision made ski areas responsible for almost every injury to skiers. Others were not as fearful, but were still unsure about the extent to which ski areas would be liable for injuries in the future.

This uncertainty led to increased insurance rates to cover the increased potential liability caused by the decision. This increase is particularly burdensome because of the limited number of insureds, about four hundred ski areas nationwide, making it more costly to spread the risk. A spokesman for one of the two major ski area insurers speculated that they could be forced to increase ski insurance rates to such an extent that ski areas may not be able to pass these costs along to the skiers.

An example of this problem was available within a year of the trial court holding. Many areas' insurance rates doubled and tripled, and at some resorts the percentage of a lift ticket price allocated to insurance increased from below 3% to about 15%. There was also talk of the possibility of a $20 to $25 dollar lift ticket to cover these increased rates. Some thought these increases might decrease business by as much as 25% as well as force some smaller areas to close. In Vermont alone the impact of decreased ski business and ski area closings could well have robbed the state of much of its $150 million annual ski tourism business.

(b) Legislation.

State legislatures responded to *Sunday* by codifying the shared responsibilities of the ski area and the skier. They grappled with questions such as the following. What risks are inherent in the sport insofar as they are obvious and necessary and therefore should be assumed by the skier? What is the extent of the ski area's duty to exercise reasonable care? Are industry standards a proper measure of whether the ski area has discharged its duty, or is more required?

Generally, four types of statutes attempt to define liability for ski injuries. The first type reaffirms the pre-*Sunday* standard and mandates that the skier assume all risks inherent in the sport insofar as they are obvious and necessary.

The Vermont statute, tit. 12, § 1037, properly resurrects the doctrine of primary assumption of risk, reassuring ski area operators and their insurers that they will not be liable for injuries due to inherent risks in the sport. Furthermore, the statute imposes the doctrine "as a matter of law." This could be interpreted in two ways. In one sense, it may mean the defendant is entitled to a jury instruction on assumption of risk as a matter of law. Alternatively, it could mean that the issue of whether the injury was due to an inherent risk may be determined by the judge rather than the jury. This type of statute is typically accompanied by a statement of legislative intent, making clear the need to limit ski area operators' liability in order to maintain reasonable insurance rates to stay in business.

The primary assumption of risk statute does fail, however, to provide a basis for determining which risks are inherent insofar as they are obvious and necessary, thus leaving open the possibility of another decision like *Sunday*.

The second type of ski liability law, Massachusetts Ann. Laws ch. 455, §§ 71N-71P, both recites the doctrine of assumption of risk and lists each party's responsibilities and duties. The statute requires that the jury consider whether the standard of due care has been met, whether the injury resulted from the skier's negligence and whether the injury was the result of an inherent risk in the sport.

This statute's main advantage is its clarification of the standard for determining due care and responsibility for injuries. Compliance with the standards set forth provides evidence of compliance with the statute. It also permits consideration of a variety of issues bearing on the accident, not limited to those enumerated. But compliance with the listed duties does not automatically relieve the area operator of liability for injuries. This again gives the jury tremendous discretion to determine liability. Because this discretion could be abused, this statute does little to decrease uncertainty in determining when the area operator has discharged its duty. To avoid this problem, a thorough list should be drawn up considering a variety of possible accidents and responsibility for them.

The third type of statute, New Mexico Stat. Ann. §§ 24-15-7, 24-15-10, 24-15-11, 24-15-13, is similar to the second as it includes both assumption of risk and an enumeration of the responsibilities of each party. This statute is different, however, in requiring the jury to find the injury is causally related to a breach of one of the enumerated duties. This statute sets out clear standards of liability and decreases the chances of recovery for injuries due to inherent risks.

This statute's principal drawback is the possible incompleteness of the list of duties. This statute also removes any discretion from the jury in determining liability. Thus there is a possibility that legitimate claims may be barred. This problem should be rectified by drawing up a list of duties in light of a wide variety of possible injury situations and delineating who should be responsible for them. A fourth statute, Montana Rev. Code Ann. §§ 23-2-733, 23-2-736, 23-2-737, expressly defines which risks are inherent and bars recovery if the injury was due to one of these specified risks. This statute provides the most direct and reasonable solution to the problem of liability. It precludes recovery for injuries due to inherent risks, yet it allows jury discretion in determining liability for injuries not due to inherent risks.

(c) Determining the Duties of Skiers and Ski Areas.

As mentioned earlier, skiers are business invitees of ski areas. Under this relationship the ski area owes the skiers the duty to exercise ordinary care to protect them from hazards that may be reasonably discovered and preventable by the operator. This includes the duty to remove or warn the skier of hidden dangers known to the area but unknown and not reasonably apparent to the skier.

There are three major considerations which complicate determination of whether the duty has been discharged. First, the combination of challenge, risk and natural setting provides the greatest attraction of the sport as well as the greatest element of danger. Second, skiers possess a wide range of abilities and sensibilities which are difficult if not impossible for the operator to ascertain. Third, natural conditions such as slope grade, vegetation, snow cover and weather conditions make the trail conditions highly variable and difficult to manage.

Because it is commonly agreed that ski areas are not liable for injuries due to risks inherent in the sport, it is important to define exactly what these risks are. To this it has been posited that inherent risks are those which are beyond the reasonable control of ski area operators. One method for determining whether a danger is beyond the reasonable control of the area operator is to look to industry standards for trail cleaning, grooming and maintenance as well as other regularly practiced safety measures. Thus if the area complied with industry standards, there is evidence that the area did not shirk its duty. This method, however, is not always conclusive.

There is another method for ascertaining whether the hazard is beyond the reasonable control of the area operator. This method looks to which party is in the best position to prevent the accident. This determination requires consideration of the nature of the danger: whether it is natural or man-made, whether it is obvious or concealed and whether it existed for such a time and in such a location that it should have been observed and corrected by the area operator.

Under this analysis the skier would be responsible for most injuries caused by obvious natural and man-made obstacles. Since these obstructions are obvious the skier is charged with knowledge of the dangers and should maintain enough control to avoid them. However, there may be exceptions to the general rule. For example, placing equipment in the center of a heavily traveled run may constitute negligence, especially if it is not necessary to the continued use of the slopes.

Ski areas should be responsible for most injuries caused by concealed or not obvious man-made hazards. The ski area is liable for such accidents because the skier does not know the hazard exists, whereas the operator should know of the danger. The operator has a duty to remove or mark the hazard since it is in the best position to protect skiers from the danger.

As *Sunday* proves, confusion exists in determining whether concealed natural objects are beyond the reasonable control of area operators and are therefore risks inherent in the sport. There are varying instances when the ski area is and is not liable for injuries caused by concealed natural obstacles.

Distinct and obvious hazards which exist through a summer maintenance program may constitute negligence if not eliminated. An example of this type of hazard is a deep eroded gully created by melting snow. These hazards are distinguished from less obtrusive and more pervasive conditions, such as vegetative or geologic variations. Recently developed obstacles may also be beyond the reasonable control of the area operator. The difference may be only a matter of degree, as the condition in the previous example may not be negligent if the gully is not abrupt, or less developed. Skiers should be held to have knowledge of the potential existence of such conditions due to the general understanding that the ski operator cannot possibly manage every condition which may arise in a natural setting.

It is especially interesting to apply the theories of control and ability to avoid collisions to recently decided cases. There is no reported case other than *Sunday* where a skier has been awarded damages for a collision with a natural object, whether obvious or not. These collisions are generally risks assumed by the skier.

There have been several actions brought for collisions with man-made obvious obstacles, such as lift towers and utility poles, which have produced divergent decisions. In *Leopold v. Okemo Mountain Inc.,* 420 F. Supp. 781 (D. Vt. 1976), the plaintiff's husband was killed when he collided with an unfenced and unpadded lift tower. The action arose prior to *Sunday* and thus prior to the enactment of Vermont's assumption of risk statute, Vermont Stat. Ann., tit. 12, § 1037. Nonetheless, the court held that assumption of risk as defined in *Wright,* 96 F. Supp. 786, was a bar to recovery because the tower was an obvious and observable obstacle. The court found no duty and thus no negligence in the placement of the tower or the design of the slope because the tower was an obstacle on the run, even though it was a foreseeable danger. The court also observed the area was not negligent for failing to pad the tower since no adequate pad was available. Further, the area was not negligent in placing the ladder on the uphill side of the tower in spite of the foreseeability of the possible aggravation of injuries due to such collisions.

In a similar case, *Green v. Sherburne,* 403 A.2d 278 (Vt. 1979), the minor plaintiff was injured when he collided with an unfenced and unpadded utility pole. The cause of action arose prior to the adoption of the Vermont assumption of risk statute, but after *Sunday.* The jury found the plaintiff skier 51% negligent and the defendant ski area 49% negligent, and the court entered a judgment for the ski area.

The plaintiff appealed, claiming that the jury was improperly charged as to the proper standard of care owed by the ski area operator to the skier. Specifically, the plaintiff claimed the charge did not detail the standard of care enough to raise the issue in the jury's mind of whether the pole was an obvious and necessary danger to be assumed by the skier. The court held the charge was adequate to apprise the jury on the issue of the duty of care because the trial court specifically included the pole as an obvious observable obstacle rather than a hidden or latent danger. The court also rejected a challenge to the charge for including the same standard of care for both the defendant and the plaintiff, who was held to have an equal duty toward his own safety.

These two cases rejected the plaintiff's contentions that the area should be liable because it exercised control over the design of the slope and the placement of the obstacles. Preventing recovery on these theories recognizes that skiers are in the best position to avoid collisions with visible obstacles. This theory prevents recovery based on foreseeability of injury and looks instead to who exercised the greater control over the cause of the accident.

The Tenth Circuit Court of Appeals reached a different result in *Rosen v. LTV Recreational Development, Inc.,* 569 F.2d 1117 (10th Cir. 1978). The plaintiff in this case was injured when he collided with a sign pole after crashing into another skier. The plaintiff alleged that the defendant was negligent in maintaining the steel pole where it created a foreseeable risk of injury of the kind that occurred. The defendant claimed the pole was obvious and thus the skier assumed the risk of injury because he should have maintained his control to avoid the collision.

The court held the intervening collision did not affect defendant's negligent placement of the sign and that it was the main cause of a foreseeable injury.

The sign created an unreasonable risk of injury to persons such as the plaintiff, one which they could not reasonably be expected to discover themselves. Thus the steel signpost was an independent hazard capable of producing liability in spite of the prior collision.

The court declared that assumption of risk no longer applied in Colorado due to the enactment of the state's comparative negligence statute and because assumption of risk was only a phase of contributory negligence. The court also denied the defense of waiver because plaintiff did not expressly exonerate the ski area for negligent conditions by signing his season pass agreement. Moreover, it upheld the $200,000 jury award as not excessive in light of the plaintiff's injury, a severe broken leg which required extensive surgery and resulted in permanent disability.

Under the theory stated above, *Rosen* was wrongly decided because the plaintiff should have maintained enough control over his course to avoid the initial collision and hence the collision with the sign. It is also questionable to impose the foreseeable injury standard in skiing cases. If this standard were widely accepted, the ski areas would be liable for a multitude of injuries resulting from every condition maintained on the ski area premises which may sooner or later be involved in a collision. This result may be justified, however, on the ground that the operator exercised discretion and control over the placement of the sign because it was not as necessary to the operation of the area as was the lift tower in *Leopold* and utility pole in *Green*.

The element of control also surfaces in cases involving the ski area's potential duty to prevent collisions. In *Davis v. Erickson*, 345 P.2d 942 (Cal. App. 1959), the California court dealt with the operator's duty to prevent collisions between skiers and ski school students. The court determined operators of the ski school could be found negligent for injuries when an overtaking skier struck a student if the acts were foreseeable because the student was reasonably under the control of the instructor. That the instructor took the beginner plaintiff to a hill crowded with skiers of all levels of ability constituted negligence because such an intervening cause of the accident was foreseeable. Here the ski area was in the best position to prevent the accident.

In accidents where the collision is not due to the negligence of a ski instructor but the negligence of another skier, the issue again becomes one of who was in the best position to avoid the accident, and control is determinative of liability for injury.

In *Ninio v. Hight*, 385 F.2d 350 (10th Cir. 1967), the Tenth Circuit Court of Appeals held that the unwritten rule that an overtaking skier is required to yield to skiers below is admissible to the jury as evidence of lack of ordinary care. Essentially, the court held the uphill skier had a duty to maintain control over his course and speed to such an extent that he could have avoided the collision.

In most decisions the courts have reached conclusions consistent with the general theories of control and ability to avoid collisions. Awareness and application of these basic principles in determining liability, either by statute or judicial decision, would help clarify the crucial issues. This would reduce confusion and hence decrease the possibility of inequitable results in ski injury litigation.

§ 7.3(C). Conclusion.

In *Sunday,* the Vermont Supreme Court followed the general doctrine set down in *Wright* that skiers assume the inherent risks of the sport. The court, however, adopted a significantly narrower view of inherent risks due to improvements in grooming techniques which have concededly changed the nature of the sport.

The main problem with the decision in *Sunday* is that it broadens ski areas' potential liability without setting general standards for determining their duties or which risks inhere in the sport. Holding ski areas liable for concealed natural obstacles in every instance is not consistent with the realities of the sport.

Some conditions are simply beyond a ski area's reasonable control and knowledge. Skiers should generally be aware that such conditions exist and cannot be eliminated, no matter what grooming methods are employed. Determining these risks and, ultimately, liability for skiing injuries involves many complex theoretical and practical considerations. Nevertheless, the final determination should be premised upon the basic idea that responsibility should be imposed on the party in the best position to reasonably prevent the injury.

---

§ 7.4. The Law of Public Assembly Facilities.

By James Oshust

§ 7.4(A). Introduction.

The current dilemma facing most personnel who manage public assembly facilities concerns the increasing list of laws that must be obeyed, requirements that must be met, codes that must be complied with totally, as weighed against the ever-increasing need to provide sensitive and responsive customer service for any and all activities in which a facility is engaged.

In certain cases, the decision is very clear-cut, having been formed by precedents in various legal cases. In the main, however, it normally comes down to a management decision, or at times, a lack thereof.

§ 7.4(B). Need for Legal Assistance.

In order to act within the law and still maintain services, the manager will need the assistance of an attorney. In order for him to make the best choices for actions to take, he will need to develop an understanding of the facility. Only when the legal counsel has been given sufficient information on the particular type of operation and some of the nuances that distinguish it from other similar operations, can he or she best prepare defense for an initiated legal action, offer substantive legal advice concerning a particular question, or provide ongoing direction and guidance in formulating rules and regulations in operational procedures.

The reader is cautioned that, like all aspects of society, the law itself changes. As social mores and conduct of society in general shift ever so slightly in one direction or another, so does the interpretation of the law; with these changes are the variations in the final judicial findings regarding any particular reflected issue brought before the court. Know the general concept of law. Stay on top of current industry standards and/or procedures found effective elsewhere. And most of all, ask for help early from those trained and schooled to provide appropriate legal consultation. To delay in requesting help, providing information or determining facts necessary for later decisions is to face potential disaster. At best, it can cast a shadow over the credibility of the operation and of the facility's position in the community.

§ 7.4(C). Access and Availability of Facility.

Access to and availability of facilities for various purposes has become an extremely sensitive item in certain areas of the country lately. A conflict in what was considered community standards and the legal aspects of access to a facility arose in Green Bay, Wisconsin in early 1983 concerning the imminent concert presentation of the then controversial rock star Ozzy Osbourne. The facility in Green Bay is operated under a management contract between a private group and the county. Local interests opposed the appearance of Osbourne and prevailed on county authorities to recommend to the management company that the existing contract for the concert be cancelled.

The management group's contract gave them total authority to handle all booking. Yet, trying to maintain a decent rapport with their client, the county, the management firm stated they would accede to the county officials' wishes if they, the county, took full legal liability for the decision. The county's corporation counsel, however, intervened saying that such a decision by either party was in direct conflict with existing law and applied constitutional freedoms. Fortunately for all concerned, Ozzy Osbourne reportedly became ill at an earlier concert elsewhere and the event was cancelled by the promoter.

In another instance, a facility was to be rented by a somewhat unusual group of individuals, by current social standards, for the purpose of holding a "Gay Beauty Contest." Local church and school groups protested violently; this event was cancelled due to a lack of ticket sales and inability of the promoter to provide necessary deposit funding.

At another facility there were doubts as to whether the building could be rented to a group that advocated policies very similar to those espoused by the Communist Party, and other groups, whose past history had indicated less than favorable local support in many urban areas of the United States. Again, that group's proposed meeting never materialized due to lack of sufficient funding and the logistics of providing necessary security requirements.

In all cases, however, the question arose — what right does a public assembly facility have to restrict or, if desired, to bar presentation of an event or availability to an individual for a public program? One person in an entertainment-industry meeting in early 1984 quipped, "You have no rights to stop them — and your ability to do so deteriorates from that point on."

When a facility is designed and constructed to serve the purpose of housing groups of individuals in attendance at a meeting, trade show, an entertainment presentation, dramatic production, music concert or similar programs, it does not matter who owns the facility and what its normal day-to-day use is. The example that follows will possibly contribute to an understanding.

Wholesome University has built a basketball arena which also houses athletic department offices. The facility is used for the school's varsity basketball games, volleyball, commencements, occasional artistic presentations of school groups like the university's symphonic choir and orchestra, and the daily physical education programs. During the summer, however, the facility sits vacant. Students are gone, sports activities are absent and the university has been called upon to make it accessible possibly for rock concerts. There are a certain number of major stars who tour the area from time to time. Since the facility holds 7,500 to 12,500 or more, it becomes a candidate for the staging of many types of artists or groups.

Although the facility is not intended as a profit-making structure, it suddenly comes into its own when it is found that there is not a competitive or like facility within miles of the campus. In addition, the university's financial advisors, recognizing the inflationary spiral, express admonitions to the university administration concerning the need to find funds for yearly operations and at some time in the future, needed repairs and/or additions. Thus with the specter of increasing deficit facing the facility, devices, such as rock show promoters, major artists, the overnight event, etc., for acquiring needed and speedy funds become an attractive possibility.

There is sufficient parking; the university has the manpower and the facilities with which to provide for the events. A large enough consuming public exists in and around the university area to assure fairly consistent success. Now what shall the university do?

The growing inclination, of course, is to provide the facility, making it available for such profit-making events, normally within certain predetermined conditions. Regardless of these conditions, once a facility is offered for such public use, it cannot be doled out in a miserly fashion. It cannot be acceptable one day to host "Kenny Rogers" because his is one of those types of acts or events the community will enjoy, and on the other hand discourage or, simply put, refuse to deal with legitimate promoters who may wish to bring in "The Blasters," even though "The Blasters" have had some reported problems in other parts of the country.

To forestall the playing of "The Blasters," one must also give up "Kenny Rogers," and in turn, depending on the nature of inherent litigation, must cease all such operations. This may be what a university feels it will have to do. But, once out of the entertainment game, they must stay out. For to re-enter would be in fact to become "selective." This is one of the most serious complaints leveled against facilities today. What a facility, its community, that community's leadership, or the operators of the facility feels is "normal" and "acceptable" to local community standards and needs may not, in the eyes of the court, be broad or general enough in its scope to preclude the claim of First Amendment rights ostensibly being exercised by those requesting dates or usage in the facility.

A program of usage should be consistent with the style of the facility. A theater, upholstered and boasting such refinements as chandeliers, extensive wood paneling and carpeting throughout, has a right to restrict those types of activities which are not considered normal for its type of decor. Rock concerts, trade shows, and other events that might be considered injurious to the facility's interior and equipment can be refused on legally justifiable grounds.

A symphony orchestra often finds the large basketball arena to be unsuitable for its needs. Theater productions are difficult to stage in large-roofed buildings having no built-in "grid" or suspension system for the hanging of sets. All these are physical matters and very easy to resolve.

§ 7.4(D). Access to Records, Booking Schedules and Operational Details.

When any facility "goes public," so do many of its records. There are certain protections given the privately owned and operated building. Certain university facilities have a greater degree of protection than do those outwardly owned and operated by cities, counties and states. Yet, any claims regarding availability of dates or violation of First Amendment rights or overly-restrictive policies place the facility in the position of possibly being required to reveal certain documents. This could include booking schedules, most financial data, and operational procedures. Any stated policy or consistent procedure should be put in writing, and should be reviewed by an ongoing monitoring process. To merely stipulate that something exists as a policy or something else is a standard method of achieving a certain end is insufficient when faced with the potential for litigation.

Privacy is a word once considered the definition of a right intrinsic to everything one did and inalienable in all aspects of personal societies. That is no longer true today. The courts have ruled that if one person's or group's privacy creates a situation or allows a hindrance to exist that diminishes or prohibits another individual's or group's right to needed information, then that prior bastion of privacy may be severely intruded upon.

§ 7.4(E). Access to Premises.

Courts have ruled that access to the premises of any public assembly facility shall be granted under conditions which form a rather large umbrella encompassing numerous types of protests, solicitation and public commentary. This is not to say that anyone may enter upon the premises of any facility at any time to do whatever they wish; however, in order to protect guarantees of free speech, the courts have stated that access to the general populace cannot be severely restricted or unnecessarily hindered. If the facility is located well within the confines of a secluded campus area, and there is little daily traffic, or its location in fact is quite isolated from normal public contact, it may experience little or no confrontational incidents.

(1) *Sale of Items.*

It should be remembered, however, that one of the primary rules prohibiting the development of any contact with the general public or attending patron at an event concerns the sale, merchandising or distribution of any type of material which is in direct conflict to the operation of the facility in question. More simply put, the coliseum that has granted a promoter or his acts or performers the right to sell T-shirts, can ban nonlicensed sellers of such goods from the premises. Food stands can be prohibited on the premises whether they are for the sale of a product or for the giving away of samples.

(2) *Distribution of Written Materials.*

The distribution of handbills, leaflets and other such written materials can be restricted so long as the restrictions do not in themselves stop the supplier from coming on the premises and having at least what is considered by the court a "reasonable degree of access" to passing patrons or general public.

(3) *Soliciting Funds.*

The question of soliciting for funds is at best difficult. Most facilities prohibit any solicitation for funds either on premises or inside the facility. Once inside the physical structure of the building, management policies supersede the previously broad powers allowed by first amendment criteria to all citizens. What we have been discussing are things that would, could, shall or might take place on the physical grounds or "premises" of a building, on the escarpment leading to the doorway and the sidewalks surrounding the property and/or facility.

(4) *First Amendment Rights.*

The law is clear regarding first amendment rights granted an individual only because that particular constitutional amendment is so very broad in its interpretive scope. Our forefathers did not designate place nor time nor attitude. It might be best to remember that an overt attempt to regulate excessively, to restrict by imposition of hindrances, or to impede by ignoring requests, creates a basic ground on which most litigation is founded.

The soliciting of funds can be restricted from the facility itself and its immediate environs. As to the soliciting on the premises, this is best handled through a clear understanding and interpretation of existing local ordinances. As for the distribution of leaflets and other types of written material, this clearly falls within the first amendment rights of all individuals. If, however, such activities bar, hinder, impede or create the atmosphere thereof as concerns the access of any individuals to and from the entry portals of a facility, then such activities can be controlled by management or local law enforcement agencies.

It is helpful to designate areas for such individuals to stand. Furthermore, there should be certain simple procedures by which those desiring such rights inform the facility that they intend to protest or use that particular facility's event as a public forum. However, a conscientious attempt to provide such groups these alternatives must still exist. Be specific about procedures concerning solicitations, handbilling and other such methods of protest or desired access to transient public. Have copies of such regulations or procedures available for distribution to interested parties who may wish to gather on premises or utilize the area for their form of public demonstration.

Such procedures should be made a part of any formal record kept at the highest level of authority such as the city clerk's office, county commissioner's office, dean of student activities office, superintendent of facilities office, or the office of the facility and/or university's legal counsel.

§ 7.4(F). Search and Seizure.

Much has been written about this subject. At the present time, there appears to be no truly definitive case pending regarding search and seizure or methods of surveilling customers attending events to preclude unwanted objects such as glass containers, alcohol, weapons and similar objects. This does not mean, however, that the question has been resolved. It merely lies in abeyance due to the pressure of other legal matters that have arisen in the industry. It should be noted that when situations arise wherein there shall be those that will protest methods by which facility personnel check individual patrons coming into a building, the courts will again be asked to intervene.

The following items can be included in anyone's list or inventory of suggested procedures:

1. All checks, searches, close surveillance, requests for the checking of baggage, parcels, purses or whatever, should be done by civilian-clothed individuals rather than uniformed police officers.
2. The language of any and all prohibitions should be very plainly marked at each and every portal and distributed in a fashion so as to clearly reflect the essence of the prohibition, and the methods of its implementation.
3. Courteous, clear, but direct conversation with the patrons being questioned regarding suspicious items, bulges in clothing, or parcels is far more effective than the blunt direction of requests or demands to search when reasonable cause may not exist.
4. Review the procedure with every individual that may be concerned — event staff, management personnel, legal counsel and law enforcement officers. Continually monitor application of procedure at each and every occasion.

§ 7.4(G). Crowd Control.

The amount of security forces necessary to provide for the well-being of the patrons and participants in any event cannot be found on any chart of standards. It is not part of any handbook or authoritative research material. It is principally a matter of management's judgment based on given circumstances, past history, information gleaned from the industry regarding like facilities and situations — and very possibly, a certain degree of luck.

Security is vital not only to control an unruly crowd and to protect of the event's participants, but also to provide needed help in the event of major emergencies and, at times, some basic customer services. Certain law enforcement detachments have individuals trained in paramedic services. Others can provide preliminary fire protection support as well as radio systems allowing a communications network often far more sophisticated than the facility can afford or find practical to utilize at all times.

At no time can management of the facility and its owner ever give up the right to reasonable levels of security personnel for all events, including their positioning, and specific duties. To relinquish these rights is to endanger the safety and welfare of the patrons who are the primary responsibility of facility management.

§ 7.4(H). Availability of Required and Desired Accouterments.

(1) *Patrons with Disabilities.*

Much is written today about providing seating for the disabled, ramps for the use of wheelchairs, and particularly, parking facilities for the disabled. Developing and providing facilities for disabled patrons is just good business. Many of these individuals have been kept from attending events not only because of personal physical difficulties but also, and more importantly, because of the lack of adequately modified facilities.

Federal and state governments have written volumes of regulations and procedures regarding such situations. In simple terms, those with basic physical handicaps, but with the mental alertness to provide their own thought processes independent of other assistance, need parking facilities, ramp access for wheelchairs and/or crutches, and minimization of difficulties in utilization of restrooms. The government has and can provide architectural plans for those desiring to construct new or renovated existing facilities.

Only recently have those with severely limited hearing been "heard," as it were. Recent technical developments allow facilities, particularly smaller theaters, to be adapted for the hearing impaired. The process is fairly simple. It involves the installation of an electronic coil or wiring system by which signals can be transmitted to separate receiving units utilized by the patron. Or in some cases, it can actually raise certain elements of sounds so as to be more defined to those utilizing hearing aids.

It is important, however, that the facility manager be aware of these new developments and, when funds become available he or she should implement whatever system meets both budgetary and technical limitations existing in the facility in question.

Investigate, recognize, develop and implement any and all procedures that will aid the disabled — it is good business, it is a worthwhile effort, and it expresses a sensitivity of management toward the potential patron who must remain the most important part of any program.

(2) *Emergency Medical Care.*

Recognition of the emergency care needs of any group of attending or participating patrons should come as a result of review and consultation with qualified preventative and emergency medical care specialists.

Categorize possible patrons as to age, emotion potential, and consider the nature and duration of the event. Proper equipment and medical personnel can be expensive, but certainly worthwhile.

There may be pressure concerning the expense of acquiring technically sophisticated cardiopulmonary equipment. The maintenance of even basic emergency care supplies, bandages, splints, medicines, stretchers and oxygen tanks can severely stretch the most carefully prepared budget. Yet the "landlord" must be prepared for the worst — or at least the tragic possibility. Heart failure, pulmonary complications, sprained or broken limbs are constant specters when any large group gathers.

Coordinate on-site facilities with the closest permanent medical facilities. Develop response codes and assess the emergency medical care needs of patrons.

The type of accident reporting system used is vitally important. Clear-cut lines of organization normally define who does what. This may be fine for most management situations — until an accident occurs or a medical emergency is at hand. During such a crisis the natural inclination of sensitive man to sympathize, to commiserate, to reach out and help becomes dominant. When the emergency at hand has passed, the cold reality of administrative need and potential legal requirement takes precedence, often revealing a lack of information on what has most recently taken place.

Remember that proper response to those in need includes appropriate record-keeping. Review all accident and medical reports. Critique pertinent staff. Learn from these incidents since they provide the most graphic example of what might exist that portends hazard or indicates need for possible change.

§ 7.4(I). Conclusion.

There exists no simple answer to the numerous legal and socio-political questions that will arise regarding the operation of any public assembly facility. If you look for the all-encompassing formula to create the proper mix between professional management needs and the often fickle nature of public demand you will find none.

What you can use is a practiced discipline in dealing with every situation, every problem, every opportunity. Accept the preeminence of law as that cohesive element required in any society. Communicate your needs clearly, concisely and sincerely so as to acquire the broadest, most effective audience. Understand that flexibility and mobility in the blade of the fencing foil adds a dimension of strength and a capacity for endurance. It has been written that civilization hinges on the habit of obedience to criminal law and to some lesser degree civil law. Although this respect for civil law is less constant and not as engrained, it is still no less important. Professional management that strives for the better in whatever is undertaken requires patience, skill and ethical stamina. Less than this precludes the success of any worthwhile venture.

Index

A

ACTIONS.
Litigation generally.
See LITIGATION.
ADMINISTRATIVE ISSUES.
Amateur sports organizations.
Public responsibilities, §2.4.
Defamation of character, §2.7.
Due process, §2.2.
Generally, §§2.1 to 2.7.
Seattle case.
General provisions, §2.1.
See SEATTLE CASE.
Title IX.
Grove City implications, §2.5.
Violence in sports.
Legislating against violence in sports, §2.6.
Waivers, §2.3.
Warnings, §2.3.
AMATEUR SPORTS ORGANIZATIONS.
Access to public records, §2.4(A).
Conclusion, §2.4(G).
Delegation of a public responsibility, §2.4(F).
Conclusion, §2.4(G).
Facilities.
Public funding of athletic facilities, §2.4(E).
Conclusion, §2.4(G).
Football.
Televised college football games.
Public access, §2.4(B).
Conclusion, §2.4(G).
Court of appeals decision, §2.4(C).
Supreme court's decision, §2.4(D).
Public responsibilities, §2.4.
Conclusion, §2.4(G).
Delegation of a public responsibility, §2.4(F).
Conclusion, §2.4(G).
Records.
Access to public records, §2.4(A).
Conclusion, §2.4(G).
Television.
Public access to televised college football games, §2.4(B).
Conclusion, §2.4(G).
Court of appeals decision, §2.4(C).
Supreme court's decision, §2.4(D).
APPEALS.
Medical issues.
Drug testing, §5.2(G).

255

ASSEMBLIES.
  Public assembly facilities.
    Generally, §7.4.

ASSOCIATIONS.
  Amateur sports organizations.
    See AMATEUR SPORTS ORGANIZATIONS.

ASSUMPTION OF RISK.
  Skiing.
    Attacks on assumption of risk as defense, §7.3(B).
    Conclusion, §7.3(C).
    Downhill skiers, §7.3(A).
  Spectators.
    Baseball, §6.3(A).
    Football, §6.3(A).
    Golf, §6.3(A).
    Hockey, §6.3(A).
  Violence in sport.
    Degree of risk assumed, §6.1(E).
  Warnings.
    Inherent risk, §2.3(A).

ATHLETES.
  Litigation.
    Historical perspective, §1.2.
  Officials.
    Liability for official for player injuries, §6.2(E).
  Schools.
    Student-athlete issues.
      General provisions, §§4.1 to 4.5.
        See STUDENT-ATHLETE ISSUES.

ATHLETIC TRAINERS.
  Trainers generally.
    See TRAINERS.

ATTORNEYS AT LAW.
  Litigation.
    Historical perspective, §1.4.
  Public assembly facilities.
    Need for legal assistance, §7.4(B).

AUDITORIUMS.
  Public assembly facilities, §7.4.

C

COACHES.
  Certification, §3.2.
    Conclusion, §3.2(C).
    Consequences, §3.2(B).
    Legal ramifications, §3.2(B).
    Preparation of coaches, §3.2(A).
    Pros and cons, §3.2(C).
  Constitutional rights.
    Employment of coaches, §3.1(F).
  Defamation.
    Privilege, §2.7(A).

COACHES—Cont'd
Discrimination.
  Employment of coaches.
    Racial discrimination, §3.1(C).
    Reverse discrimination, §3.1(D).
    Sex bias, §3.1(E).
Dismissal.
  Employment, §3.1(B).
  School coaches, §3.1(B).
Employment, §3.1.
  College coaches, §3.1(G).
  Conclusion, §3.1(H).
  Constitutional rights, §3.1(F).
  Discrimination, §3.1(D).
  Dismissal, §3.1(B).
  Racial discrimination, §3.1(C).
  Schools.
    Secondary school coaches, §3.1(A).
  Tenure, §3.1(B).
Equipment.
  Football coaches.
    Maintenance of equipment, §3.3(C).
    Providing quality equipment, §3.3(B).
Football.
  Coach as codefendant, §3.3.
  Conclusion, §3.3(G).
  Equipment.
    Maintenance of equipment, §3.3(C).
    Providing quality equipment, §3.3(B).
  Insurance.
    Providing adequate insurance, §3.3(F).
  Precautionary steps for coaches, §3.3(E).
  Role of coach, §3.3(A).
  Warning.
    Failure to warn, §3.3(D).
Insurance.
  Football coaches.
    Providing adequate insurance, §3.3(F).
Litigation.
  Historical perspective, §1.5.
Preparation of coaches.
  Certification, §3.2(A).
Racial discrimination.
  Employment of coaches, §3.1(C).
    Reverse discrimination, §3.1(D).
Reverse discrimination.
  Employment of coaches, §3.1(D).
Schools.
  Employment of coaches.
    Collegiate coaches, §3.1(G).
    Dismissal, §3.1(B).
    Secondary school coach, §3.1(A).
    Tenure, §3.1(B).
Seattle case.
  Shift from products liability analysis to responsibility of coaches and school districts, §2.1(A).

COACHES—Cont'd
Sex discrimination, §3.1(E).
  Employment of coaches, §3.1(E).
Tenure.
  Employment, §3.1(B).
Warnings.
  Football coaches.
    Failure to warn, §3.3(D).

COLLEGES.
Schools generally.
  See SCHOOLS.
Student athletes.
  College participants, §4.4.

CONFIDENTIALITY.
Medical issues.
  Drug testing, §5.2(E).

CONGRESS.
Due process of law.
  Concern for due process, §2.2(B).

CONSENT.
Medical issues.
  Drug testing.
    Informed consent, §5.2(B).

CONTRABAND.
Public assembly facilities.
  Searches and seizures, §7.4(F).

CONTRACTS.
Student-athlete issues.
  Scholarships.
    Contractual relationship of athletic scholarship, §4.4(B).

CONTROLLED SUBSTANCES.
Drug testing.
  Generally, §5.2.

CRIMINAL LAW.
Violence in sport.
  Courts as referees, §6.1(C).

CROWDS.
Spectators generally.
  See SPECTATORS.

D

DAMAGES.
Equipment.
  Punitive damages, §7.1(I).

DEFAMATION.
Coaches.
  Privilege, §2.7(A).
Conclusion, §2.7(E).
Defenses, §2.7(A).
Elements of tort, §2.7(A).
Fair comment.
  Privilege of fair comment, §2.7(A).

DEFAMATION—Cont'd
New York Times rule.
  Constitutional privilege, §2.7(B).
Overview, §2.7(A).
Per quod, §2.7(A).
Per se, §2.7(A).
Privileges, §2.7(A).
  Constitutional privilege.
    New York Times rule, §2.7(B).
Public figures.
  Cases where plaintiff not public figure, §2.7(C).
  Controversy.
    Public nature of controversy, §2.7(C).
  Interest.
    Public interest, §2.7(C).
  Officials.
    Public officials, §2.7(C).
  Prominent position, §2.7(C).
  Repose.
    Rule of repose, §2.7(D).
Repose.
  Rule of repose, §2.7(D).
Scope of law of defamation, §2.7(A).

DEFENSES.
Assumption of risk.
  General provisions.
    See ASSUMPTION OF RISK.
Defamation, §2.7(A).
Violence in sport, §6.1(F).

DEFINITIONS.
Due process of law, §2.2(C).

DISABLED PERSONS.
Public assembly facilities.
  Patients with disabilities.
    Requirements, §7.4(H).
Student athletes, §4.3.

DISCIPLINE.
Student-athlete issues.
  Disciplinary and behavioral rights, §4.1(C).

DISCRIMINATION.
Coaches.
  Employment of coaches.
    Racial discrimination, §3.1(C).
    Reverse discrimination, §3.1(D).
    Sex bias, §3.1(E).
Sex discrimination.
  Title IX.
    See TITLE IX.
Student-athlete issues.
  Disabled athletes.
    Legalized discrimination, §4.3(A).
Title IX.
  General provisions.
    See TITLE IX.

DRUGS.
 Testing, §5.2.
DUE PROCESS OF LAW.
 Administrators.
  Concern for due process, §2.2(B).
 Conclusion, §2.2(E).
 Congress.
  Concern for due process, §2.2(B).
 Constitutional provisions, §2.2(C).
 Definitions, §2.2(C).
 Litigation, §2.2.
 NCAA.
  Adoption of policy, §2.2(A).
  Concern for due process, §2.2(B).
 Penalties.
  Context for due process cases, §2.2.
 Procedural due process.
  Requirements to ensure due process, §2.2(D).
 Requirements to ensure due process, §2.2(D).
 Student-athlete issues.
  Rights of athletes, §4.1(B).
  Scholarships.
   Contractual basis for property interest in eligibility, §4.5.
 Substantive due process.
  Requirements to ensure due process, §2.2(D).

E

EDUCATION.
 Student-athlete issues.
  Conclusion, §4.2(E).
  Educational rights, §4.1(C).
  Exploitation of athletes.
   Educational exploitation, §4.2.
   Meeting exploitation challenge, §4.2(D).
  Judicial interference disrupting administration of schools, §4.2(C).
  Malpractice.
   Educational malpractice, §4.2(B).
  Pressures making it difficult for athletes to get a good education, §4.2(A).
  Scholarships.
   Contractual basis for property interest in eligibility, §4.5.
EMERGENCIES.
 Medical issues.
  Emergency medical services for large crowds.
   Public assembly facilities, §7.4(H).
   Spectators, §5.3.
EMPLOYMENT.
 Coaches.
  See COACHES.
EQUIPMENT.
 Coaches.
  Football coaches.
   Maintenance of equipment, §3.3(C).
   Providing quality equipment, §3.3(B).
 Damages.
  Punitive damages, §7.1(I).

EQUIPMENT—Cont'd
  Gymnastic facilities.
    Attempt by manufacturers to follow standards, §7.2(B).
    Conclusion, §7.2(D).
    Recommendations for upkeep, §7.2(C).
  Products liability.
    Design defects, §7.1(A).
      Standard of liability, §7.1(G).
    Failure to warn.
      Standard of liability, §7.1(G).
    Federal product liability reform, §7.1(D).
      Effect of proposed reform, §7.1(J).
      Search for federal legislative solution, §7.1(E).
    Generally, §7.1.
    Historical efforts to address problem, §7.1(B).
    Predictions for reform, §7.1(J).
    Preemption of state law by federal law, §7.1(F).
    Proposed reforms at state level, §7.1(C).
    Punitive damages, §7.1(I).
    Responsibility in product liability action, §7.1(H).
    Warnings.
      Failure to warn, §7.1(A).
      Standard of liability, §7.1(G).
  Punitive damages, §7.1(I).
  Warnings.
    Failure to warn.
      Liability, §7.1(A).
      Standard of liability, §7.1(G).

EXAMINATIONS.
  Drug testing.
    Generally, §5.2.

F

FACILITIES.
  Amateur sports organizations.
    Public funding of athletic facilities, §2.4(E).
      Conclusion, §2.4(G).
  Gymnastic facilities.
    Effective design and upkeep, §7.2.
  Public assembly facilities, §7.4.
  Public funding of facilities, §2.4(E).
    Conclusion, §2.4(G).
  Skiers.
    Liability of ski areas for downhill skiers, §7.3.

FIRST AID.
  Public assembly facilities.
    Emergency medical services for large crowds, §7.4(H).
  Spectators.
    Emergency medical services for large crowds, §5.3.

FOOTBALL.
  Amateur sports organizations.
    Televised college football games.
      Public access, §2.4(B).
        Conclusion, §2.4(G).
        Court of appeals decision, §2.4(C).

FOOTBALL—Cont'd
  Amateur sports organizations—Cont'd
    Televised college football games—Cont'd
      Public access—Cont'd
        Supreme court's decision, §2.4(D).
  Coaches.
    Coach as codefendant, §3.3.
    Conclusion, §3.3(G).
    Equipment.
      Maintenance of equipment, §3.3(C).
      Providing quality equipment, §3.3(B).
    Insurance.
      Providing adequate insurance, §3.3(F).
    Precautionary steps for coaches, §3.3(E).
    Role of coach, §3.3(A).
    Warning.
      Failure to warn, §3.3(D).
  Spectators.
    Participatory risks, §6.3(A).

G

GOLF.
  Spectators.
    Participatory risks, §6.3(A).
GROVE CITY CASE.
  Title IX.
    Implications of Grove City on Title IX, §2.5.
GYMNASTIC FACILITIES.
  Effective design and upkeep.
    Conclusion, §7.2(D).
    Generally, §7.2.
  Equipment.
    Attempt by manufacturers to follow standards, §7.2(B).
    Conclusion, §7.2(D).
    Recommendations for upkeep, §7.2(C).
  Growth of gymnastics, §7.2(A).
    Requirement for standards to be set, §7.2(A).
  Trampolines.
    Generally, §7.2.

H

HANDBILLS.
  Public assembly facilities.
    Access to premises, §7.4(E).

I

INJURIES.
  Officials.
    Player injuries.
      Liability for injuries to player, §6.2(E).
INSPECTIONS.
  Public assembly facilities.
    Searches and seizures, §7.4(F).

INSURANCE.
  Coaches.
    Football coaches.
      Providing adequate insurance, §3.3(F).
  Officials.
    Liability for player injuries, §6.2(E).

L

LEAFLETS.
  Public assembly facilities.
    Distribution of written materials.
      Access to premises, §7.4(E).
LIBEL.
  Defamation, §2.7.
LITIGATION.
  Athletes.
    Historical perspective, §1.2.
  Attorneys at law.
    Historical perspective, §1.4.
  Coaches.
    Historical perspective, §1.5.
  Due process, §2.2.
  Historical perspective.
    Athletes, §1.2.
    Athletic directors, §1.1.
    Attorneys, §1.4.
    Coaches, §1.5.
    Officials, §1.6.
    Products liability.
      Expertise in products liability cases, §1.7.
    Trainers, §1.3.
  Officials.
    Historical perspective, §1.6.
  Products liability.
    Generally.
      See PRODUCTS LIABILITY.
    Historical perspective.
      Expertise in products liability cases, §1.7.
  Sports-related legal issues, §2.2(A).
  Trainers.
    Historical perspective, §1.3.
  Violence in sport.
    Courts as referees, §6.1(C).
    Defenses, §6.1(F).
    Enforcing civility, §6.1(D).
    Survey of law, §2.6(B).

M

MALPRACTICE.
  Student-athlete issues.
    Educational malpractice, §4.2(B).
MEDICAL ISSUES.
  Appeals.
    Drug testing, §5.2(G).

MEDICAL ISSUES—Cont'd
  Confidentiality.
    Drug testing, §5.2(E).
  Consent.
    Drug testing.
      Informed consent, §5.2(B).
  Drug testing.
    Accurate information, §5.2(F).
    Appeals, §5.2(G).
    Banned list, §5.2(A).
    Conclusion, §5.2(H).
    Confidentiality, §5.2(E).
    Consent.
      Informed consent, §5.2(B).
    False negatives.
      Prevention, §5.2(D).
    False positives.
      Prevention, §5.2(C).
    Generally, §5.2.
    Information.
      Accurate information, §5.2(F).
    Informed consent, §5.2(B).
    Prevention of false negatives, §5.2(D).
    Prevention of false positives, §5.2(C).
  Emergencies.
    Emergency medical services for large crowds.
      Public assembly facilities, §7.4(H).
      Spectators, §5.3.
  Physical therapists, §5.1(D).
    Categories regarding physical therapy laws, §5.1(B).
    Licensure, §5.1(A).
    Statutory requirements by state, §5.1(C).
  Public assembly facilities.
    Emergency medical services for large crowds, §§5.3, 7.4(H).
  Spectators.
    Emergency medical services for large crowds.
      Benefits of program.
        Conclusion, §5.3(H).
      Complexity of program, §5.3(G).
      Duty to provide emergency medical capability, §5.3(B).
      Example of emergency medical system in action, §5.3(E).
      Introduction, §5.3(A).
      Level of care.
        Facilities and state law may dictate, §5.3(D).
      Planning for emergency medical response, §5.3(F).
      Public assembly facilities, §7.4(H).
      Scope of treatments.
        Standards and guidelines to specify, §5.3(C).
  Trainers.
    Conclusion, §5.1(D).
    Legal status of athletic trainer, §5.1.
    Physical therapists.
      Categories regarding physical therapy laws, §5.1(B).
      Conclusion, §5.1(D).
      Licensure, §5.1(A).
      Statutory requirements by state, §5.1(C).

N

NEGLIGENCE.
Officials.
Injuries caused by negligence, §6.2(C).
Seattle case.
Theory of the case.
School district negligence, §2.1(D).

NEW YORK TIMES RULE.
Defamation.
Constitutional privilege, §2.7(B).

O

OFFICIALS.
Athletes.
Liability of official for player injuries, §6.2(E).
Duties of officials.
Game duties, §6.2(G).
Liability for game rulings, §6.2(H).
Pregame duties, §6.2(F).
Equipment.
Ensuring use of proper equipment, §6.2(F).
Pregame duties of officials, §6.2(F).
Game duties of officials.
Liability for game rulings, §6.2(H).
Playing conditions, §6.2(G).
Supervision and control, §6.2(G).
Weather conditions, §6.2(G).
Injuries.
Intentional injuries, §6.2(B).
Negligent injuries, §6.2(C).
Player injuries.
Liability for injuries to player, §6.2(E).
Recovery for injuries, §6.2(A).
Insurance.
Liability for player injuries, §6.2(E).
Intentional injuries, §6.2(B).
Legal rights and duties.
Conclusion, §6.2(I).
Generally, §6.2.
Litigation.
Historical perspective, §1.6.
Negligence.
Injuries caused by negligence, §6.2(C).
Playing conditions.
Game duties of officials, §6.2(G).
Pregame duties of officials, §6.2(F).
Pregame duties of officials.
Failure to enforce rules, §6.2(F).
Playing conditions, §6.2(F).
Weather conditions, §6.2(F).
Recovery for injuries, §6.2(A).
Intentional injuries, §6.2(B).
Negligent injuries, §6.2(C).
Weather conditions.
Game duties of officials, §6.2(G).

OFFICIALS—Cont'd
   Weather conditions—Cont'd
      Pregame duties of officials, §6.2(F).
   Workers' compensation.
      When permitted, §6.2(D).

                                    P

PENALTIES.
   Due process of law.
      Context for due process cases, §2.2.
PHYSICAL THERAPISTS.
   Medical issues, §5.1(D).
      Categories regarding physical therapy laws, §5.1(B).
      Licensure, §5.1(A).
      Statutory requirements by state, §5.1(C).
PRIVILEGES.
   Defamation, §2.7(A).
      Constitutional privilege.
         New York Times rule, §2.7(B).
PRODUCTS LIABILITY.
   Equipment.
      Design defects, §7.1(A).
         Standard of liability, §7.1(G).
      Failure to warn.
         Standard of liability, §7.1(G).
      Federal product liability reform, §7.1(D).
         Effect of proposed reform, §7.1(J).
         Search for federal legislative solution, §7.1(E).
      Generally, §7.1.
      Historical efforts to address problem, §7.1(B).
      Predictions for reform, §7.1(J).
      Preemption of state law by federal law, §7.1(F).
      Proposed reforms at state level, §7.1(C).
      Punitive damages, §7.1(I).
      Responsibility in product liability action, §7.1(H).
      Warnings.
         Failure to warn, §7.1(A).
         Standard of liability, §7.1(G).
   Litigation.
      Historical perspective.
         Expertise in products liability cases, §1.7.
   Seattle case.
      Shift from products liability analysis to responsibility of coaches and school
         districts, §2.1(A).
PUBLIC ASSEMBLY FACILITIES.
   Access to facilities, §§7.4(C), 7.4(E).
      Premises, §7.4(E).
   Attorneys at law.
      Need for legal assistance, §7.4(B).
   Availability of facilities, §7.4(C).
   Booking schedules.
      Access to records, booking schedules and operational details, §7.4(D).
   Conclusion, §7.4(I).
   Contraband.
      Searches and seizures, §7.4(F).

PUBLIC ASSEMBLY FACILITIES—Cont'd
Crowd control, §7.4(G).
Disabled persons.
    Patients with disabilities.
        Requirements, §7.4(H).
Distribution of written materials.
    Access to premises, §7.4(E).
First amendment rights.
    Access to premises, §7.4(E).
Generally, §§7.4(A), 7.4(I).
Handbills.
    Access to premises, §7.4(E).
Inspections.
    Searches and seizures, §7.4(F).
Introduction, §7.4(A).
Leaflets.
    Distribution of written materials.
        Access to premises, §7.4(E).
Medical issues.
    Emergency medical services for large crowds, §§5.3, 7.4(H).
Premises.
    Access to premises, §7.4(E).
Records.
    Access to records, booking schedules and operational details, §7.4(D).
Sales.
    Access to premises.
        Sale of items, §7.4(E).
Searches and seizures, §7.4(F).
Soliciting funds.
    Access to premises, §7.4(E).
Spectators.
    Crow control, §7.4(G).

PUNITIVE DAMAGES.
Equipment, §7.1(I).

R

RACIAL DISCRIMINATION.
Coaches.
    Employment of coaches, §3.1(C).
        Reverse discrimination, §3.1(D).

RECORDS.
Amateur sports organizations.
    Access to public records, §2.4(A).
        Conclusion, §2.4(G).
Public assembly facilities.
    Access to records, booking schedules and operational details, §7.4(D).

REFEREES.
Officials generally.
    See OFFICIALS.

REVERSE DISCRIMINATION.
Coaches.
    Employment of coaches, §3.1(D).

S

SALES.
Public assembly facilities.
  Access to premises.
    Sale of items, §7.4(E).

SCHOLARSHIPS.
Student-athlete issues.
  Athletic scholarships differing from other financial aid, §4.4(A).
  Conclusion, §4.4(E).
  Contractual basis for property interests in eligibility, §4.5(B).
    Conclusion, §4.5(F).
    Enforcement procedures, §4.5(E).
    Legal contract, §4.5(D).
    Liberty interest, §4.5(C).
    Property right theories, §4.5(A).
    State action, §4.5(B).
  Taxation of athletic scholarships, §4.4(D).

SCHOOLS.
Athletes.
  Student-athlete issues.
    General provisions, §§4.1 to 4.5.
      See STUDENT-ATHLETE ISSUES.
Coaches.
  Employment of coaches.
    Collegiate coaches, §3.1(G).
    Dismissal, §3.1(B).
    Secondary school coach, §3.1(A).
    Tenure, §3.1(B).
Seattle case.
  Negligence of school district.
    Theory of the case, §2.1(D).
  Shift from products liability analysis to responsibility of coaches and school districts, §2.1(A).

SEARCHES AND SEIZURES.
Public assembly facilities, §7.4(F).

SEATTLE CASE.
Coaches.
  Shift from products liability analysis to responsibility of coaches and school districts, §2.1(A).
Conclusion, §2.1(F).
Failure to adequately instruct.
  Theory of the case, §2.1(C).
Implications of case, §2.1(E).
Lessons of case, §2.1(E).
Negligence.
  Theory of the case.
    School district negligence, §2.1(D).
Products liability.
  Shift from products liability analysis to responsibility of coaches and school districts, §2.1(A).
Schools.
  Negligence of school district.
    Theory of the case, §2.1(D).
  Shift from products liability analysis to responsibility of coaches and school districts, §2.1(A).

SEATTLE CASE—Cont'd
Scope of case, §2.1(E).
Theory of the case.
  Failure to adequately instruct, §2.1(C).
  Failure to warn, §2.1(B).
  Negligence of school district, §2.1(D).
  Products liability.
    Shift from products liability to responsibility of coaches and school districts, §2.1(A).
Warnings.
  Failure to warn.
    Theory of the case, §2.1(B).

SEX DISCRIMINATION.
Coaches.
  Employment of coaches, §3.1(E).
Title IX.
  General provisions.
    See TITLE IX.

SIGNATURES.
Warnings, §2.3(B).

SKIING.
Assumption of risk.
  Attacks on assumption of risk as defense, §7.3(B).
  Conclusion, §7.3(C).
  Downhill skiers, §7.3(A).
Downhill skiers.
  Assumption of risk, §7.3(A).
    Attacks on assumption of risk as defense, §7.3(B).
    Conclusion, §7.3(C).
  Conclusion, §7.3(C).
  Legal relationship between ski area operators and skiers, §7.3(A).
  Liability of ski areas, §7.3.
    Historical development, §7.3(A).

SLANDER.
Defamation, §2.7.

SOLICITING FUNDS.
Public assembly facilities.
  Access to premises, §7.4(E).

SPECTATORS.
Assumption of risk.
  Baseball, §6.3(A).
  Football, §6.3(A).
  Golf, §6.3(A).
  Hockey, §6.3(A).
Baseball.
  Participatory risks, §6.3(A).
Bleachers.
  Safe premises, §6.3(C).
Conclusion, §6.3(D).
Crowd control, §6.3(B).
  Public assembly facilities, §7.4(G).
First aid.
  Emergency medical services for large crowds, §5.3.
Football.
  Participatory risks, §6.3(A).

SPECTATORS—Cont'd
General consideration, §6.3.
Golf.
  Participatory risks, §6.3(A).
Hockey.
  Participatory risks, §6.3(A).
Medical issues.
  Emergency medical services for large crowds.
    Benefits of program.
      Conclusion, §5.3(H).
    Complexity of program, §5.3(G).
    Duty to provide emergency medical capability, §5.3(B).
    Example of emergency medical system in action, §5.3(E).
    Introduction, §5.3(A).
    Level of care.
      Facilities and state law may dictate, §5.3(D).
    Planning for emergency medical response, §5.3(F).
    Public assembly facilities, §7.4(H).
    Scope of treatments.
      Standards and guidelines to specify, §5.3(C).
Participatory risks, §6.3(A).
Public assembly facilities generally, §7.4.
  Crow control, §7.4(G).
  First aid, §7.4(H).
Safe premises, §6.3(C).
Stairs.
  Safe premises, §6.3(C).
Violence in sport.
  Historical perspective of spectator violence, §6.1(B).
Walkways.
  Safe premises, §6.3(C).

SPORTS LITIGATION.
Litigation generally.
  See LITIGATION.

SPORTS MEDICINE ISSUES, §§5.1 to 5.3.
See MEDICAL ISSUES.

STADIUMS.
Public assembly facilities, §7.4.

STATUTES.
Violence in sport.
  Suggestions for statutory control, §6.1(G).

STUDENT-ATHLETE ISSUES.
College participants.
  Conclusion, §4.4(E).
  Nature of college participation, §4.4.
  Scholarships.
    Athletic scholarships differing from other financial aid, §4.4(A).
    Conclusion, §4.4(E).
    Contractual relationship of athletic scholarship, §4.4(B).
    Taxation of athletic scholarships, §4.4(D).
  Workers' compensation.
    Applicability, §4.4(C).
Constitutional rights, §4.1(C).
Contracts.
  Scholarships.
    Contractual relationship of athletic scholarship, §4.4(B).

STUDENT-ATHLETE ISSUES—Cont'd
  Disabled athletes, §4.3.
    Conclusion, §4.3(E).
    Discrimination.
      Legalized discrimination, §4.3(A.
    Future predictions, §4.3(D).
    Ignorance of the law.
      Problems confronting individuals with disabilities, §4.3(B).
    Predictions for the future, §4.3(D).
    Problems confronting individuals with disabilities, §4.3(B).
    Progress in sports for the disabled, §4.3(C).
  Discipline.
    Disciplinary and behavioral rights, §4.1(C).
  Discrimination.
    Disabled athletes.
      Legalized discrimination, §4.3(A).
  Due process of law.
    Rights of athletes, §4.1(B).
    Scholarships.
      Contractual basis for property interest in eligibility, §4.5.
  Education.
    Conclusion, §4.2(E).
    Educational rights, §4.1(C).
    Exploitation of athletes.
      Educational exploitation, §4.2.
      Meeting exploitation challenge, §4.2(D).
    Judicial interference disrupting administration of schools, §4.2(C).
    Malpractice.
      Educational malpractice, §4.2(B).
    Pressures making it difficult for athletes to get a good education, §4.2(A).
    Scholarships.
      Contractual basis for property interest in eligibility, §4.5.
  Eligibility.
    Scholarships.
      Athletic scholarship as contractual basis for property interest in eligibility, §4.5.
  Financial rights, §4.1(C).
  Human and personal rights, §4.1(C).
  Malpractice.
    Educational malpractice, §4.2(B).
  Protective rights, §4.1(C).
  Rights of athletes, §4.1.
    Categories, §4.1(C).
    Constitutional rights, §4.1(C).
    Disciplinary and behavioral rights, §4.1(C).
    Educational rights, §4.1(C).
    Ethical or moral rights, §4.1(A).
    Financial rights, §4.1(C).
    Human and personal rights, §4.1(C).
    Landmark case, §4.1(B).
    Legal rights of athletes, §4.1(A).
    Protective rights, §4.1(C).
  Scholarships.
    Athletic scholarships differing from other financial aid, §4.4(A).
    Conclusion, §4.4(E).
    Contractual basis for property interest in eligibility.
      Conclusion, §4.5(F).

STUDENT-ATHLETE ISSUES—Cont'd
  Scholarships—Cont'd
    Contractual basis for property interest in eligibility—Cont'd
      Enforcement procedures, §4.5(E).
      Legal contract, §4.5(D).
      Liberty interest, §4.5(C).
      Property right theories, §4.5(A).
      State action, §4.5(B).
    Contractual relationship of athletic scholarship, §4.4(B).
    Taxation of athletic scholarships, §4.4(D).
  Taxation.
    College participants.
      Scholarships, §4.4(D).
  Workers' compensation.
    College participants.
      Applicability of workers' compensation provisions, §4.4(C).

SUITS.
  Litigation generally.
    See LITIGATION.

                       T

TAXATION.
  Student-athlete issues.
    College participants.
      Scholarships, §4.4(D).

TELEVISION.
  Amateur sports organizations.
    Public access to televised college football games, §2.4(B).
      Conclusion, §2.4(G).
      Court of appeals decision, §2.4(C).
      Supreme court decision, §2.4(D).

TITLE IX.
  Grove City implications.
    Conclusion to provisions, §2.5(C).
    Future of Title IX, §2.5(B).
    Generally, §2.5.
    Physical education and sports programs, §2.5(A).
  Sports-related legal issues, §2.2(A).

TORTS.
  Defamation, §2.7.
  Injuries.
    Intentional injuries, §6.2(B).
  Malpractice.
    Educational malpractice, §4.2(B).
  Negligence.
    See NEGLIGENCE.
  Violence in sport.
    Generally, §6.1.

TRAINERS.
  Litigation.
    Historical perspective, §1.3.
  Medical issues.
    Conclusion, §5.1(D).
    Legal status of athletic trainer, §5.1.

TRAINERS—Cont'd
  Medical issues—Cont'd
    Physical therapists.
      Categories regarding physical therapy laws, §5.1(B).
      Conclusion, §5.1(D).
      Licensure, §5.1(A).
      Statutory requirements by state, §5.1(C).
TRAMPOLINES.
  Generally, §7.2.

U

UMPIRES.
  Officials generally.
    See OFFICIALS.
UNIVERSITIES.
  Schools generally.
    See SCHOOLS.
  Student athletes.
    College participants, §4.4.
URINALYSIS.
  Drug testing, §5.2.

V

VIOLENCE IN SPORT.
  Assumption of risk.
    Degree of risk assumed, §6.1(E).
  Criminal law.
    Courts as referees, §6.1(C).
  Defenses, §6.1(F).
  Degree of risk assumed, §6.1(E).
  Excessive violence.
    Conclusion, §2.6(C).
    Pressure to perform, §2.6(A).
  General considerations, §6.1.
    Conclusion, §6.1(H).
  Legislating against violence in sports, §2.6.
  Litigation.
    Conclusion to provisions, §2.6(C).
    Courts as referees, §6.1(C).
    Defenses, §6.1(F).
    Enforcing civility, §6.1(D).
    Survey of law, §2.6(B).
  Pressure to perform, §2.6(A).
  Spectators.
    Historical perspective of spectator violence, §6.1(B).
  Statutes.
    Suggestions for statutory control, §6.1(G).
  Theories for increased violence, §6.1(A).
  Winning.
    Emphasis placed on winning as reason for increased violence, §6.1(A).

W

WAIVERS.
Contractual nature of waiver, §2.3(C).
Judicial scrutiny of waiver, §2.3(C).
Nature of waiver, §2.3(C).

WARNINGS.
Assumption of risk.
Inherent risk, §2.3(A).
Coaches.
Football coaches.
Failure to warn, §3.3(D).
Conclusion, §2.3(D).
Contents, §2.3(B).
Dating of warning, §2.3(B).
Equipment.
Failure to warn.
Liability, §7.1(A).
Standard of liability, §7.1(G).
Inherent risk, §2.3(A).
Seattle case.
Failure to warn.
Theory of the case, §2.1(B).
Signatures, §2.3(B).
Waiver, §2.3(C).
Written warnings, §2.3(B).

WORKERS' COMPENSATION.
Officials.
When permitted, §6.2(D).
Student-athlete issues.
College participants.
Applicability of workers' compensation provisions, §4.4(C).